DEPARTMENT OF THE ENVIRONMENT   WATER DATA UNIT

SCOTTISH DEVELOPMENT DEPARTMENT

DEPARTMENT OF THE ENVIRONMENT FOR NORTHERN IRELAND

Surface Water: United Kingdom 1971–1973

A register of United Kingdom gauging stations with selected hydrometric statistics, catchment rainfalls and river water temperatures covering the years 1971, 1972 and 1973. A description of the Water Data Unit processing and data retrieval systems is given.

LONDON: HER MAJESTY'S STATIONERY OFFICE

ISBN 0 11 751244 3*

Contents

Appendix

Publications of the International Standards Organization and of the British Standards Institution relating to Methods of Measurement of Liquid Flow in Open Channels

List of Figures

Pocket   **1:1,250,000 Map of the United Kingdom showing Gauging Stations, Water Authority and Hydrometric Area Boundaries**

1 Introduction

This volume is the eighteenth edition of the former Surface Water Year Books now renamed 'Surface Water: United Kingdom'. This change was made to be more in keeping with the longer period involved — 1971 to 1973, and to mark the inclusion of the first records from Northern Ireland.

The first edition, with records from twenty eight gauging stations,was published in 1938 for the water year 1935–1936; the edition for 1936–1937 followed in 1939. Both of these publications were prepared under the direction of the Inland Water Survey Committee appointed by the Minister of Health and by the Secretary of State for Scotland. The Inland Water Survey under Mr W. Allard and the Scottish Office continued this work after the war and the Year Book for the years 1937–1945 was published in one volume in 1952.

Due to economic stringency, the Survey was suspended in 1952 for a period of 2½ years, but in 1954 was reformed as the Surface Water Survey Centre of Great Britain, the Engineer-in-charge from 1954 to 1964 being Mr A. Gerard Boulton. A Year Book covering the years 1945–1953 was published in 1955.

In 1964 the Survey was transferred to the Water Resources Board (Director, Sir Norman Rowntree) until 1974 when the work of collection and publishing surface water information in England and Wales was again transferred, this time to the Water Data Unit (Director, Mr D H Newsome) of the Department of the Environment.

Year Books were published jointly each year by these organisations and the Scottish Office for the water years 1953–1954 to 1965–1966, but thereafter information for the five calendar years 1966 to 1970 was published in one volume in 1974.

The three editions for 1935–1936, 1936–1937 and 1953–1954 contained daily stream flow data; the remainder gave summaries either monthly and annually or, latterly, for the period of record. The first metric edition was the Year Book for 1964–1965.

A large volume of data is held in a computer based archive supported by an efficient retrieval system. This has made it practicable to give the prospective data user a number of retrieval options for the detailed information for the station in which he is interested. There is therefore less need for the publication of detailed information and the present volume continues the trend of reducing the number of published flow records. However, the list of gauging stations has been augmented to include stations which may not have met the selection criteria of previous year books and their limitations are indicated in the 'Station details' column. In all 1205 stations are listed compared with 782 in the 1966–70 edition.

Flow data up to 1973 are held in the Water Data Unit archive for 869 stations. Data for the remaining stations will be added as they become available.

With the exception of the period of record areal rainfalls assessed by the Thames Conservancy Division, rainfall data have been provided by the Meteorological Office in Bracknell who have also written the note on the computation and accuracy of the estimates of rainfall and evaporation data. The Meteorological Office in Belfast have provided the rainfall data for the catchments in Northern Ireland. The number of catchments for which rainfall data are available is steadily increasing.

The computer capabilities of the Water Data Unit used in the preparation and archiving of hydrometric data are available to users at modest charges which can be given to enquirers on request. The services which are available include the reading of tape and cards, the translation of 16 track tape to 5 and 8 track tape, the editing, processing, archiving and retrieval of data and the calibration of flow measurement stations. The output of the various options can be produced on a line-printer, on punched tape, on magnetic tape and on the graph plotter.

During the International Hydrological Decade 1965–1975 organised by the United Nations Educational Scientific and Cultural Organisation, the Water Data Unit was a participant in the United Kingdom programme. This edition of 'Surface Water: United Kingdom' is part of the United Kingdom's contribution to that Decade, so fulfilling an undertaking to collect, exchange and disseminate hydrological information.

The Water Data Unit, the Scottish Development Department and the Department of the Environment for Northern Ireland, acknowledge and extend their sincere appreciation to all those who have co-operated in the collection of information for this book.

2 Textual arrangements and Explanatory notes

2.1 Scope and Sources of Information

'Surface Water: United Kingdom' provides a variety of information relating to the network of gauging stations and data on streamflows and the rainfall on the gauged catchment areas. Some records from river temperature stations are also included. The contents have been compiled from reports provided by water authorities, river purification boards, research bodies and by private and public undertakings, and from the basic measurements which have been processed by these organisations, or by the Water Data Unit. Some slight variations from contributors' figures may occur; these may be due to different methods of computation or to provide uniformity in presentation.

2.2 The Form of Presentation of Information

The format of this book follows closely that of the previous edition and is one of the beneficial consequences of the use of the computer based systems for archiving and retrieval of data. Central to this presentation is an extended register of gauging stations (Section 4) with sufficient information to enable the user to select whichever stations are of the greatest interest to him. The locations of the gauging stations are plotted on the map in the pocket at the end of the book and they are also defined by grid references in the index. The area of the catchments is given and a measure of the outflow is provided as the mean discharge over the period of the record with the extremes which occurred. The length of the record may be found and an assessment of the quality, or the limitations in its range where they exist, may frequently be obtained from the comments.

There are several ways in which data can be presented to an enquirer; examples of the standard options follow sub-sections 5.2 Data Retrieval of Services offered by the Water Data Unit. A request form included in the book will help to ensure that sufficient specification of any request is given.

To augment the information given in the Index, two groups of hydrographs are presented which continue the sequence for the preceding five years in The Surface Water Year Book 1966–1970. The first group, Section 7, is a widely representative selection of flow types plotted as a daily mean discharge graph. The second smaller group, Section 8, selected from the first gives additional information for 1973 as follows:

a. Weekly areal rainfall and actual and potential evaporation.
b. Gauged daily mean discharges with extreme values for the period of record.
c. Gauged and naturalized monthly mean discharges, with extremes for the period of record. (The dual plot may be obscured when the gauged and naturalized flows are identical.)

Distribution curves of the catchment areas (Figure 1) and of lengths of record (Figure 2) summarise the state of the national network in 1973. The average length of record of gauging stations is less than 9 years and the average size of basin gauged is 380 km^2.

Following a register of river water temperature stations, a further set of curves (Section 10) presents the monthly mean and the monthly highest and lowest values of water temperature for 1973, together with the extremes for the period of record.

A directory of contributors to this book is included should information be required which is not available in the Water Data Unit.

An auxiliary list of gauging stations in alphabetical order will assist in the identification of a station when the name only is known.

FIGURE 1
DISTRIBUTION CURVE OF CATCHMENT AREAS FOR 869 GAUGING
STATIONS IN THE ARCHIVE ON 31st DECEMBER 1973

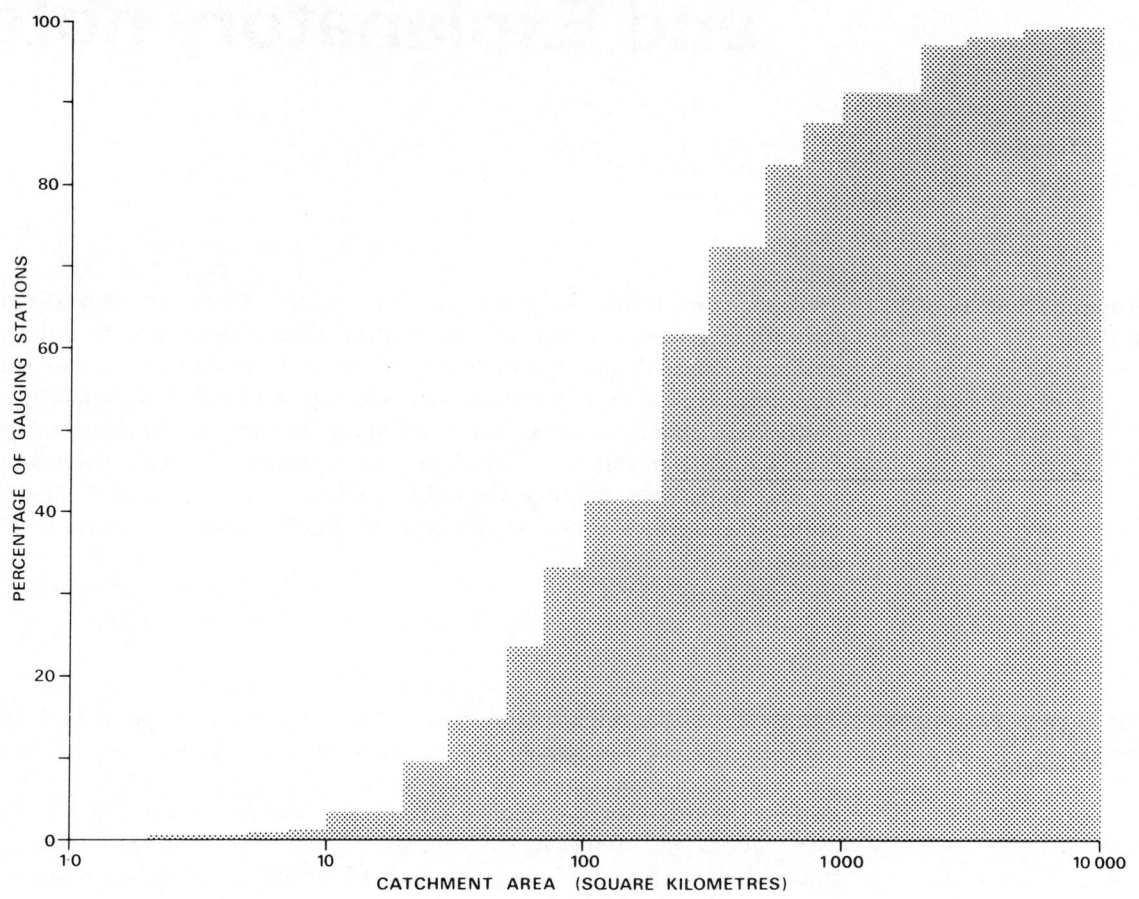

FIGURE 2
DISTRIBUTION CURVE OF LENGTHS OF RECORD FOR 869
GAUGING STATIONS IN THE ARCHIVE ON 31st DECEMBER 1973

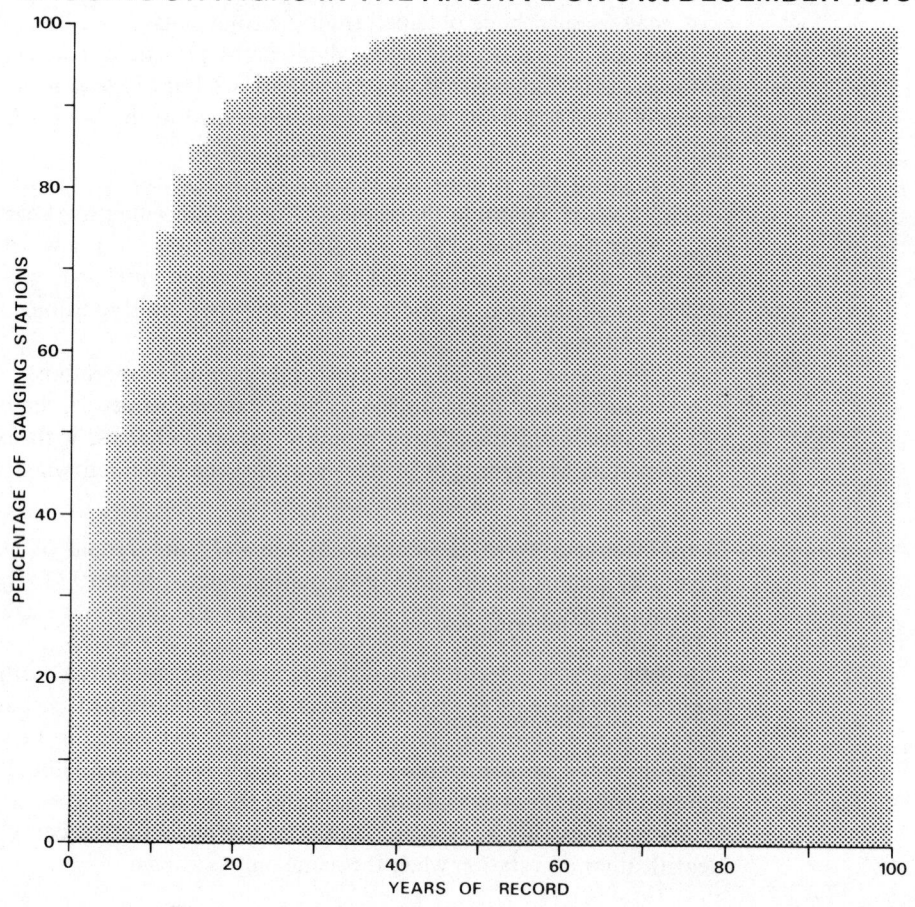

As in the previous edition, all records are presented as calendar year series and conform with the time base used in the Groundwater Year Book and in British Rainfall. Metric (SI) units are used throughout.

2.3 Arrangement of the Register of Gauging Stations

All references to contributors in this register are given in their current (1977) style, as the majority of independent organisations in England and Wales collecting hydrometric data during the period covered by this book have had their functions transferred to the water authorities. Individual acknowledgement of those smaller entities is precluded only by lack of space. The present nomenclature in England and Wales derives from the implementation of the 'Water Act 1973' on 1 April 1974, and in Scotland from the 'Local Government (Scotland) Act 1973' on 16 May 1975. In Northern Ireland reorganisation was effective from 1 October 1973 resulting from the 'Water Act (Northern Ireland) 1972' and subsequent legislation.

As far as possible stations are listed in number order. The first digit of the number is a regional identifier being 0 for the mainland of Britain, 1 for the islands and 2 for Northern Ireland. This number is followed by the hydrometric area number; hydrometric areas are river catchments having one or more outlets to the sea or tidal estuary, or for convenience may include several smaller catchments having topographical similarity with separate tidal outlets. These numbers run in clockwise order commencing in N.E. Scotland for Britain and in the River Foyle catchment in Northern Ireland, and it is this order which controls the grouping in the index.

2.4 Information given in the Register of Gauging Stations

The gauging station number used in the last Surface Water Year Book has been augmented to incorporate a wider variety of stations and has become a six-digit number. As before, the first digit identifies the region and the second and third the hydrometric area within the region. The fourth digit denotes the characteristics of a station or of its flow record and the significance of the code from 0 to 9 is as follows:

0   an orthodox network station;

1   not in use;

2   a station which is complementary to an orthodox gauging station commonly where by-pass channels are monitored and two discharges have to be summed for the catchment outflow. Alternatively it may be used for the crest tapping of a Crump weir or a similar auxiliary record;

3   a temporary station;

4   a complementary station where the channel configuration requires a third record to measure the total catchment outflow;

5   a computer requirement for the summation of the discharge of complementary stations. In practice the total discharge may be referenced by the orthodox station number, it being understood that separate discharges were originally derived;

6   a reservoir or lake level recorder station which may be additional to a discharge station at the outfall;

7   a nominal station whose discharges are derived by such indirect techniques as correlation, integration and modelling;

8   a station listed by the NERC Flood Study but not yet absorbed into the WDU numbering system;

and

9   a discontinued station.

Inevitably some anomalies will occur owing to the use of some of the prefixes, usually 3 and 9, prior to the introduction of these conventions. Where an ambiguity cannot otherwise be reconciled a new number will be allocated to one of the stations.

The number of the gauging station within the hydrometric area, usually allocated in a chronological sequence, is represented by the fifth and sixth digits.

Accompanying the station reference number are the river and station names. When the station name only is known, the reference number may be obtained from the alphabetical list of names on pages 177 to 188.

The Grid Reference of the gauging station is given by the reference letters of the 100km grid (National Grid in Great Britain; Irish Grid in Northern Ireland) and by six figures defining multiples of 100m.

The catchment area of each station is given in square kilometres to not more than three significant figures.

Under the column heading 'Records Start' is the year from which reasonably continuous records are maintained. Where earlier records exist the year of commencement of these is shown in brackets but such records may be incomplete, unreliable or discontinuous and may be available only from the measuring authority. The next column indicates with an asterisk whether the data are archived by the Water Data Unit. The number of such stations increases progressively and gaps within station records are being reduced. Flow data given in the index but not archived at the Water Data Unit have been provided by the measuring authority in summary form only.

Under the heading 'Measuring Authority' is given the body responsible for the day to day operation of the gauging station; the full names of the abbreviations and their addresses are to be found in the Directory of Contributors (pages 105–108).

The level of the station and the highest point in the catchment are given in metres above ordnance datum; the Belfast datum is used for Northern Ireland stations.

Rainfall in millimetres, as the average annual areal value over the catchment, is given for the standard period 1916 to 1950 in Great Britain or 1931 to 1960 in Northern Ireland and, for comparative purposes, for the period of the stream flow record up to 31 December 1973.

The block heading 'Discharges determined during the period of record to 31 December 1973' presents under sub-headings a brief summary including the mean and the range of the flow. The mean gauged discharge in cubic metres per second is the averaged flow which actually passed through the gauging station, whilst the mean annual naturalized run-off represents an estimate of the flow which would have occurred had it not been modified by artificial storage, abstractions, releases and returns of effluents which are termed variations. It is expressed as the equivalent water depth over the catchment in millimetres, providing a direct comparison with the catchment rainfall. The naturalized run-off is an idealized concept which is increasingly difficult to compute as river systems becomes more highly developed. When details of variations are available the naturalized run-off is computed from the mean gauged discharge modified by the net abstraction or augmentation in the catchment. Where there are no significant variations due to transfers of water to or from the catchment or to changes in storage, the natural and gauged discharges are the same. Estimates of the naturalized discharge are not always available for each year of the gauged discharge record and a minimum of five years of these estimates has been required as a criterion for including their mean annual value in the register.

The extremes of flow are the highest instantaneous value and the lowest daily mean discharge. Because the lowest daily mean discharge may occur more than once the following procedure is adopted to indicate whether or not this is the case. A date without an asterisk is the first in the year in which the lowest flow is recorded; an asterisk with the date indicates that the same flow also occurred in a later second year. When no date is given, the lowest flow is recorded in three or more years.

The column headed 'Abstractions and Returns' gives, by means of the following code, an indication of the nature of the principal variations in flow that predominate in the particular catchment:

S— Impounding Reservoir. Natural river flows will be affected by water stored in a reservoir situated in the catchment above the gauging station.

R— Regulated River. Under certain flow conditions the river will be augmented from surface and ground water storage above the gauging station.

P— Public Water Supplies. Natural river flows are reduced by an amount equivalent to the quantity abstracted from a reservoir, or by a river intake, if the water is conveyed outside the catchment area defined by the gauging station.

G— Groundwater Abstraction. Natural river flows may be reduced or augmented by groundwater abstractions.

E— Effluent Return. Outflows from sewage disposal works and from industries augment river flows if the effluents originate from a different catchment.

I— Industrial and Agricultural Abstractions. Direct industrial and agricultural abstractions from surface and underground sources may reduce the natural river flow.

H— Hydro-Electric Power. The river flow is regulated to suit the need for power generation.

The column headed 'Station Details' states briefly the type and history of the gauging station, and where relevant, it includes the dimensions, performance characteristics and limitations. A river section denotes that the rating, which is regularly checked, is derived from velocity/area measurements regardless of whether the control is the natural channel or an artificial addition. The Crump weir is now generally recognised and its specifications include a horizontal crest with 1:2 and 1:5 upstream and downstream slopes and vertical flanking walls. The Crump profile flat V weir is of a similar design but the crest is modified to incorporate cross-falls to the centre of either 1:10 or 1:20 slope. The modular limit, which is applied to Crump weirs in particular, is the submergence ratio when the flow just begins to be affected by the downstream level. (The submergence ratio is the ratio of the downstream total head to the upstream total head of a weir, the crest being taken as the datum.) The approximate stage at which the modular limit is reached is quoted in a number of the entries. A flume, which is essentially an artificial channel with clearly specified shape and dimensions, can be of the Venturi type (where stage measurements are required both upstream of and at the flume contraction), or of the critical depth type (where only one set of stage measurements is required, at a point upstream of the constriction).

2.5 Computation and Accuracy of Gauged Flows

Gauged flows are calculated by the conversion of records of stage or water level using a stage-discharge relationship which is often referred to as the rating or calibration. Stage is measured and recorded against time by instruments usually actuated by a float in a stilling well, although a pressure sensor may be used as the transducer. The instrument records the level either continuously by pen and chart or digitally on punched paper tape at regular (normally 15-minute) intervals. The stage-discharge relationship is obtained either by building a gauging structure (usually a weir or flume) with known hydraulic characteristics, or by measuring the stream velocity and cross-sectional area throughout the range of flows at a site characterised by its ability to maintain this relationship.

The accuracy of processed gauged discharges therefore depends upon several factors:

i   Accuracy and reliability in measuring and recording water levels

ii   Accuracy and reliability of the derived stage-discharge relationship

iii   Concurrency of the rating and the stage record with respect to changes in the control.

British and International Standards are followed as far as possible in the design, installation and operation of gauging stations. Most of these Standards include a section devoted to accuracy which results in recommendations for reducing uncertainties in discharge measurements, and for estimating the extent of the uncertainties which do arise. A list of Standards which are now available or are in preparation is given in the Appendix.

Measuring authorities have assumed responsibility for the effective calibration and operation of gauging stations and for ensuring that reliable records are produced. The Water Data Unit provides a medium for co-operation and standardisation in these matters between the various authorities as well as a direct service for the computation of the calibration of stations from field data, and for the processing of the recorded data.

2.6 Computation and Accuracy of Estimates of Areal Rainfall and Evaporation Data

The long-period (1916 to 1950 in Great Britain, 1931 to 1960 in Northern Ireland) average annual rainfall for each catchment was first obtained. Rainfall at each station within the catchment network for each month was then expressed as a percentage of station annual average rainfall for a selected number of stations chosen to represent the catchment. The percentage values of rainfall for each station were summed and their mean obtained to give a catchment percentage value for the month which was then converted to monthly mean rainfall (mm). Accuracy therefore depends largely on the reliability of the assessment of the areal annual average and on the adequacy of the network of stations used to represent an area. For a few areas exemplified by the Lee at Feildes Weir, the monthly rainfall values were obtained by the more accurate method of mapping all available rainfall data and assessing areal rainfall by planimetry.

The method of estimating seven-day rainfalls for each of the ten selected areas for 1973 (Section 8, p 157) was similar to that used in estimating monthly rainfalls, i.e. daily falls were expressed as percentages of station annual averages in order to get daily areal estimates. Daily estimates were then totalled to obtain the seven-day estimates. The station networks used were considered adequate for the estimation of monthly rainfall but a denser network would have been desirable for the evaluation of seven-day estimates.

The method of calculating seven-day estimates of potential evaporation for the ten areas was basically the same as that used to evaluate areal rainfall except that station evaporation was calculated (Penman 1963) by taking the mean of the appropriate meteorological variables for seven days (rather than by estimating evaporation daily and summing for seven-day periods). The values obtained are much less reliable than those for rainfall because there is greater uncertainty about the map of long-period average evaporation.

In many upland areas a crude altitude-evaporation relationship was used to construct the map, there being little confirmatory data. In most cases the network of 'evaporation stations' is quite inadequate to represent an area. The most reliable estimates are for Thames and Wissey; estimates for upland areas are much less certain and the estimates for Spey and Nith are the least satisfactory. The seven-day estimates of actual evaporation were derived from estimates of areal rainfall and potential evaporation using the method outlined by Grindley (1969). The method was first proposed by Penman (1950) and adopts his concept of 'root constant'. The root constant defines a specified amount of soil moisture (expressed in equivalent depth in mm) which can be extracted from the soil without difficulty by a given vegetation type. A further 25mm of moisture can be extracted with increasing difficulty and extraction thereafter becomes minimal. As the rate of extraction falls below the potential rate so actual evaporation falls below potential evaporation. In the model used, allowance was made for evaporation from six different vegetation types with different root constants and, where necessary, for evaporation from fallow soil, impervious areas, riparian zones and open water. The proportion of land occupied by each of the different vegetation types and other land uses was estimated for each of the ten areas.

The accuracy of the estimate of actual evaporation depends primarily on the accuracy of the estimates of rainfall and potential evaporation (as noted, the latter are uncertain for many areas). It also depends on the validity of the model used. The estimates for the ten areas were based on 'lumped' (mean areal catchment rainfall and potential evaporation) data. A more desirable procedure might be to integrate values calculated on a point basis using a close grid network, each point having its appropriate spectrum of land use values. Limited experience has shown little difference in areal estimates obtained by the two methods.

References

Penman, H. L. 1950 The water balance of the Stour catchment area. Jnl. Instn. Wat. Engrs., 4, 457–465.

Penman, H. L. 1963 Woburn irrigation 1951–1959; (1) Purpose, design and weather. J. Agric. Sci., 58, 343–348.

Grindley, J. 1969 The calculation of actual evaporation and soil moisture deficit over specified catchment areas. Meteorological Office, Hydrological Memorandum No. 38.

2.7 River Water Temperature Stations

A list is included of temperature stations for which records are available in the archives either of the Unit or of the water authorities. The 1973 records from six of these stations are presented as graphs of monthly mean temperatures together with extremes for the periods of record up to 1972. The temperatures, given in degrees Celsius (°C), are measured in flowing water about 0.5 metres below the water surface and one or two metres from the river bank. Both continuous recording and daily read thermometers are used and the method in each case is given in the register of river water temperature stations. This register also lists for each temperature station the number of the Hydrometric Area, with the number of the gauging stations when the two sites coincide, the river on which the station is located, the National Grid Reference of the site and the year of commencement of the record. Copies of the tables of river water temperatures may be obtained on request from the Water Data Unit or from the appropriate water authority.

3 Units of Measurement and Conversion Factors

The data published in this book are in metric units. The relevant conversions between metric and imperial units are as follows:

1 millimetre	mm	=	0.039 37 in
1 metre	m	=	3.281 ft
1 square kilometre	km^2	=	0.386 1 $mile^2$
1 cubic metre per second (cumec)	m^3/s	=	35.31 ft^3/s
1 litre per second per square kilometre	$1/s\ km^2$	=	0.091 46 $ft^3/s\ mile^2$
Degrees Celsius	°C	=	5 (°F − 32)/9

1 inch	in	=	25.400 mm
1 foot	ft	=	0.304 8 m
1 square mile	$mile^2$	=	2.590 km^2
1 cubic foot per second (cusec)	ft^3/s	=	0.028 32 m^3/s
1 million gallons per day	mgd	=	0.052 62 m^3/s
1 cubic foot per second per square mile	$ft^3/s\ mile^2$	=	10.933 $1/s\ km^2$
Degrees Fahrenheit	°F	=	(9°C/5) + 32

4 Register of Gauging Stations

Station number	River	Station name	National grid reference	Catchment area	Records start	Data archived	Measuring authority	Level of station	Highest point in the catchment	Annual average areal rainfall; mm	
										Standard average for 1916-1950	Period of record average to 31.12.7
				km^2				m.O.D.	m.O.D.		

HIGHLAND RIVER PURIFICATION BOARD AREA

Station number	River	Station name	National grid reference	Catchment area	Records start	Data archived	Measuring authority	Level of station	Highest point in the catchment	Standard average for 1916-1950	Period of record average to 31.12.7
002001	Helmsdale	Kilphedir	NC 997181	551	1973	*	SDD	16.99	623		
003901	Shin	Lairg	NC 581062	495	1950	*	NSHEB	81.7	873		1494
003002	Carron	Sgodachail	NH 490920	241	1973		SDD	70.74	951		
003804	Cassley	Intake	NC 386170	45.1	1962		NSHEB		998		
004001	Conon	Moy Bridge	NH 482547	962	1945	*	SDD	10.4	1110	1758	1805
004302	Glass	Redburn	NH 566672	108	1971		HRCWD		955		
004003	Alness	Alness	NH 654695	201	1973		SDD	11.95	838		
005901	Beauly	Erchless	NH 426405	850	1950	*	NSHEB	43.9	1180	2139	2174
006901	Ness	Ness Castle Farm	NH 639410	1790	1935		NSHEB	9.1	1120	1824	1757
006903	Moriston	Invermoriston	NH 416169	391	1929		RFR	35.1	1120		
006904	Garry	Invergarry	NH 316011	386	1929		RFR	33.5	1040		
006906	Allt Bhlaraidh	Invermoriston	NH 377168	27.5	1951		NSHEB	107	678		1555
006007	Ness	Ness Side	NH 645427	1840	1973	*	SDD	7.32	1120	1808	
007001	Findhorn	Shenachie	NH 828339	416	1962 (1960)	*	SDD	254.42	941	1337	1178
007002	Findhorn	Forres	NJ 018583	782	1958	*	SDD	9.60	941	1202	998
090001	Leven	Blackwater Reservoir	NN 202602	171	1950		BAC	299	939	2146	
091001	Lochy	Lochaber Water Power Area	NN 126752	780	1949		BAC	22.9	1340	2019	
091802	Allt Leachdach	Intake	NN 261781	6.5	1938		BAC	210	1067		
091901	Mucomir Cut	Gairlochy	NN 179843	383	1929		NSHEB	28.3	982		
094001	Ewe	Poolewe	NG 859803	441	1970	*	SDD	4.61	1009	2249	
097001	Calder Burn	Loch Calder	ND 085596	24.5	1956		HRCWD	64.5	245	970	
097002	Thurso	Halkirk	NU 131595	413	1971		SDD	30.23	580	995	

Mean gauged discharge	Mean annual natural runoff	Highest instantaneous gauged discharge	Date	Lowest daily mean gauged discharge	Date	Abstractions and returns	Station details	Station number
m³/s	mm	m³/s		m³/s				
							River section	002001
16.43 *0.033*		126.01	27.12.54	0.48	1. 9.55	H	River section. Records ceased November 1955	003901
							River section	003002
							Compound broad crested weir	003804
				0.57	24. 9.56	H	River section. The natural catchment has been progressively increased to 1170 km² by diversions from external areas from 1956 onwards	004001
						H	Compound Crump weir	004302
							River section	004003
44.44 *0.052*		594.66	12. 2.62	7.36	31. 8.55	H	River section. Station ceased 1963	005901
73.14 *0.041*		591.83	20.12.36	7.33	2. 9.55	H	River section – artificial control. Station ceased 1962 and replaced by 006007. Abstraction to Caledonian Canal of about 3 cumecs	006901
						H	River section. Station ceased 1945	006903
						H	River section. Station ceased 1944	006904
0.86 *(0.031)*		23.22	27.10.57	0.00	17. 7.55	H	Compound weir. Station ceased 1962	006906
76.60 *(0.042)*		264.43	18.11.73	14.36	26. 8.73		River section. Replaces 006901	006007
12.46 *(0.03)*		505.17	17. 8.70	1.37	19. 9.71		River section	007001
18.05 *(0.023)*		2410.00	17. 8.70	2.18	6. 6.60		River section	007002
						H	Thin plate weir. Monthly summaries only	090001
						H	Venturi meters at Lochaber Power Station. Possible inaccuracies in measurements due to hydrometric complication. Monthly summaries only	091001
							Compound V notch in rectangular thin plate weir	091802
							River section. Station ceased 1962. Caledonian Canal brings water from river Ness basin and takes water out unmeasured.	091901
24.75 *(0.013)*		95.01	18.11.76	4.24	20.10.72		River section	094001
						S	Broad crested weir at outlet from Loch	097001
6.87 *(0.017)*		80.77	3.12.73	0.43	29. 7.72*		River section	097002

Station number	River	Station name	National grid reference	Catchment area	Records start	Data archived	Measuring authority	Level of station	Highest point in the catchment	Annual average areal rainfall; mm	
										Standard average for 1916-1950	Period of record average to 31.12.7
				km²				m.O.D.	m.O.D.		

NORTH EAST RIVER PURIFICATION BOARD AREA

Station number	River	Station name	National grid reference	Catchment area	Records start	Data archived	Measuring authority	Level of station	Highest point	Standard average 1916-1950	Period of record average to 31.12.7
007003	Lossie	Sheriffmills	NJ 198626	216	1963	*	SDD	17.6	521	864	777
008001	Spey	Aberlour	NJ 278439	2650	1945 (1938)	*	SDD	78.6	1310	1168	1084
008002	Spey	Kinrara	NH 881082	1010	1951	*	SDD	210	941	1364	1250
008003	Spey	Ruthven Bridge	NN 759996	534	1951	*	SDD	221	941	1448	1373
008004	Avon	Dalnashaugh	NJ 186352	543	1952	*	SDD	150	1309	1119	
008005	Spey	Boat of Garten	NH 946191	1270	1951	*	SDD	197	1300	1311	
008006	Spey	Boat o' Brig	NJ 318518	2860	1957 (1952)	*	SDD	43.0	1310	1153	1083
008007	Spey	Invertruim	NN 687962	400	1957 (1952)	*	SDD	243	941	1491	1395
008008	Tromie	Tromie Bridge	NN 789995	130	1958 (1952)	*	SDD	240	782	1460	1354
008009	Dulnain	Balnaan Bridge	NH 977247	272	1958 (1952)	*	SDD	224	838	1101	
008010	Spey	Grantown	NJ 034268	1750	1953	*	SDD	193	1290	1237	1108
008901	Spey	Laggan Bridge	NN 614943	220	1935		BAC	243			
008902	Feshie	Feshie Bridge	NH 851043	232	1951		SDD	235			
009001	Deveron	Avochie	NJ 532464	442	1962 (1959)	*	SDD	82.0	775	991	983
009002	Deveron	Muiresk	NJ 705498	955	1962 (1960)	*	SDD	25.3	775	940	879
009003	Isla	Grange	NJ 494506	176	1960	*	SDD			1087	
009801	Allt Deveron	Kingsford Bridge	NJ 379288		1948		GRWD				
010001	Ythan	Ardlethan	NJ 924308	448	1965	*	NERPB	7.5	381	881	785
010002	Ugie	Inverugie	NK 101485	325	1970	*	NERPB	8.5	234	881	
011001	Don	Parkhill	NJ 887141	1270	1970	*	NERPB	32.4	872	927	
011002	Don	Haughton	NJ 756201	787	1969	*	NERPB	55.0	872	963	
011003	Don	Bridge of Alford	NJ 566170	499	1973	*	NERPB	135.0	872	994	
011304	Urie	Urieside	NJ 771229	239	1969		GRWD			901	
012001	Dee	Woodend	NO 632960	1370	1935 (1929)	*	NERPB	70.5	1310	1146	1104
012002	Dee	Park	NO 798983	1840	1972	*	NERPB	22.6	1310	1113	
012801	Glen Dye	Bridge of Dye	NO 651851		1957		GRWD			1215	

TAY RIVER PURIFICATION BOARD AREA

Station number	River	Station name	National grid reference	Catchment area	Records start	Data archived	Measuring authority	Level of station	Highest point	Standard average 1916-1950	Period of record average to 31.12.7
014001	Eden	Kemback	NO 415158	307	1967	*	TRPB	6.20	522	839	701
014002	Dighty	Balmossie Mill	NO 477324	127	1969	*	TRPB	16.1	455	835	658
015001	Isla	Forter	NO 187647	70.7	1956 (1949)	*	TRWSD	285	1070	1427	1416
015002	Newton	Newton	NO 230605	15.4	1949	*	TRWSD	256	829	1288	1291
015003	Tay	Caputh	NO 088395	3210	1947 (1937)	*	TRWSD	36	1210	1648	1541
015004	Inzion	Loch of Lintrathen	NO 280559	24.7	1949 (1927)	*	TRWSD	199	670	1107	1112

Mean gauged discharge m³/s	Mean annual natural runoff mm	Highest instantaneous gauged discharge m³/s	Date	Lowest daily mean gauged discharge m³/s	Date	Abstractions and returns	Station details	Station number
2.58	0.012 486 62.5	89.83	17. 8.70	0.49	28. 8.72		River section. Weir control	007003
55.86	0.021 674 62.2	1300.00	17. 8.70	7.98	25. 8.55	H	River section. 399 km² Developed for hydro-electric power production	008001
19.92	0.02	317.00	18.12.66	3.09	7. 8.55	H	River section. 399 km² Developed for hydro-electric power production	008002
9.33	0.017	222.40	18.12.66	1.29	30. 8.55	H	River section. 287 km² Developed for hydro-electric power production	008003
14.70	0.027	525.00	17. 8.70	1.93	17. 2.55		River section	008004
27.73	0.022	373.60	18.12.66	4.22	4. 8.55	H	River section. 399 km² Developed for hydro-electric power production	008005
62.80	0.022	1675.00	17. 8.70	9.31	16. 8.55	H	River section. 399 km² Developed for hydro-electric power production	008006
5.61	0.014	259.50	18.12.66	0.93	5. 9.58	H	River section. 287 km² Developed for hydro-electric power production	008007
2.41	0.019	117.45	28. 9.61	0.35	4. 8.55	H	River section. 112 km² Developed for hydro-electric power production	008008
5.64	0.021	230.00	17. 8.70	0.67	4. 9.59		River section	008009
35.19	0.02	461.30	19.12.66	6.68	1. 9.55	H	River section. 399 km² Developed for hydro-electric power production	008010
							River section. From 1944 a broad crest weir measures compensation and flood flows from Spey and Mashie Dams	008901
							River section	008902
8.65	0.02	236.46	17. 8.70	1.51	4.10.59		River section	009001
15.96	0.017	506.57	6. 5.68	2.54	9.10.72		River section	009002
1.99	0.011	48.80	17. 8.70	0.44	21. 6.73		River section	009003
							Compound broad crested weir	009801
6.52	0.015	66.22	6. 5.68	1.08	11.11.72		River section	010001
3.02	0.009	67.86	19. 3.71	0.65	29. 8.72		River section – weir control	010002
16.01	0.013	251.19	17. 8.70	3.22	12.11.72		River section	011001
11.21	0.0142	113.73	25.11.71	3.21	8.11.72		River section	011002
		70.79	26.12.73	2.61	13. 9.73		River section	011003
							Temporary station	011304
35.70	0.0261	1132.68	24. 1.37	1.05	21. 1.50		River section	012001
27.00	0.0147	209.79	27.12.73	6.91	15. 9.73		River section	012002
							Low flow flume set in broad crested weir	012801
3.09	0.010	47.48	5. 5.68	0.64	30. 8.73		River section	014001
1.10	0.0087	20.50	18. 1.70	0.16	30. 6.73		River section	014002
2.70	0.0382	99.11	30. 9.62	0.31	21. 2.63		Compound critical depth flume	015001
0.50	0.0325	14.73	30. 9.62	0.10	13. 7.62		Thin plate compound weir	015002
28.91	0.0402	1481.21	5.11.51	8.07	12. 8.55	H	River section. 1980 km² developed for hydro-electric power production	015003
0.57	0.0231	24.93	30. 9.62	0.06	20. 7.68		Thin plate compound weir	015004

Station number	River	Station name	National grid reference	Catch-ment area	Records start	Data archived	Measuring authority	Level of station	Highest point in the catch-ment	Annual average areal rainfall; mm	
										Standard average for 1916-1950	Period of record average to 31.12.73
				km²				m.O.D.	m.O.D.		

TAY RIVER PURIFICATION BOARD AREA (CONTD)

015005	Melgam	Loch of Lintrathen	NO 275558	40.9	1949 (1927)	*	TRWSD	212	631	1166	1149
015006	Tay	Ballathie	NO 147367	4590	1956 (1952)	*	SDD	26.2	1210	1471	1392
015007	Tay	Pitnacree	NN 924534	1150	1962 (1957)	*	SDD	61.1	1210	1946	1763
015008	Dean	Cookston	NO 340479	177	1958	*	SDD	45.0	455	879	
015010	Isla	Wester Cardean	NO 295466	367	1972		TRPB	36.4	1068	1117	
015011	Lyon	Comrie Bridge	NN 786486	391	1972 (1960)	*	TRPB	92.10	1215	2049	
015012	Tummel	Ballinluig	NN 977521	1720	1973	*	TRPB	58.67	1145	1550	
015013	Almond	Almondbank	NO 067258	175	1972	*	TRPB	20.37	930	1508	
015016	Tay	Kenmore	NN 782467	601	1974 (1960)		TRPB	100.44	1215	2129	
015808	Almond	Lednock Intake	NN 758332	17.7	1961		NSHEB			1829	
015809	Muckle Burn	Eastmill	NO 223604	16.5	1940		TRWSD				
015902	Lyon	Moar	NN 534448	161	1949	*	NSHEB	244	1080		
016001	Earn	Kinkell Bridge	NN 933167	590	1947	*	SDD	15.5	983	1608	1417
016002	Earn	Aberuchill	NN 754216	177	1958 (1955)	*	SDD	62.2	981	1859	1673
016003	Ruchill	Cultybraggan	NN 764204	99.5	1970 (1959)	*	SDD			2059	
016004	Earn	Forteviot Bridge	NO 043184	782	1972	*	TRPB	7.84	983	1497	1022

FORTH RIVER PURIFICATION BOARD AREA

017001	Carron	Headswood	NS 832820	122	1970	*	FRPB	17.1	570		
017002	Leven	Leven	NO 369006	424	1970	*	FRPB	4.05	522		
017003	Bonny Water	Bonnybridge	NS 824804	50.5	1972	*	FRPB	23.0	185		
017004	Ore	Balfour Mains	NT 330997	162	1973	*	FRPB	23.1	364		
017005	Avon	Polmonthill	NS 952797	195	1972	*	FRPB	4.27	312		
017006	Carron	Langhill Weir	NS 772846	77.7	1971		CRWD				
017007	Red Burn	Glen Cottage	NS 782766	12.7			CDC				
017308	South Queich	Kinross	NO 122015	33.7			ITE				
018001	Allan Water	Kinbuck	NN 792053	161	1958	*	FRPB	93.0	633	1381	
018002	Devon	Glenochil	NS 858960	181	1959	*	FRPB	5.49	720	1273	1214
018003	Teith	Bridge of Teith	NN 725011	518	1957	*	FRPB	14.7	1165	1996	1790
018904	Devon	Devonvale	NS 920964	142	1956		SDD	11.9	720		
018005	Allan Water	Bridge of Allan	NS 786980	210	1972	*	FRPB	11.2	633	1325	
018306	Goodie Water	Netherton	NS 660987	58.0	1956		FRPB				
018008	Leny	Anie	NN 585096	190	1974	*	FRPB	120.2	1165	2229	
019001	Almond	Craigiehall	NT 165752	369	1957	*	FRPB	22.9	518	914	852
019002	Almond	Almond Weir	NT 004652	43.8	1962	*	FRPB	128	296	1062	1034

16

Mean gauged discharge	Mean annual natural runoff	Highest instantaneous gauged discharge	Date	Lowest daily mean gauged discharge	Date	Abstractions and returns	Station details	Station number
m³/s	mm	m³/s		m³/s				
1.02 /0.025		36.82	2. 3.66	0.02	12. 8.68	S	Thin plate compound weir. Backwater Reservoir completed in 1969	015005
52.21 /0.0332		1386.70	12. 2.62	11.46	6. 8.55	H	River section. 1980 km² developed for hydro-electric power production	015006
50.77 /0.0441		486.76	12. 2.62	8.66	24.10.72	H	River section. 295 km² developed for hydro-electric power production	015007
2.39 /0.0135		39.90	23.10.60	0.27	28.11.73	E	River section	015008
4.05 /0.0110		48.24	5.11.73	1.53	9. 7.73	H	River section. 170 km² developed for hydro-electric power production. Jointly operated with Dundee University	015010
4.64 /0.0119		124.62	18.11.73	0.61	21.10.72	P	River section. 73 km² controlled for water supply purposes	015011
54.89 /0.0319		282.38	27.12.73	20.27	11.10.73	H	River section. Approx 98% (1690 km²) developed for hydro-electric power production	015012
2.71 /0.0155		70.50	19. 6.73	0.61	21.10.72	H P	River section. 30 km² of headwaters controlled by NSHEB. Minor water supply abstraction from lower tributary	015013
						H	River section. 120 km² developed for hydro-electric power production	015016
							Complex of diversion weir, fish pass and flood spillway	015808
							Compound thin plate rectangular weirs set in broad crest flanking weir	015809
10.48 /0.0651		291.67	28.12.55	0.20	8. 8.55	H	River section. Station ceased September 1958	015902
20.17 /0.0342		339.80	25.12.49	0.72	6. 8.55	H	River section. 189 km² developed for hydro-electric power production	016001
10.08 /0.057		133.01	15. 1.62	0.76	29. 6.57	H	River section. 162 km² developed for hydro-electric power production	016002
3.70 /0.0372		221.33	18. 6.73	0.29	19. 9.72		River section	016003
15.51 /0.0198		189.59	12.12.72	3.77	2.10.72	H P	River section. 189 km² developed for hydro-electric power production 43 km² controlled for water supply purposes. Jointly operated with Dundee University	016004
2.55 /0.0209		105.76	2.11.69	0.26	22.10.72	S E	River section	017001
3.94 /0.0093		38.66	23.11.70	0.51	30. 9.73	R E I	River section	017002
0.92 /0.0182		30.72	5. 8.71	0.17	9. 7.71	E I	River section	017003
0.57 /0.0035		9.19	19.12.73	0.09	21. 8.73	E I	River section	017004
2.19 /0.0112		40.65	11.12.72	0.47	26. 8.73	E I	River section	017005
						S	Flume	017006
							Compound flume and weir – records ceased in 1968	017007
							River section: periodically modified by fish hakes	017308
4.76 /0.0296		101.38	28. 7.58	0.53	7.10.72		River section	018001
4.26 /0.0235		109.05	8. 8.72	0.00	1. 3.72	S I	River section	018002
19.83 / 1561		214.10	18.12.66	2.60	10. 8.68	S	River section	018003
0.0383						S	River section. Station ceased 1963	018904
4.70 / 0.0224		79.68	21.10.71	0.75	19. 7.71	I	River section	018005
							River section	018306
		49.13	19.11.73	2.56	2.11.73		River section	018008
5.16 /0.014 455 44.0		174.8	22.11.69	0.24	9.10.59	E I P	River section	019001
0.96 /0.0219 692 66.9		23.09	22.11.69	0.10	28. 6.68	E	Broad crested compound weir	019002

Station number	River	Station name	National grid reference	Catchment area	Records start	Data archived	Measuring authority	Level of station	Highest point in the catchment	Annual average areal rainfall; mm	
										Standard average for 1916-1950	Period of record average to 31.12.7
				km²				m.O.D.	m.O.D.		

FORTH RIVER PURIFICATION BOARD AREA (CONTD)

019003	Breich Water	Breich Weir	NT 014639	51.8	1962	*	FRPB	136	359	980	942
019004	North Esk	Dalmore Weir	NT 252616	81.6	1960	*	FRPB	132	579	1003	959
019005	Almond	Almondell	NT 086686	229	1963	*	FRPB	73.2	518	968	882
019006	Water of Leith	Murrayfield	NT 228732	107	1963	*	FRPB	37.5	562	935	816
019007	Esk	Musselburgh	NT 339723	330	1962		FRPB	3.36	651	892	865
019008	South Esk	Prestonholm	NT 325623	112	1964	*	FRPB	76.8	651	921	836
019009	Bog Burn	Cobbinshaw	NT 026591	8.5	1963	*	FRPB	256	301	990	
019010	Braid Burn	Liberton	NT 273707	16.2	1969	*	FRPB	49.5	493		
019011	North Esk	Dalkeith Palace	NT 333678	137	1963		FRPB		579		
020001	Tyne	East Linton	NT 591768	307	1961	*	FRPB	16.5	528	759	710
020002	Peffer West	Luffness	NT 489811	26.2	1968	*	FRPB	4.15	138	643	
020003	Tyne	Spilmersford Bridge	NT 456689	161	1965	*	FRPB	69.3	472	762	
020004	Peffer East	Lochhouses	NT 610824	13.1	1967	*	FRPB	3.51	180	652	
020005	Birns Water	Saltoun Hall	NT 457688	93.0	1965	*	FRPB	71.5	451		
020006	Biel Water	Belton House	NT 645768	51.8	1973		FRPB	13.9	433		
020007	Gifford Water	Lennoxlove	NT 511717	64.0	1973		FRPB	51.2	527	809	

TWEED RIVER PURIFICATION BOARD AREA

021901	Fruid Water	Fruid	NT 088205	23.7	1947	*	LRWD	277	808	1755	1755
021902	Whiteadder Water	Hungry Snout	NT 663633	45.6	1955	*	LRWD	215	533	884	951
021003	Tweed	Peebles	NT 257400	694	1950 (1939)	*	TWRPB	155	839	1252	1235
021004	Watch Water	Watch Water Reservoir	NT 664566	10.7	1955	*	LRWD	252	464	940	
021005	Tweed	Lyne Ford	NT 206397	373	1961	*	TWRPB	167	839	1364	1260
021006	Tweed	Boleside	NT 498334	1500	1961	*	TWRPB	94.5	839	1270	1224
021007	Ettrick Water	Lindean	NT 486315	499	1961	*	TWRPB	99.1	839	1455	1358
021008	Teviot	Ormiston Mill	NT 702280	1110	1961 (1960)	*	TWRPB	43.2	608	1046	960
021009	Tweed	Norham	NT 898477	4390	1962 (1959)	*	TWRPB	4.27	839	1024	962
021010	Tweed	Dryburgh	NT 588320	2080	1963 (1959)	*	TWRPB	66.8	839	1166	1072
021011	Yarrow Water	Philiphaugh	NT 439277	231	1963 (1962)	*	TWRPB	128	839	1488	1325
021012	Teviot	Hawick	NT 522159	323	1963 (1960)	*	TWRPB	90.1	608	1262	
021013	Gala Water	Galashiels	NT 479374	207	1964 (1963)	*	TWRPB	120	651	975	908
021014	Tweed	Kingledores	NT 109285	139	1961	*	TWRPB	214	839	1622	
021015	Leader Water	Earlston	NT 565388	239	1966	*	TWRPB	103	528	861	
021016	Eye Water	Eyemouth Mill	NT 942635	119	1967	*	TWRPB	2.90	414	747	
021017	Ettrick Water	Brockhoperig	NT 234132	37.5	1965	*	TWRPB	259	692	1881	
021018	Lyne Water	Lyne Station	NT 209401	175	1968	*	TWRPB	168	562	1004	
021019	Manor Water	Cademuir	NT 217369	61.6	1968	*	TWRPB	197	818	1534	
021020	Yarrow Water	Gordon Arms	NT 309247	155	1967	*	TWRPB	226	839	1669	
021021	Tweed	Sprouston	NT 752354	3330	1969	*	TWRPB	24.5	839	1106	
021022	Whiteadder Water	Hutton Castle	NT 881550	503	1969	*	TWRPB	29.0	533	826	
021023	Leet Water	Coldstream	NT 838396	113	1970	*	TWRPB	12.05	223	699	

Discharges determined during period of record to 31 December 1973

Mean gauged discharge	Mean annual natural runoff	Highest instantaneous gauged discharge	Date	Lowest daily mean gauged discharge	Date	Abstractions and returns	Station details	Station number
m^3/s	mm	m^3/s		m^3/s				
0.95	570	24.25	14. 8.66	0.03	18. 6.71	E	Broad crested weir	019003
1.48	573	37.10	14. 8.66	0.23	18. 9.72	E I	Broad crested ogee section weir. Paper mills on river	019004
3.59	604	132.62	22.11.69	0.19	14.10.72	E I P	River section – flat V control constructed 1970. Abstraction for canal	019005
1.29	445	66.83	14. 8.66	0.14	17.10.73	S	River section	019006
3.75	463	175.56	14. 8.66	0.70	24. 7.66	E I S P	River section	019007
1.24	483	70.79	14. 8.66	0.22	16. 4.73	S	Crump weir	019008
0.14	529	2.58	31.10.70	0.00	1. 3.73	S	Thin plate rectangular weir replaced by trapezoidal flume in 1973	019009
0.09	187	5.58	19. 3.71	0.02	18.10.69		Combined Crump weir and trapezoidal flume	019010
							River section	019011
2.66	289	112.70	4. 8.66	0.33	6. 9.69		River section	020001
0.11	145	4.39	16. 5.67	0.00	8. 7.73	I	Combined Crump weir and trapezoidal flume	020002
1.29	253	103.07	4. 8.66	0.20	3.12.73		River section with artificial control	020003
0.15	149	3.83	23.11.69	0.00	25. 8.73	I	Combined Crump weir and trapezoidal flume	020004
							River section with artificial control	020005
							River section	020006
							River section	020007
0.68	1324	28.88	15. 1.62	0.06	1.10.59	S P	Compound rectangular thin plate weir. Fruid Reservoir completed in 1969 and weir removed in 1971	021901
1.02	736	63.23	4. 8.66	0.08	10.11.59	S P	Broad crested weir with central concrete flume. Whiteadder Reservoir completed 1969 and weir removed	021902
4.49	762	481.39	15. 1.62	1.93	7.10.59	S P	River section. Station moved in 1959; earlier records correlated	021003
0.10		1.58	12. 5.68	0.03	1.10.65*	S	Thin plate compound weir	021004
8.12	879	266.18	15. 1.62	1.19	7.10.72	S P	River section	021005
33.58	827	605.98	16. 1.62	3.46	7.10.72	S P	River section	021006
4.20		362.46	15. 1.62	0.77	5.10.72		River section	021007
8.20		475.73	6. 3.63	1.78	25.10.72		River section	021008
73.85	582	1186.47	6. 3.63	9.07	8.10.72	S P	River section	021009
41.43	711	622.97	11. 1.65	4.98	5. 8.64	S P	River section	021010
6.22		102.22	11. 1.65	0.41	26.10.72		River section	021011
7.54		228.60	27. 2.67	0.60	6.10.72		River section	021012
3.38		62.30	27. 3.65	0.37	12. 9.73		River section with artificial control	021013
2.52		87.46	11.12.72	0.46	6.10.72	S P	River section. Variable stage-discharge relationship at high flows due to backwater from tributary	021014
2.97		94.79	1.11.67	0.34	4.10.73		River section	021015
1.06		37.13	15. 7.68	0.08	5. 7.73		River section with artificial control	021016
1.57		76.30	11.12.72	0.12	7.10.72		River section	021017
2.25		40.49	31.10.70	0.53	23. 9.73	S P	River section	021018
1.25		25.89	11.12.72	0.19	26.10.72	P	River section with artificial control	021019
4.16		55.52	11.12.72	0.29	26.10.72		River section	021020
6.58		698.37	11.12.72	6.99	27.10.72	S P	River section	021021
4.50		185.96	22.11.69	0.42	26.11.73	S P	Compound Crump weir	021022
0.41		20.68	20. 3.71	0.01	11. 9.73		River section with artificial control and trapezoidal flume for low flow measurement	021023

Station number	River	Station name	National grid reference	Catch-ment area	Records start	Data archived	Measuring authority	Level of station	Highest point in the catch-ment	Annual average areal rainfall; mm Standard average for 1916-1950	Period of record average to 31.12.7
				km²				m.O.D.	m.O.D.		

TWEED RIVER PURIFICATION BOARD AREA (CONTD)

021024	Jed Water	Jedburgh	NT 655214	139	1971	*	TWRPB	67.51	553	1004	
021025	Ale Water	Ancrum	NT 634244	174	1972	*	TWRPB	61.23	445	1003	
021026	Tima Water	Deephope	NT 278138	31.0	1973	*	TWRPB	232.2	545	1692	
021027	Blackadder Water	Mouth Bridge	NT 826530	159	1973	*	TWRPB	56.60	447	804	
021028	Menzion Burn	Menzion Farm	NT 092234	5.7	1953	*	LRWD	267	689		
021029	Tweed	Glenbreck	NT 063215	34.0	1964		LRWD	290	628		
021030	Megget Water	Henderland	NT 231232	56.7	1968	*	TWRPB	259	839	1824	
021033	Baddinsgill Burn	Intake	NT 118557	3.8	1963		LRWD			1232	
021034	Yarrow Water	Craig Douglas	NT 288244	116	1968		TWRPB	238	839	1720	

NORTHUMBRIAN WATER AUTHORITY AREA

021031	Till	Etal	NT 927396	648	1958	*	NWA	25.3	816	838	844
021032	Glen	Kirknewton	NT 918310	199	1966	*	NWA	54.3	816		
022001	Coquet	Morwick	NU 234044	570	1966	*	NWA	77.7	776	921	874
022002	Coquet	Bygate	NT 870083	59.6	1957 (1948)	*	NWA	213	776	1053	994
022003	Usway Burn	Shillmoor	NT 886077	21.4	1952	*	NWA	207	776	1103	1068
022004	Aln	Hawkhill	NU 211129	205	1966	*	NWA	13.9	404	789	862
022005	Wansbeck	Highford Dam	NZ 175858	287	1963		NWA	30.5	440		
022006	Blyth	Hartford Bridge	NZ 243800	270	1966	*	NWA	24.6	259	726	697
022007	Wansbeck	Mitford	NZ 175858	287	1968	*	NWA	31.4	440	839	731
022008	Alwin	Clennell	NT 925063	27.7	1969	*	NWA	156.4	616	1044	
022009	Coquet	Rothbury	NU 067016	346	1972		NWA	70.7	776	962	
023001	Tyne	Bywell	NZ 038617	2180	1956	*	NWA	16.2	893	1044	1046
023002	Derwent	Eddy's Bridge	NZ 041508	118	1954	*	S&SSW	181	560	932	962
023003	North Tyne	Reaverhill	NY 906732	1010	1959	*	NWA	64.9	600	1062	1107
023004	South Tyne	Haydon Bridge	NY 856647	751	1962	*	NWA	58.5	893	1172	1221
023005	North Tyne	Tarset	NY 776861	285	1963 (1960)	*	NWA	117	602	1255	1259
023006	South Tyne	Featherstone	NY 672611	322	1966	*	NWA	131.7	893	1357	1453
023007	Derwent	Rowlands Gill	NZ 168581	242	1963 (1962)	*	NWA	29.3	560	853	905
023008	Rede	Rede Bridge	NY 868832	344	1968	*	NWA	107.1	579	1002	
023009	South Tyne	Alston	NY 716465	119	1969	*	NWA	264	893	1572	
023010	Tarset Burn	Greenhaugh	NY 789879	96.0	1969	*	NWA	136	504	1032	
023011	Kielder Burn	Kielder	NY 644946	59.6	1970	*	NWA	214	602	1341	
023012	East Allen	Wide Eals	NY 802583	88.0	1971	*	NWA	148.6	673	1175	
023013	West Allen	Hindley Wrae	NY 791583	75.1	1971	*	NWA	155.1	673	1234	
023314	North Tyne	Kielder	NY 631931	27.0	1971	*	NWA		602	1343	
023902	North Tyne	Barrasford	NY 924721	1040	1939	*	NGWC		602	1054	997
023903	Rede	Catcleugh Reservoir	NT 750030	39.9	1910		NGWC	248.4	579	1254	
024001	Wear	Sunderland Bridge	NZ 264376	658	1957 (1955)	*	NWA	40.2	747	945	952
024002	Gaunless	Bishop Auckland	NZ 215306	93.0	1958	*	NWA	64.8	461	752	752

Mean gauged discharge m³/s	Mean annual natural runoff mm	Highest instantaneous gauged discharge m³/s	Date	Lowest daily mean gauged discharge m³/s	Date	Abstractions and returns	Station details	Station number
1.44	0.0104	56.98	11.12.72	0.29	13.10.72		River section	021024
1.05	0.006	32.07	11.12.72	0.15	12.10.72	S P	River section	021025
		22.97	10.12.73	0.08	16. 6.73		River section with artificial control	021026
		6.61	19.12.73	0.20	26.11.73		River section	021027
							Compound thin plate weir	021028
							River section: concrete control	021029
1.65	0.0287	104.36	11.12.72	0.12	5. 1.71		River section	021030
							Diverted flow only measured	021033
							Trapezoidal flume	021034
8.75	0.0135	149.23	20.11.65	0.09	1.10.72		River section	021031
2.64	0.0133	75.27	20. 3.71	0.28	6.10.72		River section with flat V Crump profile control weir	021032
8.12	0.0142	207.31	5.11.67	0.00	13. 9.68		River section	022001
1.17	0.0196	32.28	16.10.67	0.04	23.12.71		Critical depth flume and broad crested weir	022002
0.53	0.0248	26.16	15. 7.68	0.04	4. 9.59		Thin plate weir	022003
2.83	0.0138	122.90	5.11.67	0.03	5. 6.68		River section	022004
						S P	River section with round top, brick, skew weir 42.7 m long, superseded by Mitford 022007 in 1968	022005
1.94	0.00719	94.26	18.12.68	0.00	29. 4.67	E	Originally river section. Flat V weir 24.4 m long constructed in 1968. Slopes 1:2, 1:2, 1:20	022006
2.86	0.0099	134.74	18. 3.71	0.12	4.10.70	S	Broad crested weir with a low flow flume	022007
0.57	0.0206	19.54	22.11.69	0.06	16.11.72		Flat V weir	022008
				0.81	5.10.72	S P	River section, weir control	022009
3.45	0.0133 684 65.4	1585.75	17.10.67	3.31	22. 6.70	S	River section	023001
1.59	0.013 664 69.0	58.05	15. 7.61	0.04	11.11.56	S	Critical depth flume	023002
0.04	0.0198	631.47	9.12.64	0.00	16. 1.68	S	River section. Replaces Barrasford, 023902	023003
8.24	0.0242	516.29	16.10.67	0.92	9. 9.69		River section, with informal flat V low flow weir installed 1973	023004
7.64	0.0268	327.32	23. 3.68	0.00	3. 7.67*		River section, with informal flat V low flow weir installed 1973	023005
9.59	0.0298	257.75	3.10.67	1.01	19. 7.71		Compound Crump weir. 2 crests 15.2 m and 29.6 m long	023006
3.15	536 0.013	97.98	5.11.67	0.39	19. 4.72	S R P E I	Two triangular section weirs on the invert of bridge	023007
5.05	0.0147	282.72	19. 2.70	0.47	26.11.73	S	Flat V weir 54.9 m long, with 1:2, 1:2 and 1:20 slopes and cableway	023008
3.58	0.03	145.00	21. 2.70	0.00	3.11.73		River section	023009
1.33	0.0138	128.86	31.10.70	0.11	17. 7.71		River section	023010
1.38	0.0232	128.76	31.10.70	0.12	5. 7.70		Flat V weir 12 m long, with 1:2, 1:2 and 1:20 slopes, and cableway	023011
1.78	0.0202	75.47	13. 8.71	0.13	24. 8.71		River section	023012
1.48	0.0197	50.60	16. 3.72	0.08	4. 7.73		River section	023013
0.72	0.0267	54.12	4.11.71	0.03	6.10.73		River section	023314
8.62	586 58.8	1019.41	19. 1.54	1.30	13. 7.49	S P	Critical depth flume. Replaced by Reaverhill, 023003, in 1959	023902
	0.0179					S P	Rectangular orifice and overflow spillway	023903
0.48	0.0159	576.71	5.11.67	0.90	4.10.59	S E	Compound broad crested weir, 39 m long, within the arches of Sunderland bridge. Lowest crest 9.9 m long	024001
0.96	0.0103	142.72	9.12.65	0.11	10. 8.70	I	Crump weir, 9 m long	024002

Station number	River	Station name	National grid reference	Catch-ment area	Records start	Data archived	Measuring authority	Level of station	Highest point in the catch-ment	Annual average areal rainfall; mm	
										Standard average for 1916-1950	Period of record average to 31.12.7:
				km²				m.O.D.	m.O.D.		

NORTHUMBRIAN WATER AUTHORITY AREA (CONTD)

Station number	River	Station name	National grid reference	Catch-ment area	Records start	Data archived	Measuring authority	Level of station	Highest point in the catch-ment	Standard average for 1916-1950	Period of record average to 31.12.7:
024003	Wear	Stanhope	NY 984391	172	1958	*	NWA	202	747	1318	1322
024004	Bedburn Beck	Bedburn	NZ 118322	74.9	1959	*	NWA	109	531	853	913
024005	Browney	Burn Hall	NZ 259387	181	1954	*	NWA	43.9	363	770	776
024006	Rockhope Burn	Eastgate	NY 952390	36.5	1960	*	NWA	241	611	1156	1214
024007	Browney	Lanchester	NZ 165462	44.6	1968	*	NWA	110	384	768	
024008	Wear	Witton Park	NZ 174309	372	1972		NWA	76.8	747		
024801	Burnhope Burn	Burnhope Reservoir	NY 855395	21.0	1937		NWA		747		
025001	Tees	Broken Scar	NZ 259137	818	1956	*	NWA	37.2	893	1207	1184
025902	Tees	Dent Bank	NY 932260	217	1959	*	NWA	227	893	1717	1687
025003	Trout Beck	Moor House	NY 759336	11.4	1957	*	NWA	533	847	2182	1855
025004	Skerne	South Park	NZ 284129	250	1956 (1954)	*	NWA	34.1	222	671	679
025005	Leven	Leven Bridge	NZ 445122	196	1959	*	NWA	5.18	454	790	753
025006	Greta	Rutherford Bridge	NZ 034122	86.2	1960	*	NWA	223	596	1179	1102
025007	Clow Beck	Croft	NZ 282101	78.2	1961	*	NWA	29.4	447	758	698
025008	Tees	Barnard Castle	NZ 047165	509	1966	*	NWA	133	636	1412	1388
025009	Tees	Low Moor	NZ 364105	1260	1969	*	NWA	4.00	893	1020	
025010	Baydale Beck	Mowden Bridge	NZ 260156	31.1	1957	*	NWA	47.3	206	672	
025011	Langdon Beck	Langdon	NY 852309	13.0	1970	*	NWA	373	700	1521	
025012	Harwood Beck	Harwood	NY 849309	25.1	1970	*	NWA	374	714	1669	
025313	Billingham Beck	Thorpe Thewles	NZ 408237	61.4	1969	*	NWA	18.3	114	648	
025018	Tees	Middleton-in-Teesdale	NY 950250	242	1971	*	NWA	211.2	893	1650	
025019	Leven	Easby	NZ 585087	14.8	1971	*	NWA	101.3	335	884	
025020	Skerne	Preston-Le-Skerne	NZ 292238	147	1972	*	NWA	67.5	222	683	
025021	Skerne	Bradbury	NZ 318285	70.1	1973	*	NWA	72.45	193	687	
025022	Balder	Balderhead Reservoir	NY 928183	20.4	1965		NWA	284.4	562		
025023	Tees	Cow Green Reservoir	NY 814289	58.2	1971	*	NWA	465.4	893	2006	

ean uged scharge m³/s	Mean annual natural runoff mm	Highest instantaneous gauged discharge m³/s	Date	Lowest daily mean gauged discharge m³/s	Date	Abstractions and returns	Station details	Station number
3.59 _0.0209_	778 _58.9_	237.86	23. 3.68	0.24	6. 9.59	S E	Compound Crump weir, 19.1 m long overall, low crest 7.6 m long	024003
1.20 _0.016_		38.51	7. 3.63	0.09	1.10.59		Compound Crump weir 10.3 m long, low crest 2.4 m long	024004
1.75 _0.0097_		64.65	18.12.68	0.15	11.10.59	I	Compound broad crested weir 17.6 m long, low crest 5.5 m long	024005
0.80 _0.022_		33.98	23. 3.68	0.06	22.10.72	E	Compound Crump weir, 8.8 m long, low crest 1.5 m long	024006
0.48 _0.0107_		17.58	13. 8.71	0.05	18.10.70		Compound Crump weir, with crest tapping, 10 m long, low crest 2 m long	024007
						S P	River section with informal flat V low flow weir	024008
						SP	Compound rectangular notch/broad crested weir and overflow spillway	024801
6.54 _0.0202_	784 _66.2_	679.35	23. 3.68	0.02	16.10.59	S R P	Compound Crump weir 64m long with two low sills each 4.6 m long. Excess flows from Cocker Beck (R Skerne) diverted into catchment via Baydale Beck. See 025010 Mowden Bridge	025001
7.46 _0.0343_		467.54	23. 3.68	0.10	20. 6.57	R	Compound Crump weir 39.3 m long. Replaced by Middleton-in-Teesdale 025018 in 1971	025902
0.52 _0.0456_		27.89	29. 3.62	0.01	3. 6.59		Compound Crump weir 12.8 m long, low crest 1.5 m long	025003
1.90 _0.0076_	265 _39.0_	40.21	6. 3.63	0.41	7. 4.66	G E I	Compound broad crested weir. Pumped mine water augments flow. Excess flow from Cocker Beck diverted to Tees catchment above Broken Scar 025001. See also 025010 Mowden Bridge	025004
1.82 _0.00929_		98.91	2.11.68	0.14	1.10.59	E	Compound broad crested weir 17.4 m long with a by-pass Crump weir 4.6 m long	025005
2.15 _0.0249_		110.44	13. 8.66	0.09	5. 8.64		Compound Crump weir 20 m long, low crest 3 m long	025006
0.74 _0.0095_		39.36	6. 3.63	0.03	20.10.64	I	Compound rectangular thin plate weir, 6.6 m long, low crest 2 m long	025007
2.65 _0.0100_		509.71	23. 3.68	0.00	1. 6.66	S R I	Compound Crump weir 52.4 m long, low crest 7 m long	025008
9.46 _0.0154_		269.48	12.12.72	1.87	23.10.70	S R P G E I	River section	025009
0.25 _0.0080_		11.01	18.12.68	0.00	2. 7.73		Concrete weir with adjustable timber crest. Measures only excess flows diverted from River Skerne catchment into the river Tees	025010
0.36 _0.0277_		15.30	7. 1.71	0.02	19. 6.70		Flat V weir with 1:2, 1:2, 1:10 slopes	025011
0.79 _0.0315_		32.93	16. 3.72	0.05	5. 7.73		Flat V weir with 1:2, 1:2, 1:10 slopes	025012
0.26 _0.0042_		24.23	14. 8.71	0.02	14. 7.72	G	River section with timber weir control (Discontinued 1974)	025013
		255.08	16. 3.72	0.10	24.12.72	R	River section with informal flat V low flow weir. Replaces Dent Bank, 025902	025018
0.17 _0.0115_		4.31	3. 2.72	0.06	15. 7.71		Flat V, Crump profile weir, slopes 1 in 10	025019
		4.42	23. 4.73	0.19	7. 9.73	G S P E	River section	025020
		1.51	16. 7.73	0.17	8. 9.73	G S P E	River section with informal flat V low flow weir	025021
						S R P	Compound Crump weir, low crest 6.2 m long	025022
		18.56	11. 1.72	0.44	18.12.71	S R	Flat V weir	025023

Station number	River	Station name	National grid reference	Catch-ment area km²	Records start	Data archived	Measuring authority	Level of station m.O.D.	Highest point in the catch-ment m.O.D.	Annual average areal rainfall; mm Standard average for 1916-1950	Period of record average to 31.12.

YORKSHIRE WATER AUTHORITY AREA

Station number	River	Station name	National grid reference	Catch-ment area	Records start	Data archived	Measuring authority	Level of station	Highest point in the catchment	Standard average for 1916-1950	Period of record average to 31.12.
026001	West Beck	Wansford Bridge	TA 064560	192	1953	*	YWA	4.88	246	754	760
026002	Hull	Hempholme	TA 080498	378	1962 (1961)	*	YWA	3.04	246	724	620
026003	Foston Beck	Foston Mill	TA 093548	57.2	1959	*	YWA	6.40	164	719	756
026004	Gypsey Race	Bridlington	TA 165675	254	1970	*	YWA	11.00	211	747	
027001	Nidd	Hunsingore Weir	SE 428530	484	1953 (1934)	*	YWA	18.3	704	993	986
027002	Wharfe	Flint Mill Weir	SE 422473	759	1955	*	YWA	14.2	704	1161	1117
027003	Aire	Beal Weir	SE 534255	1930	1962 (1931)	*	YWA	6.10	594	975	1014
027004	Calder	Newlands	SE 365220	899	1960 (1927)	*	YWA	18.9	531	1026	1076
027005	Nidd	Gouthwaite Reservoir	SE 141683	114	1937 (1901)	*	YWA(W)	123	704	1367	1343
027006	Don	Hadfields Weir	SK 390910	373	1965	*	YWA	33.3	547	970	1045
027007	Ure	Westwick Lock	SE 356667	914	1958 (1955)	*	YWA	15.2	713	1163	1156
027008	Swale	Leckby Grange	SE 415748	1350	1956 (1955)	*	YWA	12.8	713	879	866
027009	Ouse	Skelton Railway Bridge	SE 568554	3320	1969 (1956)	*	YWA	4.88	713	940	837
027010	Hodge Beck	Bransdale Weir	SE 627944	18.9	1954	*	YWA(E)	156	450	1057	943
027011	Washburn	Lindley Wood Reservoir	SE 219488	87.3	1953 (1895)	*	YWA(NE)	91.1	472	1021	1031
027012	Hebden Water	High Greenwood	SD 973309	36.0	1954	*	YWA (SW)	191	518	1415	1419
027013	Ewden Beck	More Hall Reservoir	SK 289957	26.4	1954 (1936)	*	YWA (S)	123	547	1161	1169
027014	Rye	Little Habton	SE 743771	679	1959 (1958)	*	YWA	22.9	454	851	829
027015	Derwent	Stamford Bridge	SE 714557	1600	1961 (1932)	*	YWA	5.65	454	787	747
027016	Little Don	Underbank Reservoir	SK 253992	38.6	1956 (1915)	*	YWA(S)	166	534	1234	1218

an ged charge /s	Mean annual natural runoff mm	Highest instantaneous gauged discharge m³/s	Date	Lowest daily mean gauged discharge m³/s	Date	Abstractions and returns	Station details	Station number
2.54 *0.0132*		11.61	10.12.65	0.28	10. 3.65	G	Compound rectangular critical depth flume. Affected by heavy weed growth downstream during summer months	026001
3.62 *0.0096*		16.17	6.11.67	0.58	5.10.72*	G	2 tilting gate weirs each 7.2 m wide with a rectangular notch 0.915 m wide x 0.308 m deep in the upper edge	026002
.69 *0.0121*		2.89	21. 1.69	0.08	13. 9.73		Rectangular thin plate weir 2.8 m long. The weir plate is adjustable to control upstream water level and the height of the weir crest is allowed for by means of differential gearing between float and weir	026003
		0.57	12. 2.71	0.00	13. 7.71*	G	Crump weir 2.75 m wide	026004
7.99 *0.0165*	569 *57.7*	271.84	17.10.67	0.22	28. 8.43	S R P	Broad crested weir. Width 49.8 m. Rated by formula and checked by current meter gauging	027001
7.21 *0.0227*	793 *70.9*	362.46	17.10.67	0.43	23. 6.57	S P	Broad crested weir. 47.3 m wide, rated by current meter gauging from a cableway 1.5 km upstream of the station	027002
5.89 *0.0191*	639 *63.0*	339.60	1. 4.69	3.46	18.10.59	S E I	Weir with crest 33.5 m wide; 25 m consist of timbers on edge which can be laid flat in flood periods. Rating by formula to 1962, now calibrated by current meter	027003
8.19 *0.0202*	661 *61.4*	382.28	27.11.60	3.26	21.10.62		Velocity-area station. Replaced Kirkthorpe Weir, 80.5 m masonry and timber structure, in October 1968	027004
2.70 *0.0237*		138.67	17.10.67	0.21	6.12.64	S P	Rectangular notch 12 m wide set in broad crested weir, total width 29 m. Sited at downstream end of stilling basin	027005
5.52 *0.0148*	655 *62.7*	265.09	12. 4.70	0.91	10.10.71	S E I	Broad-crested weir 45 m wide rated by hydraulic model test and by current meter gauging	027006
9.95 *0.0218*	679 *58.7*	413.15	24. 3.68	0.02	4. 9.72	S P	River section	027007
9.22 *0.0142*		255.70	7. 3.63	0.86	27. 9.59		River section	027008
.45 *0.0122*		220.9	5. 4.73	7.34	13. 9.73	S R P	River section	027009
.34 *0.0180*		102.71	26. 2.60	0.00	23. 1.63		A three-stage thin plate rectangular weir 6.1 m wide with short lengths of broad crested weir at each end	027010
.63 *0.0072*		61.07	2.11.68	0.01	8.10.55	S P	An orifice for measurement of compensation water discharge and a broad crested weir for measurement of reservoir overflow	027011
.69 *0.0192*	942 *66.4*	21.58	9.12.65	0.07	2. 1.70	S P	A compound rectangular thin plate weir. The installation is a statutory compensation gauge	027012
.29 *0.011*	734 *62.8*	21.24	21.11.63	0.00	14. 5.67	S P	Compound weir; thin plate weir 6 m wide set in middle of a broad crested weir, overall width 36.5 m	027013
.43 *0.0139*		168.20	10.10.60	0.97	30. 9.70		River section	027104
.38 *0.0102*		123.46	22. 2.66	3.05	22. 8.72	P	Broad crested weir 31 m wide replaced by river section in 1967. In 1973 superseded by 027041 Buttercrambe. Excess flows from 88.8 km² of catchment diverted into New Cut. See 027033 Scarborough	027015
.63 *0.0163*	904 *74.2*	35.40	9.12.65	0.00	15. 3.70	S P	Orifice and weir 11.7 m wide	027016

Station number	River	Station name	National grid reference	Catch-ment area km²	Records start	Data archived	Measuring authority	Level of station m.O.D.	Highest point in the catch-ment m.O.D.	Annual average areal rainfall; mm	
										Standard average for 1916-1950	Period of record average to 31.12.

YORKSHIRE WATER AUTHORITY AREA (CONTD)

027017	Loxley	Damflask Reservoir	SK 286906	43.5	1956	*	YWA(S)	124	534	1140	1156
027018	Ryburn	Ryburn Reservoir	SE 025187	10.7	1956 (1934)	*	YWA(SW)	163	435	1326	1364
027019	Booth Dean Clough	Booth Wood Mill Reservoir	SE 033166	15.9	1956	*	YWA(SW)	207	480	1359	1414
027020	Scout Dike	Scout Dike Reservoir	SE 236047	10.5	1956 (1928)	*	YWA(SW)	207	381	1034	1062
027021	Don	Doncaster	SE 569040	1260	1960 (1941)	*	YWA	10.7	547	798	794
027922	Don	Rotherham	SK 427928	826	1960 (1924)	*	YWA	23.2	547	856	870
027023	Dearne	Barnsley Weir	SE 350073	119	1960 (1953)	*	YWA	43.6	381	767	791
027024	Swale	Richmond	NZ 146006	381	1961 (1960)	*	YWA	106	713	1300	1206
027025	Rother	Woodhouse Mill	SK 432857	352	1961 (1959)	*	YWA	29.3	367	762	761
027026	Rother	Whittington	SK 394744	165	1963 (1960)	*	YWA	58.7	367	800	834
027027	Wharfe	Ilkley	SE 112481	443	1961 (1960)	*	YWA	71.4	704	1382	1325
027028	Aire	Armley	SE 281340	692	1961 (1960)	*	YWA	30.5	594	1059	1098
027029	Calder	Elland	SE 124219	342	1961 (1953)	*	YWA	58.9	518	1219	1264
027030	Dearne	Adwick	SE 477020	311	1963	*	YWA	12.9	381	701	766
027031	Colne	Colnbridge	SE 174199	245	1964	*	YWA	48.4	582	1107	1194
027032	Hebden Beck	Hebden	SE 025643	23.3	1965	*	YWA	228	412	1429	
027033	Sea Cut	Scarborough	TA 028908	33.2	1969	*	YWA	20.6	299		
027034	Ure	Kilgram Bridge	SE 190860	510	1968	*	YWA	87.6	713	1390	
027035	Aire	Kildwick Bridge	SE 013457	282	1969	*	YWA	87.4	594	1201	
027037	Went	Kirk Smeaton	SE 529164	54.5	1970 (1969)		YWA	9.75	85		
027038	Costa	Gate Houses	SE 774836	7.8	1970	*	YWA	22.9	27	704	
027040	Doe Lea	Staveley	SK 443746	67.9	1970	*	YWA	48	196	720	
027041	Derwent	Buttercrambe	SE 731587	1570	1973		YWA	9.50	454	788	
027042	Dove	Kirkby Mills	SE 705855	51.8	1972	*	YWA	35.6	429	958	
027047	Snaizeholme Beck	Low Houses	SD 832883	10.2	1972	*	YWA	260	587	1778	

...ean ...uged ...scharge	Mean annual natural runoff	Highest instantaneous gauged discharge	Date	Lowest daily mean gauged discharge	Date	Abstractions and returns	Station details	Station number
³/s	mm	m³/s		m³/s				
0.59 (0.0136)	672 [58,1]	29.73	9.12.65	0.00		S P	A weir about 23 m wide measuring reservoir overflow and orifices measuring compensation water	027017
0.16 (0.015)	1031 [75,6]	9.85	7. 2.66	0.00		S P	A compound rectangular thin plate weir	027018
0.23 (0.0145)	971 [68,7]	13.00	12. 4.70	0.00	19. 9.67	S P	A compound rectangular wooden weir with thin plate crest	027019
0.10 (0.0095)		7.24	9.12.65	0.00		S P	Thin plate weir 12 m wide measuring part of reservoir overflow and a V notch measuring compensation and balance of overflow	027020
4.89 (0.0118)		272.33	13. 4.70	3.06	4.10.64	S E I	River section	027021
1.75 (0.0142)		259.46	13. 4.70	1.98	19.10.64	S E I H	A weir 60 m wide calibrated at a river section 360 m downstream. Terminated 1971	027922
1.35 (0.0113)	457 [52,8]	68.88	13. 4.70	0.13	17. 9.61	I	Compound broad crested weir about 12 m overall width rated by hydraulic model tests	027023
0.68 (0.028)		380.06	23. 3.68	0.84	25.10.72	P	River section	027024
4.06 (0.0115)	352 [46,3]	78.14	13. 4.70	0.02	14. 4.70	S E I	River section	027025
1.76 (0.011)	398 [47,7]	79.95	15. 7.73	0.00	31. 5.68	S E I	River section	027026
3.98 (0.0316)		300.1	31. 3.69	1.15	10. 9.69	S P	River section	027027
4.32 (0.0207)	661 [60,2]	212.38	17.10.67	1.23	12. 9.71	S E I H	River section	027028
8.11 (0.0237)	798 [63,1]	183.75	18.10.71	1.23	8. 7.62	S E I H	A broad crested weir. Modifications carried out to crest in 1969 and a low flow Crump profile section 5 m wide incorporated	027029
3.34 (0.0107)	361 [47,1]	58.42	13. 4.70	0.67	25.10.64	S E I	Compound weir 17.5 m overall, consisting of middle Crump weir section 5.5 m wide with broad crested flanking weirs	027030
4.71 (0.0192)	884 [74,0]	210.57	23. 9.68	0.00	31. 1.68	S E I	Compound Weir 52 m overall having central Crump profile weir section 3.8 m wide and broad crested flanking weirs	027031
0.15 (0.0064)		5.81	1. 7.68	0.02	18. 5.70	P	Crump weir 3.5 m wide and 90° V Notch. Area upstream of gauge contains limestone outcrops with underground streams; catchment area difficult to define	027032
							Compound broad crested weir with 2.9 m centre section and two 9.2 m flank sections at 0.152 m higher level. Excess flows from 88.8 km² upper Derwent diverted into New Cut during floods. See also 027015, 027041 and 027048	027033
3.66 (0.0268)		367.10	23. 3.68	0.00	16. 3.68		River section with bridge invert as control	027034
.00 (0.0177)		98.13	5.12.72	0.26	26. 6.70	S	River section	027035
						I	River section	027037
0.59 (0.0756)		1.53	22.11.71	0.44	1.11.73	G	Crump weir 5.2 m wide with crest tappings. Costa Beck has a spring source 1.6 km upstream of the station	027038
0.64 (0.0094)		13.10	16. 7.73	0.15	1. 9.70	I	Rectangular critical depth flume. Throat width 3.05 m	027040
						P	Crump weir 19.987 m wide. For total flow see 027033 Scarborough	027041
0.64 (0.0123)		36.68	3. 2.72	0.22	1.10.72		Flat V, Crump profile weir. 8.0 m wide	027042
0.44 (0.043)		10.10	9.11.72	0.02	1.10.72		Trapezoidal critical depth flume. Throat width 1.219 m	027047

Station number	River	Station name	National grid reference	Catchment area	Records start	Data archived	Measuring authority	Level of station	Highest point in the catchment	Annual average areal rainfall; mm	
										Standard average for 1916-1950	Period of record average to 31.12.
				km²				m.O.D.	m.O.D.		

③

YORKSHIRE WATER AUTHORITY AREA (CONTD)

027048	Derwent	West Ayton	SE 990853	93.8	1972 (1964)	*	YWA	34.2	299	823	
027050	Esk	Sleights Weir	NZ 865081	308	1970	*	YWA	5.03	435		
027051	Crimple	Burn Bridge, Harrogate	SE 282518	8.1	1972	*	LU	109	245	831	
027852	Little Don	Langsett Reservoir	SE 215005	21.1	1910		YWA				

④

SEVERN TRENT WATER AUTHORITY AREA

028001	Derwent	Yorkshire Bridge	SK 198851	127	1906	*	DD	160	636	1410	1420
028002	Blithe	Hamstall Ridware	SK 109192	163	1937	*	TAU	63.9	278	790	790
028003	Tame	Water Orton	SP 169915	407	1955	*	TAU	75.0	290	742	753
028004	Tame	Lea Marston	SK 206935	795	1956	*	TAU	66.1	290	734	752
028005	Tame	Elford	SK 173105	1470	1955	*	TAU	50.3	290	714	712
028006	Trent	Great Haywood	SJ 994231	325	1955	*	TAU	69.5	330	825	776
028007	Trent	Shardlow	SK 448299	4400	1955	*	TAU	29.3	548	775	744
028008	Dove	Rocester Weir	SK 112399	399	1954	*	TAU	86.3	550	1029	1060
028009	Trent	Colwick	SK 620399	7490	1958	*	TAU	15.7	636	785	782
028010	Derwent	Longbridge Weir	SK 356363	1120	1935	*	TAU	44.4	636	996	991
028011	Derwent	Matlock Bath	SK 296586	689	1958	*	TAU	83.2	636	1105	1066
028012	Trent	Yoxall	SK 131177	1230	1959	*	TAU	56.4	318	775	783
028013	Soar	Zouch	SK 498240	1280	1961		TAU	31.4	278	700	
028014	Sow	Milford	SJ 975215	591	1959	*	TAU	69.2	195	754	680
028015	Idle	Mattersey	SK 690895	529	1961		TAU	3.7	195	663	
028016	Ryton	Serlby Park	SK 641897	228	1965	*	TAU	5.5	143	631	
028017	Devon	Cotham	SK 787476	284	1966	*	TAU	11.0	53	622	
028018	Dove	Marston-on-Dove	SK 235288	883	1962	*	TAU	47.2	555	950	967
028019	Trent	Drakelow Park	SK 239204	3070	1966	*	TAU	43.0	290	732	746
028020	Churnet	Rocester	SK 103389	236	1954	*	TAU	81.7	475	968	956
028021	Derwent	Draycott	SK 443327	1180	1965	*	TAU	30.0	636	981	
028022	Trent	North Muskham	SK 801601	8230	1968	*	TAU	5.6	636	771	
028023	Wye	Ashford	SK 182696	154	1965	*	TAU	139	497	1145	
028024	Wreake	Syston Mill	SK 615124	414	1967	*	TAU	47.7	230	664	
028025	Sence	Ratcliffe Culey	SP 321996	170	1966	*	TAU	67.6	183	707	
028026	Anker	Polesworth	SK 263034	368	1967		TAU	60.4	177	690	
028027	Erewash	Stapleford	SK 482364	181	1965	*	TAU	33.2	190	721	777
028028	Soar	Wanlip	SK 603109	480	1970		TAU	47.0	221	655	

Mean gauged discharge m³/s	Mean annual natural runoff mm	Highest instantaneous gauged discharge m³/s	Date	Lowest daily mean gauged discharge m³/s	Date	Abstractions and returns	Station details	Station number
0.23 *0.00245*		1.32	7. 7.73	0.02	30. 9.72	P	Compound thin plate weir. Centre section 3.05 m wide with side sections each 4.19 m wide at 0.275 m higher level. For total flow see 027033 Scarborough	027048
3.89 *0.0126*				0.46	6.10.72		River section with broad crested weir control 25.0 m wide	027050
0.08 *0.00988*		3.86	27. 9.73	0.01	1.10.72*		Flat V Crump profile weir 3.5 m wide	027051
						S R P	Reservoir compensation flow gauge. Records ceased 1932	027852
2.12 *0.0167*	1017 *71.6*	150.65	9.12.65	0.30	11.12.59	S R P	Compound critical depth flume immediately downstream from Ladybower Reservoir. 0.876 m³/s compensation water	028001
1.34 *0.0082*	335 *42.4*	38.74	17. 3.47	0.20	30. 7.48	S R P G I	Rectangular concrete critical depth flume with side contractions; Blithfield reservoir constructed 1952	028002
5.90 *0.0145*		106.76	8. 9.72	0.69	8. 8.59	N I	River section, inaccurate at high flows	028003
14.07 *0.0177*		78.84	11. 7.68	4.08	12.10.59	E I	River section	028004
19.05 *0.0129*		137.50	12. 7.68	0.29	28. 9.69	E I	River section	028005
4.66 *0.0143*		46.16	5.12.60	1.66	13. 9.64	G E S	River section. Control unstable affecting low flows	028006
52.55 *0.0119*		447.41	5.12.60	1.03	1.10.66	S R P G	River section. Influence from Derwent floods backwater	028007
7.49 *0.0188*		144.42	9.12.65	0.60	27. 9.59	G E	River section	028008
32.21 *0.011*		923.13	5.12.60	0.00	30. 9.69	S R P G E I	River section	028009
16.81 *0.0150*		520.87	10.12.65	0.00		S R P G E I A	River section	028010
13.05 *0.0189*		436.08	9.12.65	0.00	4. 4.69	S R P G E I A	River section	028011
12.99 *0.0106*		126.58	5.12.60	5.15	5.10.59	S R P G E I	River section	028012
						S R P G E	River section. Discharge affected by Leicester Canal	028013
5.52 *0.0093*		50.12	5.12.60	1.00	2.11.69	G E	River section	028014
						S R G E A	River section	028015
2.27 *0.0099*		18.36	2.11.68	0.41	12. 8.65	E A	River section. Subject to severe weed growth during summer months	028016
1.49 *0.0052*		116.89	16. 9.68	0.10	4.11.71	E A	River section subject to seasonal weed growth	028017
15.28 *0.0173*		137.05	9.12.65	3.11	11.10.71	S R P G	River section subject to seasonality	028018
36.55 *0.0119*		209.00	7. 5.69	0.00	19. 6.68	P G E	River section. Due to regrading scheme records from 1960/1965 not compatible with those of 1965/70	028019
3.61 *0.0153*		34.09	11. 8.71	0.60	16. 8.59	S R P G E	River section	028020
23.26 *0.0197*		165.72	2.11.68	0.99	31. 7.70	S R P G E I A	River section	028021
85.66 *0.0104*		392.97	23. 2.70	25.37	5. 8.70	S R P G E I	River section	028022
2.93 *0.019*		15.72	8. 9.65	0.01	5. 1.71	P G E	River section	028023
2.27 *0.0055*		29.86	2.11.68	0.21	18.10.70	G E A	Crump weir, modular to 19.5 m³/s	028024
1.58 *0.0093*		62.24	5.11.67	0.19	14. 9.67	G E A	Crump weir, double gauged with upstream and downstream tapping points. Modular limit dependent upon backwater effects of river Anker	028025
						G E A	Crump profile weir with cableway	028026
0.93 *0.0052*		15.31	10.12.65	0.00	27. 3.67	E I A	River section with twin concrete channels	028027
						E	Double gauged compound Crump weir. Upstream and downstream tapping point	028028

Station number	River	Station name	National grid reference	Catchment area	Records start	Data archived	Measuring authority	Level of station	Highest point in the catchment	Annual average areal rainfall; mm	
										Standard average for 1916-1950	Period of record average to 31.12.7
				km²				m.O.D.	m.O.D.		

SEVERN TRENT WATER AUTHORITY AREA (CONTD)

Station number	River	Station name	National grid reference	Catchment area	Records start	Data archived	Measuring authority	Level of station	Highest point in the catchment	Standard average for 1916-1950	Period of record average to 31.12.7
028029	Kingston Brook	Kingston Hall	SK 503277	56.0	1966	*	TAU	30.0	152	652	
028030	Blackbrook	Blackbrook Flume	SK 466171	8.4	1967	*	TAU	111	247	761	
028031	Manifold	Ilam	SK 140507	149	1968	*	TAU	131	513	1081	1025
028032	Meden	Church Warsop	SK 558680	63.0	1965	*	TAU	55.5	100	710	745
028033	Dove	Hollingsclough	SK 063668	8.1	1965	*	TAU	284	549	1392	
028034	Maun	Haughton	SK 681728				TAU	25.8	191	675	
028035	Leen	Triumph Road, Nottingham	SK 549392	111	1968		TAU	24.3	192	697	
028036	Poulter	Twyford Bridge	SK 700752	125	1969	*	TAU	16.8	187	666	
028037	Derwent	Mytham Bridge	SK 205825	206			TAU	137	636	1416	
028038	Manifold	Hulme End	SK 106595	45.6	1968		TAU	213	513	1145	
028039	Rea	Calthorpe Park	SP 071847	74.3	1967	*	TAU	104	286	808	
028040	Trent	Stoke-on-Trent	SJ 892467	80.3	1968	*	TAU	113	213	869	
028041	Hamps	Waterhouses	SK 082502	39.6	1968		TAU	210	489	1064	
028042	Churnet	Cheddleton	SJ 979520	136	1958		TAU	133	472	954	
028043	Derwent	Chatsworth	SK 261683	218	1972	*	TAU	100	636	1193	
028044	Poulter	Cuckney	SK 563714	64.8	1969	*	TAU	45.4	187	692	
028045	Meden	Bothamsall	SK 680732	267	1965 (1958)	*	TAU	24.3	191	678	
028046	Dove	Izaak Walton	SK 146509	83.0	1969	*	TAU	135	549	1143	1102
028047	Oldcoates Dyke	Blyth	SK 615876	85.2	1970		TAU	10.7	145	620	
028048	Amber	Wingfield Park	SK 376520	138	1970		TAU	71.0	329	783	
028049	Ryton	Worksop	SK 575794	77.0	1970		TAU	31.7	143	658	
028050	Torne	Auckley	SE 646012	141	1970		TAU	1.6	134	596	
028051	Soar	Narborough	SP 551985	202	1971		TAU	60.3	151	671	
028052	Sow	Great Bridgeford	SJ 883270	163	1971		TAU	79.39	168	765	
028053	Penk	Penkridge	SJ 923144	272	1971		TAU	76.2	151	654	
028054	Sence	Blaby	SP 566985	133	1971		TAU	62.54	213	867	
028055	Ecclesbourne	Duffield	SK 320447	50.0	1971		TAU	69.35	227		
028056	Rothley Brook	Rothley	SK 580121	94.0	1973		TAU	47.0	170		
028057	Trent	Cromwell Lock	SK 808612	8230	1968		TAU	5.5	636	690	
028059	Maun	Mansfield	SK 548623	28.8	1965	*	TAU	78.6	191	734	
028060	Dover Beck	Lowdham	SK 653479	63.9	1972		TAU	28.3	121		
028062	Trent	Fledborough	SK 815715		1971		TAU		636		

Mean gauged discharge	Mean annual natural runoff	Highest instantaneous gauged discharge	Date	Lowest daily mean gauged discharge	Date	Abstractions and returns	Station details	Station number
m³/s	mm	m³/s		m³/s				
		4.06	10. 6.72	0.01	16. 7.72	E A	Double gauged compound Crump weir – backwater from River Soar floods results in non-modularity	028029
		5.86	14. 5.67	0.00		G E	Trapezoidal critical depth flume	028030
3.33	0.0223	137.03	10. 8.71	0.62	10. 9.69	P E	Crump profile weir, modular to bankfull	028031
0.66	0.010	11.34	14. 7.68	0.16	1. 9.65	G E A	River section with trapezoidal critical depth flume	028032
0.27	0.0333	11.04	15. 7.73	0.03	9. 7.73		Compound Crump weir	028033
							Obsolete number, see 028245	028034
						G E I	River section	028035
		3.57	9. 9.72	0.38	2. 9.72	S R G E A	Crump weir. Modular except when affected by backwater from River Idle floods	028036
						S R P E	River level records for flood forecasting only	028037
						P E	River section	028038
0.80	0.0108	41.25	19. 8.70	0.23	24. 9.72	E	Crump profile low flow weir with horizontal berms for medium flows Rated by model tests above modular limit	028039
0.81	0.0101	10.04	6. 5.69	0.16	8.10.71	E	Crump profile weir, modular to bankfull	028040
						E	Triangular profile flat V weir 1:2, 1:2, 1:10. Vertical side walls	028041
						S R P G	River section, replaced by Basford Bridge 028061 in December 1974	028042
		149.85	2.11.68	1.66	6.10.71	S R P	River section. Levels prior to 1.12.72 unavailable	028043
0.26	0.0040	1.08	13. 4.70	0.18	30. 9.71	G F A	Crump weir. Modular throughout range of flows	028044
1.73	0.0065					G E A	Trapezoidal critical depth flume added 1965 to improve measurement in low flow range. Complementary station on bifurcation, Haughton 028245 previously 028034, similarly improved by construction of trapezoidal flume	028045
1.87	0.0225	20.69	21.11.71	0.48	2.11.69	E	Crump profile flat V weir, 1:10 – with vertical side walls; modular to 30.5 m³/s	028046
						E A	Crump profile flat V weir, 1:10. Trapezoidal channel cross-section	028047
						S R P	Crump profile flat V weir, 1:10. Trapezoidal channel cross-section	028048
						G E A	Flow modular to 7.08 m³/s	
						G E A	Crump profile flat V weir. 1:10. Trapezoidal channel cross-section. Rated by gauging for discharges above modular limit	028049
						G E A	Crump profile flat V weir, 1:10. Trapezoidal channel cross-section. Rated by gaugings above modular limit	028050
						E	Crump profile, flat V weir – affected by downstream levels	028051
						G	Crump profile, flat V weir	028052
						E I	River section	028053
						E I	Crump profile, flat V weir	028054
							Crump profile, flat V weir	028055
							Crump profile, flat V weir	028056
						S R P	Water level recorder at tidal limit of	028057
						G E I	Trent; for land drainage and navigation purposes	
0.46	0.016	11.21	14. 7.68	0.18	27. 8.67	G E A	River section with trapezoidal critical depth flume	028059
						G	Crump profile, flat V weir	028060
						S P G E I	Tidal recorder	028062

Station number	River	Station name	National grid reference	Catchment area km²	Records start	Data archived	Measuring authority	Level of station m.O.D.	Highest point in the catchment m.O.D.	Annual average areal rainfall; mm Standard average for 1916-1950	Period of record average to 31.12.7

SEVERN TRENT WATER AUTHORITY AREA (CONTD)

Station number	River	Station name	National grid reference	Catchment area	Records start	Data archived	Measuring authority	Level of station	Highest point	Standard avg	Period of record avg
028065	Trent	Torksey	SK 836793		1971		TAU		636		
028066	Cole	Coleshill	SP 183874	130	1973		TAU	78.0	190		
028067	Derwent	Church Wilne	SK 438316	1200	1973		TAU	31.0	636		
028068	Lathkill	Pickering Wood	SK 223648	89.7	1964		TAU	107	396	1120	
028069	Tame	Tamworth	SK 206037	1410	1955		TAU	57.0	290	700	
028070	Burbage Brook	Burbage	SK 259804	9.1	1925		TAU	290	436	1090	
028071	Amber	Ogston Reservoir	SK 379598	40.0	1959		DD	99.0	329	830	
028804	Trent	Trent Bridge	SK 582384	7490	1888		TAU		636		
054001	Severn	Bewdley	SO 782762	4330	1921	*	SAU	17.4	827	945	914
054002	Avon	Evesham	SP 034431	2210	1937	*	SAU	19.8	320	683	665
054003	Vyrnwy	Vyrnwy Reservoir	SJ 019191	94.3	1937 (1879)	*	NWWAWD	226	624	1908	1931
054004	Sowe	Stoneleigh	SP 332731	264	1951	*	SAU	55.2	183	709	677
054005	Severn	Montford	SJ 413145	2030	1953	*	SAU	52.4	827	1179	1180
054006	Stour	Kidderminster	SO 828769	324	1953	*	SAU	30.8	316	721	722
054007	Arrow	Broom	SP 087532	319	1957 (1956)	*	SAU	28.7	291	709	715
054008	Teme	Tenbury Wells	SO 598685	1130	1956	*	SAU	48.5	546	871	881
054010	Stour (Warwicks)	Alscot Park	SP 208507	319	1959	*	SAU	38.1	290	711	691
054011	Salwarpe	Harford Hill	SO 868619	184	1961 (1958)	*	SAU	19.2	291	691	657
054012	Tern	Walcot	SJ 592123	852	1960 (1959)	*	SAU	44.8	366	729	719
054013	Clywedog	Cribynau	SN 944855	57	1959 (1958)	*	SAU	175	622	1803	1973
054014	Severn	Abermule	SO 165958	580	1963 (1962)	*	SAU	83.2	740	1257	1248
054015	Bow Brook	Besford Bridge	SO 927463	156	1969	*	SAU	13.4	152	668	
054016	Roden	Rodington	SJ 589141	259	1961	*	SAU	48.2	208	721	699
054017	Leadon	Wedderburn Bridge	SO 777234	293	1962	*	SAU	9.14	339	737	704
054018	Rea Brook	Hookagate	SJ 465092	178	1962	*	SAU	64.6	502	787	770
054019	Avon	Stareton	SP 333715	347	1962	*	SAU	54.9	210	676	673
054020	Perry	Yeaton	SJ 435193	181	1963	*	SAU	61.3	356	792	787
054022	Severn	Plynlimon	SN 850872	8.8	1953	*	IH	331	740	2449	2627
054023	Badsey Brook	Offenham	SP 063449	95.8	1968	*	SAU	23.9	320	680	
054024	Worfe	Burcote	SO 746954	258	1969	*	SAU	33.2	120	704	684

Mean gauged discharge	Mean annual natural runoff	Highest instantaneous gauged discharge	Date	Lowest daily mean gauged discharge	Date	Abstractions and returns	Station details	Station number
m³/s	mm	m³/s		m³/s				
						SPGEI	Tidal recorder	028065
						EI	Crump profile, flat V weir	028066
						SPEI	Crump profile, flat V weir; used with 028021, Draycott	028067
							Thin plate weir rated by theoretical formula — believed to be modular throughout range of flows	028068
						EI	River level recording only for flood forecasting purposes	028069
							Compound thin plate weir	028070
						SRPG	Thin plate weir	028071
						SPGEI	Level recorder	028804
62.70 *0.0145*	476 *52.1*	634.30	6.12.60	5.38	4. 9.40	SRPGEI	River section. The aqueduct site (SO776783) recorder was superseded in January 1970 by the gauging section recorder. Variations used to derive the natural flow include storage changes in Lakes Vyrnwy and Clywedog and abstractions for public water supplies from the river	054001
14.43 *0.0065*		370.95	11. 7.68	1.27		PGEI	River section	054002
2.10 *0.0223*	1426 *73.8*	99.00	9.12.65	0.24	4.10.49	SR	Rectangular notch	054003
2.75 *0.0104*		54.09	26. 3.55	0.00	1. 1.73*	GE	Two critical depth flumes at site of old mill. Discharges above 34 m³/s are estimated	054004
40.98 *0.020704*	*59.7*	467.23	5.12.60	1.98	10. 5.54	SRP	River section	054005
2.89 *0.0089*		81.55	27. 3.55	0.99	16. 6.57*	GEI	River section	054006
2.79 *0.0087*		77.87	11. 7.68	0.43	19. 9.59	GEI	River section. Flows exceeding 31 m³/s are estimated	054007
13.70 *0.0121*		266.46	4.12.60	0.22	26.10.68		River section	054008
2.17 *0.0068*		113.27	11. 7.68	0.11	21. 9.64		Compound broad crested weir 17.7 m long overall	054010
1.39 *0.0076*		32.57	11. 7.68	0.32	28.10.72	G	River section	054011
7.21 *0.0085*		48.71	3. 7.68	1.36	2.10.64	G	River section. Discharges above 15.5 m³/s are estimated	054012
2.19 *0.0384*		111.57	13.12.64	0.03	4. 7.61	SR	Compound triangular section weir	054013
13.29 *0.0229*		419.09	13.12.64	0.63	16. 6.70	SR	River section	054014
		19.59	13. 1.72	0.08	25. 8.73		Thin plate weir in summer season; rated section in winter	054015
2.15 *0.0083*		30.58	2. 7.68	0.34	12. 9.64		Compound broad crested weir for low and medium flows. River section for flood flows	054016
2.16 *0.0074*		36.53	11. 7.68	0.21	30. 9.64	GE	Compound broad crested weir for low flows. River section for medium and high flows	054017
1.75 *0.0098*		38.51	9.12.65	0.11	23. 9.64		Compound broad crested weir for low and medium flow. River section for high flows	054018
2.48 *0.0071*		71.36	11. 7.68	0.34	25. 7.69	SEI	Crump weir. Gauged flow includes the effluent discharge of about 0.16 m³/s from Baginton Sewage Disposal Works (Coventry B.C.)	054019
1.78 *0.0098*		14.49	22.12.69	0.31	18. 9.64	G	Crump weir	054020
0.51 *0.0579*		26.53	5. 8.73	0.00	15. 8.55		Combined thin plate and broad crested weir, overall length 18.4 m. Last published records for 1957/8. Replaced by trapezoidal flume in 1967	054022
0.78 *0.0081*		11.73	26. 5.69	0.04	1. 9.72	P	Trapezoidal flume	054023
1.34 *0.0052*		16.09	25. 5.69	0.44	18. 6.73	PGEI	Crump weir	054024

Station number	River	Station name	National grid reference	Catchment area	Records start	Data archived	Measuring authority	Level of station	Highest point in the catchment	Annual average areal rainfall; mm	
										Standard average for 1916-1950	Period of record average to 31.12.7
				km²				m.O.D.	m.O.D.		

SEVERN TRENT WATER AUTHORITY – (CONTD)

Station number	River	Station name	National grid reference	Catchment area	Records start	Data archived	Measuring authority	Level of station	Highest point in the catchment	Standard average for 1916-1950	Period of record average to 31.12.7
054025	Dulas	Rhos y Pentref	SN 950824	52.7	1969	*	SAU		570	1298	
054026	Chelt	Slate Mill	SO 892264	34.5	1969	*	SAU	16.9	305	734	
054027	Frome	Ebley Mill	SO 831047	198	1969	*	SAU	31.1	267	903	
054028	Vyrnwy	Llanymynech	SJ 252196	778	1970	*	SAU		624	1334	
054029	Teme	Knightsford Bridge	SO 735557	1480	1970	*	SAU	21.3	546	845	
054032	Severn	Saxon's Lode	SO 863392	6850	1970	*	SAU	7.5	827	777	
054034	Dowles Brook	Dowles	SO 768764	40.8	1971	*	SAU	24.2	198	781	
054036	Isbourne	Hinton on the Green	SP 023408	90.7	1971	*	SAU	25.2	330	726	
054038	Tanat	Llanyblodwel	SJ 252225	229	1973	*	SAU	77.0	827	1283	
054040	Meese	Tibberton	SJ 680205	168	1973	*	SAU	56.4	152	732	
054041	Tern	Eaton Mill	SJ 649231	189	1972	*	SAU	53.5	226	739	
054042	Clywedog	Dam (Lower Weir)	SN 914867	46.6	1968	*	SAU	212.43	622	1859	
054043	Severn	Upton on Severn	SO 863399	6850	1955	*	AD	7.5	827	777	
054044	Tern	Ternhill	SJ 629316	92.6	1972	*	SAU	62.22	218	759	
054045	Perry	Perry Farm	SJ 347303	49.1	1973		SAU	78.99	358	886	
054352	Bailey Brook	Ternhill	SJ 629316	34.4	1970	*	SAU	62.22	128	737	
054353	Corve	Ludlow	SO 510752	164	1970	*	SAU	81.37	540	785	
054354	Onny	Onibury	SO 454790	235	1971	*	SAU		537	850	
054355	Rea	Neen Sollars	SO 664724	129	1971	*	SAU		540		
054356	Clun	Clungunford	SO 394786	195	1971	*	SAU		496	935	
054357	Severn	Haw Bridge	SO 844279	9900	1971	*	SAU	6.4	827	748	
054358	Stoke Park Brook	Stoke Park	SJ 644260	14.3	1972	*	SAU	58.58			
054359	Allford Brook	Allford	SJ 654223	10.2	1972	*	SAU	55.96			
054360	Potford Brook	Potford Bridge	SO 634220	25.0	1972	*	SAU				
054361	Hodnet Brook	Hodnet	SJ 628288	5.1	1972	*	SAU	61.41			
054362	Stoke Brook	Stoke	SJ 637280	13.7	1972	*	SAU	58.76		724	
054363	Stour	Prestwood Hospital	SO 865858	89.9	1971	*	SAU	51.05	316		
054365	Roden	Stanton	SJ 565241	210	1973	*	SAU		208	730	
054366	Platt Brook	Platt	SJ 628229	15.7	1973	*	SAU			699	
054367	Smestow Brook	Swindon	SO 861906	81.3	1973		SAU	60.41	267		

ANGLIAN WATER AUTHORITY AREA

Station number	River	Station name	National grid reference	Catchment area	Records start	Data archived	Measuring authority	Level of station	Highest point in the catchment	Standard average for 1916-1950	Period of record average to 31.12.7
029001	Waithe Beck	Brigsley	TA 253016	108	1960	*	LRD	15.5	162	698	685
029002	Great Eau	Claythorpe Mill	TF 416793	77.4	1962	*	LRD	6.58	145	644	662
029003	Lud	Louth	TF 337876	55.2	1968	*	LRD	15.4	159	657	
029004	Ancholme	Bishopbridge	TF 032911	54.5	1968	*	LRD	3.81	66	630	
029005	Rase	Bishopbridge	TF 032912	66.5	1967	*	LRD	4.05	161	644	

Mean gauged discharge	Mean annual natural runoff	Highest instantaneous gauged discharge	Date	Lowest daily mean gauged discharge	Date	Abstractions and returns	Station details	Station number
m³/s	mm	m³/s		m³/s				
1.21	0.0229	24.78	5. 8.73	0.04	22. 7.70		Trapezoidal flume	054025
0.48	0.0139	6.97	3. 2.72	0.11	22. 4.72	S P E I	Trapezoidal flume	054026
2.22	0.0112	17.44	20.11.70	0.60	4.11.72	P I	Calibrated weir	054027
16.27	0.0209	406.72	6. 8.73	1.64	20.10.72	S P	River section	054028
16.00	0.0108	220.91	6.12.72	2.00	1. 9.73	P	River section	054029
77.51	0.0113	485.26	8.12.72	15.42	24.10.72	S R P G E I	River section	054032
0.37	0.0091	9.84	6.12.72	0.04	1. 9.72		Flat V Crump weir	054034
				0.11	3.11.73		Crump weir	054036
		118.20	6. 8.73	0.53	13. 7.73		River section	054038
		2.09	8.12.73	0.85	3.11.73	G	Crump weir	054040
1.59	0.0084	16.11	7. 8.73	0.69	19. 7.72	G	Double crested Crump weir	054041
1.69	0.0362	5.65	10. 4.72	0.00	18. 4.73	S R	Rectangular notch	054042
99.53	0.0145			13.90		G E I S R P	River section. Levels read frequently	054043
0.81	0.0087	15.19	6. 8.73	0.44	13. 7.73	G	Rectangular notch	054044
							Flat V Crump weir	054045
0.29	0.0084	7.14	6. 8.73	0.00	1. 9.72	G	Rectangular notch	054352
0.81	0.0049	24.45	7.12.72	0.16	4.10.72		Rated section. Temporary station	054353
1.89	0.008	69.53	6.12.72	0.28	4.10.72		Rated section. Temporary station	054354
0.92	0.0071	32.80	6.12.72	0.35	24. 8.72*		Rated section. Temporary station	054355
1.36	0.007	31.32	6. 8.73	0.00	1.11.73		Rated section. Temporary station	054356
94.35	0.0035			20.23	4. 9.72	S R P	Rated section	054357
0.09	0.0063	3.25	6. 8.73	0.03	5. 7.73		Flat V Crump weir. Temporary station in Shropshire Groundwater Investigation	054358
0.08	0.0078	3.63	5. 8.73	0.01	9. 7.73		Flat V Crump weir. Temporary station in Shropshire Groundwater Investigation	054359
0.12	0.0048	1.78	6. 8.73	0.05	9.7.73		Flat V Crump weir. Temporary station in Shropshire Groundwater Investigation	054360
0.02	0.0039	2.00	19. 7.73	0.01	4.10.73	G	Flat V Crump weir. Temporary station in Shropshire Groundwater Investigation	054361
0.10	0.0073	3.63	6. 8.73	0.04	13. 9.73		Flat V Crump weir. Temporary station in Shropshire Groundwater Investigation	054362
0.90	0.010	18.23	9. 9.72	0.43	4.10.73	G E I	Rated section. Temporary station	054363
0.70	0.0033	6.41	17. 7.73	0.00	1. 1.73		Rated section. Temporary station	054365
0.04	0.0025	0.97	6. 8.73	0.00	1. 1.73		Flat V Crump weir. Temporary station in Shropshire Groundwater Investigation	054366
						G E	Rated section. Temporary station	054367
0.28	0.0026	4.18	15. 7.73	0.05	11. 3.65	G E	Trapezoidal critical depth flume. Range 0.05-17.0 m³/sec Installed cableway	029001
0.62	0.0080	13.31	11. 7.68	0.10	5.12.70		River section, with Crump profile weir for range 0.03-1.0 m³/sec.	029002
0.35	0.0063	6.77	2.11.68	0.05	2.12.70		Crump weir. Range 0.03-14.0 m³/sec.	029003
0.34	0.0062	9.37	16. 7.73	0.00	13. 6.70*	E	Compound Crump weir. Range 0.03-11.5 m³/sec.	029004
0.31	0.0047	9.88	16. 7.73	0.05	11.10.71*	P E	Crump weir equipped for measurement under non-modular flow conditions with crest and wing-wall tapping	029005

Station number	River	Station name	National grid reference	Catchment area	Records start	Data archived	Measuring authority	Level of station	Highest point in the catchment	Annual average areal rainfall; mm	
										Standard average for 1916-1950	Period of record average to 31.12.73
				km^2				m.O.D.	m.O.D.		

ANGLIAN WATER AUTHORITY AREA–(CONTD)

Station number	River	Station name	National grid reference	Catchment area	Records start	Data archived	Measuring authority	Level of station	Highest point	Standard average	Period of record
030001	Witham	Claypole Mill	SK 842480	298	1959	*	LRD	16.9	158	625	601
030002	Barling's Eau	Langworth Bridge	TF 066766	210	1960	*	LRD	4.06	114	617	638
030003	Bain	Fulsby Lock	TF 241610	197	1962	*	LRD	10.1	149	671	669
030004	Partney Lymn	Partney Mill	TF 402676	61.6	1962	*	LRD	14.9	142	673	732
030005	Witham	Saltersford	SK 927335	126	1968	*	LRD	57.7	158	639	
030011	Bain	Goulceby Bridge	TF 246795	62.5	1971 (1967)	*	LRD	52.25	149	709	
030012	Stainfield Beck	Cream Poke Farm, Stainfield	TF 127739	37.4	1970	*	LRD	7.70	134	653	
030014	Pointon Lode	Pointon	TF 128313	11.1	1972	*	LRD	2.66	79	612	
030803	Miningsby Beck	Revesby Reservoir	TF 312632	7.7	1973 (1927)		LRD	45	112		
031001	Eye Brook	Eye Brook Reservoir	SP 853942	60.1	1939	*	CDWC	54.6	221	671	630
031002	Glen	Kate's Bridge	TF 106149	342	1960	*	WNRD	6.10	129	612	624
031004	Welland	Tallington Weir	TF 095078	717	1967	*	WNRD	13.1	228	620	
031005	Welland	Tixover	SP 970997	404	1963		WNRD	30.0	228		
031006	Gwash	Belmesthorpe	TF 038097	150	1967	*	WNRD	24.0	207	630	
031007	Welland	Barrowden	SP 948999	400	1967	*	WNRD	34.9	228	642	
031008	East Glen	Manthorpe Bridge	TF 068159	136	1970	*	WNRD	15.6	129	614	
031009	West Glen	Shillingthorpe	TF 074113	173	1968	*	WNRD	13.8	126	616	
031010	Chater	Fosters Bridge	SK 960030	68.9	1968	*	WNRD	38.4	228	641	
031011	West Glen	Burton Coggles	SK 988261	31.6	1969	*	WNRD	61.4	128	625	

an aged charge /s	Mean annual natural runoff mm	Highest instan- taneous gauged discharge m³/s	Date	Lowest daily mean gauged discharge m³/s	Date	Abstrac- tions and returns	Station details	Station number
.61 *0.0054*		29.17	4.12.60	0.11	20. 6.60	P G E	Compound broad crested weir. Range 0.03–42.9 m³/s	030001
.29 *0.0061*		29.17	21.12.60	0.00	21. 9.64	G E	Originally river section only. Design flow 38.0 m³/sec. Compound Crump weir built 1965. Range 0.03–3.40 m³/sec.	030002
.16 *0.0059*		29.65	29.11.65	0.07	18. 6.73	S P E I	Combined round crested weir (main channel) and thin plate weir (subsidiary channel). Range 0.06–45.0 m³/s	030003
).50 *0.0081*		13.38	11. 7.68	0.00	1. 5.62	S	Crump weir. Range 0.05–14.0 m³/sec	030004
.06 *0.0084*		14.98	6. 5.69	0.10	26.10.70	P E	Full range compound weir with round-crested notch and symmetrical broad crested flanking weirs. Range 0.03–22.8 m³/sec.	030005
).23 *0.0037*		2.46	27. 1.72	0.07	16. 6.73		Rated section with drop replaced by Crump weir, 4.8768 m wide in 8/1971	030011
).17 *0.0045*		17.57	16. 7.73	0.01	22. 7.71		Full range symmetric compound Crump weir. Range 0.03–10.0 m³/sec Facilities for measuring non-modular conditions, i.e. crest and wing-wall tappings incorporated	030012
		1.47	28. 6.73	0.00	1. 6.72		Simple Crump weir with 2.445 m crest: double gauged	030014
						I	Rectangular thin plate weir; flow range 0–0.13 cumecs	030803
).18 *0.003*	209 *33.2*	22.37	4.12.60	0.00	20. 1.40*	S	Two Crump weirs, one for compen- sation water and one for high flows.	031001
.16 *0.0034*				0.01	1.10.61*	G	Critical depth flume replaced in November 1971 by flat V Crump profile weir (slope 1 : 20, width 9.7 m) rated up to 0.998 m (21.99 cumec) with complementary critical depth flume 031202 King Street Bridge at TF109106 on Greatford Cut for flood diversions which join the Welland River. The groundwater abstraction takes place outside the catchment.	031002
.87 *0.0040*		46.33	6. 5.69	0.00		S E	Compound broad crested weir 13.1 m long with two complementary Crump weirs, 031204 on West Deeping Mill Stream, 12.6 m crest and 031404, Lolham Mill Stream, 12.9 m crest	031004
						S	River section for measuring high flows above 6.5 m³/s. Low and medium flows measured at 031007 Barrowden	031005
.14 *0.0076*		40.70	9.12.69	0.18	4.10.67		Crump weir, crest 8.5 m long	031006
.37 *0.0034*		50.37	3.11.68	0.00	19.11.70	S	Crump weir crest 3.04 m long. High flows measured at Tixover 031005	031007
		2.89	16. 7.73	0.00			Simple Crump weir, crest 1.3 m long. Rated up to 0.520 m (3.789 cumecs). Low flows only.	031008
		3.74	8. 3.72	0.03	12.11.71		Simple Crump weir, crest 1.83 m long. Rated up to 0.490 (3.000 cumecs). Low flows only.	031009
.49 *0.0071*		20.64	11. 7.68	0.00	1. 1.68		Compound Crump weir, low flow notch 1.05 m long, total length 6.08 m.	031010
		1.70	6.12.72	0.00	1. 2.69*		Simple Crump weir, crest 1.82 m long. Rated up to 0.484 m (1.950 cumecs). Low flows only.	031011

Station number	River	Station name	National grid reference	Catchment area	Records start	Data archived	Measuring authority	Level of station	Highest point in the catchment	Annual average areal rainfall; mm	
										Standard average for 1916-1950	Period of record average to 31.12.?
				km²				m.O.D.	m.O.D.		

ANGLIAN WATER AUTHORITY—(CONTD)

Station number	River	Station name	National grid reference	Catchment area	Records start	Data archived	Measuring authority	Level of station	Highest point in catchment	Standard average for 1916-1950	Period of record average
031012	Tham	Little Bytham	TF 016179	24.9	1969	*	WNRD	35.7	122	623	
031013	East Glen	Irnham	TF 038273	71.5	1969	*	WNRD	42.6	129	622	
031014	Grimsthorpe Brook	Grimsthorpe Park	TF 046203	21.0	1969	*	WNRD	28.6	98	617	
031015	Chater	Ridlington	SK 848037	18.5	1969	*	WNRD	92.0	229	691	
031016	North Brook	Empingham	SK 957088	36.5	1969	*	WNRD	50.4	153	633	
031017	Stonton Brook	Welham Road Bridge	SP 759918	42.8	1970	*	WNRD	66.4	210	665	
031018	Langton Bridge	Welham Road Bridge	SK 755907	55.1	1970	*	WNRD	66.2	200	649	
031019	Medbourne Brook	Medbourne	SP 798939	27.9	1970	*	WNRD	65.7	192	644	
031020	Morcott Brook	South Luffenham	SK 939019	19.6	1970	*	WNRD	28.2	170	625	
031021	Welland	Ashley	SP 819915	250	1970	*	WNRD	55.7	210	653	
031022	Jordan	Market Harborough	SP 740867	20.8	1970	*	WNRD	75.3	158	643	
031023	West Glen	Easton Wood	SK 965259	4.4	1972	*	WNRD	81.0	120	627	
031024	Holywell Brook	Holywell	TF 026148	22.3	1972	*	WNRD	27.0	128	617	
032001	Nene	Orton	TL 166972	1630	1939	*	WNRD	4.27	224	627	623
032002	Willow Brook	Fotheringhay	TL 067933	89.6	1938	*	WNRD	15.2	136	602	608
032003	Harper's Brook	Old Mill Bridge	SP 983799	74.3	1938	*	WNRD	30.3	146	617	629
032004	Ise Brook	Harrowden Old Mill	SP 898715	195	1943	*	WNRD	45.4	197	648	638
032005	Nene	Northampton	SP 755597	570	1945		WNRD	79.5	213	657	
032006	Nene (Kislingbury Branch)	Upton Mill	SP 721592	223	1939	*	WNRD	61.6	224	668	665
032007	Nene (Brampton Branch)	St Andrew's Mill	SP 747617	233	1939	*	WNRD	59.4	204	655	655
032008	Nene (Kislingbury Branch)	Dodford	SP 627607	107	1945	*	WNRD	79.2	214	673	671

~an ~ged ~scharge m³/s	Mean annual natural runoff mm	Highest instantaneous gauged discharge m³/s	Date	Lowest daily mean gauged discharge m³/s	Date	Abstractions and returns	Station details	Station number
		0.67	17. 3.69	0.00	12. 3.69		Simple Crump weir, crest 1.82 m long. Rated up to 0.30 m (0.677 cumecs). Low flows only	031012
		0.61	17.11.69	0.00			Simple Crump weir, crest 1.82 m long. Rated up to 0.304 m (0.673 cumecs). Low flows only.	031013
		0.67	17. 3.69	0.00			Simple Crump weir, crest 1.82 m long. Rated up to 0.304 m (0.670 cumecs). Low flows only. Catchment area contains large artificial lake.	031014
		3.33	28. 9.73	0.00	17. 7.70*		Simple Crump weir, crest 1.82 m long. Rated up to 0.306 (0.626 cumecs). Low flows only.	031015
0.18 0.0049		0.97	13. 3.69	0.00	1. 2.69		Simple Crump weir, crest 2.36 m long. Rated up to 0.584 m (2.503 cumecs). Low flows only.	031016
		0.71	21. 1.73	0.01	3.10.70*		Simple Crump weir, crest 1.81 m long. Rated up to 0.304 m (0.653 cumecs). Low flows only	031017
		2.28	20. 1.73	0.03	22.10.72		Simple Crump weir, crest 1.83 m long. Rated up to 0.300 m (0.636 cumecs). Low flows only.	031018
		0.64	21. 1.73	0.01	31.10.71		Simple Crump weir, crest 1.82 m long. Rated up to 0.306 m (0.658 cumecs). Low flows only.	031019
		0.66	20. 1.73	0.01	4. 9.72		Simple Crump weir, crest 2.0 m long. Rated up to 0.300 m (0.689 cumecs). Low flows only. River section up to 1.8 m (22.1 cumecs)	031020
1.37 0.0055		26.59	6.12.72	0.12	7. 9.72	E	Simple Crump weir, crest 6.97 m long. Structure rated up to 0.500 metres (4.816 cumecs)	031021
		1.10	20.12.72	0.00	22. 7.70		Simple Crump weir, crest 1.47 m long. Rated up to 0.354 metres (0.673 cumecs). Low flows only	031022
		1.27	20. 7.73	0.00	30. 5.72*		Flat V Crump profile weir 8.05 m wide. Rated to 0.90 m (10.722 cumecs)	031023
0.08 0.0036		0.89	8. 3.72	0.01	30.11.72	G	Simple Crump weir 2.498 m wide. Rated to 0.494 m (1.788 cumecs). Low flows only	031024
8.97 0.0055	157 25.2	382.28	18. 3.47	0.09	29. 7.48	S P E I	Group of weirs and sluices with regulated by-pass channels. High flows measured at Wansford 032010. Some river regulation by sluices.	032001
0.74 0.0093	171 28.1	15.01	17. 3.47	0.06	8. 8.44	F I	Rectangular critical depth flume	032002
0.41 0.0055		15.21	16. 3.47	0.01	22.10.70		Compound Crump weir, total crest length 3.7 m. Centre low flow notch 1.22 m long.	032003
1.30 0.0067	210 32.9	19.54	2. 7.58	0.05	11. 8.44	S E	Compound Crump weir, total crest length 5.5m. Centre low flow notch 1.22 m long	032004
							Crump weir, crest 2.66 m long	032005
1.27 0.0057	182 27.4	20.84	11. 7.68	0.07	28. 9.44	S P	Rectangular critical depth flume. Rated up to 1.0 metres (12.721 cumecs). Complementary simple Crump weir, 6.118 m crest, 032206, on by-pass, replaced broad crest weir in April 1969	032006
1.09 0.0047	192 29.3	27.84	22.11.40	0.00	13. 6.73	S P	Rectangular critical depth flume. Complementary broad crested weir 032207 in by-pass channel	032007
1.55 0.0051	167 24.9	11.61	11. 7.68	0.00	4. 3.68		In 1966, Crump weir crest length 2.66 m replaced original structure comprising thin plate notch set in a broad crested weir	032008

Station number	River	Station name	National grid reference	Catchment area	Records start	Data archived	Measuring authority	Level of station	Highest point in the catchment	Annual average areal rainfall; mm	
										Standard average for 1916-1950	Period of record average to 31.12.
				km²				m.O.D.	m.O.D.		

⑤

ANGLIAN WATER AUTHORITY AREA–(CONTD)

Station number	River	Station name	National grid reference	Catchment area	Records start	Data archived	Measuring authority	Level of station	Highest point in the catchment	Standard average for 1916-1950	Period of record average to 31.12.
032009	Willow Brook	Blatherwyke	SP 981967	64.8	1938		CDWC	57.0			
032010	Nene	Wansford	TL 081996	1530	1939	*	WNRD	7.92	224		
032012	Wootton Brook	Lady Bridge	SP 738571	53.3	1968	*	WNRD	65.4	131	642	
032013	Nene	Wollaston	SP 887647	645	1944		WNRD	43.1	224		
032014	Nene	Lilford	TL 025837	1260	1970		WNRD	21.8	224		
032015	Willow Brook Central Stream	Tunwell Loop	SP 896891	7.1	1969	*	WNRD	96.7	140	617	
032016	Willow Brook South Stream	Stanion Lane	SP 901886	7.6	1969	*	WNRD	101	140	620	
032018	Ise	Barford Bridge	SP 961831	62.4	1969	*	WNRD	66.8	197	665	
032019	Slade Brook	Kettering	SP 873763	58.3	1970	*	WNRD	56.2	160	642	
032020	Wittering Brook	Wansford	TL 089995	46.9	1970	*	WNRD	9.15	92	579	
032023	Grendon Brook	Ryeholmes Bridge	SP 883633	47.5	1970	*	WNRD	140	371	617	
032024	Southwick Brook	Southwick Brook	TL 025921	20.5	1971	*	WNRD	25.0	100	605	
032025	Nene (Whilton Branch)	Surney Bridges	SP 620658	63.4	1971	*	WNRD	92.0	221	686	
032026	Nene (Brampton Branch)	Brixworth	SP 737708	58.0	1971	*	WNRD	28.5	206	669	
032027	Billing Brook	Chesterton	TL 117949	24.3	1971	*	WNRD	14.0	72	592	
032029	Flore Experimental Catchment		SP 660610	7.0	1964		WNRD	80.2	146		
032902	Sywell Brook	Sywell Reservoir	SP 833651	7.08	1955 (1907)		NWD				
033001	Great Ouse	Brownshill Staunch	TL 369727	3030	1936	*	GORD	1.83	247	615	610
033002	Great Ouse	Bedford	TL 055495	1460	1936	*	GORD	24.4	247	650	655
033003	Cam	Bottisham	TL 508657	803	1936	*	GORD	2.75	168	587	589

...an ged charge	Mean annual natural runoff	Highest instan- taneous gauged discharge	Date	Lowest daily mean gauged discharge	Date	Abstrac- tions and returns	Station details	Station number
/s	mm	m³/s		m³/s				
						E I	Reservoir spillway	032009
						S P E I	River section, for flows over 28.3 cumecs. Low and medium flows measured at Orton 032001	032010
		1.12	2. 6.69	0.00	1. 6.69*		Simple Crump weir, crest 1.83 m long. Rated up to 0.250 metres (0.488 cumecs). Low flows only	032012
						S P E I	Complex of weirs replaced in 1968 by simple Crump weir, crest 4.87 m long. Rated up to 1.698 cumecs. Low flows only. Some interference from navigation locks upstream	032013
						S P E I	Simple Crump weir, crest 4.87 m long. Rated up to 0.500 metres (4.403 cumecs). Low flows only. Some interference from lock gates upstream.	032014
		0.65	12. 3.70	0.00			Simple Crump weir, crest 1.82 m long. Rated up 0.304 metres (0.646 cumecs). Low flows only.	032015
		0.67	10. 8.71	0.00	1.10.72*	I	Simple Crump weir, crest 1.83 m long. Rated up to 0.304 metres (0.651 cumecs). Low flows only.	032016
		3.59	20. 1.73	0.04	5. 9.72	E	Simple Crump weir, crest 2.44 m long. Rated up to 0.310 m (1.019 cumecs). Low flows only..	032018
		1.00	20. 1.73	0.07	27.11.73	S	Simple Crump weir, crest 2.42 m long. Rated up to 0.300 m (0.848 cumecs). Low flows only.	032019
.16 0.0034		0.73	17. 7.73	0.06	8. 6.73		Simple Crump weir, crest 2.44 m long. Rated up to 0.308 m (0.896 cumecs). Low flows only.	032020
		0.44	21.11.73	0.02	7. 9.72		Simple Crump weir, crest 1.83 m long. Rated up to 0.300 m (0.616 cumecs). Low flows only.	032023
		0.77	7. 3.72	0.01	27.11.72	G E	Simple Crump weir 2.00 m wide. Rated to 0.300 m (0.670 cumecs) Low flow only.	032024
		1.73	10. 6.72	0.08	9.10.72	R E	Simple Crump weir 2.530 m wide. Rated to 0.348 m (1.177 cumecs) Low flows only	032025
		0.87	2. 4.73	0.02	2. 9.72		Simple Crump weir, crest 2.48 m long. Rated up to 0.350 m (1.086 cumecs). Low flows only.	032026
		2.51	6. 3.72	0.00		E	Simple Crump weir 2.00 m wide. Rated to 0.280 m (0.635 cumecs). Low flows	032027
							Trapezoidal critical depth flume rated to 1.92 m (8.49 cumecs)	032029
							Compound thin plate weir in con- crete channel	032902
.16 0.0047	126 20.7	311.49	16. 3.47	0.00		S P G E I	Three radial sluice gates 4.27 m wide and navigation lock; some flow regulation by sluices. Publication discontinued 1962, records continued by 033017, St. Ives Staunch	033001
.46 0.0065	221 33.7	278.10	15. 3.47	0.01	15. 8.34	S P G E I	Three broad crested weirs for low flows, and three vertically lifting sluice gates for high flows	033002
.67 0.0046		72.78	14. 3.47	0.00	25. 6.44	G E I	Broad crested weir with low flow notch 2.4 m wide, two vertically lifting sluice gates and navigation lock; some flow regulation by sluices	033003

Station number	River	Station name	National grid reference	Catch-ment area km²	Records start	Data archived	Measuring authority	Level of station m.O.D.	Highest point in the catch-ment m.O.D.	Annual average areal rainfall; mm Standard average for 1916-1950	Period of record average to 31.12.

ANGLIAN WATER AUTHORITY AREA–(CONTD)

Station number	River	Station name	National grid reference	Catchment area km²	Records start	Data archived	Measuring authority	Level of station m.O.D.	Highest point m.O.D.	Standard average 1916-1950	Period of record average to 31.12.
033004	Lark	Isleham	TL 648760	466	1949		GORD	2.5	113	620	609
033005	Great Ouse	Thornborough Mill	SP 736353	389	1951	*	GORD	72.8	177	673	665
033006	Wissey	Northwold	TL 771965	275	1956	*	GORD	6.10	95	660	656
033007	Nar	Marham	TF 723119	153	1953	*	GORD	4.88	91	691	698
033908	Little Ouse	Thetford No. 1 Staunch	TL 863832	702	1958	*	GORD	7.19	97		
033009	Great Ouse	Harrold Mill	SP 951565	1320	1955	*	GORD	42.7	247	655	674
033010	Great Ouse	Bromhall Mill	TL 011508	1440	1963		GORD	27.4	247		
033011	Little Ouse	Euston (County Bridge)	TL 892801	129	1960	*	GORD	13.4	67	616	565
033012	Kym	Meagre Farm	TL 155631	138	1960	*	GORD	17.2	101	594	577
033013	Sapiston	Rectory Bridge, Euston	TL 896791	206	1960	*	GORD	15.6	97	615	579
033014	Lark	Temple Weir	TL 758730	272	1960	*	GORD	8.84	113	622	597
033015	Ouzel	Willen Weir	SP 883409	277	1962	*	GORD	56.7	243	655	668
033016	Cam	Jesus Lock	TL 450593	761	1959		GORD	5.2	168	592	541
033017	Great Ouse	St Ives Staunch	TL 314705	2880	1961		GORD	3.13	247	620	
033018	Tove	Cappenham Bridge	SP 714488	138	1962	*	GORD	80.8	182	696	663
033019	Thet	Melford Bridge	TL 880830	316	1962	*	GORD	10.7	64	637	605
033020	Alconbury Brook	Brampton	TL 208717	202	1963	*	GORD	9.45	73	581	480
033021	Rhee	Burnt Mill	TL 413522	303	1962	*	GORD	8.84	168	587	543
033022	Ivel	Blunham	TL 153509	541	1964	*	GORD	18.9	160	597	601
033023	Lea Brook	Beck Bridge	TL 662733	102	1962	*	GORD	10.5	107	551	562
033024	Cam	Dernford	TL 466506	194	1963	*	GORD	14.8	137	603	603
033025	Babingley	West Newton Mill	TF 696256	39.6	1963	*	GORD	40.4	76	696	783
033026	Great Ouse	Offord	TL 217669	2570	1970		GORD	10.9	247	625	

ean uged scharge	Mean annual natural runoff	Highest instantaneous gauged discharge	Date	Lowest daily mean gauged discharge	Date	Abstractions and returns	Station details	Station number
³/s	mm	m³/s		m³/s				
1.94 *0.042*	120 *19.7*	28.00	17. 9.68	0.00	23. 6.57	G E I	Sluice gate plus weir at high levels. Flows estimated using lock keeper's record.	033004
2.50 *0.0064*	209 *31.4*	35.11	11. 7.68	0.07	21. 9.59	S P G E I	Broad crested weir 10.2 m long with low flow rectangular notch plate, also two sluice gates 3.6 m wide;	033005
1.86 *0.068*	210 *32.0*	9.85	25. 2.69	0.31	5. 8.57		Rectangular critical depth flume measures flows up to 11.5 m³/s	033006
1.18 *0.0077*	264 *37.8*	5.07	1. 3.58	0.31	25.11.59	P G	Critical depth flume with central low flow notch 0.3 m wide, total crest length 7.47 m	033007
2.94 *0.042*		25.34	9. 1.59	0.00	12. 7.64	G E I	Two vertical lift gates 5.3 m and 7.2 m wide, replaced by 033034 Abbey Heath in 1968; some river regulation by sluices	033908
9.51 *0.0072*		141.59	2.11.60	0.43	27. 5.56	S P G E I	Compound broad crested weir overall length 17.2 m; one broad crested weir 15.4 m long and one weir 2.5 m long; some flow regulation by sluices	033009
						S P G E I	Thin plate weir for low flow measurement; some flow regulation by sluices	033010
0.39 *0.0030*		5.66	2.11.60	0.03	23. 9.64	G	Compound broad crested weir with trapezoidal cross-section	033011
0.51 *0.0037*		33.98	21.12.60	0.01	29. 5.60*	E I	Compound broad crested weir with trapezoidal cross-section	033012
0.60 *0.0029*		8.95	17. 9.68	0.02	2. 9.65	G E I	Rectangular thin plate weir, crest 8.8 m long	033013
1.24 *0.0046*		22.06	17. 9.68	0.29	26. 8.73	G E I	Compound broad crested weir with rectangular cross section, overall length 5.8 m; some flow regulation by sluices	033014
1.82 *0.0066*		23.87	11. 7.68	0.12	5. 7.73	G E I	Compound broad crested weir measuring up to 20 m³/s; some flow regulation by sluices	033015
2.72 *0.0036*		34.83	21.12.60	0.26	23. 8.64	G E I	Thin plate weir plus two sluice gates	033016
						S P G E I	Seven vertically lifting sluice gates and navigation lock, supersedes Brownhill Staunch 033001; some river regulation by sluices. Abandoned 1965	033917
0.97 *0.0070*		33.96	27. 6.73	0.11	25. 1.63*	E	Compound broad crested weir measures flow up to 14 m³/s; some flow regulation by sluices	033018
1.70 *0.0054*		11.55	25. 2.69	0.27	2.10.64	G E	Triangular profile weir, crest 6.25 m long. Some flow regulation by groundwater abstraction	033019
0.58 *0.0029*		28.09	16. 3.64	0.00	19. 7.72	E I	Compound broad crested weir with low flow notch	033020
0.96 *0.0032*		9.54	11.12.66	0.14	15. 9.73	G E I	Triangular profile weir with trapezoidal cross section; some flow regulation by sluices	033021
2.72 *0.0050*		23.09	13. 3.69	0.61	14. 9.73	G E I	Crump weir, crest 7.31 m long; some flow regulation by sluices	033022
0.22 *0.0022*		4.76	14. 3.69	0.00	16. 9.64	G E I	Crump weir, 4 m long. Groundwater catchment area approximately 60 per cent of the surface catchment	033023
0.97 *0.005*		10.99	17. 9.68	0.03	3. 7.49	G E I	Rectangular thin plate aerated weir, crest 5.79 m long	033024
0.40 *0.01*		1.17	17. 3.69	0.08	5.11.72	G I	Rectangular thin plate weir; some flow regulation by sluices	033025
1.35 *0.044*				1.60	6.10.72	S P G E I	Automatic adjustable tilting gate 15.2 m wide, Crump weir 15.3 m wide, compound broad crested weir and navigation lock. Some flow regulation by sluices. Major intake just upstream	033026

Station number	River	Station name	National grid reference	Catchment area km²	Records start	Data archived	Measuring authority	Level of station m.O.D.	Highest point in the catchment m.O.D.	Annual average areal rainfall; mm Standard average for 1916-1950	Period of record average to 31.12.

ANGLIAN WATER AUTHORITY AREA–(CONTD)

Station number	River	Station name	National grid reference	Catchment area km²	Records start	Data archived	Measuring authority	Level of station m.O.D.	Highest point in the catchment m.O.D.	Standard average for 1916-1950	Period of record average to 31.12.
033027	Rhee	Wimpole	TL 333485	119	1965	*	GORD	17.9	167	583	573
033028	Flit	Shefford	TL 143393	119	1966		GORD	36.6	162	610	
033029	Stringside	White Bridge	TF 716006	93.5	1965	*	GORD	2.54	82	637	
033030	Clipstone Brook	Hockcliffe Weir	SP 933255	40.2	1966		GORD	83.5	161	666	
033031	Broughton Brook	Broughton	SP 892405	66.6	1970	*	GORD	58.0	170	630	
033032	Heacham	Heacham Mill	TF 685375	89.3	1965	*	GORD	12.1	88	672	
033033	Hiz	Arlesey	TL 190379	108	1973	*	GORD	35.7	172	625	
033034	Little Ouse	Abbey Heath	TL 851844	699	1968	*	GORD	7.23	98	624	
033035	Great Ouse	Denver Sluice	TF 588010	3430	1925		GORD	1.5	167	615	591
033037	Great Ouse	Newport Pagnell	SP 877442	800	1969		GORD	53.6	189	665	
033039	Great Ouse	Roxton	TL 160535	166	1972	*	GORD	15.4	247	641	
033040	Rhee	Ashwell	TL 267401	1.0	1971	*	GORD	39.9	100	587	
033044	Thet	Bridgham	TL 957856	278	1967		GORD	15.1	76	641	
033045	Whittle	Quidenham	TM 027878	28.3	1967		GORD	23.8	55	648	
033046	Thet	Red Bridge	TL 996923	145	1967		GORD	20.1	64	651	
033348	Larling Brook	Stonebridge	TL 927907	21.4	1969		GORD	24.7	52	622	
033349	Stamford Water	Buckenham Tofts	TL 836952	44.5	1967		GORD	13.9	58	635	
033051	Cam	Chesterford	TL 505426	141	1965		GORD	35.4	137		
033052	Swaffham Lode	Swaffham Bulbeck	TL 553629	36.4	1963		GORD	3.1	119		
033353	Granta	Stapleford	TL 471515	114	1949		GORD	14.7	126		
033805	Beechamwell Brook	Beechamwell	TF 738036	34.4	1964		GORD	6.0	82	649	
033809	Bury Brook	Bury Weir	TL 286837	65.3	1963		GORD	2.2	51	554	
033813	Mel	Meldreth	TL 378466	8.6	1965		GORD	18.2	100	597	
033901	Little Ouse	Thetford Bridge	TL 860832	702	1958		GORD				
033902	Ouzel	Orchard Mill	SP 885308	205	1956		GORD	70	243		
034001	Yare	Colney	TG 182082	232	1960	*	NSRD	8.18	69	661	66:
034002	Tas	Shotesham	TM 226994	147	1957	*	NSRD	9.6	65	688	61
034003	Bure	Ingworth	TG 192296	165	1959	*	NSRD	12.2	87	699	68
034004	Wensum	Costessey Mill	TG 177128	536	1960	*	NSRD	5.18	94	688	68:
034005	Tud	Costessey Park	TG 170113	73.2	1961	*	NSRD	9.45	85	680	
034006	Waveney	Needham Mill	TM 229811	370	1963	*	NSRD	16.5	65	643	69

Mean gauged discharge	Mean annual natural runoff	Highest instantaneous gauged discharge	Date	Lowest daily mean gauged discharge	Date	Abstractions and returns	Station details	Station number
^{3}/s	mm	m^3/s		m^3/s				
0.48	0.004	6.14	18.12.68	0.02	3.10.73	G E I	Trapezoidal critical depth flume	033027
0.64	0.0054	5.86	1. 2.71	0.00	10.12.66	G E I	Trapezoidal critical depth flume	033028
0.67		4.08	22.11.71	0.07	2.10.70	G I	Trapezoidal critical depth flume	033029
	0.0072			0.00			Crump weir, crest 4.2 m long	033030
0.16	0.0024	3.80	19.10.71	0.04	15. 7.72*	G E	Trapezoidal flume	033031
0.22	0.0025	0.90	27. 6.70	0.00	16. 5.69	G I	Two Crump weirs, total crest length 3.0 m. The groundwater catchment area is approximately half the surface catchment	033032
0.35	0.0032	2.02	27. 6.73	0.27	12. 9.73	G E I	Crump type weir	033033
3.85	0.0055	21.61	24. 2.69	0.85	14. 9.73	G E I	Crump weir with crest and downstream tappings, crest 12.2 m long; some flow regulation by groundwater abstraction	033034
15.70	0.0046			0.00		G E I	Complex of sluice gates and a navigation lock. Long term records, but unreliable and no continuous recorder; flows regulated by sluice gates	033035
2.81	0.0035	44.60	1. 2.71	0.30	23.10.70		Compound Crump weir, complemented by simple Crump at Mill, 033237 measuring flows to 72 m^3/s	033037
3.98	0.024	34.35	8.12.72	0.47	27. 9.73	P G E I	Flat V Crump profile weir	033039
0.04	0.04	0.23	2. 4.72	0.02	30. 7.73	G	Trapezoidal flume	033040
0.72	0.0026	2.26	20. 6.73	0.30	7. 9.73	G E	Two broad crested weirs under road bridge, total crest length 7.4 m Some river flow regulation by groundwater	033044
0.04	0.0014	0.21	6. 5.73	0.01	11. 9.73		Compound broad crested weir, total crest length 3.05 m	033045
		1.69	20. 6.73	0.09	12. 9.73	G	Crump weir 3.96 m wide	033046
0.02	0.00093	0.12	19. 6.73	0.01	12. 9.73	I	Triangular critical depth flume	033348
0.17	0.0038	0.39	10.12.73	0.11	11. 9.73		Broad crested weir, 2.76 m wide	033349
						G E I	Compound broad crested trapezoidal weir	033051
						G	Crump type weir, reconstructed 1972 and 1973	033052
						G	Thin plate weir. Some flows derived. Monthly means only valid	033353
						G	Abandoned February 1975	033805
							Rectangular compound weir. Drowns completely at high flows	033809
						G	Thin plate weir in mill race	033813
							Occasional measurements	033901
1.39	0.0068	23.5	21. 1.59	0.17	5. 8.58	G E I	Compound weir and sluice gate. Abandoned January 1960	033902
1.47	0.0063	21.61	17. 9.68	0.22	10. 8.64	I G	Compound weir, total crest length 11.9 m. Low flow notch broad crested weir, remainder Crump profile; measures flows accurately up to 19 m^3/s	034001
0.78	0.0053	62.30	16. 9.68	0.08	5. 9.64	I	Irregular rectangular flume 5.5 m wide. Reconstructed to flat V Crump profile weir in 1970. Measures flows up to 14 m^3/s	034002
1.09	0.0066	11.94	7. 4.60	0.43	14. 9.64	I	Two ogee weirs measuring flows accurately up to 4.3 m^3/s	034003
3.82	0.0071	24.44	6.12.60	0.90	16. 6.73	I	Three broad crested weirs and flood gates; measures flows up to 19 m^3/s	034004
0.35	0.0048	5.76	28. 1.72	0.05	12. 9.73	I	Four trapezoidal critical depth flumes; measures flows up to 4 m^3/s	034005
1.72	0.0046	113.27	16. 9.68	0.19	23. 8.73	I	Two Crump weirs, one with low flow notch; measures flows up to 23 m^3/s	034006

Station number	River	Station name	National grid reference	Catchment area	Records start	Data archived	Measuring authority	Level of station	Highest point in the catchment	Annual average areal rainfall; mm	
										Standard average for 1916-1950	Period of record average to 31.12.7.
				km²				m.O.D.	m.O.D.		

⑤

ANGLIAN WATER AUTHORITY AREA—(CONTD)

Station number	River	Station name	National grid reference	Catchment area	Records start	Data archived	Measuring authority	Level of station	Highest point in the catchment	Standard average for 1916-1950	Period of record average to 31.12.7.
034007	Dove	Oakley Park	TM 174772	134	1966	*	NSRD	21.0	67	633	
034008	Ant	Honing Lock	TG 331270	47.3	1966	*	NSRD	1.88	59		
034010	Waveney	Billingford Bridge	TM 168782	149	1968	*	NSRD	20.3	61	651	
034011	Wensum	Fakenham	TF 919294	127	1966	*	NSRD	33.7	91	706	
034012	Burn	Burnham Overy	TF 842428	80.0	1966	*	NSRD	2.59	81	655	
034013	Waveney	Ellingham Mill	TM 364917	670	1970	*	NSRD	1.6	63	645	
034014	Wensum	Swanton Morley	TG 020184	363	1969	*	NSRD	17.8	92	701	
034016	Glaven	Bayfield	TG 055396	80.5	1970		NSRD	7.5	95		
034018	Stiffkey	Warham	TM 944414	77.1	1972	*	NSRD	5.3	95	663	
034320	Stiffkey	Little Walsingham	TF 935366	49.3	1966		NSRD		94		
034321	Mundesley Beck	Mundesley Hospital	TG 296364	19.4	1968		NSRD		76	657	
034322	Dove	Abbey Bridge	TM 151738	122	1972		NSRD		66		
034323	Dove	Standwell Green	TM 130702	36.6	1973		NSRD		64		
034324	Finningham Watercourse	Stoke Ash	TM 111707	50.2	1972		NSRD		66		
034325	Yaxley Watercourse	Eye	TM 146741	13.5	1972		NSRD		61		
034326	Thorndon Watercourse	Catbridge	TM 138707	10.2	1972		NSRD		63		
035001	Gipping	Constantine Weir	TM 154441	311	1961	*	NSRD	1.70	94	635	
035002	Deben	Naunton Hall	TM 322534	163	1964	*	NSRD	5.49	62	635	633
035003	Alde	Farnham	TM 360601	63.9	1961	*	NSRD	5.18	63	625	577
035004	Ore	Beversham	TM 359593	54.9	1965	*	NSRD	2.43	53	640	635
035008	Gipping	I.C.I. Stowmarket	TM 058570	129	1966	*	NSRD	25.1	94	618	
035009	Blyth	Blyford Bridge	TM 425765	96.4	1965		NSRD	1.22	59	634	
035010	Gipping	Bramford	TM 127465	298	1968	*	NSRD	6.25	78	626	
035011	Belstead Brook	Belstead	TM 143420	40.4	1968		NSRD	1.83	91		

Mean gauged discharge	Mean annual natural runoff	Highest instantaneous gauged discharge	Date	Lowest daily mean gauged discharge	Date	Abstractions and returns	Station details	Station number
m³/s	mm	m³/s		m³/s				
0.71 *0.0053*		38.51	16. 9.68	0.11	12. 9.73	I	Compound Crump weir; measures flows up to 24 m³/s. Centre low flow notch 1.22 m wide, overall crest length 7.92 m	034007
						I	Simple Crump weir	034008
		1.70	6.12.72	0.04	10. 9.73	I E	Compound Crump weir and thin plate crested sluice gate; measures flows up to 6.4 m³/s	034010
0.72 *0.0057*		5.23	31. 8.66	0.00	20. 9.67		Compound Crump weir and thin plate crested sluice gate; measures flows up to 8.2 m³/s	034011
0.29 *0.0036*		1.34	27. 5.67	0.04	29.12.72	I	Compound Crump weir measures flows up to 2.9 m³/s. Centre low flow notch 0.61 m wide, overall crest length 3.04 m	034012
		0.82	3. 8.72	0.07	6.11.73		Simple Crump weir, 0.86 m crest. Complementary simple Crump weir 1.515 m crest, 034213, with variable level gates for high flows at sluice	034013
				0.16	18. 8.72		Twin compounded Crump weirs totalling 4.4013 m crest. Complementary triple compounded Crump weirs, 034214, totalling 11.59 m crest.	034014
						I	Crump weir	034016
		2.65	20. 6.73	0.00	1.10.73	I G	Flat V Crump weir, measures up to 5 m³/s	034018
						I G	Compound Crump weir	034320
						I	90° triangular thin plate weir	034321
						I G	Temporary steel Crump weir, 2.74m wide crest	034322
							Temporary steel Crump weir, 0.91m wide crest	034323
							Temporary steel Crump weir, 0.91m wide crest	034324
							Temporary steel Crump weir, 0.91 m wide crest	034325
							Temporary steel Crump weir, 0.91 m wide crest	034326
		17.36	1.12.65	0.06	15. 8.65	I G	Broad crested weir with low flow notch converted to compound flat V and horizontal Crump crest in 1973. Tides influence low flows which are measured at 035010. Mainly used as high flow station for flows up to 70 m³/s.	035001
0.75 *0.0046*		29.45	17. 9.68	0.03	30. 8.64	I G	Compound Crump weir measures flows up to 12 m³/s	035002
0.27 *0.0042*		15.63	10.12.65	0.04	3. 7.73	I G	Ogee weir crest 10.6 m long, with low flow notch. Measures flows up to 7 m³/s	035003
0.34 *0.0062*		9.77	4. 9.65	0.00	8. 9.70	I	Compound Crump weir measures flows up to 15 m³/s	035004
0.55 *0.0043*		24.19	14. 9.68	0.05	26. 8.73		Compound Crump weir measures flows up to 32 m³/s. Centre low flow notch 0.91 m wide, overall crest length 7.40 m	035008
						I	Rectangular thin plate notch in lifting sluice gate	035009
0.82 *0.0028*		21.22	21.11.71	0.07	17. 6.73	I G	Compound Crump weir and thin plate crested sluice gate measures flows up to 13 m³/s. High flows measured at 035001, Constantine weir	035010
							Compound Crump weir	035011

Station number	River	Station name	National grid reference	Catch-ment area	Records start	Data archived	Measuring authority	Level of station	Highest point in the catch-ment	Annual average areal rainfall; mm	
										Standard average for 1916-1950	Period of record average to 31.12.7.
				km²				m.O.D.	m.O.D.		

ANGLIAN WATER AUTHORITY AREA–(CONTD)

Station number	River	Station name	National grid reference	Catch-ment area	Records start	Data archived	Measuring authority	Level of station	Highest point	Standard average	Period average
035013	Blyth	Holton	TM 406769	92.9	1969	*	NSRD	12.3	61	635	
035314	Mill River	Newbourn	TM 270420	27.1	1948		IWD		36		
035315	Newbourn Stream	Newbourn	TM 274432	8.1	1948		IWD		35		
035316	Fromus	Benhall Bridge	TM 388618	18.5	1970		NSRD		48		
035317	Shottisham	Shottisham	TM 315444	8.6	1970		NSRD	0.1	27		
036001	Stour	Stratford St. Mary	TM 042340	844	1928	*	EWC	5.43	128	615	601
036002	Glem	Glemsford	TL 846472	87.3	1960	*	ERD	33.6	128	625	568
036003	Box	Polstead	TL 985379	53.9	1960	*	ERD	15.9	86	617	560
036004	Chad Brook	Long Melford	TL 868459	47.4	1965	*	ERD	34.6	128		572
036005	Brett	Hadleigh	TM 025429	156	1962	*	ERD	18.0	102	612	568
036006	Stour	Langham	TM 020344	578	1962	*	ERD	6.40	128	610	595
036007	Belchamp Brook	Bardfield Bridge	TL 848421	58.6	1964	*	ERD	27.0	86	587	536
036008	Stour	Westmill	TL 827463	224	1960	*	ERD	33.2	126	617	570
036009	Brett	Cockfield	TL 914525	25.7	1967	*	ERD	59.4	102		552
036010	Bumpstead Brook	Broad Green	TL 689418	28.3	1968	*	ERD	55.8	112		555
036011	Stour Brook	Sturmer	TL 696441	34.5	1968	*	ERD	54.6	119		532
036012	Stour	Kedington	TL 708450	76.2	1968	*	ERD	52.5	122	624	539
036013	Brett	Higham	TM 032354	195	1969		ERD	5.87	102		
036015	Stour	Lamarsh	TL 897358	481	1970	*	ERD	17.5	128	610	475
036016	Ramsey	Great Oakley	TM 202286	13.9	1960		ERD				
037002	Chelmer	Rushes Lock	TL 794090	534	1932	*	ERD	11.3	125	602	590
037003	Ter	Crabb's Bridge	TL 786107	77.8	1963	*	ERD	14.5	96	587	565
037005	Colne	Lexden	TL 962261	238	1959	*	ERD	8.23	114	599	568
037006	Can	Beach's Mill	TL 690072	228	1962	*	ERD	23.3	103	617	578
037007	Wid	Writtle	TL 686060	136	1948	*	ERD	27.1	114	620	612
037008	Chelmer	Springfield	TL 713071	190	1965	*	ERD	23.1	125	595	570
037009	Brain	Guithavon Valley	TL 818147	60.7	1962	*	ERD	16.2	98	597	576
037010	Blackwater	Appleford Bridge	TL 845158	247	1962	*	ERD	14.6	127	605	570
037011	Chelmer	Churchend	TL 629233	72.5	1963	*	ERD	51.8	125	607	571
037012	Colne	Poolstreet	TL 771364	65.1	1963	*	ERD	43.0	114	607	526
037013	Sandon Brook	Sandon Bridge	TL 755055	60.6	1963	*	ERD	19.8	110	577	556
037016	Pant	Copford Hall	TL 668313	62.5	1965	*	ERD	57.9	127	614	612
037017	Blackwater	Stisted	TL 793243	139	1969	*	ERD	31.8	127	611	537
037020	Chelmer	Felsted	TL 670193	132	1970	*	ERD	40.1	125	601	
037021	Roman	Bounstead Bridge	TL 985205	52.6	1965	*	ERD	4.60	114	581	
037022	Holland Brook	Thorpe-le-Soken	TM 179212	54.9	1970	*	ERD	0.76		574	
037024	Colne	Earls Colne	TL 855298	154	1971	*	ERD	25.15	114	606	
037325	Bourne Brook	Perces Bridge	TL 822276	32.1	1964		ERD			614	
037326	Tenpenny Brook	Tenpenny Bridge	TM 079207	29.0	1960		ERD	4.05			
037327	Sixpenny Brook	Ship House Bridge	TM 054214	5.1	1960		ERD	16.1			
037328	Bentley Brook	Saltwater Bridge	TM 109193	12.1	1960		ERD	2.11			
037329	St Osyth Brook	Main Road Bridge	TM 134159	8.0	1960		ERD	3.30			
037330	Holland Brook	Cradle Bridge	TM 171217	48.6	1962		ERD			575	

Mean gauged discharge	Mean annual natural runoff	Highest instantaneous gauged discharge	Date	Lowest daily mean gauged discharge	Date	Abstractions and returns	Station details	Station number
m³/s	mm	m³/s		m³/s				
0.29 *0.0031*		17.35	23. 1.71	0.06	4. 7.73	I	Compound Crump weir, crest lengths 0.92 m and 4.86 m	035013
						I	Compounded thin plate weir, with orifice, measures flows up to 0.44 m³/s	035314
							Compounded thin plate weir with orifice. Measures flows up to 0.09 m³/s	035315
							Compound Crump weir	035316
						I	Compound Crump weir	035317
2.78 *0.0033*		42.16	18. 9.68	0.08	23. 8.49	S R P G E I	A system of weirs, sluices and meters	036001
0.41 *0.0047*	158 *27.8*	18.09	13. 3.69	0.05	10. 8.65	S G E I	Trapezoidal critical depth flume	036002
0.19 *0.0035*	114 *20.3*	5.46	13. 3.69	0.03	10. 9.73	S G E I	Trapezoidal critical depth flume	036003
0.22 *0.0046*	159 *27.8*	10.85	13. 3.69	0.02	9. 9.67	S G I	Modified flat V Crump profile weir with low flow side weir	036004
0.63 *0.0040*	141 *24.8*	17.64	27. 1.72	0.04	30. 6.65	S G E I	Modified flat V Crump profile weir with low flow side weir	036005
2.53 *0.0044*	149 *25.0*	36.74	28. 1.72	0.00	14. 3.69	S R G E I	Twin-throated trapezoidal critical depth flume	036006
0.15 *0.0026*		8.30	13. 3.69	0.00	27. 8.61	S G I	Trapezoidal critical depth flume	036007
1.04 *0.0046*	146 *25.6*	84.00	16. 9.68	0.02	10. 9.66	S G E I	Compound trapezoidal critical depth flume	036008
0.11 *0.0043*		8.12	15. 9.68	0.00	15. 8.73		Modified flat V Crump profile weir	036009
0.13 *0.0046*		21.00	16. 9.68	0.00	6. 9.69*	S G I	Modified flat V Crump profile weir	036010
0.20 *0.0058*		25.30	11. 9.68	0.02	21. 3.73	S G E I	Modified flat V Crump profile weir	036011
0.62 *0.0081*		85.00	16. 9.68	0.01	20. 9.71	S G E I	Modified flat V Crump profile weir	036012
		3.78	7. 3.72	0.05	9. 9.73	S G E I	Modified flat V Crump profile weir	036013
0.99 *0.00712*		13.05	7.12.72	0.23	6.10.72	S G E I	Flat V weir with low flow notch	036015
						S E I	Thin plate weir	036016
1.63 *0.0031*	91 *15.4*	18.23	10.12.65	0.00	29. 5.57	S P G E I	Broad crested weir with timber crest 21.3 m long	037002
0.29 *0.0037*	125 *22.1*	7.56	13. 3.69	0.04	19. 8.65	S R E I	Trapezoidal critical depth flume	037003
1.01 *0.0042*	133 *23.4*	23.80	13. 3.69	0.03	30. 8.65	S G E I	Compound trapezoidal critical depth flume	037005
1.18 *0.0052*		27.93	23. 1.71	0.11	1. 8.63	S E I	Triple throated rectangular critical depth flume	037006
0.79 *0.0058*	178 *29.1*	26.45	18.12.68	0.06	28.10.70	S E I	Modified flat V Crump profile weir	037007
0.96 *0.0051*	155 *27.2*	21.75	13. 3.69	0.15	14. 9.73	S G E I	Modified flat V Crump profile weir	037008
0.34 *0.0056*	161 *27.9*	6.30	13. 3.69	0.09	20. 7.64	S G E I	Modified flat V Crump profile weir	037009
1.12 *0.0045*	139 *24.4*	21.71	14. 3.69	0.09	6.10.64	S G E I	Twin throated trapezoidal critical depth flume	037010
0.33 *0.0046*	156 *27.3*	13.20	13. 3.69	0.04	14. 8.65	S G E I	Trapezoidal critical depth flume	037011
0.24 *0.0037*	130 *24.7*	18.76	13. 3.69	0.00	2. 8.73	S G I	Trapezoidal critical depth flume	037012
0.28 *0.0046*	140 *25.2*	12.22	13. 3.69	0.01	18. 7.65	S R	Modified flat V Crump profile weir	037013
0.36 *0.0058*	174 *28.4*	16.80	16. 9.68	0.01	18. 8.65	S G E I	Modified flat V Crump profile weir	037016
0.76 *0.0055*		17.14	12. 3.70	0.12	18. 7.72	S G E I	Modified flat V Crump profile weir	037017
0.47 *0.0036*		12.00	23. 1.71	0.09	14. 9.73	S G E I	Modified flat V Crump profile weir	037020
0.16 *0.0030*		4.26	27. 1.72	0.04	26.10.73	S G E I	Temporary weir, replaced in 1969 by a modified flat V Crump profile weir	037021
0.12 *0.0022*		6.00	27. 1.72	0.00	10. 7.73	S G E I	Modified flat V Crump profile weir	037022
0.41 *0.0027*		12.01	27. 1.72	0.09	13. 9.73	S G E I	Modified flat V Crump profile weir	037024
						S E I	Compound thin plate weir	037325
						I	Thin plate weir	037326
							Thin plate weir. Discontinued December 1971	037327
						I	Thin plate weir	037328
							Twin throated trapezoidal flume	037329
						E I	Thin plate weir, superseded by Thorpe-le-Soken, 037022 in 1970	037330

Station number	River	Station name	National grid reference	Catchment area	Records start	Data archived	Measuring authority	Level of station	Highest point in the catchment	Annual average areal rainfall; mm	
										Standard average for 1916-1950	Period of record average to 31.12.7
				km²				m.O.D.	m.O.D.		

ANGLIAN WATER AUTHORITY AREA–(contd)

037331	Crouch	Wickford	TQ 748934	71.8	1961		ERD				
037332	Eastwood Brook	Lambeth Road	TQ 842889	6.2	1965		ERD	33.6			
037035	Salary Brook	Spring Valley	TM 041279	6.7	1965		ERD	20.0	40		
037036	Ely-Ouse outfall	Great Sampford	TL 646351		1971	*	ERD	68.65			
037901	Ter	Hatfield Peverel	TL 793103	80.3	1932	*	ERD	17.0	98	587	583
037902	Wid	Margaretting	TL 672000	98.6	1951	*	ERD	36.08	111		

THAMES WATER AUTHORITY AREA

037001	Roding	Redbridge	TQ 415884	303	1950	*	LD	5.72	117	635	622
037904	Blackwater	Langford	TL 836092	337	1932	*	LD	11.3	125	662	589
037014	Roding	High Ongar	TL 560040	95.1	1963	*	LD	41.0	113	630	571
037015	Cripsey Brook	Chipping Ongar	TL 548035	62.2	1966		LD	57.9	127	614	
037018	Ingrebourne	Gaynes Park	TQ 553862	47.9	1970	*	LD	7.01	76	603	
037019	Beam	Breton's Farm	TQ 515853	49.8	1970	*	LD	1.98	108	593	
037023	Roding	Loughton	TQ 442955	269	1970	*	LD	18.0	113	634	
038001	Lee	Feildes Weir	TL 390092	1040	1932 (1851)	*	LD	28.3	229	649	639
038002	Ash	Mardock	TL 393148	80.3	1936		LD	36.3	140		
038003	Mimram	Panshanger Park	TL 282133	134	1952	*	LD	47.1	193	665	666
038004	Rib	Wadesmill	TL 359174	137	1959		LD	47.1	168		
038005	Ash	Easneye	TL 380138	85.2	1960	*	LD	32.3	140	648	598
038006	Rib	Herts Training School	TL 335158	148	1961	*	LD	40.8	168	650	625
038007	Canons Brook	Elizabeth Way	TL 431103	21.5	1950	*	LD	37.4	110	640	
038008	Lee, New Cut	Chalk Bridge	TQ 356913	1240	1967		LD	7.10	229		
038010	Dagenham Brook	Leyton	TQ 373864	10.4	1969		LD	3.60	54		
038011	Mimram	Fulling Hill	TL 225169	98.7	1955	*	LD	67.5	193	668	
038013	Upper Lee	Luton Hoo	TL 118185	70.7	1960		LD	99.5	229		

Discharges determined during period of record to 31 December 1973						Abstractions and returns	Station details	Station number
Mean gauged discharge	Mean annual natural runoff	Highest instantaneous gauged discharge	Date	Lowest daily mean gauged discharge	Date			
m³/s	mm	m³/s		m³/s				
						E	Rated concrete channel with low flow Crump weir	037331
						E	Crump weir, not accurate at low flows	037332
						S E	Originally 2 x 90° V notch weirs. 1969 onwards – compound ½ x 90° V plus rectangular notch weir. Operated in conjunction with Ardleigh Reservoir Committee	037035
						R	1 : 20 Flat V thin plate weir	037036
0.22 *0.002)*	87			0.01		S E I	Abandoned 1964. Replaced by Crabbs Bridge, 037003	037901
		9.54	13.10.58	0.03	10. 9.59	S E I	Compound rectangular notch	037902
1.66 *0.0055*		38.51	16. 3.64	0.00	13. 7.53	S E I	Broad crested weir replaced by a modified flat V Crump profile weir in 1962	037001
1.21 *0.0036*	144	18.89	13. 3.69	0.00		S P G	A system of weirs, sluices and abstraction meters. Records not archived after 1-8-68	037904
0.43 *0.0045*	157	12.07	10.12.65	0.01	24.11.72	S E I	Modified flat V Crump profile weir	037014
						S E I	Compound rectangular weir; incomplete record	037015
0.26 *0.0054*		13.52	21. 5.73	0.06	17. 8.72	S E I	Modified flat V Crump profile weir	037018
0.32 *0.0064*		11.75	15. 9.68	0.01	7.11.73	S E I	Modified flat V Crump profile weir	037019
0.78 *0.0029*		15.19	28. 1.72	0.04	18. 8.72		Modified flat V Crump profile weir	037023
3.74 *0.0036*		118.00	16. 3.47	0.00		P G E	Series of sluice gates and weirs with navigation lock. Total gate width 14.9 m. Monthly flows are available since 1858, and intermittent readings since 1851	038001
							Rectangular critical depth flume, range 1.4 to 10.6 m³/sec, used in conjunction with low flow station at TL 380138 (Easneye) 038005	038002
0.53 *0.0040*		3.46	15. 9.68	0.15	8. 9.73		Trapezoidal critical depth flume measures up to 11.3 m³/sec	038003
							Trapezoidal control weir rated by current meter for high flows in excess of 2.10 m³/sec. Used in conjunction with the low flow station at TL 335158 (Herts Training School)	038004
0.29 *0.0034*		9.16	17.12.68	0.00	22.10.66		Compound rectangular thin plate weir for low flows, used in conjunction with high flow station at TL 393148 (Mardock) 038002	038005
0.62 *0.0042*		21.83	10.12.66	0.07	1. 7.65		Compound thin plate weir with Crump weir for low and medium flows. All other flows measured at TL 359174 (Wadesmill). 038004	038006
0.18 *0.0084*		10.97	31. 7.72	0.00	4. 6.73		Crump weir for low flows up to 0.28 m³/sec, rectangular critical depth flume for higher flows	038007
						P G E	Two thin plate weirs, total crest length 8.5 m, measuring low and medium flows	038008
							Trapezoidal critical depth flume	038010
0.20 *0.0020*				0.01	28. 8.65		Two thin plate weirs to record discharges for groundwater study	038011
							Thin plate rectangular weir 0.92 m wide for flows up to 0.33 m³/sec; higher flows over broad crested weir 10.0 m wide	038013

51

Station number	River	Station name	National grid reference	Catchment area	Records start	Data archived	Measuring authority	Level of station	Highest point in the catchment	Annual average areal rainfall; mm	
										Standard average for 1916-1950	Period of record average to 31.12.7
				km²				m.O.D.	m.O.D.		

(6) THAMES WATER AUTHORITY AREA–(CONTD)

Station number	River	Station name	National grid reference	Catchment area	Records start	Data archived	Measuring authority	Level of station	Highest point in the catchment	Standard average for 1916-1950	Period of record average to 31.12.7
038014	Salmon Brook	Edmonton	TQ 343936	20.5	1956		LD	12.0	131		
038015	Intercepting Drain	Enfield	TQ 354932	7.7	1969	*	LD	9.60	37	632	
038016	Springs	Stansted Mountfitchet	TL 500247		1969	*	LD	60.4		639	
038017	Mimram	Whitwell	TL 184212	39.1	1970	*	LD	88.1	193	671	
038018	Upper Lee	Water Hall	TL 299099	150	1971	*	LD	43.6	229	665	
038020	Cobbins Brook	Sewardstone Road	TQ 387999	38.0	1971	*	LD	17.2	117	629	
038021	Turkey Brook	Albany Park	TQ 359985	42.2	1971	*	LD	16.6	127	665	
038022	Pymmes Brook	Edmonton (Silver Street)	TQ 340925	42.6	1954		LD	11.2	107		
038024	Small River Lee	Enfield Lock	TQ 370988	41.5	1973	*	LD	15.3	113	631	
039001	Thames	Teddington	TQ 173713	9950	1883	*	TCD	4.7	330	735	736
039002	Thames	Days Weir	SU 568935	3440	1938	*	TCD	46.0	330	734	731
039003	Wandle	Connolly's Mill	TQ 265705	176	1962	*	GLC	10.4	267	754	533
039004	Wandle	Beddington	TQ 296655	122	1952 (1936)	*	GLC	33.1	267	800	781
039005	Beverley Brook	Wimbledon Common	TQ 216717	43.5	1935	*	GLC	11.0	117	640	628
039006	Windrush	Newbridge	SP 402019	363	1950	*	TCD	63.4	319	785	792
039007	Blackwater	Swallowfield	SU 731648	355	1952	*	TCD	42.4	226	719	731
039008	Thames	Eynsham	SP 445087	1620	1954	*	TCD	59.7	330	770	772
039009	Thames	Bray	SU 909797	6920	1959	*	TCD	21.0	330	732	722
039010	Colne	Denham	TQ 052864	743	1953	*	TCD	34.4	256	726	709
039011	Wey	Tilford	SU 874434	396	1954	*	TCD	48.2	273	869	872
039012	Hogsmill	Kingston	TQ 182688	69.2	1956	*	TCD	6.1	185	691	696
039013	Colne	Berrygrove	TQ 123982	352	1954	*	TCD	55.2	243	699	684
039014	Ver	Hansteads	TL 151016	132	1956	*	TCD	61.0	244	719	696
039015	Whitewater	Lodge Farm	SU 731523	44.5	1957	*	TCD	71.6	226	790	813
039016	Kennet	Theale	TU 649708	1030	1961	*	TCD	43.6	297	808	797
039017	Ray	Grendon Underwood	SP 680211	18.6	1962	*	IH	65.7	190	660	660
039018	Ock	Abingdon	SU 486969	234	1962	*	TCD	51.3	261	681	705
039019	Lambourn	Shaw	SU 470682	234	1962	*	TCD	75.6	261	775	779

Mean gauged discharge /s	Mean annual natural runoff mm	Highest instantaneous gauged discharge m³/s	Date	Lowest daily mean gauged discharge m³/s	Date	Abstractions and returns	Station details	Station number
0.09 0.0117		5.77	4. 8.71	0.01	15. 6.69		Compound broad crested weir	038014
							Trapezoidal critical depth flume	038015
0.06		0.23	24. 1.71	0.00	5. 7.69*		Two thin plate weirs measuring spring flows. Intermittent records from 1964 to 1969	038016
0.05 0.0013		0.20	11. 6.72	0.01	6.10.73		Crump weir, crest 1 m long	038017
0.85 0.0057		6.74	6.12.72	0.37	30. 9.73	E	Crump weir, crest 6 m long	038018
0.11 0.0029		4.95	5. 3.72	0.00	25. 7.71		Trapezoidal critical depth flume	038020
0.12 0.0028		6.51	6.12.72	0.00	14. 9.73		Flat V triangular profile weir	038021
							Concrete lined channel section till 1972 when simple Crump weir installed	038022
		2.28	21. 6.73	0.02	3. 3.73		Flat V triangular profile weir	038024
7.40 0.0068	246 33.4			0.88	29.11.34	S P G E I	A low flow gauging weir with adjustable crest 21.3 m long, two roller sluices each 10.7 m wide, 35 vertically lifting gates total width, 236.4 m, and 34 radial gates each 3.07 m wide	039001
8.88 0.0084	263 35.9	349.14	17. 3.47	0.54	31. 8.61	S E I	A weir 45.3 m long with radial and buck gates. Modified in 1969 to comprise an adjustable thin plate weir for low flows, 5.48 m long and 15 radial gates total width 35.5. m.	039002
0.95 0.0054		18.14	20. 9.73	0.22	29. 1.63	G E	Critical depth flume supersedes station Wandle Park, 039901	039003
0.13 0.0011		5.11	20. 9.73	0.00	11.11.72*		Originally a broad crested weir, reconstructed in 1964 to compound Crump weir with crest 7.5 m long	039004
0.53 0.0122		22.43	7. 4.60	0.08	5. 8.62*	G E	Critical depth flume	039005
3.71 0.0102	323 40.8	21.62	6.12.60	0.45	12.11.59	P I	Two broad crested weirs 1.9 m and 6.3 m long on the main channel, and a broad crested weir 14.9 m long on side channel	039006
2.69 0.0076	239 32.7	41.06	16. 9.68	0.46	18. 8.53	E	Critical depth flume and side weir 9 m long. 1970 onwards 2 Crump weirs, main 4.57 m long, side 2.7 m long	039007
	276 35.8	82.6	7.12.60	0.62	6.10.64	S E	The station comprises 8 radial gates, total width 13.4 m for low flow measurement, 3 lifting gates total width 10.2 m for flood flows and compound thin plate weir	039008
5.63 0.0066	208 28.8	199.05	29. 1.60	5.70	15. 6.73	S E I	Sluices and a broad crested weir 48.5 m long	039009
3.80	161 22.7	13.99	2.11.58	1.08	27.11.57	G E I	Curved broad crested weir 30 m long	039010
0.0051		79.00	16. 9.68	0.65	27. 7.56	G I	Broad crested weir 27 m long. 21.1.72 onwards, Crump weir 27 m long	039011
0.94 0.0135	427 61.4	23.59	15. 9.68	0.20	23. 9.67	E	Broad crested weir 9.1 m long	039012
0.56 0.0016	50 7.3	7.48	14. 1.68	0.00	9.73	G I	Thin plate compound weir 9 m long	039013
0.47 0.0036	113 16.2	2.44	5.12.60	0.04	14. 9.73	G I	Broad crested weir 8.3 m long and side channel. Modified in 1969 to compound Crump weir with low flow crest 2.44 m long	039014
0.37 0.0083	259 31.9	1.93	14. 9.68	0.11	15. 8.65	G	Thin plate weir 3.25 m long	039015
0.60 0.0093	293 36.8	70.79	11. 6.71	2.92	3. 7.65	G I	Crump weir 6.8 m long	039016
0.12 0.0065		8.47	18.11.63	0.00			Trapezoidal critical depth flume	039017
1.45 0.0062	195 27.7	15.83	6. 3.72	0.19	23.10.63	E I	Crump 3.4 m long and 2 broad crested weirs 2.6 m and 2.5 m long	039018
1.69 0.0072	227 29.1	4.39	9. 3.67	0.52	16. 8.65	G	Crump weir 10.7 m long	039019

Station number	River	Station name	National grid reference	Catchment area km²	Records start	Data archived	Measuring authority	Level of station m.O.D.	Highest point in the catchment m.O.D.	Standard average for 1916-1950	Period of record average to 31.12.

THAMES WATER AUTHORITY AREA – (CONTD)

Station number	River	Station name	National grid reference	Catchment area km²	Records start	Data archived	Measuring authority	Level of station m.O.D.	Highest point in the catchment m.O.D.	Standard average for 1916-1950	Period of record average to 31.12.
039020	Coln	Bibury	SP 122062	107	1963	*	TCD	101.0	330	831	803
039021	Cherwell	Enslow Mill	SP 482193	552	1965	*	TCD	65.0	239	715	688
039022	Loddon	Sheepbridge	SU 720652	164	1965	*	TCD	42.4	228	738	767
039023	Wye	Hedsor	SU 896867	137	1964	*	TCD	26.8	247	772	768
039024	Gatwick Stream	Gatwick	TQ 288402	31.1	1952	*	TCD	57.6	172	853	943
039025	Enborne	Brimpton	SU 568648	148	1967	*	TCD	59.4	297	834	805
039026	Cherwell	Banbury	SP 458411	199	1966	*	TCD	88.7	222	726	698
039027	Pang	Pangbourne	SU 634766	171	1968	*	TCD	39.6	230	722	675
039028	Dun	Hungerford	SU 321685	101	1968	*	TCD	99.0	265	818	751
039029	Tillingbourne	Shalford	TQ 000478	59	1968	*	TCD	32.0	294	822	742
039030	Gade	Croxley Green	TQ 082952	184	1970	*	TCD	49.7	246	748	
039031	Lambourn	Welford	SU 411731	176	1962		TCD	95.7	261		
039032	Lambourn	East Shefford	SU 390745	154	1966		TCD	102.0	261	725	
039033	Winterbourne	Bagnor	SU 453694	49.2	1962		TCD	80.5	230	708	
039034	Evenlode	Cassington Mill	SP 448099	430	1969	*	TCD	60.2	267	742	
039035	Churn	Cerney Wick	SU 076963	124	1969	*	TCD	82.2	298	868	821
039036	Law Brook	Albury	TQ 045468	16.1	1968		TCD		260		
039037	Kennet	Marlborough	SU 187686	142	1972		TCD	126.5	299	829	
039038	Thame	Shabbington	SP 670055	442	1968		TCD	51.8	260		
039039	Wye	High Wycombe	SU 850937	68.0	1968		TCD		247		
039040	Thames	Cricklade	SU 094942	185	1972		TCD	78.5	210	802	
039042	Leach	Lechlade	SU 227994	76.9	1972		TCD	71.6	249	763	
039043	Kennet	Knighton	SU 295710	295	1962		TCD	106.0	294	828	775
039044	Hart	Bramshill	SU 755593	84.0	1972		TCD	48.9	187	720	
039049	Silk Stream	Colindeep Lane	TQ 217895	29.0	1973	*	GLC	39.9	146	687	
039051	Sor Brook	Adderbury	SP 475346	106	1967	*	TCD	28.2	226	720	
039052	The Cut	Binfield	SU 853713	50.2	1957		TCD	44.8			
039053	Mole	Horley	TQ 271434	89.9	1967		TCD	51.6	238		
039054	Mole	Gatwick Airport	TQ 260399	31.1	1961		TCD	56.6	238	828	
039359	Cole	Coleshill	SU 234935	120	1969		TCD	69.2	277		
039360	Evenlode	Ascott-Under-Wychwood	SP 301191	184	1972		TCD	90.6	267		
039361	Letcombe Brook	Letcombe Bassett	SU 375853	2.6	1971		TCD	105.8	261		
039362	Trib. of Letcombe Brook	Manor Farm, Wantage	SU 397864	2.4	1971		TCD	96.7	224		
039363	Childrey Brook	West Challom	SU 367884	4.3	1971		TCD	72.3	242		
039364	Ewelme Brook	Cottesmore Farm	SU 636920	15.3	1971		TCD	63.2	230		
039365	Ewelme Brook	Ewelme	SU 642916	12.6	1970		TCD	65.9	230		
039366	Winterbourne Stream	Winterbourne	SU 453715	40.3	1967		TCD	84.5	220		
039367	Cove Brook	Hawley Road Bridge	SU 862581	66.1	1970		TCD	47.9	98		

Mean gauged discharge m³/s	Mean annual natural runoff mm	Highest instantaneous gauged discharge m³/s	Date	Lowest daily mean gauged discharge m³/s	Date	Abstractions and returns	Station details	Station number
1.35 *0.0126*	399 *49.7*	5.10	22.12.65	0.36	30.11.72	G	Crump weir 9.1 m long	039020
2.46 *0.0045*	140 *20.3*	24.55	12. 7.68	0.40	24.10.70	P E	Compound Crump weir 6.096 m and 3.048 m long and broad crested outfall	039021
2.19 *0.0134*	421 *54.9*	26.42	16. 9.68	0.75	13. 9.73	G E I	2 Crump weirs 6.9 m and 2.1 m long	039022
1.03 *0.0075*	236 *30.7*	3.20	13. 3.69	0.35	17.10.65	G I	Crump weir 6.1 m long	039023
0.45 *0.0145*	460 *48.8*	18.69	15. 9.68	0.03	20.10.59	E	River section	039024
1.27 *0.0086*	270 *33.5*	23.20	23. 1.71	0.14	12. 9.73	I	Compound Crump weir 3.04 and 4.58 m long	039025
1.20 *0.0060*	190 *27.2*	27.18	11. 7.68	0.00	5.11.72	P	Compound Crump weir 3.04 m and 8.92 m	039026
0.67 *0.039*	123 *18.2*	3.74	13. 3.69	0.19	7. 9.73	G I	Crump weir 3.96 m long	039027
0.68 *0.067*	212 *28.2*	3.27	5. 3.72	0.22	31.10.70	G	Crump weir 10.7 m long	039028
0.58 *0.098*	310 *41.8*	3.65	15.11.70	0.30	7. 9.73	G I	Crump weir 5.5 m long	039029
0.68 *0.0037*	116	3.03	6.12.72	0.10	26. 7.73	G I	Compound Crump weir in 3 sections, overall width 10.1 m and a broad crested weir 10.6 m long measuring flow from the Grand Union Canal	039030
1.03 *0.0058*	184	2.95	10. 4.67	0.39	9.65	G	Compound Crump weir low crests 2 x 2.92 m long. High crest 2.92 m long with .61 m notch	039031
0.79 *0.0051*	163	2.47	7. 2.69	0.16	5.11.70	G	Compound Crump weir, 4.57 m and 4.57 m long	039032
0.17 *0.035*	106	0.57	9. 3.67	0.01	3.11.69		Crump weir 3.02 m long	039033
3.23 *0.0075*	237	23.93	5. 2.72	0.63	4.11.72	E I	Compound Crump weir 4 m and 3.7 m long. Crump weir 4.6 m long and broad crested 7.5 m long	039034
0.81 *0.0065*	205 *24.9*	6.72	31. 1.71	0.00	24.10.72	G E I	Compound Crump weir 1.83 m and 3.66 m long	039035
0.11 *0.0068*	222	0.63	17.12.68	0.07	11. 7.73	G I	Thin plate weir 2.7 m long	039036
		3.11	8. 3.72	0.14	30.11.72	E A P	Compound Crump weir, 6.11 m and 6.01 m long	039037
2.33 *0.0053*	166	16.48	24. 1.71	0.24	19.10.72		Broad crested weir 10.5 m long	039038
0.20 *0.0029*	91	1.08	2. 8.69	0.00	9.73		Two thin plate weirs 1.8 m and 1.4 m long	039039
						E I A P	Compound Crump weir 2.5 m and 4.5 m long	039040
0.48 *0.0062*		2.85	12.72	0.07	26.10.72		Crump weir 4.5 m long	039042
2.39 *0.0081*	255 *32.9*	13.25	11. 6.71	0.56	9.10.65		2 Crump weirs 13.7 m and 1.7 m long	039043
0.41 *0.049*		8.50	12.72	0.15	14. 9.73	E	Crump weir 4 m long	039044
		5.24	23.12.73	0.02	2.12.73		Flat V, Crump profile, weir	039049
0.82 *0.0077*		5.21	13. 3.69	0.13	30.10.70	E A I	Broad crested weir 3.45 m long below 1 ft. head: 3.58 m long above 1ft. head	039051
0.69 *0.0137*		15.77	15. 9.68	0.01	6. 9.67	E A I P	Broad crested weir 13.71 m long; sluice 1.219 m long	039052
1.19 *0.0132*		64.00	9.68	0.00	2. 8.70	E P	Broad crested weir 10.97 m long; notch 2.44 m long	039053
4.37 *0.0119*		22.34	15. 9.68	0.01	7. 9.72	E	Compound broad crested weir 2 x 10.97 m long, 1 x 2.44 m long	039054
							River section	039359
							River section	039360
							Rectangular notch 1.0 m long	039361
							Rectangular notch 0.5 m long	039362
							Rectangular notch 0.75 m long	039363
							Rectangular notch 1.50 m long	039364
							Rectangular notch 1.524 m long	039365
							Rectangular notch 1.067 m long	039366
							River section	039367

Station number	River	Station name	National grid reference	Catch-ment area	Records start	Data archived	Measuring authority	Level of station	Highest point in the catch-ment	Annual average areal rainfall; mm	
										Standard average for 1916-1950	Period of record average to 31.12.
				km²				m.O.D.	m.O.D.		

THAMES WATER AUTHORITY AREA–(CONTD)

Station number	River	Station name	National grid reference	Catch-ment area	Records start	Data archived	Measuring authority	Level of station	Highest point	Standard average 1916-1950	Period of record
039368	Mole	Castle Mill	TQ 179502	316	1971		TCD	38.8	238		
039369	Mole	Kinnersley Manor	TQ 262462	142	1972		TCD	48.0	238		
039820	Dollis Brook	Hendon Lane Bridge	TQ 240895	25.1	1952		GLC	46.6	142	688	
039821	Brent	Monks Park	TQ 202580	118	1939		GLC	24.5	146	678	
039822	Crane	Marsh Farm	TQ 154734	81.0	1939		GLC	7.4	124		
039824	Ravensbourne East	Bromley South	TQ 405687	10.3	1962		GLC	44.3	265	657	
039825	Ravensbourne West	Hayes Lane	TQ 405679	4.3	1963		GLC	46.2	265	692	
039828	Quaggy	Manor House Gardens	TQ 394748	33.5	1961		GLC	13.3	135	661	
039829	Quaggy	Chinbrook Meadows	TQ 410720	15.0			GLC	35.1	135		
039832	Wandle	Carshalton	TQ 279647	1.0	1948		GLC	31.8	267		
039833	Silk Stream	Sheaveshill Road	TQ 214895	29.0	1962		GLC	39.0	146		
039834	Brent	Hanwell	TQ 151801	132	1961		GLC	8.8	146		
039836	Duke of Northum-berland's Stream	Mogden (Lower Dukes)	TQ 153753	35.0	1964		GLC	8.7	29		
039837	Duke of Northumber-land's Stream	Feltham	TQ 088742	35.0	1961		GLC	21.6	29		
039838	Longford	Feltham	TQ 085741	30.0	1969		GLC	20.7	29		
039901	Wandle	Wandle Park (Wimbledon)	TQ 266703	17.6	1936	*	GLC	10.7	267		701
040012	Darent	Hawley	TQ 551718	191	1963		TCD	11.1	246	754	726
040013	Darent	Otford	TQ 525584	101	1969		TCD	60.0	259	802	
040016	Cray	Crayford	TQ 511746	120	1969		TCD			720	
040018	Darent	Lullingstone	TQ 530643	118	1968		TCD	44.0	251	790	

SOUTHERN WATER AUTHORITY AREA

Station number	River	Station name	National grid reference	Catch-ment area	Records start	Data archived	Measuring authority	Level of station	Highest point	Standard average 1916-1950	Period of record
040001	Medway	Weir Wood Reservoir	TQ 407353	26.9	1952	*	NWSWD	61.8	189	871	908
040002	Darwell	Darwell Reservoir	TQ 722213	9.6	1950	*	ESWDD	21.0	195	904	978
040003	Medway	Teston	TQ 708530	1260	1956	*	KRWD	7.01	267	759	773
040004	Rother	Udiam	TQ 773245	206	1962	*	KRWD	1.94	197	851	907
040005	Beult	Stile Bridge	TQ 758478	277	1958	*	KRWD	11.5	160	696	724
040006	Bourne	Hadlow	TQ 632497	49.7	1959	*	KRWD	22.6	233	724	744
040007	Medway	Chafford	TQ 517405	255	1960	*	KRWD	30.8	241	874	824
040008	Great Stour	Wye	TR 049470	230	1962	*	KRWD	29.0	205	749	764

56

an ged charge	Mean annual natural runoff	Highest instan- taneous gauged discharge	Date	Lowest daily mean gauged discharge	Date	Abstrac- tions and returns	Station details	Station number
/s	mm	m³/s		m³/s				
							Mill weir, velocity-area rated	039368
							Rectangular flume 7 m long at throat and rectangular side sluice 1.86 m long	039369
							Compound broad crest weir with rectangular thin plate weir inset	039820
							Critical depth flume in concrete channel	039821
							Critical depth flume	039822
							Critical depth flume	039824
							Rectangular thin plate weir	039825
							Critical depth flume	039828
							Critical depth flume	039829
							Rectangular thin plate weir	039832
							River section	039833
							River section with low flow weir	039834
							Compound thin plate rectangular weir	039836
							River section	039837
							River section	039838
.67 *0.095*		9.09	8. 7.56	0.57	3. 7.38		Critical depth flume; abandoned 1960	039901
.66 *0.0035*		10.05	16. 9.68	0.00	19. 8.73		Crump weir 7.61 m long	040012
.45 *0.0045*		12.93	21. 9.73	0.07	8. 9.73		Compound Crump weir 1 x 3.048 m long, 2 x 2.286 m long	040013
.33 *0.0028*		12.67	20. 9.73	0.00	14. 9.73		Compound Crump weir 3 m and 7.6 m long	040016
.55 *0.0047*		4.85	12. 3.69	0.06	13. 9.73		Broad crested weir 11 m long	040018
.16 *0.0059*		11.84	24. 1.60	0.02	2.10.53	S	Trapezoidal critical depth flume with low flow notch	040001
.03 *0.0031*	401 *41.0*	11.84	29. 1.61	0.01		S	Compound thin plate weir for low flows, rectangular critical depth flume for higher flows. Reservoir storage augmented by pumping from R. Rother downstream	040002
.97 *0.0087*	292 *37.8*	294.50	4.11.60	0.68	30. 9.59	S P G	Low and medium flows measured at group of weirs and sluices with navigation lock: high flows measured at river section 040203, East Farleigh	040003
.11 *0.0102*		51.82	9.12.65	0.11	1.11.69	S G E	River section with paved bed and weir control. Catchment includes pumped storage reservoir scheme. See Darwell 040002	040004
.16 *0.0078*		80.99	4.11.60	0.01	14. 8.73	E	Broad crested weir with low flow notch, and river section for high flows	040005
.39 *0.0078*		11.98	22.10.66	0.03	3. 7.68	E	Trapezoidal critical depth flume	040006
.84 *0.0111*	358 *43.4*	127.43	3.11.60	0.10	13.10.61	S E	Low flows measured at broad crested weir, 5.48 m long; high flows at river section, 040207, Chafford Colliers	040007
.13 *0.0093*		35.03	20. 9.73	0.13	6.10.62	G E	Crump weir crest 7.61 m long for low and medium flows; river section for high flows	040008

Station number	River	Station name	National grid reference	Catchment area km²	Records start	Data archived	Measuring authority	Level of station m.O.D.	Highest point in the catchment m.O.D.	Annual average areal rainfall; mm Standard average for 1916-1950	Annual average areal rainfall; mm Period of record average to 31.12.

(7) SOUTHERN WATER AUTHORITY AREA–(CONTD)

Station number	River	Station name	National grid reference	Catchment area km²	Records start	Data archived	Measuring authority	Level of station m.O.D.	Highest point in the catchment m.O.D.	Standard average for 1916-1950	Period of record average to 31.12.
040009	Teise	Stone Bridge	TQ 718399	136	1961	*	KRWD	24.5	201	797	797
040010	Eden	Penshurst	TQ 520437	224	1961	*	KRWD	27.8	267	775	814
040011	Great Stour	Horton	TR 116554	345	1964	*	KRWD	12.5	205	766	804
040014	Wingham	Durlock	TR 276576	37.7	1969	*	KRWD	4.05	134		
040015	White Drain	Fairbrook Farm	TR 055606	31.8	1969	*	KRWD	7.55	171	707	
040017	Dudwell	Burwash	TQ 679240	27.5	1969	*	KRWD	27.6	197	904	
040020	Eridge Stream	Hendal Bridge	TQ 522367	53.7	1966		KRWD		240		
040021	Hexden Channel	Hopemill Bridge Sandhurst	TQ 813290	32.4	1973		KRWD	5.2	131		
040022	Great Stour	Chart Leacon	TQ 973423	72.5	1966		KRWD		193		
040023	East Stour	South Willesborough	TQ 017407	77.7	1966		KRWD		182		
040024	Bartley Mill Stream	Bartley Mill	TO 633357	25.1	1958		KRWD				
041001	Nunningham Stream	Tilley Bridge	TQ 662128	16.9	1964 (1950)	*	SRWD	3.80	137	807	921
041002	Ash Bourne	Hammer Wood Bridge	TQ 684142	18.4	1953	*	SRWD	6.10	169	859	911
041003	Cuckmere	Sherman Bridge	TQ 532051	135	1959	*	SRWD	3.96	183	825	884
041004	Ouse	Barcombe	TQ 433148	396	1955	*	SRWD	5.25	248	846	771
041005	Ouse	Gold Bridge	TQ 429214	182	1960	*	SRWD	11.6	203	859	874
041006	Uck	Isfield	TQ 459190	87.8	1964	*	SRWD	11.3	221	850	935
041010	Adur	Hatterell Bridge	TQ 178197	109	1961	*	SRWD	3.66	99	785	806
041011	Rother	Iping Mill	SU 852229	154	1967	*	SRWD	26.7	271	925	
041012	Adur (E. Branch)	Sakeham	TQ 219189	93.3	1967	*	SRWD	3.04	248	799	
041013	Huggletts Stream	Henley Bridge	TQ 672138	14.4	1964 (1950)	*	SRWD	6.40	137	847	
041014	Arun	Pallingham Quay	TQ 047229	379	1970		SRWD	2.8	294	752	
041015	Ems	Westbourne	SU 755074	57.7	1967	*	SRWD	9.60	242	907	
041016	Cuckmere	Cowbeech	TQ 611151	18.7	1967	*	SRWD	29.8	183	875	
041017	Combe Haven	Crowhurst	TQ 765102	30.5	1968		SRWD	1.90	140		
041018	Kird	Tanyards	TQ 045255	66.8	1969	*	SRWD	8.70	280	780	
041019	Arun	Alfoldean	TQ 117331	139	1970		SRWD	21.4	294		
041020	Bevern Stream	Clappers Bridge	TQ 423161	34.6	1969	*	SRWD	9.62	248	861	
041021	Clayhill Stream	Old Ship	TQ 448154	7.1	1969	*	SRWD	6.25	38	813	
041022	Lod	Halfway Bridge	SU 931223	52.0	1970	*	SRWD	14.3	274	865	
041023	Lavant	Graylingwell	SU 871064	87.2	1970	*	SRWD	20.7	255	933	
041024	Shell Brook	Ardingly	TQ 335286	22.6	1971	*	SRWD	37.50	183	889	
041025	Loxwood Stream	Drungewick	TQ 060309	91.6	1972	*	SRWD	13.15	260	803	

an ged charge /s	Mean annual natural runoff mm	Highest instantaneous gauged discharge m³/s	Date	Lowest daily mean gauged discharge m³/s	Date	Abstractions and returns	Station details	Station number
.30	0.0096	41.91	9.12.65	0.10	6. 9.73	P G E	Broad crested weir 5.95 m long and river section for high flows	040009
.89	0.0084	40.09	4.11.67	0.03	14. 9.62	S E	Flows up to 4.25 cumecs measured at Crump weir; high flows at river section, 040210, Vexour Bridge	040010
.26	0.0094	29.38	21. 9.73	0.74	8. 9.73	G E	Broad crested weir 10.6 m long measures flows up to 20 m³/sec; higher flows by means of paved river section	040011
.03	0.00094	0.09	26. 6.73	0.00	13. 6.73		Thin plate weir, 120° V notch	040014
.14	0.0051	2.21	14. 6.71	0.01	12. 7.73		Trapezoidal critical depth flume	040015
		8.97	6. 3.72	0.03	15.10.72		Crump weir, crest 4.88 m long	040017
							River section	040020
							Trapezoidal critical depth flume	040021
							River section	040022
							River section	040023
							Broad crested weir with low flow notch	040024
.19	0.0112	11.53	4.11.67	0.00	1.11.50		Compound critical depth flume for winter flow and compound thin plate weir for summer flow	041001
.24	0.013	13.11	17.11.63	0.01	14. 9.59*		Compound critical depth flume for winter flow and compound thin plate weir for summer flow	041002
.68	0.0124	83.54	30. 1.61	0.03	12. 9.71	S P	Compound broad crested weir with river section for high flows	041003
.27	0.0133	170.47	3.11.60	0.01	29. 8.73	S P G E	Compound Crump and broad crested weirs with sub-atmospheric syphon; high flow station at Hamsey 041204, 4.8 km downstream	041004
.94	0.0107	58.62	3.11.60	0.12	1. 9.61	P G E	Compound broad crested weir with river section for high flows	041005
.14	0.0130	48.17	16.11.69	0.07	8.11.64	E	Crump weir with crest 7.5 m long	041006
.98	0.0090	19.81	23. 1.71	0.00	5. 9.73		Critical depth flume, with 2 side sections for winter flows	041010
.95	0.0127	30.09	28. 2.67	0.53	4.10.72	G E	Compound Crump weir, crest lengths 3.04 m and 5.03 m	041011
.52	0.0056	31.15	4.11.67	0.10	10. 8.67	E	Compound Crump weir, crest lengths 3.04 m and two 3.50 m	041012
.18	0.0125	9.77	4.11.67	0.01	5.10.72		Compound thin plate weir, and compound critical depth flume for winter flow	041013
				0.11	2. 9.72	E	Broad crested weir and river section	041014
		1.88	9. 1.68	0.00	10.11.69*	G	Compound Crump weir, crest lengths 0.61 m and 4.12 m. Compensation water at rate of 0.013 cumec added when natural flow falls below 0.026 cumec	041015
.15	0.0080	12.89	18. 6.71	0.01	14. 9.73	P G	Compound Crump weir, crest lengths 0.54 m and 2.13 m	041016
				0.01	24.10.69	G	Compound Crump weir, crest lengths 2.44 m and two 2.13 m	041017
		0.82	12. 5.72	0.00	25. 8.72*		Crump weir, crest 8.7 m long	041018
				0.10	7.10.71		Compound Crump weir, crests 4 m and 6 m long	041019
		0.85	4. 6.72	0.01	4. 8.70		Crump weir, crest 6 m long	041020
		0.10	12. 5.72	0.00			Crump weir, crest 3 m long	041021
		0.91	11. 5.72	0.03	14. 7.70		Crump weir, crest 7 m long	041022
		0.32	1. 5.72	0.03	29. 6.72		Flat V Crump profile weir, crest length 5 m, transverse slope 1:10	041023
		0.60	31. 7.72	0.04	18. 9.71		Simple Crump weir, crest 4 m long	041024
		1.66	20.11.72	0.03	16. 9.73		Compound Crump weir, crest lengths 2 m and 4 m	041025

Station number	River	Station name	National grid reference	Catchment area	Records start	Data archived	Measuring authority	Level of station	Highest point in the catchment	Annual average areal rainfall; mm	
										Standard average for 1916-1950	Period of record average to 31.12.
				km²				m.O.D.	m.O.D.		

SOUTHERN WATER AUTHORITY AREA–(CONTD)

Station number	River	Station name	National grid reference	Catchment area	Records start	Data archived	Measuring authority	Level of station	Highest point in the catchment	Standard average for 1916-1950	Period of record average to 31.12.
041026	Cockhaise Brook	Holywell	TQ 376262	36.1	1972	*	SRWD	28.55	203	886	
041027	Rother	Princes Marsh	SU 772271	37.2	1973	*	SRWD	56.40	252	927	
041028	Chess Stream	Chess Bridge	TQ 217173	24.0	1964		SRWD	4.57	206	842	
042001	Wallington	North Fareham	SU 587075	111	1951	*	HRWD	3.67	248	843	902
042002	Itchen	Highbridge	SU 468214	360	1958	*	HRWD	16.8	208	851	835
042003	Lymington	Brockenhurst Park	SU 318019	98.9	1960	*	HRWD	6.10	114	871	790
042004	Test	Broadlands	SU 354188	1040	1957	*	HRWD	10.1	297	808	836
042005	Wallop Brook	Broughton	SU 311330	53.6	1955	*	HRWD	35.9	168	803	796
042006	Meon	Mislingford	SU 589141	72.8	1958	*	HRWD	29.3	233	912	923
042007	Alre	Alresford	SU 575325	57.0	1969	*	HRWD	56.5	216	873	
042008	Cheriton Stream	Sewards Bridge	SU 574322	75.1	1970		HRWD	55.8	234	897	
042009	Candover Brook	Borough Bridge	SU 569324	71.2	1970		HRWD	54.4	208		
042011	Hamble	Durley Mill	SU 523149	56.6	1972		HRWD	9.41	169		
042012	Anton	Fullerton	SU 379392	185	1973		HRWD	40.52	253	793	
101001	Eastern Yar	Alverstone Mill	SZ 577857	57.5	1957		IoWRWD	3.66	239	874	
101002	Medina	Upper Shide	SZ 503874	29.8	1960	*	IoWRWD	10.4	167	861	

WESSEX WATER AUTHORITY AREA

Station number	River	Station name	National grid reference	Catchment area	Records start	Data archived	Measuring authority	Level of station	Highest point in the catchment	Standard average for 1916-1950	Period of record average to 31.12.
043901	Avon	Ringwood	SU 142054	1650	1954	*	ADD	13.7	294	851	734
043002	Stour	Ensbury	SZ 089964	1210	1959		ADD	4.14	277		
043003	Avon	East Mills Flume	SU 158144	1450	1963	*	ADD	25.2	294	851	830
043004	Bourne	Laverstock Mill	SU 157303	164	1964	*	ADD	45.9	267	790	782
043005	Avon	Queens Falls, Amesbury	SU 151414	324	1965	*	ADD	67.1	294	795	801
043006	Nadder	Wilton Park	SU 098308	221	1965	*	ADD	51.2	277	895	930
043007	Stour	Throop Mill	SZ 113958	1070	1973	*	ADD	4.35	277	866	
043008	Wylye	South Newton	SU 086343	445	1966	*	ADD	55.5	288	876	774
043009	Stour	Hammoon	ST 820147	523	1968	*	ADD	40.9	259	846	853

60

Mean gauged discharge	Mean annual natural runoff	Highest instantaneous gauged discharge	Date	Lowest daily mean gauged discharge	Date	Abstractions and returns	Station details	Station number
m³/s	mm	m³/s		m³/s				
		2.07	30.11.72	0.02	10. 9.73	P G	Simple Crump weir measuring up to mean annual flood. Crest 3.5 m long. River section for higher flows	041026
				0.15	14. 9.73	E G	Simple Crump weir, crest 5 m long	041027
		1.55	11. 5.72	0.00	7. 9.72*		Rectangular thin plate weir in summer, with 3.35 m wide rectangular flume for winter flows	041028
0.64	0.0058	9.20	1.11.53	0.00	11. 9.59	G	Compound critical depth flume	042001
5.37	0.0149	13.14	28. 1.69	2.46	18.10.59	P G	River section until 1971 when simple Crump weir, 7.75 m crest, installed. Complementary rectangular thin plate weir, Allbrook, 042202	042002
0.99	0.010	7.10	8.10.68	0.01	18. 7.62		Compound thin plate weir with flat V notch	042003
2.45	0.0120			4.73	6. 1.65		River section. Unstable rating curve checked by monthly current meter gaugings at adjacent site.	042004
0.40	0.0075	1.73	26. 1.59	0.01	11.10.59		Thin plate rectangular weir	042005
0.99	0.0136	5.66	4.12.60	0.11	15.10.59		Critical depth flume	042006
1.41	0.0247	2.17	18. 3.71	0.87	30.11.69		Simple Crump weir, 2.5 m crest. Complementary Crump weir, 1.5 m crest, 042207, on subsidiary channel. The groundwater catchment is approximately twice the surface catchment	042007
							Crump weir, crest 3 m long	042008
						G	Crump weir, crest 3 m long	042009
							Simple Crump weir, 3 m crest. Ground water catchment area 51.4 km²	042011
							Crump weir, crest 4.75 m. Complementary Crump weir, crest 1.0 m, 042212, on by-pass. Monthly gauging since 1956. Groundwater catchment area 192.3 km²	042012
						P	Compound thin plate weir	101001
		6.00	20. 2.66	0.06	1. 8.73		Trapezoidal critical depth flume	101002
7.73	0.0107	116.10	9.10.60	4.81	26. 9.62		River section at bridge with 3 spans. Unstable section, station abandoned 1968	043901
							River section with cableway, unreliable for low and medium flows and replaced by 043007, Throop Mill, for this range in 1974	043002
9.97	0.0069	33.27	19.11.63	4.15	1. 1.68		Critical depth rectangular flume with complementary compound Crump weir having a central broad crest fish pass, 043203	043003
0.71	0.0043	3.94	4. 3.66	0.00	11. 6.70		Crump weir crest length 3.05 m. The groundwater catchment is approximately half the surface catchment	043004
3.42	0.0106	15.04	11. 3.67	0.99	13. 9.73		Crump weir 9.14 m long with a broad crested weir on both sides	043005
2.72	0.0123	21.92	5.11.66	0.74	12. 9.73		Crump weir crest 18.3 m long	043006
		39.61	21. 1.73	1.89	14. 9.73		Compound Crump weir. High flows measured at 043002, Ensbury; river section	043007
3.76	0.0084	15.15	9. 3.67	0.46	2.10.68		Crump weir crest 10.7 m long	043008
5.38	0.0103	100.00	6.12.72	0.36	31. 7.73		Compound Crump weir with low flow notch 6.10 m long, total length 18.3 m	043009

Station number	River	Station name	National grid reference	Catch- ment area	Records start	Data archived	Measuring authority	Level of station	Highest point in the catch- ment	Annual average areal rainfall; mm	
										Standard average for 1916-1950	Period of record average to 31.12.7
				km²				m.O.D.	m.O.D.		

WESSEX WATER AUTHORITY AREA–(CONTD)

Station number	River	Station name	National grid reference	Catch- ment area	Records start	Data archived	Measuring authority	Level of station	Highest point in the catch- ment	Standard average for 1916-1950	Period of record average to 31.12.7
043010	Allen	Loverley Mill	SU 006085	94.0	1968	*	ADD	37.3	277	899	
043011	Ebble	Bodenham	SU 162263	109	1969		ADD	41.5	245	899	
043012	Wylye	Norton Bavant	ST 909428	112	1969	*	ADD	96.7	288	942	997
043013	Mude	Somerford	SZ 184936	12.4	1966	*	ADD	56.4	75.6	822	
043014	East Avon	Upavon	SU 133559	86.2	1970	*	ADD	92.0	239	815	831
043015	Wylye	Longbridge Deverill	ST 868413	69.1	1970	*	ADD	118	238	969	
043017	West Avon	Upavon	SU 133559	75.8	1970	*	ADD	91.7	217	801	822
043019	Shreen Water	Colesbrook	ST 807278	29.1	1973	*	ADD	71.78	245	901	
044001	Frome	East Stoke Mill	SY 866867	414	1960	*	ADD	7.73	266	996	976
044002	Piddle	Baggs Mill	SY 913876	183	1963	*	ADD	2.04	275	973	979
044003	Asker	Bridport	SY 470928	49.1	1962	*	ADD	6.40	236	989	1067
044004	Frome	Dorchester	SY 708903	206	1969	*	ADD	51.1	262	1058	1204
044006	Sydling Water	Sydling St. Nicholas	SY 632997	12.4	1969	*	ADD	110	262	1021	1222
051001	Doniford Stream	Swill Bridge	ST 088428	75.8	1966	*	SD	9.30	491	928	
051002	Horner Water	West Luccombe	SS 898458	20.8	1973	*	SD	60.96	520		
051801	Washford	Beggearn Huish	ST 040395	36.3	1966		SD	67.05	424		
052001	Axe	Wookey	ST 527458	18.1	1956	*	BWW	30.48	285	1117	1240
052002	Yeo	Sutton Bingham Reservoir	ST 556116	30.3	1955	*	SD	41.5	252	909	997
052003	Halse Water	Bishop's Hull	ST 206253	87.8	1961	*	SD	16.2	391	909	900
052004	Isle	Ashford Mill	ST 361188	90.1	1962	*	SD	14.6	274	904	878
052005	Tone	Bishop's Hull	ST 206250	202	1961	*	SD	16.2	409	993	987
052006	Yeo	Pen Mill	ST 573162	213	1962	*	SD	23.9	252	896	896
052007	Parrett	Chiselborough	ST 461144	74.9	1966	*	SD	20.7	219	846	967
052008	Tone	Clatworthy Reservoir	ST 044313	18.1	1960	*	SD	196.7	409	1273	1233
052009	Sheppey	Fenny Castle	ST 498439	59.6	1963	*	SD	5.79	296	996	975

Mean gauged discharge	Mean annual natural runoff	Highest instantaneous gauged discharge	Date	Lowest daily mean gauged discharge	Date	Abstractions and returns	Station details	Station number
m³/s	mm	m³/s		m³/s				
1.02 *0.0109*		4.86	12. 3.72	0.13	21.11.73	G	Crump weir 1.84 m long and calibrated side hatches	043010
		2.65	31. 1.71	0.02	26. 9.70		River section and Crump weir 2.82 m long	043011
0.85 *0.0076*		5.47	6.12.72	0.23	16.11.71		Crump weir crest 6.09 m long	043012
0.06 *0.0048*		1.18	7. 3.72	0.02	1. 9.73		Crump weir 2.59 m long	043013
0.73 *0.0085*		4.61	6.12.72	0.42	14. 9.73		Crump weir crest 3.04 m long (adjacent to station no. 043017)	043014
		0.75	1. 4.73	0.16	26. 9.72		Rectangular thin plate weir for low and medium flows up to 1.7 m³/sec	043015
0.48 *0.0063*		7.15	6.12.72	0.09	14. 9.73	I	Crump weir crest 4.57 m long, (adjacent to station no. 043014)	043017
		2.36	22.12.73	0.16	5.12.73		Crump weir, crest 3 m long	043019
5.41 *0.0131*		21.28	30. 1.70	1.80	14. 9.73		Rectangular critical depth flume 3.04 m long bounded by two broad crested weirs, with a complementary Crump weir, 044201, crest 3.565 m long on by-pass channel	044001
2.39 *0.0131*		9.37	13. 3.69	0.35	2.10.68		Rectangular critical depth flume	044002
0.52 *0.0106*		16.06	28. 6.68	0.17	12. 9.73		Crump weir crest 7.3 m long with flood relief hatch	044003
1.81 *0.0088*		12.88	29. 1.70	0.28	10. 9.73		At Loud's Mill two Crump weirs, 10.66 m crest and 1.52 m crest (on side channel), with complementary Crump weir, 044204, 3.04 m crest in Stinsford channel	044004
0.16 *0.0129*		0.70	22. 1.71	0.05	21.11.73		Crump weir, crest 1.85 m long	044006
0.99 *0.0131*		42.48	10. 7.68	0.00	26. 9.70		River section	051001
		3.15	7.12.73	0.02	7.11.73		Single crested Crump with crest tapping. Compensation flow in summer	051002
							River section	051801
0.58 *0.0320*		5.01	20.11.63	0.04	27. 6.61		Compound critical depth flume. Minimum flow may be affected by operation of sluice in by-pass channel. Maximum measured discharge limited to 4.2 m³/s	052001
0.40 *0.0132*	519 *52.1*	35.82	10. 7.68	0.03			Critical depth flume and broad crested weir. Reservoir station	052002
1.02 *0.0116*		28.32	10. 7.68	0.15	13. 9.73		River section. Levels affected by backwater from floods in River Tone. Flows in excess of 7.0 m³/s by-pass station	052003
1.22 *0.0135*		28.45	2.12.72	0.09	28. 6.64		Crump weir for low flows, crest 6.71 m River section for higher flows. Maximum measurable discharge 28.7 m³/s	052004
2.87 *0.0142*	476 *48.2*	112.72	11. 7.68	0.34	24. 9.72		River section, improved by Crump weir of length 12.2 m in 1968. Contained measurable flow 0.22/62.26 m³/s	052005
2.40 *0.0113*		55.18	22. 2.69	0.05	6.11.71		Crump weir of length 4.57 m for low flows. Rated river section for higher flows. Maximum discharge measurable 55 m³/s	052006
0.99 *0.0132*		114.33	18.11.70	0.00	22. 2.69		Crump weir with crest tapping, length 7.87 m. Backwater affects very high flows. Measurable discharges 0.07/25.19 m³/s	052007
0.30 *0.0166*		4.96	27.10.60	0.05	21. 6.67		Two thin plate weirs in broad crested weir. Compensation flow	052008
1.02 *0.0171*		9.29	10. 7.68	0.10	13. 9.64		Crump weir of length 5.18 m for low flows. River section for higher flows. Weed growth affects high summer flows. Discharge measurement range 0/9.9 m³/s	052009

Station number	River	Station name	National grid reference	Catchment area km²	Records start	Data archived	Measuring authority	Level of station m.O.D.	Highest point in the catchment m.O.D.	Annual average areal rainfall; mm Standard average for 1916-1950	Period of record average to 31.12.7

WESSEX WATER AUTHORITY AREA–(CONTD)

Station number	River	Station name	National grid reference	Catchment area km²	Records start	Data archived	Measuring authority	Level of station m.O.D.	Highest point in the catchment m.O.D.	Standard average for 1916-1950	Period of record average to 31.12.7
052010	Brue	Lovington	ST 590318	135	1964	*	SD	19.8	244	909	959
052011	Cary	Somerton	ST 498291	82.4	1965	*	SD	8.83	152	751	790
052014	Tone	Greenham	ST 078202	57.2	1966	*	SD	77.1	409	1143	
052015	Land Yeo	Wraxall	ST 483716	23.3	1971	*	SD	11.4	235	916	
052016	Currypool Stream	Currypool	ST 221382	15.7	1971	*	SD	49.0	384	918	
052017	Congresbury Yeo	Iwood	ST 452631	66.6	1973 (1964)	*	SD	7.40	325	825	
052020	Gallica Stream	Gallica Bridge	ST 571100	16.4	1966	*	SD	29.3	223	886	
052801	Tone	Wadhams Farm	ST 055268	32.1	1967		SD	152.4	409		
052803	Aisholt Brook	Hawkridge	ST 201359	3.0	1963		SD	91.5	384		
052804	Merridge Brook	Hawkridge	ST 201361	3.0	1963		SD	91.5	365		
053001	Avon	Melksham	ST 903641	666	1953 (1937)	*	BAD	30.02	260	815	783
053002	Semington Brook	Semington	ST 907605	158	1953 (1947)	*	BAD	33.25	225	785	756
053903	Avon	Bath	ST 753645	1600	1953 (1939)	*	BAD	17.07	305	861	847
053004	Chew	Compton Dando	ST 648647	130	1958	*	BAD	16.76	305	1013	1012
053005	Midford Brook	Midford	ST 763611	147	1961	*	BAD	27.43	220	998	997
053006	Frome (Bristol)	Frenchay	ST 637772	149	1961	*	BAD	19.96	193	820	796
053007	Frome (Somerset)	Tellisford	ST 805564	262	1961	*	BAD	35.05	305	983	986
053008	Avon	Great Somerford	ST 966832	303	1964	*	BAD	57.61	207	838	821
053009	Wellow Brook	Wellow	ST 741581	72.6	1966	*	BAD	43.74	220	1025	951
053013	Marden	Stanley	ST 955729	99.2	1969	*	BAD	47.33	260	783	
053014	Spring	Three Ashes	ST 655464		1972	*	BAD	239.26		1110	
053015	Spring	Tiswell	ST 902524		1973 (1965)	*	BAD	79.90		810	
053016	Spring	Dunkerton	ST 803399		1973	*	BAD	149.03		975	
053017	Boyd	Bitton	ST 681698	47.9	1973	*	BAD	15.5	237	861	
053018	Avon	Bathford	ST 786671	1550	1969	*	BAD	18.0	305		
053019	Woodbridge Brook	Crabb Mill	ST 949866	46.6	1969 (1964)		BAD	65.53	157	810	
053020	Gauze Brook	Rodbourne	ST 937840	28.2	1968 (1963)		BAD	65.99	128	810	
053021	The Malago	Bristol	ST 583703	12.1	1956		BAD	10.50	233	875	

Mean gauged discharge	Mean annual natural runoff	Highest instantaneous gauged discharge	Date	Lowest daily mean gauged discharge	Date	Abstractions and returns	Station details	Station number
m³/s	mm	m³/s		m³/s				
1.83 *(0.0136)*		76.60	10. 7.68	0.06	1.10.64		Crump weir of length 6.71 m for low flows. River section for higher flows. Weed growth affects high summer flows. Maximum discharge measurable 80.7 m³/s	052010
0.81 *(0.0098)*		12.04	6.11.66	*0.03	27. 8.67		Compound Crump weir of centre section 3.05 m and two side sections 1.22 m for low flows. River section for high flows. Weed growth affects high summer flows. Maximum discharge in weir 12.93 m³/s	052011
1.07 *(0.0187)*		25.49	10. 7.68	0.00	18. 9.69		River section, with unstable bed condition	052014
0.20 *(0.0086)*		4.94	19.10.71	0.05	13. 9.73		Crump weir	052015
0.16 *(0.0102)*		4.70	19. 8.71	0.06	12. 9.73		Crump weir, flows below 0.13 m³/s only	052016
		4.45	15. 7.73	0.00	15.12.73		Crump weir	052017
							Villemonte weir	052020
							Crump weir, compensation flows in summer	052801
							Rectangular thin plate weir	052803
							Rectangular thin plate weir	052804
7.04 *(0.0106)*		195.39	10. 7.68	0.28	14. 8.55*	G I	River section with cableway	053001
1.25 *(0.0079)*		32.00	6.12.72	0.08	11.10.53		Trapezoidal section installed 1969 with cableway, replacing river section downstream	053002
20.67 *(0.0129)*		365.29	5.12.60	1.42	19. 8.55*	G P I	River section with cableway. Station closed 1969 (Sept). Replaced by 053018, Bathford	053903
1.02 *(0.0078)*	475 *(46.9)*	226.54	9. 7.68	0.05	31. 5.71	S P	Trapezoidal critical depth flume. Range 0.028/85.0 m³/s	053004
2.05 *(0.0139)*		55.73	10. 7.68	0.08	28. 5.71		Trapezoidal critical depth flume. Range 0.028/56.6 m³/s	053005
1.75 *(0.0117)*		166.00	17. 1.69	0.05	21. 5.71		Trapezoidal critical depth flume. Range 0.028/56.6 m³/s	053006
3.70 *(0.0141)*		108.11	10. 7.68	0.10	22. 5.71	G I	Trapezoidal critical depth flume. Range 0.028/113.2 m³/s	053007
4.17 *(0.0138)*		200.09	11. 7.68	0.17	22.11.64	G	Compound Crump weir. Range 0.085/109 m³/s	053008
1.22 *(0.0168)*		29.54	10. 7.68	0.16	25. 9.71		Trapezoidal critical depth flume. Range 0.028/42.4 m³/s	053009
1.11 *(0.0112)*		34.22	11. 6.71	0.21	29. 9.70	P I	Trapezoidal critical depth flume. Range 0.028/56.6 m³/s	053013
		0.01	6. 8.73	0.00	1. 8.72*	P	90° V notch weir plate. Range 0/0.124 m³/s	053014
		0.00	1.10.72	0.00	1. 9.72*		¼ x 90° V notch weir plate. Range 0/0.017 m³/s	053015
		0.01	7. 7.73	0.00	1. 7.73	P	90° V notch weir plate. Range 0/0.124 m³/s	053016
						I	Flat V Crump profile weir	053017
						G P I	River section. Range to 150 m³/s. Replaces station 053003	053018
						P G	Compound rectangular thin plate weir. Range 0.028/1.4 m³/s	053019
						G	Rectangular thin plate weir. Range 0.028/0.566 m³/s	053020
							Trapezoidal critical depth flume. Range 0/19.6 m³/s. Operated jointly with Bristol District Council	053021

Station number	River	Station name	National grid reference	Catchment area	Records start	Data archived	Measuring authority	Level of station	Highest point in the catchment	Annual average areal rainfall; mm	
										Standard average for 1916-1950	Period of record average to 31.12.7:
				km²				m.O.D.	m.O.D.		

SOUTH WEST WATER AUTHORITY AREA

Station number	River	Station name	National grid reference	Catchment area	Records start	Data archived	Measuring authority	Level of station	Highest point in the catchment	Standard average for 1916-1950	Period of record average to 31.12.7:
045001	Exe	Thorverton	SS 936016	601	1956	*	SWWA	25.85	519	1280	1263
045002	Exe	Stoodleigh	SS 943178	422	1961 (1960)	*	SWWA	74.52	519	1407	1362
045003	Culm	Wood Mill	ST 021058	226	1962	*	*SWWA	43.97	293	965	1042
045004	Axe	Whitford	SY 262953	289	1964	*	SWWA	7.27	316	1009	1011
045005	Otter	Dotton	SY 087885	203	1963 (1962)	*	SWWA	14.52	299	1005	981
045006	Quarme	Enterwell	SS 919356	20.4	1964	*	SWWA	187.50	519	1584	1671
045801	Back Brook	Hawkerland	SY 058887	2.5	1967		UE		176	889	
045806	Creedy	Cowley	SX 901967	263	1964		SWWA	14.17	286	903	
046001	South Teign	Fernworthy Reservoir	SX 671844	10.0	1951 (1943)		SWWA	323.00	537	2022	
046002	Teign	Preston	SX 856746	380	1956	*	SWWA	3.83	604	1267	1283
046003	Dart	Austin's Bridge	SX 751659	248	1958	*	SWWA	22.43	604	1821	1747
046004	Avon	Avon Reservoir	SX 680651	12.0	1959 (1957)		SWWA	312.12	515	2261	
046005	East Dart	Bellever	SX 657775	21.5	1964	*	SWWA	309.00	604	2103	2129
046006	Erme	Ermington	SX 642532	43.5	1973		SWWA	7.90	473		
046007	West Dart	Dunnabridge	SX 643742	47.9	1972		SWWA	283.76	564	2122	
046801	Erme	Erme Intake	SX 640632	14.9	1960 (1954)		SWWA	294.14	473	2003	
046802	Swincombe	Swincombe Intake	SX 633719	14.2	1924		SWWA	316.98	480	1966	
046805	Bala Brook	Bala Intake	SX 672629	5.9	1933		SWWA	246.55	472	2003	
046806	Avon	Avon Intake	SX 681641	14.0	1939 (1936)		SWWA	273.68	515	2197	
047001	Tamar	Gunnislake	SX 426725	917	1956	*	SWWA	8.21	586	1229	1278
047902	Tamar	Werrington	SX 343886	232	1956	*	SWWA			1153	
047003	Tavy	Lopwell	SX 474650	206	1956	*	SWWA	2.67	604	1595	
047004	Lynher	Pillaton Mill	SX 368624	136	1963 (1961)	*	SWWA	8.54	396	1436	1397
047005	Ottery	Werrington Park	SX 336866	121	1963 (1961)	*	SWWA	54.66	308	1166	1137
047006	Lyd	Lifton Park	SX 388842	218	1963 (1962)	*	SWWA	47.76	586	1356	1239
047007	Yealm	Puslinch	SX 574511	54.9	1963 (1962)	*	SWWA	5.49	492	1449	1483
047008	Thrushel	Tinhay	SX 398856	113	1969	*	SWWA	55.47	299	1289	
047009	Tiddy	Tideford	SX 343595	37.2	1969	*	SWWA	4.23	274	1302	
047010	Tamar	Crowford Bridge	SX 290991	76.7	1972	*	SWWA	84.02	227	1164	
047011	Plym	Carn Wood	SX 522613	79.2	1971	*	SWWA	15.49	577	1644	

Mean gauged discharge	Mean annual natural runoff	Highest instan- taneous gauged discharge	Date	Lowest daily mean gauged discharge	Date	Abstrac- tions and returns	Station details	Station number
m³/s	mm	m³/s		m³/s				
5.75 *0.0262*		492.26	4.12.60	1.14	8.10.72	P G I E	River section. Modified in 1973 by the construction of a low level bed control	045001
2.13 *0.0287*		232.20	19.12.65	0.95	8.10.72	P G I E	River section	045002
3.68 *0.0163*	498 *47.8*	202.18	11. 7.68	0.65	4. 7.73	P G I E	River section. Modified in 1973 by the construction of a low level bed control	045003
4.94 *0.0171*		228.80	11. 7.68	0.97	14. 9.73	P G I E	Compound Crump weir. Total crest length 21.3 m low flow crest length 7.6 m	045004
3.19 *0.057*		346.88	11. 7.68	0.60	15. 9.71	S R P G I E	River section. Modified in 1971 by the construction of a low level bed control	045005
0.72 *0.0353*		18.92	18.12.65	0.07	1.10.64	G	Compound broad crested weir	045006
							Flat V Crump profile weir. Jointly operated with University of Exeter	045801
						G E	River section	045806
						S R P	Thin plate compound weir 28 m long	046001
9.37 *0.0246*	826 *63.4*	198.22	25. 2.66	0.67	25. 9.59	S R P G I E	River section. Modified in 1967 by the construction of low level bed control	046002
11.13 *0.0449*		327.61	30. 9.60	0.68	5.10.59	S R P G I E	River section	046003
						S R P	Thin plate weir	046004
1.23 *0.0572*		65.13	23. 7.67	0.15			River section	046005
						P G I E	River section with low level bed control	046006
						P	River section with low level bed control	046007
						P	Thin plate notch 0.3 m x 0.3 m in 9 metre long broad crested weir.	046801
						P	Group of thin plate weirs	046802
						P	Thin plate rectangular weir	046805
						S R P	Compound rectangular thin plate weir	046806
3.29 *0.0254*		410.60	26.11.59	0.69	4.10.59	S R P G I E	River section. Because of the presence of large boulders, low flows are measured at a ford about 1.6 km upstream	047001
6.38 *0.0275*		220.87	27.10.60	0.01	3.10.59		Discontinued 1961	047902
7.34 *0.0356*		91.12	25. 4.59	0.45	22. 9.59	P G I E H	Weir with Crump profile main and secondary crests, and with compound thin plate crests on fish pass	047003
4.58 *0.0337*		150.08	4.11.67	0.64	22. 7.70	P G E	River section	047004
2.48 *0.0205*		80.00	30.11.71	0.00		G E	River section	047005
5.82 *0.0267*		226.54	17.11.65	0.02	1.10.71	G I E	River section. Modified in 1968 by the construction of a rectangular critical depth flume for low and medium flows	047006
1.69 *0.0308*		28.88	28. 6.68	0.04	28. 8.72	P G I E	River section. Modified in 1967 by the construction of a rectangular critical depth flume for low and medium flows	047007
2.16 *0.0191*		57.13	18. 6.71	0.05	20.10.72	G E	Compound Crump weir. Total crest length 14.6 m. Low flow crest length 3.7 m	047008
0.81 *0.0218*		6.39	6.12.72	0.07	1.11.69	G E	Single crest Crump weir 5.5 m long	047009
1.95 *0.0254*		57.23	28.11.73	0.03	21.10.72	S R P G E	Compound Crump weir. Total crest length 11.0 m. Low flow crest length 3.0 m	047010
2.13 *0.0269*		46.78	18.11.72	0.29	5.10.72	S R P G I E	Compound Crump weir. Total crest length 12.5 m. Low flow crest length 3.50 m	047011

Station number	River	Station name	National grid reference	Catch-ment area	Records start	Data archived	Measuring authority	Level of station	Highest point in the catch-ment	Annual average areal rainfall; mm	
										Standard average for 1916-1950	Period of record average to 31.12.7
				km²				m.O.D.	m.O.D.		

047013	Withey Brook	Bastreet	SX 244763	16.2	1972	*	SWWA	228.69	396	1575	
048001	Fowey	Trekeivesteps	SX 227693	36.8	1957	*	SWWA	187.86	420	1678	1817
048002	Fowey	Restormel I	SX 108613	171	1963 (1961)	*	SWWA	3.83	420	1518	1478
048003	Fal	Tregony	SW 921447	87.0	1961		SWWA	6.95	226		
048004	Warleggan	Trengoffe	SX 159674	25.3	1969	*	SWWA	70.26	308	1533	
048005	Kenwyn	Truro	SW 820450	19.1	1968	*	SWWA	7.16	152	1121	
048006	Cober	Helston	SW 654273	40.1	1968	*	SWWA	4.69	251	1150	
048007	Kennall	Ponsanooth	SW 762377	26.6	1968	*	SWWA	13.56	251	1290	
048008	White	Molingey	SW 007495	29.9	1969		SWWA	11.46	313		
048009	St. Neot	Craigshill Wood	SX 184662	22.7	1971	*	SWWA	70.53	339	1614	
048010	Seaton	Trebrownbridge	SX 299596	38.1	1972	*	SWWA	26.60	369	1349	
048011	Fowey	Restormel 2	SX 098624	169	1972	*	SWWA	9.24	420	1518	
049001	Camel	Denby	SX 017682	209	1964	*	SWWA	4.61	420	1378	1357
049002	Hayle	St. Erth	SW 549342	48.9	1968 (1957)	*	SWWA	7.00	238	1075	
049003	De Lank	De Lank	SX 132765	21.7	1967	*	SWWA	226.37	420	1681	
049004	Gannel	Gwills	SW 829593	41.0	1970	*	SWWA	8.75	212	1052	
050001	Taw	Umberleigh	SS 608237	826	1961 (1958)	*	SWWA	14.14	604	1158	1120
050002	Torridge	Torrington	SS 500185	663	1962 (1960)	*	SWWA	13.95	621	1186	1133
050003	Taw	Sticklepath	SX 634938	15.6	1962 (1960)		SWWA	218.62	604	1717	
050904	Hole Water	Muxworthy	SS 705673	5.4	1964	*	SWWA	222	477	1767	
050801	Yeo	Parkham	SS 393221	7.7	1969 (1965)		SWWA	80.82	208		
050802	West Okement	Vellake	SX 557903	13.3	1967 (1951)		SWWA	300.00	621		
050803	Mole	Woodleigh	SS 660211	328	1965		SWWA	47.94	493	909	
050804	Hookmoor Brook	Gorhuish	SX 532987	11.4	1967		SWWA	150.88	287	1247	

WELSH NATIONAL WATER DEVELOPMENT AUTHORITY AREA

055901	Wye	Cadora	SO 535090	4040	1937 (1936)	*	WRD	7.92	752	1039	1023

...ean ...uged ...scharge	Mean annual natural runoff	Highest instan- taneous gauged discharge	Date	Lowest daily mean gauged discharge	Date	Abstrac- tions and returns	Station details	Station number
...³/s	mm	m³/s		m³/s				
0.46 *0.0284*		11.19	5. 8.73	0.07	16. 6.73	P	Compound Crump weir. Total crest length 4.0 m. Low flow crest length 0.9 m	047313
1.45 *0.0394*		34.26	4.11.67	0.11	5.10.59	S R P G	A compound broad crested weir. Reconstructed as compound Crump weir in 1969. Total crest length 7.0 m. Low flow crest length 1.5 m	048001
5.00 *0.0292*		223.70	3.11.67	0.69	21. 7.71	S R P G I E	River section	048002
						G I E	River section with low flow flume	048003
0.81 *0.0320*		15.38	28.11.73	0.19	17. 7.71*	G	Compound Crump weir. Total crest length 10.0 m. Low flow crest length 1.5 m	048004
0.36 *0.0188*		6.74	29.11.71	0.05	13. 9.73	G	Compound Crump weir. Total crest length 4.3 m. Low flow crest length 1.2 m	048005
0.94 *0.0234*		5.61	12.10.73	0.00	1.10.68	P G I	River section	048006
0.51 *0.0192*		6.02	12.10.73	0.09	13. 9.73	S R P G I	Single crest Crump weir 4.9 m long	048007
						G I	Trapezoidal flume	048008
0.82 *0.0361*		11.34	28.11.73	0.13	21. 7.71	G E	Compound Crump weir. Total crest length 7.2 m. Low flow crest length 1.8 m	048009
0.69 *0.0181*		6.12	5.12.72	0.21	12. 9.73	G I	Compound Crump weir. Total crest length 11.0 m. Low flow crest length 3.0 m	048010
3.89 *0.0230*		51.46	28.11.73	0.74	31. 7.73	S R P G I E	Compound Crump weir. Total crest length 16.5 m. Low flow crest length 3.5 m	048011
5.70 *0.0273*		72.49	20. 1.65	0.54	21. 7.71	P G E	River section	049001
0.87 *0.0178*		6.20	10. 1.58	0.15	1. 9.73	G	River section. Modified in 1967 by construction of compound Crump weir. Total crest length 4.6 m. Low flow crest length 1.2 m	049002
0.77 *0.0355*		18.77	24.12.68	0.06	13. 7.73	P G	Compound Crump weir. Total crest length 7.6 m. Low flow crest length 1.2 m	049003
0.61 *0.0149*		16.88	29.11.71	0.08	3.10.70	G E	Single crest Crump weir 6.0 m long	049004
7.09 *0.0207*		560.68	9. 1.68	0.69	4. 8.61	S P E	River section	050001
4.75 *0.0222*	729 *64.3*	314.32	19.12.65	0.68	24.10.72	S R P G I E	River section	050002
						P G	River section with low flow thin plate weir	050003
		6.57	18.12.65	0.04	23. 7.66		Compound broad crest weir. Aban- doned 1967	050904
						P	River section. Modified in 1969 by the construction of a flat V weir.	050801
						P	Compound thin plate and broad crested rectangular weir.	050802
						S P E	River section	050803
							River section with low flow flat V weir. Jointly operated with University of Exeter	050804
.41 *0.0177*	627 *61.3*	925.88	20. 3.47	6.91	27. 9.59	S P E	River section. Gross discharges take account of reservoirs in the Elan Valley. Replaced by Redbrook, 055023, in October 1969	055901

Station number	River	Station name	National grid reference	Catchment area km²	Records start	Data archived	Measuring authority	Level of station m.O.D.	Highest point in the catchment m.O.D.	Annual average areal rainfall; mm Standard average for 1916-1950	Period of record average to 31.12.

WELSH NATIONAL WATER DEVELOPMENT AUTHORITY AREA–(CONTD)

Station number	River	Station name	National grid reference	Catchment area km²	Records start	Data archived	Measuring authority	Level of station m.O.D.	Highest point in the catchment m.O.D.	Standard average for 1916-1950	Period of record average to 31.12.
055002	Wye	Belmont	SO 485388	1900	1937 (1935)	*	WRD	46.3	752	1267	1239
055003	Lugg	Lugwardine	SO 548405	886	1940 (1939)	*	WRD	45.1	660	836	850
055004	Irfon	Abernant	SN 892460	72.8	1937	*	WRD	230	585	1953	1868
055905	Wye	Rhayader	SN 969676	167	1937	*	WRD	195	752	1664	1640
055006	Elan	Caban Coch Reservoir	SN 926645	184	1937 (1908)	*	STWATD	251	645	1873	1819
055007	Wye	Erwood	SO 076445	1280	1937	*	WRD	107	752	1425	1402
055008	Wye	Cefn Brwyn	SN 829838	10.4	1951	*	IH	341	740	2532	2452
055909	Monnow	Kentchurch	SO 419251	357	1948	*	WRD	57.6	713	993	1032
055010	Wye	Pant Mawr	SN 843825	27.2	1955 (1952)	*	WRD	310	752	2461	2393
055011	Ithon	Llandewi	SO 105683	111	1961 (1959)	*	WRD	230	585	1166	1229
055012	Irfon	Cilmery	SN 995507	244	1966	*	WRD	136	645	1661	1691
055013	Arrow	Titley Mill	SO 328585	126	1966	*	WRD	129	542	968	961
055014	Lugg	Byton	SO 364647	203	1966	*	WRD	124	660	1033	1106
055015	Honddu	Tafolog	SO 277294	25.1	1954	*	WRD	253	713	1405	1377
055016	Ithon	Disserth	SO 024578	358	1968	*	WRD	149	585	1104	
055017	Chwefru	Carreg-y-Wen	SN 998531	29	1968	*	WRD	154	612	1500	1504
055018	Frome	Yarkhill	SO 615428	144	1968	*	WRD	55.5	244	710	781
055019	Gamber Brook	Kilbreece	SO 529235	30.3	1970	*	WRD	52.0	293	790	
055020	Pinsley Brook	Cholstrey Mill	SO 462598	24.2	1970		WRD	77.3	325	769	
055021	Lugg	Butts Bridge	SO 502589	371	1969	*	WRD	67.0	660	918	1012
055022	Trothy	Mitchel Troy	SO 503112	142	1969	*	WRD	16.2	482	913	831
055023	Wye	Redbrook	SO 528110	4010	1969	*	WRD	9.00	752	1039	1092
055025	Llynfi	Three Cocks	SO 166373	132	1970	*	WRD	85		994	1060
055026	Wye	Ddol Farm	SN 985676	174	1969	*	WRD	193	752	1659	1677
055027	Rudhall Brook	Sandford Bridge	SO 641257	13.2	1971	*	WRD	46	278	748	628
055028	Frome	Bishops Frome	SO 667489	77.7	1971	*	WRD			717	794
055029	Monnow	Grosmont	SO 504225	354	1972	*	WRD		740	993	
055030	Claerwen	Dol y Mynach	SN 910620	95.3	1925	*	STWA			695	
055031	Yazor Brook	Three Elms	SO 491414	42.3	1972	*	WRD		293	695	
056001	Usk	Chain Bridge	SO 345056	912	1957	*	URD	22.6	886	1388	1413
056002	Ebbw	Rhiwderyn	ST 259889	217	1957	*	URD	30.6	581	1491	1516
056003	Honddu	The Forge, Brecon	SO 051297	62.1	1963 (1959)	*	URD	143.9	474	1194	1231
056004	Usk	Llandetty	SO 127203	544	1965	*	URD	103.6	886	1498	1589
056005	Afon Lwyd	Ponthir	ST 330924	98.1	1966	*	URD	14.9	581	1425	1532
056006	Usk	Trallong	SN 947295	184	1963	*	URD	166	793	1708	1708
056007	Afon Senni	Pont-hen-hafod	SN 928255	19.9	1967	*	URD	220	663	2026	1605
056008	Monks Ditch	Llanwern	ST 372885	15.4	1970	*	URD	7.9	308	1059	
056010	Usk	Trostrey	SO 355042	927	1969	*	TWD	20.35	886		

...an ...ged ...charge /s	Mean annual natural runoff mm	Highest instantaneous gauged discharge m³/s	Date	Lowest daily mean gauged discharge m³/s	Date	Abstractions and returns	Station details	Station number
.67 *(0.0235)*	813 *65.6*	948.62	4.12.60	0.57	29.11.55	S	River section. Gross discharges take account of reservoirs in the Elan Valley	055002
.51 *(0.0119)*		81.22	8.12.72	0.72	1.10.55		River section	055003
.14 *(0.0431)*		129.80	5. 8.73	0.00	29. 2.56	P	River section	055004
.19 *(0.0371)*		198.30	26.11.39	0.16	7. 7.61	P	River section. Replaced by Ddol Farm 055026 in October 1969	055905
.70 *(0.0310)*	1285 *70.6*	331.88	11.11.70	0.00		S	Broad crested weir. Gross mean flows allow for supply to aqueduct, change in reservoir content and compensation water	055006
.31 *(0.0276)*	953 *68.0*	801.62	8. 2.46	2.51	11.10.59	S	River section. Gross discharges take account of reservoirs in the Elan Valley	055007
.69 *(0.0663)*		57.28	5. 8.73	0.00			Compound Crump weir	055008
.80 *(0.0162)*		201.62	24. 1.60	0.42	17.10.55		River section. Replaced by Grosmont 055029 in April 1972	055909
.64 *(0.0603)*		174.02	5. 8.73	0.05	4.10.72		River section. Informal flat V weir control from 1973	055010
.52 *(0.0227)*		72.49	14. 1.68	0.04	2. 7.61		River section	055011
.04 *(0.0370)*		249.50	6. 8.73	0.41	12. 7.67		River section	055012
.30 *(0.0183)*		44.96	13. 1.68	0.17	12. 8.71	P	River section	055013
.79 *(0.0187)*		45.56	26. 5.69	0.61	16.10.69		River section. Flat V Crump profile weir control, 1:10 slope, added Oct 1971. Crest length 12.5 m	055014
.74 *(0.0295)*		30.30	16.10.67	0.06	8. 8.70		River section. Flat V control constructed 1974	055015
.92 *(0.0165)*		133.36	26. 5.69	0.21	21. 7.70	P E	River section. Flat V Crump profile from 1972	055016
.09 *(0.0376)*		45.52	5. 8.73	0.02	14. 9.73		River section. Informal flat V weir from 1973	055017
.26 *(0.0087)*		25.89	26. 5.69	0.13	1.11.69	E	River section	055018
		0.31	4. 5.73	0.04	9.12.73		River section. Concrete rectangular channel	055019
							River section. Concrete rectangular channel	055020
.36 *(0.0144)*		52.06	26. 5.69	0.85	3.11.69		River section	055021
.42 *(0.010)*		30.91	31. 1.71	0.09	26.10.70		River section	055022
.88 *(0.0159)*		560.80	6.12.72	9.92	25.10.72	S P E	River section. Replaces the long-period station at Cadora 055901	055023
.86 *(0.0141)*		44.93	11.12.72	0.16	14. 8.70		River section. Informal flat V weir	055025
.37 *(0.0366)*		252.23	5. 8.73	0.33	21. 7.71	P	River section. Replaces the long-period station at Rhayader 055905	055026
.08 *(0.0061)*		0.72	17. 1.72	0.00	1. 1.72		1:5 flat V Crump profile weir	055027
.85 *(0.0109)*		17.50	3. 2.72	0.13	2. 9.72		River section	055028
.74 *(0.0077)*		95.23	6.12.72	0.69	14. 9.73		River section. Informal flat V weir. Replaces Kentchurch, 055909	055029
.02 *(0.0422)*				0.00	28.12.27		Twin thin plate rectangular weirs. Claerwen Reservoir constructed 1948	055030
		2.31	3. 7.73	0.02	1.11.73		Flat V Crump profile weir	055031
.37 *(0.030)*	1068 *75.6*	689.97	17.10.67	2.32	6.10.59	S	River section. Intake to canal above gauge	056001
.22 *(0.0333)*	1108 *73.1*	201.56	16.10.67	0.13	1.10.70	S	River section. Flows affected by mine water discharge	056002
.48 *(0.0238)*		41.57	16.10.67	0.11	1.10.64		Compound Crump weir	056003
.58 *(0.0305)*		559.05	16.10.67	0.19	1. 8.72	S	River section. Intake to canal above gauge	056004
.72 *(0.0277)*		53.56	27. 2.67	0.58	1.11.69*	S P G	Compound Crump weir	056005
.13 *(0.0331)*	1255 *73.5*	244.55	16.10.67	0.81	21. 7.70	S	River section	056006
.86 *(0.0432)*		29.08	18.10.71	0.01	17.10.72		Crump weir. Fish pass removed in 1973	056007
.18 *(0.0117)*		4.23	6.12.72	0.04	24. 9.72		Trapezoidal flume	056008
.93 *(0.0291)*		282.55	6. 8.73	1.22	5. 1.71		Simple Crump weir. Low flows only; high flows may be obtained from Chain Bridge, 056001	056010

Station number	River	Station name	National grid reference	Catch-ment area	Records start	Data archived	Measuring authority	Level of station	Highest point in the catch-ment	Annual average areal rainfall; mm	
										Standard average for 1916-1950	Period of record averag to 31.12.
				km²				m.O.D.	m.O.D.		

WELSH NATIONAL WATER DEVELOPMENT AUTHORITY AREA–(CONTD)

Station number	River	Station name	National grid reference	Catch-ment area	Records start	Data archived	Measuring authority	Level of station	Highest point	Standard average	Period
056011	Sirhowy	Wattsville	ST 206912	76.1	1970	*	URD	68.7	610	1547	
056012	Grwyne	Millbrook	SO 241176	82.2	1970	*	URD	82.7	811	1318	
056013	Yscir	Pontaryscir	SO 003304	62.8	1972	*	URD	61.2	474	1407	
056014	Usk	Usk Reservoir	SN 840290	15.8	1950		URD	267.0	550	1422	
057001	Taf Fechan	Taf Fechan Reservoir	SO 060117	33.7	1937 (1913)	*	TWD	298	886	2007	2029
057002	Taf Fawr	Llwynon Reservoir	SO 012111	43.0	1937 (1931)	*	TWD	236	873	2055	2018
057003	Taff	Tongwynlais	ST 132818	487	1961		GRD	23.77	885.7	1835	1882
057004	Cynon	Abercynon	ST 079956	106	1957	*	GRD	81.2	521	1801	1864
057005	Taff	Pontypridd	ST 079897	455	1968		GRD	45.2	886	1863	
057006	Rhondda	Trehafod	ST 054909	101	1968		GRD	68.3	600	2181	
057007	Taff	Fiddler's Elbow	ST 089952	195	1973	*	GRD	82.50	886	1790	
057008	Rhymney	Llanederyn	ST 225821	179	1972	*	GRD	11.78	610.0	1413	
057010	Ely	Lanelay	ST 038843	39.4	1968	*	GRD	46.0	420.0		
057803	Clun	Cross Inn	ST 053824	25.9	1968		GRD		259		
058001	Ogmore	Bridgend	SS 904794	158	1962 (1959)	*	GRD	13.8	568	1765	1786
058002	Neath	Resolven	SN 815017	191	1961		GRD		734		
058903	Ewenny	Ewenny Priory	SS 914780	62.9	1962 (1960)		GRD	8.30	300	1328	1135
058004	Afan	Cwmavon	SS 781919	85.7	1961		GRD		597.1		
058005	Ogmore	Brynmenyn	SS 904844	74.3	1969		GRD	43.1	568	2005	
058006	Mellte	Pontneath-vaughan	SN 915082	65.8	1971	*	GRD	29.1	734	2021	
058007	Llynfi	Coytrahen	SS 891855	50.2	1970		GRD	49.9	558	1833	
058008	Dulais	Cilfrew	SN 778008	43.8	1971	*	GRD	42.11	481	1665	
058009	Ewenny	Keepers Lodge	SN 920782	62.5	1971	*	GRD	8.28	300	1380	
059001	Tawe	Ynys Tanglws	SS 685998	228	1957 (1956)	*	SWWRD	9.32	802	1841	1883
059002	Loughor	Tirydail	SN 624127	46.4	1967		SWWRD	30.8	503	1514	
060001	Tywi	Ty-Castell Farm	SN 491204	1090	1958	*	SWWRD	7.23	792	1572	1566
060002	Cothi	Felin-Mynachdy	SN 508225	298	1961	*	SWWRD	16.2	485	1646	1622

an ...ged ...charge ³/s	Mean annual natural runoff mm	Highest instantaneous gauged discharge m³/s	Date	Lowest daily mean gauged discharge m³/s	Date	Abstractions and returns	Station details	Station number
.78 *0.0234*		43.79	5.12.72	0.22	12. 8.70	S	Flat V Crump profile weir, 1:10 cross slope. Flows are affected by mine water discharge above gauge	056011
.77 *0.0215*		15.73	5.12.72	0.33	23.10.72	S	Crump weir	056012
.29 *0.0205*		28.81	5. 8.73	0.15	21.10.72		Simple Crump weir	056013
						S	Measures compensation water from Usk Reservoir. Crump weir constructed 1973	056014
.78 *0..0231*	1539 *75.9*	36.81	18.12.65	0.10	23.10.73	S	Combined thin plate weir and orifice measurement. Records obtained from compensation flows, variation in reservoir level and water taken into supply	057001
.28 *0.0298*	1461 *72.4*	110.72	3. 6.58	0.00		S	Combined Venturi flume and weir downstream of dam. Records obtained from compensation flows, variation in reservoir level and water taken into supply	057002
.74 *0.0426*		481.39	18.12.65	3.06	23. 7.67	S E I	River section. Flows affected by mine water discharge above gauge	057003
.93 *0.0371*	1114 *59.8*	147.25	18.12.65	0.31	27. 6.60	S	Combined flat V weir and river section	057004
.55 *0.0342*		323.84	5.12.72	3.07	25.10.72	S E	Combined flat V weir and river section. Flows affected by mine water discharge above gauge	057005
.57 *0.0452*		100.90	12.11.72	0.66	25.10.72	S	River section. Flows affected by mine water discharge above gauge	057006
		49.84	5. 8.73	1.54	13. 9.73	S E	River section with flat V weir. Flows affected by mine water discharge upstream	057007
.90 *0.0162*		79.27	6. 8.73	0.79	12. 9.73	P	River section with flat V weir. Flows affected by mine water discharge upstream	057008
						E I	River section	057010
						E I	River section. Flows affected by mine water discharge upstream	057803
.14 *0.0389*		155.18	17.12.65	0.54	22. 7.67	P E I	River section	058001
						S I	River section – levels only	058002
.34 *0.0213*		26.39	16. 1.65	0.05	2.10.64	E	River section. Records cease March 1970; replaced by Keepers Lodge 058009	058903
							River section – levels only	058004
.90 *0.0390*		69.05	1.11.70	0.50	1. 8.73	E	Combined flat V weir and river section. Flows affected by mine water discharge above gauge	058005
.57 *0.0391*		79.67	4.11.73	0.29	7.10.72		Flat V, Crump profile weir. 1:20 cross slopes	058006
.82 *0.0363*		59.41	1.11.70	0.29	19.10.72	E I	Combined flat V weir and river section	058007
.67 *0.0381*		85.38	4.11.73	0.25	28. 7.73		Crump profile, flat V centre section 1:10 cross slopes combined with horizontal side sections without divide walls	058008
.31 *0.0209*		30.58	20.11.71	0.28	23.10.72		River section with flat V, Crump profile weir, 1:15 cross slopes. Replaces Ewenny Priory 058903	058009
.32 *0.0496*	1595 *84.7*	322.81	27. 2.67	0.45	18. 9.59	G E I	River section	059001
						P G E	River section	059002
.34 *0.0352*	1133 *72.3*	526.75	13.12.64	1.19	1. 9.59	S R P G E I	River section. Complemented by Capel Dewi 060010, for low flows	060001
.37 *0.0382*		274.68	12.12.64	0.65	9. 7.62	P E	River section. Discharges below 2 m³/s and above 35 m³/s are estimated	060002

Station number	River	Station name	National grid reference	Catch-ment area km²	Records start	Data archived	Measuring authority	Level of station m.O.D.	Highest point in the catch-ment m.O.D.	Standard average for 1916-1950	Period of record average to 31.12.

WELSH NATIONAL WATER DEVELOPMENT AUTHORITY AREA–(CONTD)

Station number	River	Station name	National grid reference	Catch-ment area	Records start	Data archived	Measuring authority	Level of station	Highest point	Standard average 1916-1950	Period of record
060003	Taf	Clog y Fran	SN 238160	217	1965	*	SWWRD	7.01	385	1411	
060004	Dewi Fawr	Glasfryn Ford	SN 290175	40.1	1967		SWWRD	10.2	284	1466	
060005	Bran	Llandovery	SN 771343	66.8	1968	*	SWWRD	63.9	517	1503	
060006	Gwili	Glangwili	SN 431220	130	1968		SWWRD	7.48	358	1521	
060007	Tywi	Dolau Hirion	SN 762362	232	1968	*	SWWRD	68.9	549	1749	
060008	Tywi	Ystrad Ffin	SN 785472	82.8	1972		SWWRD	174	549		
060009	Sawdde	Felin y Cwm	SN 712266	81.1	1970		SWWRD	55.3	750	1766	
060010	Towy	Capel Dewi	SN 485206	1090	1973		SWWRD	7.77	792		
060012	Twrch	Ddol Las	SN 650440	20.7	1971		SWWRD	151	484	1664	
060013	Cothi	Pont Ynys Brechfa	SN 537301	262	1971		SWWRD	54.5	485	1696	
061001	Western Cleddau	Prendergast Mill	SM 954177	198	1965	*	SWWRD	3.51	468	1266	1380
061002	Eastern Cleddau	Canaston Bridge	SN 072153	183	1960 (1959)	*	SWWRD	5.03	536	1461	1412
061003	Gwaun	Cilrhedyn Bridge	SN 005349	31.3	1968		SWWRD	70.3	468	1474	
061004	Western Cleddau	Redhill	SM 942184	198	1972		SWWRD	5.79	468	1266	
062001	Teifi	Glan Teifi	SN 244416	894	1959	*	SWWRD	5.18	595	1389	1355
062002	Teifi	Llanfair	SN 433406	546	1970		SWWRD	66.0	595	1479	
063001	Ystwyth	Pont Llolwyn	SN 592774	170	1963	*	SWWRD	12.0	611	1488	1441
063002	Rheidol	Llanbadarn Fawr	SN 601804	182	1965	*	SWWRD	4.02	753	1771	
063003	Wyre	Llanrhystyd	SN 542698	40.6	1969		SWWRD	19.3	358	1150	
064001	Dovey	Dovey Bridge	SH 745019	471	1962	*	GWRD	6.00	905	1863	
064002	Dysynni	Pont y Garth	SH 632066	75.1	1966	*	GWRD	2.39	892	1934	
064003	Mawddach	Ganllwyd	SH 729233	139	1967	*	GWRD	25.1	754	2160	
064004	Twymyn	Cemaes Road	SH 825047	107	1968		GWRD	29.8	544		
064005	Wnion	Dolgellau	SH 730179	111	1969		GWRD	6.18	905		
064006	Leri	Dolybont	SN 635882	48.6	1971	*	GWRD	14.58	506	1380	
065001	Glaslyn	Beddgelert	SH 592478	68.6	1962 (1961)	*	GWRD	33.0	1090	3279	3281
065002	Dwyryd	Maentwrog	SH 670415	78.2	1967	*	GWRD	3.0	770	2558	
065903	Gwyrfai	Llyn Gwellyn	SH 552557	20.6	1966		GWRD	140	1085		
065004	Gwyrfai	Bontnewydd	SH 484599	47.9	1970	*	GWRD	30.9	1090	2311	
065005	Erch	Pencaenewydd	SH 400404	18.1	1972	*	GWRD	56.13	564	1207	
065901	Dwyryd	Hydro-Electric scheme	SH 689422	46.15	1951		CEGB			2840	
066001	Clwyd	Pont-y-Cambwll	SJ 069709	404	1959	*	DCRD	15.5	555	922	904
066002	Elwy	Pant-yr-Onen	SJ 021704	220	1961	*	DCRD	35.7	518	1175	1156
066003	Aled	Bryn Aled	SH 957703	69.9	1963	*	DCRD	105	518	1171	1021
066004	Wheeler	Bodfari	SJ 105714	62.9	1970	*	DCRD	55.0	455	856	
066005	Clwyd	Ruthin Weir	SJ 122592	95.3	1970	*	DCRD	51.0	501	969	
066006	Elwy	Pont-y-Gwyddel	SH 952718	194	1972	*	DCRD	87.6	518	1226	
066707	Clwyd	Rhuddlan Bridge	SJ 021780	695	1973		DCRD	2.0	555		

Mean gauged charge m³/s	Mean annual natural runoff mm	Highest instantaneous gauged discharge m³/s	Date	Lowest daily mean gauged discharge m³/s	Date	Abstractions and returns	Station details	Station number
.60	*0.0350*	61.73	18.12.65	0.87	9. 9.69	P G E I	River section	060003
						E	River section	060004
.94	*0.0290*	86.00	14. 2.71	0.01	20.10.72	I	River section	060005
						S P E I	River section	060006
.00	*0.0302*	299.00	18. 6.71	0.40	20. 7.71	S R E I	River section	060007
						S R	Crump weir	060008
						S P	Flat V, Crump profile weir	060009
							Flat V weir, 1:20 cross slope set in horizontal flanks both with Crump profile; complements Ty Castell, 060001, for low flows	060010
							River section	060012
							River section	060013
.64	*0.0335*	51.82	27. 2.67	0.00	1.10.67	P E I	River section with levels recorded at Redhill 061004 from 1972	061001
.73	955 *70.5 0.0313*	199.35	12.12.64	0.59	22. 7.70	S R P E	River section with artificial control from June 1974. Discharges above 14 m³/s are estimated	061002
							River section	061003
							Water level record only. Complementary to Prendergast Mill, 061001	061004
.15	995 *73.5 0.0315*	259.67	19.12.65	0.91	16. 9.59	S P	River section. Discharges below 4.25 m³/s and above 85 m³/s are estimated	062001
						S P	River section	062002
.44	*0.032*	210.40	12.12.64	0.26	30. 8.68		River section	063001
.33	*0.0513*	145.27	17.12.65	0.00	15. 9.67	S P H	River section	063002
							River section	063003
.66	*0.0460*	580.50	12.12.64	1.20	29. 6.64		River section	064001
.08	*0.0543*	43.64	5. 8.73	0.00	29. 9.72		River section	064002
.64	*0.0334*	900.00	1.10.67	0.00	20. 1.69		River section	064003
							River section	064004
						I	River section	064005
.35	*0.0278*	17.83	31. 3.72	0.10	6.10.72		River section	064006
.24	*0.0764*	130.15	16. 7.73	0.00	20. 1.69*	H	River section	065001
		163.00	15. 4.70	0.00	27. 6.69	H	River section	065002
							River section downstream of outflow from Llyn Gwellyn. Abandoned 1971	065903
		21.11	11.12.72	0.12	30. 9.72		Single crest Crump weir	065004
.43	*0.0238*	6.70	9.11.73	0.07	4. 7.73		Single crest Crump weir	065005
							Abandoned 1959	065901
.08	72.21? *0.0150*	72.21	13.12.64	0.45	24. 9.64		River section. Flood discharges are affected by flood plain storage in the Vale of Clwyd upstream of the site	066001
.40	648 *56.6 0.02*	150.08	12.12.64	0.23	29. 7.62	R P S	River section, subject to rating changes at low flow	066002
.21	*0.0173*	49.27	12.12.64	0.07	28. 7.64	R P S	Compound Crump weir. Measures low flows only	066003
.74	*0.0118*	3.71	10. 8.71	0.26	14. 9.73	I	Single crest Crump weir, 3m wide	066004
.29		10.16	1. 8.72	0.08	24.10.72*		Non-standard weir with central notch	066005
	0.0135	22.75	29.12.73	3.09	6.12.73	R P S	River section upstream of road bridge with invert acting as control.	066006
.25	*0.0164*			0.10	29. 2.64*		Level recorder. Discharges synthesised from tributary flows	066707

Station number	River	Station name	National grid reference	Catch-ment area	Records start	Data archived	Measuring authority	Level of station	Highest point in the catch-ment	Annual average areal rainfall; mm	
										Standard average for 1916-1950	Period of record averag to 31.12.
				km²				m.O.D.	m.O.D.		

WELSH NATIONAL WATER DEVELOPMENT AUTHORITY AREA–(CONTD)

Station number	River	Station name	National grid reference	Catch-ment area	Records start	Data archived	Measuring authority	Level of station	Highest point in the catch-ment	Standard average for 1916-1950	Period of record averag to 31.12.
066011	Conwy	Cwm Llanerch	SH 802581	344	1964	*	GWRD	6.98	1060	2284	
066012	Lledr	Gethin's Bridge	SH 785538	72.8	1969		GWRD	37.7	603		
067001	Dee	Bala	SH 942357	262	1957 (1956)	*	DCRD	158	884	1933	1858
067902	Dee	Erbistock Rectory	SJ 357413	1040	1937	*	DCRD	23.4	884	1445	1407
067003	Brenig	Pont y Rhuddfa	SH 974539	22.0	1922	*	DCRD	325	520	1308	1306
067004	Alwen	Alwen Reservoir	SH 957528	25.5	1929 (1911)	*	DCRD	332	531	1326	1120
067005	Ceiriog	Bryn-Kinalt Weir	SJ 295373	114	1956 (1952)	*	DCRD	65.8	784	1257	1430
067006	Alwen	Druid	SJ 042436	185	1960	*	DCRD	146	611	1333	1326
067907	Dee	Glyndyfrdwy	SJ 155428	728	1964	*	DCRD	118	884	1562	1725
067008	Alyn	Pont-y-Capel	SJ 336541	227	1965	*	DCRD	38.5	562	910	940
067009	Alyn	Rhydymwyn	SJ 206667	77.8	1957 (1940)	*	DCRD	126	562	971	
067010	Afon Gelyn	Cynefail	SH 843420	13.0	1966	*	DCRD	302	695	2459	
067011	Nant Aberderfel	Nant Aberderfel	SH 851392	3.7	1966		DCRD				
067912	Afon Tryweryn	Upper Tryweryn	SH 838398	27.2	1966	*	DCRD	329	854	2198	
067013	Afon Hirnant	Plas Rhiwaedog	SH 946349	33.9	1967	*	DCRD	195	66	1747	
067014	Dee	Corwen	SJ 069433	656	1935		DCRD	134	884		
067015	Dee	Manley Hall	SJ 348815	1020	1970	*	DCRD	25.3	884	1445	
067016	Worthenbury Brook	Worthenbury	SJ 418464	146	1969	*	DCRD	10.4	133	764	
067017	Afon Tryweryn	Llyn Celyn Outflow	SH 880399	59.9	1962	*	DCRD	249	853	2168	
067018	Afon Dyfrdwy	New Inn	SH 874308	53.9	1969	*	DCRD	164	750	2065	
067019	Afon Tryweryn	Weir X, Bala	SH 932360	105	1961		DCRD	163	853		

Mean gauged discharge m³/s	Mean annual natural runoff mm	Highest instantaneous gauged discharge m³/s	Date	Lowest daily mean gauged discharge m³/s	Date	Abstractions and returns	Station details	Station number
		365.32	19.10.71	0.56	30. 9.72		River section	066011
							River section	066012
2.17 *0.0465*	1582 *85.2*	198.22	4.12.60	0.80	18. 3.62	R S	Low/medium flow control structure (modified in 1968), calibrated by gauging at non-modular high flows	067001
1.55 *0.0303*	1025 *72.9*	665.45	13.12.64	1.93	5.10.37*	I S R P	River section. Replaced by Manley Hall, 067015, in 1970.	067902
0.55 *0.025*	945 *72.4*	28.28	31. 7.72	0.01	16. 7.59		Combined V notch/rectangular thin plate weir. Flows greater than 13 cumecs not recorded on chart prior to 1968. The catchment area was revised to 22.0 sq km in November 1973 to include the drainage area of a small stream diversion (at Pant y Maen) which had been excluded from the original estimate of 20.2 sq km. Neither of these two figures includes the Llyn Bran catchment area, but flow corrections for Llyn Bran over-flow and Pant y Maen diversion have been allowed for since October 1967. For details of the errors and defi-ciencies of the river flow record, the Dee and Clwyd River Division should be consulted.	067003
0.36 *0.0141*		16.31	14.12.36	0.07	2.10.56	P S	Combined V notch/rectangular thin plate weir	067004
3.11 *0.0273*		66.11	9.12.65	0.34	6.10.59		River section upstream of weir, which was modified to a compound broad crested weir in 1969. Discharges less than 15 cumecs are estimated	067005
4.62 *0.0260*	917 *69.2*	175.57	12.12.64	0.34	26. 6.61	I P	River section. Flows greater than 60 cumecs estimated	067006
5.71 *0.0367*		552.18	12.12.64	2.28	5. 7.64	I R P	River section. Regulation of the River Dee by Llyn Tegid (since 1957) and Llyn Celyn (since 1964) affects measured low and high flows. Dis-charge record terminated October 1969	067907
2.53 *0.0111*		35.92	2.12.66	0.40	27.10.69	E I	Asymmetrical compound Crump weir	067008
0.57 *0.0073*		66.11	9.12.65	0.00			Trapezoidal flume in concrete trapezoidal channel. Flow frequently zero due to river flow entering swallow holes in limestone upstream of site	067009
0.61 *0.0469*		25.29	24. 6.67	0.04	21.10.72		Compound Crump weir	067010
						P	Compound broad crested weir	067011
		28.37	23. 3.68	0.07	11. 8.68		Compound Crump weir with modular flow less than 7 cumecs. Above this calibration is not possible. Abandoned 1974	067912
.19 *0.0351*		51.85	19. 3.68	0.00	31. 8.68		River section	067013
						R P S	Level recorder upstream of Corwen Bridge	067014
.98 *0.0255*		275.60	19.10.71	0.70	16. 2.70	I R P S	Asymmetrical compound Crump weir, superseding Erbistock, 067902, 1 km downstream. Prescribed flow station for regulation of R. Dee	067015
.61 *0.0042*		20.30	13. 1.68	0.05	12. 8.68*		River section upstream of narrow bridge	067016
.16 *0.0528*		23.80	22. 4.70	0.21	15. 3.71	R H P S	Compound broad crested weir measur-ing controlled outflow and overspill from Llyn Celyn regulating reservoir	067017
.82 *0.0523*		56.11	19.10.71	0.14	16. 6.70		River section. Measures all but flood peaks greater than 40 m³/sec	067018
						H R P S	Compound broad crested weir	067019

Station number	River	Station name	National grid reference	Catchment area	Records start	Data archived	Measuring authority	Level of station	Highest point in the catchment	Annual average areal rainfall; mm	
										Standard average for 1916-1950	Period of record average to 31.12.
				km²				m.O.D.	m.O.D.		

WELSH NATIONAL WATER DEVELOPMENT AUTHORITY AREA—(CONTD)

067020	Dee	Chester Weir	SJ 408659	1810	1969		DCRD	4.3	884		
067024	Dee	Farndon	SJ 412544		1973		DCRD	4.0	884		
067901	Dee	Bala Lake (Llyn Tegid)	SH 920355	161	1935		DCRD	161	884		1858

NORTH WEST WATER AUTHORITY AREA

068001	Weaver	Ashbrook	SJ 670633	622	1937	*	NWWARD	16.46	222	772	764
068002	Gowy	Picton	SJ 443714	156	1949	*	NWWARD	3.05	222	754	749
068003	Dane	Rudheath	SJ 668718	407	1949	*	NWWARD	12.80	547	874	897
068004	Wistaston Brook	Marshfield Bridge	SJ 674552	92.7	1955	*	NWWARD	29.54	221	785	788
068005	Weaver	Audlem	SJ 653431	207	1953 (1936)	*	NWWARD	44.68	222	772	773
068006	Dane	Hulme Walfield	SJ 845644	150	1953	*	NWWARD	66.45	547	1034	1072
068007	Wincham Brook	Lostock Gralam	SJ 697757	148	1962	*	NWWARD	16.46	148	833	864
068008	Weaver	Beam Bridge	SJ 651535	349	1969 (1938)		NWWARD	29.87	222		
068010	Fender	Ford	SJ 281880	18.4	1973		NWWARD	5.49	88	811	
068011	Arley Brook	Gore Farm	SJ 696799	36.5	1973		NWWARD	39.41	72	822	
068012	Dane	Ravenscroft	SJ 702671	212	1937		NWWARD	21.95	547		
068014	Sandersons Brook	Sandbach	SJ 754652	5.4	1969		NWWARD	49.71	79		
068015	Gowy	Huxley	SJ 497624	49.0	1973		NWWARD	16.76	222		
068016	Birket	Fornalls Green	SJ 235894	12.9	1962		NWWARD	2.74	70		
068017	Arrowe Brook	Moreton	SJ 255894	14.5	1953		NWWARD	6.61	102		
068018	Dane	Congleton Park	SJ 861632	145	1968		NWWARD	78.08	547		
068804	Dane	Northwich	SJ 660738	420	1935		NWWARD	9.45	547		
069001	Mersey	Irlam Weir	SJ 728936	679	1945 (1934)	*	NWWARD	10.33	636	1118	1138
069002	Irwell	Adelphi Weir	SJ 824987	599	1949	*	NWWARD	24.16	473	1265	1285
069003	Irk	Scotland Weir	SJ 841992	72.5	1949 (1937)	*	NWWARD	26.21	213	1064	1083
069004	Etherow	Bottoms Reservoir	SK 023971	78.2	1937 (1922)	*	NWWAED	151	628	1481	1461
069005	Glaze Brook	Little Woolden Hall	SJ 685939	152	1954 (1932)	*	NWWARD	9.04	158	950	956
069006	Bollin	Dunham Massey	SJ 727875	256	1955 (1936)	*	NWWARD	12.80	678	871	910
069007	Mersey	Ashton Weir	SJ 772936	660	1959		NWWARD	14.87	636		
069008	Dean	Stanneylands	SJ 846830	51.8	1967		NWWARD	56.98	483		
069009	Goyt	Chadkirk	SD 941899	347	1956		NWWARD	59.37	547		
069011	Micker Brook	Cheadle	SJ 855889	67.2	1968		NWWARD	34.59	408		
069012	Bollin	Wilmslow	SJ 850815	72.5	1968		NWWARD	59.15	452		

Mean gauged discharge	Mean annual natural runoff	Highest instantaneous gauged discharge	Date	Lowest daily mean gauged discharge	Date	Abstractions and returns	Station details	Station number
m³/s	mm	m³/s		m³/s				
						I R P G S E	River section, upstream of ancient weir liable to occasional tidal over-topping	067020
						S R P	Level recorder used to infer low and medium flows at Eccleston Ferry (SJ 415 622), 141 km downstream	067024
							Water level recorder, now obsolete	067901
5.58	276	212.38	8. 2.46	0.57		P G E	River section	068001
1.13		19.37	6.11.54	0.09	22. 4.71	P G	River section. Subject to variable backwater effects	068002
4.70	413	92.78	13.12.64	0.23	2.10.49	S P G E I	River section. River bed is mobile and calibration changes periodically	068003
1.21	908	16.21	14. 1.68	0.00	15. 3.67	P G E I	River section	068004
1.66	230	28.32	26. 3.55	0.15	2.10.64	P G E	Thin plate weir for low flows. River section for medium and high flows	068005
2.41		107.18	8. 9.65	0.21	5. 7.65	S P G I	River section	068006
2.13		30.03	12.12.64	0.23	2. 9.64	P G E I	River section	068007
						P G E	River section: affected by sluice gates upstream	068008
							Compound critical depth flume. Design calibration	068010
							Trapezoidal critical depth flume. Design calibration	068011
						S P G I	River section	068012
							Critical depth flume	068014
						P G	River section	068015
							River section: concrete-lined channel	068016
							River section with critical depth flume low flow control in concrete lined channel	068017
						S P G	Broad crested long mill weir	068018
						S P G E I	River section	068804
13.92		736.24	5.12.34	0.43	9. 3.70	S P G E I	Broad crested weir in two lengths each 30 m long at slightly different levels. Hydraulic model analysis calibration	069001
19.04		430.42	20. 1.54	1.05	29. 7.51	S P G E I	Broad crested weir with modular flow to moderate discharges only; hydraulic model analysis calibration. Higher flows measured at 069025 Manchester Racecourse 1½ miles upstream	069002
1.77		72.92	11. 6.70	0.14		S P G E I	Broad crested weir 18 m long. Hydraulic model analysis calibration	069003
1.26	1046	98.86	9.12.65	0.14	8.11.59	S	Compensation water is measured by two orifices and overflow by two compound thin plate weirs each about 24 m long	069004
3.09		36.17	19.10.71	0.40	2. 8.61	P G E I	River section	069005
3.85		63.02	31. 5.64	0.30	31. 5.70	S P G E I	River section, modified by canal bank burst 2. 8.71	069006
						S P G E I	Broad crested weir	069007
						S P G E I	Compound Crump weir. Designed calibration	069008
						S P G E I	Broad crested weir. Hydraulic model calibration	069009
						S P G E I	Compound Crump weir	069011
						S P G E I	Compound Crump weir. Designed calibration	069012

(handwritten annotations in left margin:)
0.0089 · 36.1
0.0072
46.0
0.0115 · ?
0.0131
0.008
0.0161
0.0144
0.0205
0.0318
0.0244
71.6
0.0161
0.0203
0.015

79

Station number	River	Station name	National grid reference	Catch-ment area km²	Records start	Data archived	Measuring authority	Level of station m.O.D.	Highest point in the catch-ment m.O.D.	Annual average areal rainfall; mm Standard average for 1916-1950	Period of record average to 31.12.7

NORTH WEST WATER AUTHORITY AREA—(CONTD)

Station number	River	Station name	National grid reference	Catch-ment area km²	Records start	Data archived	Measuring authority	Level of station m.O.D.	Highest point in the catch-ment m.O.D.	Standard average for 1916-1950	Period of record average to 31.12.7
069013	Sinderland Brook	Partington	SJ 726905	44.8	1968		NWWARD	12.98	76		
069015	Etherow	Compstall	SJ 962908	156	1969		NWWARD	73.49	628		
069016	Etherow	Melandra	SK 005949	134	1967		NWWARD	115.21	628		
069017	Goyt	Marple Bridge	SJ 964897	183	1969		NWWARD	74.38	547		
069018	Newton Brook	Newton-le-Willows	SJ 585933	32.8	1969		NWWARD	9.92	131	825	
069019	Worsley Brook	Eccles	SJ 753980	23.8	1969		NWWARD	15.16	101		
069020	Medlock	Ardwick, London Road	SJ 849975	57.5	1970		NWWARD	30.75	372		
069021	Stake Brook	Bacup	SD 876247	0.1	1962		NWWARD	–	399	1397	
069022	Irwell	Irwell Vale	SD 791201	101	1964		NWWARD	139.54	473		
069023	Roch	Blackford Bridge	SD 807077	186	1941		NWWARD	69.92	475		
069024	Croal	Farnworth Weir	SU 743068	145	1948		NWWARD	51.71	418		
069025	Irwell	Manchester Racecourse	SD 821004	557	1941		NWWARD	24.16	473		
069026	Irwell	Kearsley	SD 764049	528	1948		NWWARD	40.57	473		
069027	Tame	Portwood	SJ 906918	150	1943		NWWARD	42.99	585		
069028	Mersey	Brinksway	SJ 884900	531	1955		NWWARD	33.48	636		
069029	Mersey	Flixton Bridge	SJ 743938	673	1933		NWWARD	10.33	636		
069030	Sankey Brook	Causey Bridge	SJ 588922	154	1953	*	NWWARD	7.57	131		
069031	Netherley Brook	Greens Bridge	SJ 457867	47.9	1970		NWWARD	4.88	85		
069032	Alt	Kirkby	SJ 392983	90.1	1963		NWWARD	8.41	70		
069033	Alt	Sefton	SJ 359012	100	1953	*	NWWARD	3.05	70		
069034	Musbury Brook	Helmshore	SD 773212	3.1	1971		NWWARD	184.21	407		
069035	Irwell	Bury Bridge	SD 797109	155	1973		NWWARD	74.98	473		
069036	Eagley Brook	Longworth Clough	SD 701149	16.8	1972		NWWARD	159.49	450	1499	
069802	Etherow	Woodhead	SK 102998	13.0	1937		NWWAED				
069901	Medlock	New Viaduct Street	SJ 863987	55.9	1950 (1949)	*	NWWARD	42.4	372		1065
070001	Douglas	Rivington Reservoirs	SD 631119	39.6	1937 (1861)	*	NWWAWD	113	457	1237	1289
070002	Douglas	Wanes Blades Bridge	SD 476126	198	1966		NWWARD	4.36			
070003	Douglas	Central Park, Wigan	SD 587061	60.1	1973		NWWARD	31.73			
070004	Yarrow	U/S of Croston Mill	SD 498179	96.6	1973		NWWARD	6.85			
071001	Ribble	Samlesbury	SD 589304	1140	1964 (1960)	*	NWWARD	6.71	680	1323	1331
071002	Hodder	Stocks Reservoir	SD 71 5	37.6	1954	*	NWWARBD	182	544	1656	1692
071003	Croasdale Beck	Croasdale Flume	SD 706546	10.4	1957	*	NWWARBD	177	544	1839	1883
071004	Calder	Whalley	SD 730360	316	1963	*	NWWARD	39.9	558	1227	1264

Mean gauged discharge	Mean annual natural runoff	Highest instantaneous gauged discharge	Date	Lowest daily mean gauged discharge	Date	Abstractions and returns	Station details	Station number
m³/s	mm	m³/s		m³/s				
						P G E I	Compound Crump weir. Designed calibration	069013
						S P G E I	Crump weir with crest tapping. Designed calibration	069015
						S	Critical depth flume with broad crested flanking weir. Designed calibration	069016
						S P G E I	Compound Crump weir with crest tapping. Designed calibration	069017
						S P G E I	Compound Crump weir. Designed calibration	069018
						P G E I	Trapezoidal critical depth flume. Designed calibration	069019
						S P G E I	Weir at culvert entrance. Estimated calibration	069020
							Thin plate compound weir. Hydraulic design formula calibration	069021
						S P G E I	River section	069022
						S P G E I	River section, upstream of mill weir	069023
						S P G E I	Broad crested weir. Hydraulic model calibration	069024
						S P G E I	River section	069025
						S P G E I	Broad crested mill weir	069026
						S P G E I	Broad crested mill weir; hydraulic model calibration	069027
						S P G E I	River section	069028
						S P G E I	River section	069029
						P E I	River section	069030
						G E I	River section	069031
						G E I	River section	069032
						P E I	River section	069033
							Thin plate compound weir; hydraulic design formula calibration	069034
						S P G E I	River section	069035
							Compound thin plate weir. Manufacturer's calibration	069036
							Compound V notch and rectangular thin plate weir	069802
1.14 *0.0204*		27.61	18. 8.56	0.00	24. 8.55*		Broad crested weir 18.75 m long. Station closed in 1960	069901
0.39 *0.0098*	996 *77.3*	15.37	28.12.67	0.00	12. 7.52*	S	Compensation orifice at lowest of a series of seven reservoirs	070001
						S R E I P	River section in which weir control was built in 1973. Flood warning scheme station. Affected by tides	070002
						S R E I P	River section	070003
							Non-standard weir	070004
4.72 *0.0278*		891.25	12.12.64	2.00	1.10.72*	S E	River section. A compound weir for more accurate measurement of low and medium discharges was completed in 1970 at NGR SD 587314. Crump profile 1 : 20 flat V centre section. Horizontal flanking weirs of Crump section	071001
0.54 *0.0144*	1275	66.83	14.12.36	0.16	30. 1.69	S	Overflow weir 91.4 m long	071002
0.40 *0.0385*		25.22	9.11.72	0.04	5.10.59		Compound trapezoidal critical depth flume	071003
3.59 *0.0272*		344.20	24. 3.64	1.04	7. 9.69	E I	River section. A Crump profile flat V weir, 1 : 20, was constructed in 1970	071004

Station number	River	Station name	National grid reference	Catchment area km²	Records start	Data archived	Measuring authority	Level of station m.O.D.	Highest point in the catchment m.O.D.	Annual average areal rainfall; mm Standard average for 1916-1950	Period of record average to 31.12.7
NORTH WEST WATER AUTHORITY AREA–(CONTD)											
071005	Bottoms Beck	Bottoms Beck Flume	SD 745565	10.6	1960	*	NWWARBD	186	405	1524	1554
071006	Ribble	Henthorn	SD 721391	446	1968 (1960)		NWWARD	38.78		1338	
071007	Ribble	Hodderfoot	SD 709379	719	1965		NWWARD	33.53			
071008	Hodder	Hodder Place	SD 705399	261	1969		NWWARD	41.99			
071009	Ribble	Jumbles Rock	SD 702376	1050	1970		NWWARD	31.31			
071010	Pendle Water	Barden Lane	SD 837351	104	1971		NWWARD	92.28		1285	
071011	Ribble	Arnford	SD 839556	207	1966		NWWARD	116.81		1529	
071013	Darwen	Ewood Bridge	SD 677262	40.0	1973		NWWARD	98.29			
071802	Ribble	Halton West	SD 850552	207	1966		NWWARD				
071803	Hodder	Higher Hodder Bridge	SD 697411	258	1960		NWWARD	50.90			
071804	Dunsop	Footholme	SD 652529	24.9	1962		NWWARBD				
072001	Lune	Halton	SD 502647	995	1959	*	NWWARD	5.18	737	1577	1469
072002	Wyre	St Michael's	SD 465411	275	1963	*	NWWARD	4.69	560	1257	1270
072003	Hindburn	Wray	SD 605679	83.7	1967		NWWARD	39.30			
072004	Lune	Caton	SD 529654	983	1968	*	NWWARD	10.66			
072005	Lune	Killington New Bridge	SD 622906	226	1969		NWWARD	82.84		1780	
072006	Lune	Kirkby Lonsdale	SD 614778	507	1968		NWWARD	36.07		1384	
072008	Wyre	Garstang	SD 489447	111	1967	*	NWWARD			1391	
072009	Wenning	D/S of Wennington Road Bridge	SD 614701	140	1970		NWWARD	39.40		1318	
072010	Lune	Tebay	NY 613040	136	1968		NWWARD	172.33			
072011	Rawthey	Brigg Flatts (Sedburgh)	SD 630907	200	1968		NWWARD				
072012	Greta	Burton-in-Lonsdale	SD 653717	92.7	1964		NWWARD	60.96			
072014	Conder	Galgate	SD 482554	28.5	1966		NWWARBD	16.31			
072803	Lune	Halton Upper Weir	SD 513648	993	1940		NWWARD	9.56		1875	
072804	Lune	Broadraine	SD 621901	226	1966		NWWARD			1780	
072807	Wenning	Hornby	SD 586684	236	1940		NWWARD	22.74		1388	
072809	Wyre	Scorton Weir	SD 501500	88.8	1967		NWWARD	31.56			
072812	Stubbins Brook	Claughton	SD 512428	3.4	1971 (1965)		NWWARD	20.70			
073001	Leven	Newby Bridge	SD 371863	241	1964	*	NWWARD	38.4	873	2195	2156

ean uged scharge	Mean annual natural runoff	Highest instantaneous gauged discharge	Date	Lowest daily mean gauged discharge	Date	Abstractions and returns	Station details	Station number
3/s	mm	m3/s		m3/s				
0.34 _(0.0321)_		22.77	21.11.63	0.02	21. 6.70		Compound trapezoidal critical depth flume	071005
							River section with unstable rating. Compound broad crested weir installed August 1968	071006
							River section	071007
						S R P	Compound flat V weir, Crump profile	071008
						S R P	River section. Stage records only	071009
							Flat V weir, Crump profile	071010
							River section until flat V weir, Crump profile completed March 1972	071011
						P E I	River section	071013
							Superseded by 071011 Arnford. Abandoned 1973	071802
							Superseded by 071008 Hodder Place, September 1969	071803
							Compound thin plate weir, washed out in August 1967	071804
4.65 _(0.0348)_	1148 _78.1_	1032.27	24. 3.68	1.50	17. 6.70		River section. Subject to tidal influence by some spring tides. Broad crested weir at 072004 Caton, improved during 1967/68 provides accurate measurement of low and medium flows	072001
6.32 _(0.0229)_		165.58	11.12.64	0.05	27 2.68	P G	River section, supplemented by the construction of a flat V weir in 1969 (SD 463411); subject to tidal influence at Spring tides	072002
							Compound broad crested weir (Bazin profile)	072003
		364.24	1.11.68	2.34	12. 8.68		Compound broad crested weir (Bazin profile). See also 072001 Halton	072004
							Compound broad crested weir (Bazin profile)	072005
							River section	072006
2.06 _(0.0186)_		94.33	18.10.71	0.19	20. 6.70	P G	River section in which a flat V weir, 1 : 2, 1 : 2, and 1 : 20 slopes was installed in September 1969	072008
							Flat V triangular profile weir	072009
							River section	072010
							River section	072011
							River section	072012
							River section	072014
							River section with modified mill weir as control. Correlated with Halton 072001 d/s and Caton 072004 u/s	072803
							River section	072804
							Original broad crested weir breached in 1945. Records resumed in May 1957 at rebuilt curved (plan) weir	072807
							Old weir rated by current meter	072809
							Critical depth flume	072812
4.04 _(0.0583)_		119.54	9.10.67	0.11	7.10.72		River section with weir as low flow control. Low flow values suspect; see 073010. 1¼ km below outlet from Windermere: see 073012 Far Sawrey for lake levels	073001

Station number	River	Station name	National grid reference	Catch-ment area	Records start	Data archived	Measuring authority	Level of station	Highest point in the catch-ment	Annual average areal rainfall; mm	
										Standard average for 1916-1950	Period of record average to 31.12.7
				km²				m.O.D.	m.O.D.		

NORTH WEST WATER AUTHORITY AREA–(CONTD)

Station number	River	Station name	National grid reference	Catch-ment area	Records start	Data archived	Measuring authority	Level of station	Highest point in the catch-ment	Standard average for 1916-1950	Period of record average to 31.12.7
073002	Crake	Low Nibthwaite	SD 294882	73.0	1963	*	NWWARD	38.6	803	2247	
073004	Coniston Water	Brown How	SD 291908	63.7	1966		NWWARD	43.59			
073005	Kent	Sedgwick	SD 508874	208	1968	*	NWWARD			1925	
073006	Cunsey Beck	Eel House Bridge	SD 370940	18.9	1968		NWWARD	63.40			
073007	Troutbeck	Troutbeck Bridge	NY 404006	23.6	1967		NWWARD	60.90			
073008	Bela	Beetham	SD 496806	137	1969	*	NWWARD	15.0	338	1350	
073009	Sprint	Sprint Mill	SD 515960	33.9	1970		NWWARD	57.48		2283	
073010	Leven	Newby Bridge	SD 366863	249	1970	*	NWWARD	37.28			
073011	Mint	Mint Bridge	SD 524944	65.8	1970		NWWARD	50.29		1875	
073012	Windermere	Far Sawrey	SD 391957		1964		NWWARD	38.71			
073013	Rothay	Miller Bridge House	NY 371042	63.3	1965		NWWARD	40.84		2529	
073014	Brathay	Jeffy Knotts	NY 360034	57.4	1970		NWWARD	41.90			
073015	Keer	High Keer Bridge	SD 522719	41.2	1970		NWWARD	7.69		1197	
073803	Winster	Lobby Bridge	SD 424885	20.7	1965		NWWARD	5.49			
073805	Kent	Kendal	SD 516919	183	1963		NWWARD			1988	
074001	Duddon	Duddon Hall	SD 195895	78.2	1968	*	NWWARD	18.0	833	2187	
074002	Irt	Galesyke	NY 136038	48.0	1967	*	NWWARD	54.2	978	2994	
074003	Ehen	Ennerdale	NY 084154	44.2	1973	*	NWWARD	110.0	899	2784	
074006	Calder	Calder Hall	NY 035045	44.8	1973	*	NWWARD	26.44	667	1751	
074802	Wast Water	Low Wood	NY 145040		1970		NWWARD	60.44	978		
075001	St John's Beck	Thirlmere Reservoir	NY 309191	40.9	1935	*	NWWAED	179	950	2710	2732
075002	Derwent	Camerton	NY 037305	663	1961	*	NWWARD	16.8	950	1821	1771
075003	Derwent	Ouse Bridge	NY 198321	360	1968	*	NWWARD	67.9	950	2176	2096
075004	Cocker	Southwaite Bridge	NY 131281	117	1967	*	NWWARD	59.7	838	2094	1860
075005	Derwent	Portinscale	NY 252239	235	1971	*	NWWARD	72.56	950	2340	
075006	Newlands Beck	Braithwaite	NY 240239	33.9	1968	*	NWWARD	74.9	754	2456	2181
075007	Glenderamackin	Threlkeld	NY 323248	64.5	1969	*	NWWARD	136	868	1750	1602
075008	Bassenthwaite	Peil Wyke	NY 205308		1970		NWWARD	67.67	950		
075009	Greta	Low Briery	NY 285242	146	1971	*	NWWARD	99.69	950	2059	
075010	Marron	Ullock	NY 074237	27.7	1972	*	NWWARD	93.74	572	1490	1154
075011	Derwent Water	Fawe Park	NY 254228		1972		NWWARD		910		
075012	St John's Beck	Bridgend (High Farm)	NY 313195	41.0	1973	*	NWWARD	159.52	950		
075015	Crummock Water	Crummock Water	NY 151201		1973		NWWARD		838		

Mean gauged discharge m³/s	Mean annual natural runoff mm	Highest instantaneous gauged discharge m³/s	Date	Lowest daily mean gauged discharge m³/s	Date	Abstractions and returns	Station details	Station number
3.87	*0.0530*	30.01	9.10.67	0.00	18. 9.68		River section with weir for control at low flows. 2 km below Coniston Water. See 073004 Brown How for lake levels	073002
							Lake level recorder. See 073002 Low Nibthwaite for outflow	073004
7.61	*0.0366*	156.55	17. 9.70	0.71	7.10.72		Compound broad crested weir 27 m overall, having low crest 3 m long. River section for high flows	073005
							River section	073006
							River section	073007
2.89	*0.0211*	46.13	22. 4.70	0.36	17. 7.71		Crump profile, 1 : 20, flat V weir with river section for high flows	073008
							Flat V weir, Crump profile	073009
		64.74	13.12.72	0.11	7.10.72		Compound Crump weir complements the original station 073001	073010
							Flat V weir, Crump profile	073011
							Lake level recorder. For outflow from lake see 073001 Newby Bridge	073012
							River section	073013
							River section	073014
							Crump profile, flat V weir	073015
							River section	073803
							River section. Stage recorder at Nether Bridge; discharge measurements at Victoria Bridge, 1.3 km u/s	073805
3.97	*0.0508*	124.24	18. 1.72	0.31	17. 6.68		Compound broad crested weir 22.9 m overall, having low flow crest 7 m long	074001
2.86	*0.0596*	39.29	3.10.68	0.24	21. 6.70	I	River section, with gabion control from September 1968	074002
		22.86	15. 8.73	0.28	31. 8.73		Compound Crump weir. Measures outflow from Lake Ennerdale	074003
							Flat V, Crump profile weir: cross slope 1 : 20	074006
							Lake level recorder	074802
0.99	*0.0242*	43.13	9.12.64	0.16		S	Compensation water measured at rectangular thin plate weir below the dam. Overflows measured over 29 m long sill of dam	075001
3.84	*0.0359*	283.17	9.10.67	1.79	21. 6.70	S P	River section	075002
3.40	*0.0372*	95.08	24. 3.68	1.19	7.10.72	S	River section below Bassenthwaite Lake. Insensitive in the low flow range	075003
4.54	*0.0388*	68.40	1.10.68	0.32	2. 7.73	P	River section	075004
3.90	*0.0379*	90.25	1.12.72	0.87	7.10.72		River section	075005
.47	*0.0434*	51.05	29.11.72	0.00	9. 6.70		River section. The station is affected by water loss through the gravel bed upstream of the station	075006
2.12	*0.0329*	78.65	11.12.72	0.15	10. 6.70		River section with control stabilised by gabions	075007
							Lake level recorder	075008
.61	*0.0247*	86.70	11.12.72	0.48	7.10.72		River section	075009
.57	*0.0206*	18.17	3. 4.73	0.08	7.10.72		Flat V, Crump profile weir	075010
							Lake level recorder	075011
							Compound Crump weir, complements Thirlmere Reservoir station 075001	075012
							Lake level recorder	075015

Station number	River	Station name	National grid reference	Catchment area	Records start	Data archived	Measuring authority	Level of station	Highest point in the catchment	Annual average areal rainfall; mm	
										Standard average for 1916-1950	Period of record average to 31.12.?
				km²				m.O.D.	m.O.D.		

NORTH WEST WATER AUTHORITY AREA–(CONTD)

Station number	River	Station name	National grid reference	Catchment area	Records start	Data archived	Measuring authority	Level of station	Highest point	Standard average 1916-1950	Period of record
076001	Haweswater Beck	Thornthwaite	NY 515161	33.9	1951	*	NWWAED	189	830	2497	2471
076002	Eden	Warwick Bridge	NY 471567	1370	1959	*	NWWARD	17.8	950	1369	1379
076003	Eamont	Udford	NY 575305	396	1961	*	NWWARD	90.8	950	1882	1889
076004	Lowther	Eamont Bridge	NY 525285	159	1962	*	NWWARD	113	828	1890	1698
076005	Eden	Temple Sowerby	NY 604283	616	1964	*	NWWARD	92.4	950	1219	1120
076007	Eden	Sheepmount	NY 390571	2290	1967	*	NWWARD	7.00	950	1232	1117
076008	Irthing	Greenholme	NY 487583	335	1967	*	NWWARD	18.4	622	1049	847
076009	Caldew	Holm Hill	NY 378468	147	1968	*	NWWARD	60.1	931	922	1117
076010	Petteril	Harraby Green	NY 412545	156	1969	*	NWWARD	20.1	366	1338	829
076011	Coal Burn	Coalburn	NY 693777	1.5	1967		IH				
076912	Irthing	Gilsland	NY 629663	115	1968		NWA	120	518		
076014	Eden	Kirkby Stephen	NY 773097	69.4	1971	*	NWWARD	158.1	710	1439	1381
076015	Eamont	Pooley Bridge	NY 471248	144	1970	*	NWWARD	145	950	2302	
077001	Esk	Netherby	NY 390718	842	1963	*	NWWARD	14.5	692	1502	1449

SOLWAY RIVER PURIFICATION BOARD AREA

Station number	River	Station name	National grid reference	Catchment area	Records start	Data archived	Measuring authority	Level of station	Highest point	Standard average 1916-1950	Period of record
077002	Esk	Canonbie	NY 397751	495	1963 (1962)	*	SRPB	22.6	692	1550	1730
077003	Liddell	Rowanburnfoot	NY 415759	319	1973	*	SRPB	27.00	608	1419	
078301	Annan	St Mungo's Manse	NY 125755	730	1958	*	SRPB	34.0	821	1478	1486
078302	Water of Ae	Elshieshields	NY 068852	143	1963 (1961)	*	SRPB	54.5	697	1494	1315
078003	Annan	Brydekirk	NY 191704	925	1967	*	SRPB	10.0	821	1432	
078004	Kinnel Water	Redhall	NY 077868	76.1	1966 (1963)	*	SRPB	53.7	666	1510	1265
079001	Afton Water	Afton Reservoir	NS 631050	8.5	1950		SRCWD	386	680	2334	
079002	Nith	Friar's Carse	NX 923851	799	1957	*	SRPB	19.8	725	1598	1468
079003	Nith	Hall Bridge	NS 684129	155	1959	*	SRPB	173	680	1692	1621
079004	Scar Water	Capenoch	NX 845940	142	1963	*	SRPB	48.4	580	1700	1519
079005	Cluden Water	Fiddlers Ford	NX 928795	238	1963	*	SRPB	22.9	598	1407	1275
079006	Nith	Drumlanrig	NX 858994	471	1967	*	SRPB	52.2	725	1613	
080001	Urr	Dalbeattie	NX 822610	199	1964 (1963)	*	SRPB	4.01	432	1321	
080801	Pullaugh Burn	Diversion Works	NX 544742	18.2	1961		SSEB				
081001	Penwhirn Burn	Penwhirn Reservoir	NX 128694	18.2	1956 (1955)		DGRWD	151	269	1567	1618
081002	Cree	Newton Stewart	NX 412653	368	1963	*	SRPB	4.82	843	1715	1456
081003	Water of Luce	Airyhemming	NX 180599	171	1968	*	SRPB	19.0	438	1433	

...ean ...ged ...charge ...³/s	Mean annual natural runoff mm	Highest instantaneous gauged discharge m³/s	Date	Lowest daily mean gauged discharge m³/s	Date	Abstractions and returns	Station details	Station number
).79 *0.0233*	2062 *83.4*	25.29	25.12.60	0.11	13. 1.57	S	Compound thin plate weir 21 m long overall, in four stages: 1 km below reservoir	076001
1.02 *0.0226*		955.20	9.11.72	4.73	8.10.72	S P	River section. Weed growth influences calibration during summer months	076002
4.28 *0.0361*		299.88	23. 3.68	1.22	26.10.72	S	River section. Weed growth influences calibration in summer months	076003
3.81 *0.0239*		232.20	23. 3.68	0.00	27. 2.67	S	River section	076004
2.55 *0.0204*		346.32	23. 3.68	0.97	25. 9.72		River section. Weed growth influences calibration in summer months	076005
3.88 *0.0192*		1356.96	24. 3.68	6.96	8.10.72	S P	River section	076007
5.66 *0.0169*		222.70	23. 3.68	0.74	18. 7.71	P	River section. Control is gravel shoal which moves periodically	076008
3.50 *0.0238*		84.23	11.12.72	0.56	21. 6.70		River section	076009
1.43 *0.0092*		25.50	12.12.72	0.23	2. 7.73		River section with thin plate rectangular weir control	076010
							Compound Crump weir. Experimental catchment	076011
							River section. Abandoned 1970	076912
2.12 *0.0305*		132.80	9.11.72	0.12	6.10.72		River section with low flow broad crest control	076014
5.96 *0.0483*		49.41	24.11.70	0.52	6.10.72	P	Compound Crump weir with crest tapping, 29.3 m overall, having low crest 9.1 m long	076015
2.78 *0.0271*		1544.87	9.10.67	2.32	30. 9.72		River section. Affected by gravel abstraction downstream with consequent changes in calibration	077001
5.58 *0.0315*		562.70	9.10.67	1.51	7.10.72	S P	River section	077002
9.00		89.73	10.12.73	0.98	7.10.73		River section	077003
2.30 *0.0305*		283.17	1.12.60	1.93	9. 9.59		River section – affected by weed growth, water level only from 1961	078301
4.16 *0.0291*		130.26	18. 6.65	0.54	10.11.64		River section – unstable control, water level only from 1965	078302
2.37 *0.0242*		477.50	9.10.67	2.63	11. 8.68		River section	078003
2.20 *0.0289*		84.62	9.10.67	0.04	7.10.72		River section	078004
4.24 *0.0282*		8.69	15.12.66	0.01	1.12.65	S	Thin plate compound weir	079001
.47 *0.0361*	1010 *68.8*	1274.27	16. 1.62	1.46	2. 3.63	S P	River section	079002
.86 *0.034*	1089 *67.2*	212.38	15. 1.62	0.21	7.10.72	S P	River section	079003
.81 *0.0339*		192.40	13. 8.66	0.17	7.10.72		River section	079004
.90 *0.0289*		205.20	21. 1.69	0.27	6.10.72	S P	River section	079005
3.05 *0.0277*		378.49	11.12.72	0.95	7.10.72	S P	River section	079006
.96 *0.0249*		113.38	19. 1.72	0.14	21. 6.70		River section	080001
							Weir with flume on diversion channel: both theoretically rated. Flow regulated by Loch Grennoch	080801
.57 *0.0313*		18.43	3. 7.68	0.03	5. 4.66	S	Compound V notch and rectangular weir	081001
.07 *0.0382*		263.80	9.10.67	0.52	5.10.72		River section	081002
.07 *0.0296*		197.58	3. 4.73	0.17	28. 6.73	S P	River section	081003

Station number	River	Station name	National grid reference	Catchment area	Records start	Data archived	Measuring authority	Level of station	Highest point in the catchment	Annual average areal rainfall; mm	
										Standard average for 1916-1950	Period of record average to 31.12.
				km²				m.O.D.	m.O.D.		

CLYDE RIVER PURIFICATION BOARD AREA

Station number	River	Station name	National grid reference	Catchment area	Records start	Data archived	Measuring authority	Level of station	Highest point in the catchment	Standard average for 1916-1950	Period of record average to 31.12.
082001	Girvan Water	Robstone	NX 217997	246	1963	*	CRPB	9.14	659	1435	1286
082002	Doon	Auchendrane	NS 338160	324	1974	*	CRPB	22.2	844	1554	
082003	Stincher	Balnowlart	NX 108832	341	1973	*	CRPB	3.0	565	1456	
083001	Caaf Water	Knockendon Reservoir	NS 245514	6.0	1950 (1949)		SRCWD	208	387	1643	
083002	Garnock	Dalry	NS 293488	88.8	1963	*	CRPB	19.1	522	1742	
083003	Ayr	Catrine	NS 525258	166	1970	*	CRPB	86.9	548	1365	
083004	Lugar Water	Langholm	NS 508217	181	1972	*	CRPB	84.2	548	1351	
083005	Irvine	Shewalton	NS 345369	381	1972	*	CRPB	4.8	384	1237	
083802	Irvine	Kilmarnock	NS 430369	218	1913		GKL			1254	
084001	Kelvin	Killermont	NS 558705	335	1952 (1948)	*	CRPB	27.7	578	1245	1171
084002	Calder	Muirshiel	NS 309638	12.4	1952	*	SRCWD	229	486	2329	2346
084003	Clyde	Hazelbank	NS 835452	1090	1956	*	CRPB	51.8	732	1262	1144
084004	Clyde	Sills	NS 927424	705	1957 (1955)	*	CRPB	183	732	1339	1206
084005	Clyde	Blairston	NS 704579	1700	1958 (1955)	*	CRPB	17.7	732	1222	1109
084006	Kelvin	Bridgend	NS 672749	63.7	1963 (1956)	*	CRPB	34.6	578	1331	1235
084007	South Calder Water	Forgewood	NS 751585	93.0	1967	*	CRPB	43.8	312	978	
084008	Rotten Calder Water	Redlees	NS 679604	51.3	1967 (1966)	*	CRPB	16.5	344	1175	
084009	Nethan	Kirkmuirhill	NS 809429	66.0	1967 (1966)	*	CRPB	103	522	1296	
084011	Gryfe	Craigend	NS 415664	71.0	1963	*	CRPB	10.2	453	1729	1638
084012	White Cart Water	Hawkhead	NS 499629	235	1952 (1948)	*	CRPB	4.6	375	1264	1192
084013	Clyde	Daldowie	NS 672616	1900	1967 (1963)	*	CRPB	7.5	732	1204	
084014	Avon Water	Fairholm	NS 755518	266	1964	*	CRPB	53.0	475	1295	1179
084015	Kelvin	Dryfield	NS 638739	235	1965 (1960)	*	CRPB	31.4	578	1261	1166
084016	Luggie Water	Condorrat	NS 739725	33.9	1967 (1962)	*	CRPB	67.9	107	1086	
084017	Black Cart Water	Milliken Park	NS 411620	103	1967	*	CRPB	24.8	509	1711	
084018	Clyde	Tulliford Mill	NS 893405	933	1969 (1968)	*	CRPB	183	732	1317	
084019	North Calder Water	Calderpark	NS 681625	130	1968 (1962)	*	CRPB	12.5	285	1011	
084020	Glazert Water	Milton of Campsie	NS 656763	51.9	1968	*	CRPB	38.7	578	1551	
084921	White Cart Water	Netherlee	NS 587597	91.6	1967	*	CRPB	57.9	375	1307	
084022	Duneaton	Maidencots	NS 929259	110	1965	*	CRPB	228.3	593	1471	
084023	Bothlin Burn	Auchengeich	NS 689716	19.9	1972	*	CRPB	56.7	220	1011	
084024	North Calder Water	Hillend	NS 828678	35.7	1972	*	CRPB	167.0	301	1099	
084025	Luggie Water	Oxgang	NS 665734	69.6	1973		CRPB	47.0	220	1037	
084026	Allander Water	Milngavie	NS 558738	32.8	1972		CRPB	39.9	401		
084027	North Calder Water	Calderbank	NS 765625	60.6	1968	*	CRPB	99.0	301	1066	
084806	Clyde	Cambusnethan	NS 786522	1260	1955		SDD		748	1126	
085001	Leven	Linnbrane	NS 394803	784	1963	*	CRPB	4.3	1130	2168	1956
085002	Endrick Water	Gaidrew	NS 485866	220	1964 (1963)	*	CRPB	8.4	578	1478	

Mean gauged discharge /s	Mean annual natural runoff mm	Highest instantaneous gauged discharge m³/s	Date	Lowest daily mean gauged discharge m³/s	Date	Abstractions and returns	Station details	Station number
.91 *63.7*	819	101.60	9.10.67	0.28	9. 9.69		River section	082001
0.024						H E P	River section	082002
.28		165.84	3. 4.73	0.32	28. 6.73		River section	082003
0.0243								
						S	Thin plate compound weir	083001
85 *0.0321*		69.65	2.11.69	0.08	14. 6.69		River section with artificial control	083002
38 *0.0204*		177.04	1.10.70	0.24	17. 7.71		River section – weir control	083003
79 *0.0209*		124.54	11.12.72	0.14	28. 6.73		River section	083004
48		164.28	12.11.73	0.00	22. 7.72		River section	083005
0.0170							Broad crested skewed masonry weir; rated theoretically and checked by current meter	083802
04 *0.024*		176.98	18.10.54	0.74	4. 5.62	E	River section	084001
71 *0.0523*		15.80	13. 1.61	0.00	13. 6.69	P	Compound thin plate weir. Limit of measurement 15.8 m³/s	084002
81 *0.0218* 692 *60.4*		470.06	16. 1.62	2.20	11.10.59		River section	084003
56 821 *68.1*		410.40	14. 8.66	1.61	11.10.59		River section	084004
0.0235								
40 698 *62.9*		577.30	14. 8.66	4.50	11.10.59		River section	084005
0.022								
52		20.63	18.12.66	0.16	12. 7.69	E	River section	084006
0.0239								
68 429		39.67	31.10.70	0.59	23. 9.73	E	Compound Crump weir	084007
0.0181								
10 627		42.84	31.10.70	0.07	11. 8.68	E	Compound Crump weir	084008
0.0214								
31		58.22	31.10.70	0.08	19.12.67	E	Compound Crump weir	084009
0.0198								
16 *0.0451* 1351 *82.5*		160.86	28. 4.70	0.10	27. 3.73	E	River section – weir control	084011
76 771 *64.7*		187.10	18.12.66	0.71	5. 8.64	E	River section	084012
0.0245								
90 430		486.04	9.10.67	7.76	20.10.72	E	River section	084013
0.0194								
63 *0.0243* 807 *68.4*		585.20	13. 8.66	0.19	21. 7.71		River section	084014
43		66.22	18.12.66	0.56	18. 9.72	E	River section	084015
0.0231								
57		23.76	2.11.69	0.09	22. 7.71	E	River section-artificial control	084016
0.0198								
47 1323		55.46	2.11.69	0.18	30. 9.72	E	River section – artificial control	084017
0.0337								
18		236.48	22. 2.70	2.26	16.10.72		River section	084018
0.0206								
55 297		42.65	31.10.70	0.14	23. 9.73	E	River section	084019
0.0119								
50		35.87	2.11.69	0.00	5.11.71	E	River section – artificial control	084020
0.0289								
79		76.39	31.10.70	0.00	1. 1.72		Abandoned 1974	084921
0.0632								
		36.43	15.12.73	0.62	1.10.73		River section	084022
		6.24	15.12.73	0.18	6.10.73	E	Crump weir	084023
		0.14	31.12.73	0.10	31.10.73	R	Flat V Crump profile weir. (1 : 10)	084024
						E	River section – artificial control	084025
							River section – artificial control	084026
		3.62	19.12.73	0.16	3.11.73	E	River section with critical depth flume by-pass	084027
							Abandoned 1964	084806
75 1597 *81.6*		123.12	19.12.66	7.26	17. 4.73		River section. Regulating weir for Loch Lomond outflow completed 1971	085001
0.0507								
84 871		129.09	13. 1.69	0.28	20. 6.70		River section	085002
0.0265								

Station number	River	Station name	National grid reference	Catch-ment area	Records start	Data archived	Measuring authority	Level of station	Highest point in the catch-ment	Annual average areal rainfall; mm	
										Standard average for 1916-1950†	Period of record average to 31.12.
				km²				m.O.D.	m.O.D.		

CLYDE RIVER PURIFICATION BOARD AREA–(CONTD)

085003	Falloch	Glen Falloch	NN 321197	80.3	1970	*	CRPB	9.5	1130	3030	
086001	Little Eachaig	Dalinlongart	NS 143821	30.8	1969	*	CRPB	10.6	611	2266	
086002	Eachaig	Eckford	NS 140843	140	1969	*	CRPB	5.7	742	2436	
087801	Allt Uaine	Intake	NN 263113	3.1	1950		NSHEB	331.3	884	3454	

ISLE OF MAN WATER AND GAS AUTHORITY AREA

103801	Glass	West Baldwin Reservoir	SC 361834	6.9	1959		IoM W&G				

DEPARTMENT OF THE ENVIRONMENT FOR NORTHERN IRELAND

201001	Owenkillew	Killymore Bridge	H 438872	431	1971		DOE (NI)	46	680	1308	1147
201002	Fairy Water	Dudgeon Bridge	H 406758	161	1971		DOE (NI)	61	420	1350	
201303	Derg	Glashagh Bridge	H 226825	169	1972		DOE (NI)	52	643	1917	
201304	Strule	Stone Bridge	H 437775	818	1972		DOE (NI)	56	539	1150	
201005	Camowen	Camowen Terrace	H 460730	275	1972		DOE (NI)	66	539	1050	1008
201006	Drumragh	Campsie Bridge	H 458722	325	1972		DOE (NI)	63	341	1095	1070
203301	Lower Bann	Loughan Island	C 876287	5640	1937		DOE (NI)		667	1028	998
203302	Lower Bann	Agivey Bann Bridge	C 909229	5450	1937		DOE (NI)		667	1050	998
203303	Blackwater	Battleford Bridge	H 786526	944	1944		DOE (NI)	28	362	980	
203004	Lower Bann	Movanagher Weir	C 926160	5210	1946		DOE (NI)	9	667	1024	
203305	Lower Bann	Newferry	H 991983	4920	1948		DOE (NI)	11	667	1028	998
203306	Braid	Ballymena	D 108029	154	1951		DOE (NI)	40	439	1207	990
203307	Blackwater	Caledon Bridge	H 758447	727	1951		DOE (NI)	31	362	1023	967
203308	Lower Bann	Portna	C 938123	5180	1951		DOE (NI)	10	667	1028	998
203309	Blackwater	Verners Bridge	H 883612	1110	1969		DOE (NI)	15	362	965	901
203010	Blackwater	Maydown Bridge	H 820519	951	1970		DOE (NI)	15	362	990	889
203011	Main	Dromona	D 052086	229	1970		DOE (NI)	71	401	1390	1232
203012	Ballinderry	Ballinderry Bridge	H 926799	420	1970		DOE (NI)	16	476	1110	94
203013	Main	Andraid	J 092973	647	1970		DOE (NI)	30	540	1238	1055
203614	Lough Neagh	Derryadd Bay	J 036613		1970		DOE (NI)	12			
203315	Lower Bann	Toome (Lower Bann)	H 987 903	4840	1970		DOE (NI)	11	667	1028	998
203616	Lough Neagh	Toome (Lough Neagh)	H 988900		1970		DOE (NI)	12			
203017	Upper Bann	Dynes Bridge	J 043509	336	1970	*	DOE (NI)	13	667	1106	101
203018	Six Mile Water	Antrim	J 146867	277	1970		DOE (NI)	13	477	1080	93
203019	Claudy	Glenone Bridge	C 962037	130	1970		DOE (NI)	14	461	1156	107
203020	Moyola	Moyola New Bridge	H 955905	307	1971		DOE (NI)	16	554	1261	112
203021	Kells Water	Currys Bridge	J 106971	127	1971		DOE (NI)	35	438	1197	105
203922	Blackwater	Derrymeen Bridge	H 625530	176	1971		DOE (NI)	46	362	1010	
203023	Torrent	The Moor Bridge	H 858649	59.8	1971		DOE (NI)	15	286	1050	86
203024	Cusher	Gamble's Bridge	J 048471	177	1971		DOE (NI)	15	354	996	90
203025	Callan	Callan New Bridge	H 893524	164	1971		DOE (NI)	16	364	936	83
203026	Glenavy	Glenavy	J 149725	44.6	1971		DOE (NI)	55	328	1007	92
203027	Braid	Ballee	D 097014	177	1972		DOE (NI)	35	439	1197	99
203028	Agivey	White Hill	C 883193	98.9	1972		DOE (NI)	18	461	1106	100
203329	Six Mile Water	Ballyclare	J 282902	58.4	1973		DOE (NI)	59	477	1150	98
203330	Six Mile Water	Dunadry	J 205853	208	1973		DOE (NI)	41	477	1125	97

† Standard Average for Northern Ireland is 1931-1960.

an aged charge /s	Mean annual natural runoff mm	Highest instan- taneous gauged discharge m³/s	Date	Lowest daily mean gauged discharge m³/s	Date	Abstrac- tions and returns	Station details	Station number
.79	0.0597	266.68	22.10.71	0.16	6.10.72		River section. Artificial control from 1975	085003
.45	0.0471	87.13	6. 5.72	0.04	21. 7.71		River section – artificial control	086001
.86		90.98	2.11.69	0.94	22. 7.71		River section	086002
	0.0633							
							Weir with flume on diversion channel; both theoretically rated	087801
						S	Curved thin plate overflow weir. Reservoir	103801
							River section: unstable bed	201001
							River section	201002
							Level recording only	201303
						P E	Level recording only	201304
						P	River section with cableway	201005
							River section with cableway	201006
						R	Level recording only	203301
						R	Level recording only	203302
							Level recording only	203303
						R	Calibration of existing weir	203004
						R	Level recording only	203305
						S P E	Level recording only. Concrete lined channel	203306
							Level recording only	203307
						R	Level recording only	203308
						S	Level recording only	203309
							River section	203010
						S G	River section	203011
						S	River section	203012
						S P G E I	River section. Unstable bed	203013
							Level recording of Lough only	203614
						R	Level recording only	203315
							Level recording of Lough only	203616
.74		1397.14	20. 1.73	0.36	11. 7.73	S P E I	River section	203017
	0.0289					E I	River section	203018
							River section	203019
						S	River section	203020
						S P	River section with cableway	203021
							River section. Closed 1971	203922
						S G E I	River section	203023
							River section	203024
						S P E I	River section	203025
							River section; thin plate weir control	203026
						S P E I	River section with cableway	203027
							River section with cableway	203028
							Level recording only	203329
							Level recording only	203330

Station number	River	Station name	National grid reference	Catch-ment area km²	Records start	Data archived	Measuring authority	Level of station m.O.D.	Highest point in the catch-ment m.O.D.	Annual average areal rainfall; mm	
										Standard average for 1931-1960	Period of record average to 31.12.

DEPARTMENT OF THE ENVIRONMENT FOR NORTHERN IRELAND–(CONTD)

Station number	River	Station name	National grid reference	Catch-ment area	Records start	Data archived	Measuring authority	Level of station	Highest point in the catch-ment	Standard average for 1931-1960	Period of record average to 31.12.
204001	Bush	Seneirl	C 942362	306	1972		DOE (NI)	25	540	1220	1103
205301	Quoile	Quoile Barrier Lower	J 505495	275	1948		DOE (NI)	−3	533	990	968
205302	Quoile	Quoile Barrier Upper	J 505495	275	1948		DOE (NI)	−2	533	990	968
205003	Lagan	Dunmurry Lane	J 299679	445	1969	*	DOE (NI)	9	532	969	897
205004	Lagan	Newforge	J 329693	490	1972		DOE (NI)	2	532	969	897
205005	Ravernet	Ravernet	J 267613	69.5	1972		DOE (NI)	31	163	922	860
205306	Lagan	Blaris	J 259628	316	1972		DOE (NI)	26	532	969	897
205907	Blackwater (Ards)	Florida Bridge	J 470610	34.4	1973		DOE (NI)	43	168	850	
206001	Clanrye	Mount Mill Bridge	J 086309	133	1971		DOE (NI)	16	329	985	903
206002	Jerretspass	Jerretspass (River)	J 064332	32.4	1971		DOE (NI)	11	182	985	899
206003	Newry Canal	Jerretspass (Canal)	J 064332	56.7	1971		DOE (NI)	12	194	985	899
236301	Lower Erne	Rosscor	G 998578	4210	1957		DOE (NI)	42	664	1121	1139
236302	Lower Erne	Portora	H 223453	3510	1957		DOE (NI)	42	664	1096	1121
236303	Upper Erne	Belle Isle	H 283345	2790	1957		DOE (NI)	42	587	1035	1059
236604	Arney	Lough Macnean Lower	H 131375	477	1970		DOE (NI)	52	457	1101	

ean uged scharge	Mean annual natural runoff	Highest instan- taneous gauged discharge	Date	Lowest daily mean gauged discharge	Date	Abstrac- tions and returns	Station details	Station number
³/s	mm	m³/s		m³/s				
						S P E I	River section	204001
							Tidal level recorder	205301
						R P E	Level recording only	205302
5.09 *0.0137*		73.24	25. 4.71	0.47	21.10.72	P G E I	River section with cableway	205003
						P G E I	River section	205004
							River section	205005
						P G E I	Level recording only	205306
							Level recording only. Closed 1973	205907
							River section	206001
							River section	206002
							Canal section; thin plate weir control	206003
							Level recording only, Lower Lough Erne	236301
							Level recording only, Lower Lough Erne	236302
							Level recording only, Upper Lough Erne	236303
							Level recording only: effectively the level of the Lough	236604

ean uged scharge	Mean annual natural runoff	Highest instan- taneous gauged discharge	Date	Lowest daily mean gauged discharge	Date			
	mm	m³/s		m³/s				

5 Services offered by the Water Data Unit

5.1 The Processing System

The Water Data Unit surface water data processing system provides for the collection, processing and storage of river flow data. Much of the current data is collected in the form of 16 channel or 5 channel punched tapes of river level, a translator converting the 16 channel tapes into a computer compatible format. Daily mean discharges are computed from these records of levels using the appropriate stage-discharge relationship, and are then stored on magnetic tape with certain ancillary information. These flow data are available for further analysis and as basic data to meet requests for river flow information.

The derivation of stage-discharge relationships for most types of flow-measurement stations is undertaken by the Water Data Unit to provide calibrations for the processing system and as a service to other organisations. Velocity-area stations are rated using a standard regression program to establish the line, or lines, of best-fit through a series of gaugings. Flow-measurement structures are normally calibrated with reference to the relevant weir dimensions or by utilising the appropriate procedures recommended by the British Standards Institution.

5.2 Data Retrieval

Approximately 80 per cent of the United Kingdom's record of daily mean river flows have been archived by the Water Data Unit computer; this is a continuing task. A suite of programs has been written to provide a selection of retrieval options to meet user requirements. Clients are advised to give as much notice as possible of their data needs so that attempts can be made to fill any gaps in the archived flow record. Some retrieval options require complete annual flow records.

5.2.1 Retrieval Options

The options available within the present service are listed in Table 1 and examples are given on pages 99 to 104. Table 1 has been slightly revised from that in the previous edition of the Surface Water Year Book to accommodate additional options and to allow greater flexibility in the selection of suitable hydrograph retrievals.

The output may be obtained on the following media:

(a) Line printer listing paper

(b) Punched paper tape (ICL 1900 Series 8 track code)

(c) Magnetic tape (ICL 1900 Series, ½ inch, 9 track, 1600 c.p.i., or, ½ inch, 7 track, 556 c.p.i.)

and

(d) Hydrograph plots on a plain (p) or grid (g) base.

For each option the availability of the media (a) to (d) above is indicated by an asterisk in Table 1.

5.2.2 Cost of Service

To cover the cost of computing a moderate charge will be made depending on the output options selected and the length of the period for which records are required. Details of these charges may be obtained on request from the Water Data Unit.

5.2.3 Notes on Individual Retrievals

Option 2 enables an annual hydrograph of daily mean gauged or naturalized discharges to be plotted on either linear or logarithmic flow axes. A facility exists to truncate the hydrograph at a nominated flow and the hydrograph dimensions can be varied to meet user requirements.

Option 10 outputs 15 minute and hourly mean discharge values for specified periods and is normally only available for those gauging stations where the Water Data Unit has ready access to the appropriate punched tapes of river levels.

Option 11 provides discharge frequencies in the forms of a histogram and a discharge duration curve together with a tabulation of flows which are exceeded for a given percentage of the time. The former option 12 as described in the Surface Water Year Book 1966—70 has now been incorporated with this option.

The retrieval options 1—11 were primarily designed to provide information for water resources investigations where data are required for a small selection of river basins only. It is recognised that some data users would prefer flow information for many gauging stations in England, Scotland, Wales and Northern Ireland; options 12 and 13 have been designed to cater for this need.

Option 12 provides a concise summary, on line printer output, of the major flow parameters for each gauging station record held in the Water Data Unit archive.

Option 13 provides a magnetic tape containing the following discharge information, by months, for any specified flow measurement stations:

> Station Number
> River Name
> Station Name
> Catchment Area
> Daily Gauged Discharges
> Monthly Total Gauged Discharge
> if available { Daily Naturalized Discharges
> Monthly Total Naturalized Discharge
> Monthly Average (1916—50) Areal Rainfall
> Current Monthly Areal Rainfall

The magnetic tape will be formatted for ease of reading by most programming languages.

5.2.4 Data Requests

Requests for data should be submitted on pro-forma Table 2, a copy of which is enclosed in the wallet attached to the back cover, and addressed to:

> Department of the Environment
> Water Data Unit,
> Archive Section,
> 26—30 King's Road,
> Reading, Berkshire
> RG1 3AA

TABLE 1 COMPUTER RETRIEVAL OPTIONS

Outputs are annual unless otherwise stated
The availability of various output media is indicated by asterisks

Option No	Title	Media				Example on Page:
		(a)	(b)	(c)	(d)	
1	Table of daily mean gauged discharges in cumecs	*	*	*		99
2	Hydrograph of daily mean gauged or naturalized discharges in cumecs				*	99
3	Table of daily mean naturalized discharges in cumecs	*	*	*		100
4	Table of monthly mean gauged discharges in cumecs	*	*	*		100
5	Table of monthly mean naturalized discharges in cumecs	*	*	*		100
6	Table of monthly instantaneous peak discharges and highest and lowest daily mean gauged discharges in cumecs	*				100
7	Table of catchment monthly areal rainfall (mm)	*	*	*		101
8	Table of catchment monthly areal rainfall and naturalized runoff (mm)	*	*	*		101
9	Hydrographs of daily and monthly mean gauged or naturalized discharges with corresponding extremes from the period of record				*	101
10	Monthly table of 15 minute and hourly mean gauged discharges	*	*			102
11	Flow frequency and duration curves with tabulated duration data for one or more years	*				103
12	Concise summary of station gauged discharge data for period of record	*				104
13	Magnetic tape of monthly data for period of record			*		

Media:

(a) Line printer listing paper
(b) Punched paper tape
(c) Magnetic tape
(d) Plotted on plain (p) or grid (g) base

TABLE 2 REQUEST FORM FOR SURFACE WATER DATA FROM THE WATER DATA UNIT

NAME AND ADDRESS to whom data is to be sent

FLOW DATA is requested for the following stations

Station Number(s)	River	Station	Period of Record Required	Type of flow data for hydrograph options	
				Gauged	Natural

OPTION REQUIRED (selected from TABLE 1)

Option No / Media	1	2	3	4	5	6	7	8	9	10	11	12	13
(a)													
(b)													
(c)													
(d)													

Comments

Signed .... Date ....

1. Complete calendar years only should be requested except for option number 10 which has a monthly base. Missing values will be output as zeros.

2. If magnetic tape output is requested a blank tape must be sent with the request.

3. If options 12 or 13 are requested it is only necessary to specify the first and last gauging station in a sequence or the hydrometric areas for which you require complete data.

4. For any further guidance please contact the Water Data Unit, Archive Section.

OPTION NO. 1
TABLE OF DAILY MEAN GAUGED DISCHARGES IN CUMECS

```
                    WATER   DATA   UNIT   RETRIEVAL   LISTING

        39C01      RIVER THAMES              AT  TEDDINGTON                    GAUGED   FLOWS

   YEAR   1973
```

DAY	JAN	FEB	MAR	APR	MAY	JUN	JUL	AUG	SEP	OCT	NOV	DEC
1	46.204	51.785	30.545	10.536	29.430	18.505	19.336	12.214	9.026	10.988	8.810	8.295
2	45.967	50.175	32.691	24.149	25.921	18.221	17.905	11.546	9.189	10.404	8.826	9.068
3	45.057	39.855	33.575	32.644	32.880	15.338	11.483	9.910	9.189	10.567	8.179	8.905
4	44.305	36.020	33.548	27.242	64.782	11.940	10.557	9.910	9.147	8.306	9.273	8.916
5	41.181	40.981	35.089	26.226	67.886	9.857	14.360	12.298	9.147	9.105	13.971	9.137
6	40.681	39.797	37.772	19.167	73.125	8.032	18.489	25.585	8.095	13.723	12.345	9.216
7	42.659	38.182	37.467	17.568	83.592	9.358	25.890	38.435	8.826	17.521	10.394	11.640
8	41.538	37.725	37.725	17.074	78.684	11.814	24.822	31.265	8.453	8.621	11.561	15.380
9	40.491	38.850	34.716	17.000	52.837	10.683	22.297	22.865	8.474	8.810	10.509	11.009
10	39.545	31.455	22.660	17.000	52.553	11.030	15.938	14.770	8.116	7.906	9.805	11.467
11	36.189	28.630	23.938	18.252	25.211	13.224	8.895	11.788	8.411	8.621	10.699	9.736
12	21.992	66.334	29.430	17.626	24.427	10.778	9.152	12.229	8.284	9.468	13.681	10.341
13	26.842	67.312	33.506	18.442	26.910	9.889	8.895	11.851	8.663	8.284	10.815	10.331
14	29.919	83.592	33.322	16.422	26.773	8.137	7.422	8.179	11.072	9.673	9.831	10.993
15	64.845	60.306	28.867	15.401	27.725	8.558	44.515	8.432	9.652	9.173	10.083	7.322
16	84.902	55.877	22.823	14.912	26.179	8.810	56.834	7.822	9.726	11.535	10.362	8.369
17	63.709	45.483	21.882	12.556	22.676	9.294	45.099	9.631	10.425	10.425	6.586	8.569
18	54.888	37.888	19.714	8.895	18.189	9.826	20.461	9.536	10.231	8.221	8.100	8.742
19	46.877	39.192	24.869	10.457	19.778	23.633	46.693	9.021	9.589	8.663	9.910	8.590
20	46.514	40.355	25.984	9.831	23.980	80.972	31.292	9.500	21.519	10.246	9.410	12.435
21	70.952	40.449	21.745	13.155	23.523	43.185	24.291	9.210	51.227	10.715	9.126	41.743
22	96.516	39.708	19.231	33.932	20.588	18.278	56.534	8.747	19.935	11.051	9.473	27.399
23	50.507	36.226	18.158	49.202	25.911	12.187	39.913	7.780	9.757	10.362	9.826	65.455
24	54.189	27.347	12.024	63.362	37.393	7.890	23.954	9.073	10.962	9.494	8.079	72.604
25	59.959	26.389	12.787	25.611	22.644	9.358	17.610	9.194	10.136	8.663	8.395	48.071
26	54.999	34.080	23.849	31.676	19.835	11.209	15.470	8.684	11.525	8.200	9.889	38.719
27	56.424	31.923	24.096	25.595	19.367	17.758	14.007	11.567	11.593	8.495	8.274	31.834
28	53.110	31.644	21.019	19.593	15.554	83.429	13.708	14.281	11.104	9.373	9.231	29.835
29	52.416		17.632	23.333	16.890	87.353	11.004	10.473	8.621	9.168	11.714	18.852
30	50.275		10.452	25.295	20.698	50.943	12.393	7.054	7.780	8.895	12.424	23.486
31	50.259		7.196		19.751		11.882	9.626		9.110		32.849

```
  TOTAL   MONTHLY   FLOW:     CUMEC.DAYS

          1554.31  1200.21   788.31  660.37 1045.69  649.48  701.10  392.47  346.89  303.78  299.58  629.30
```

OPTION NO. 2
HYDROGRAPH OF DAILY MEAN GAUGED OR NATURALIZED
DISCHARGES IN CUMECS

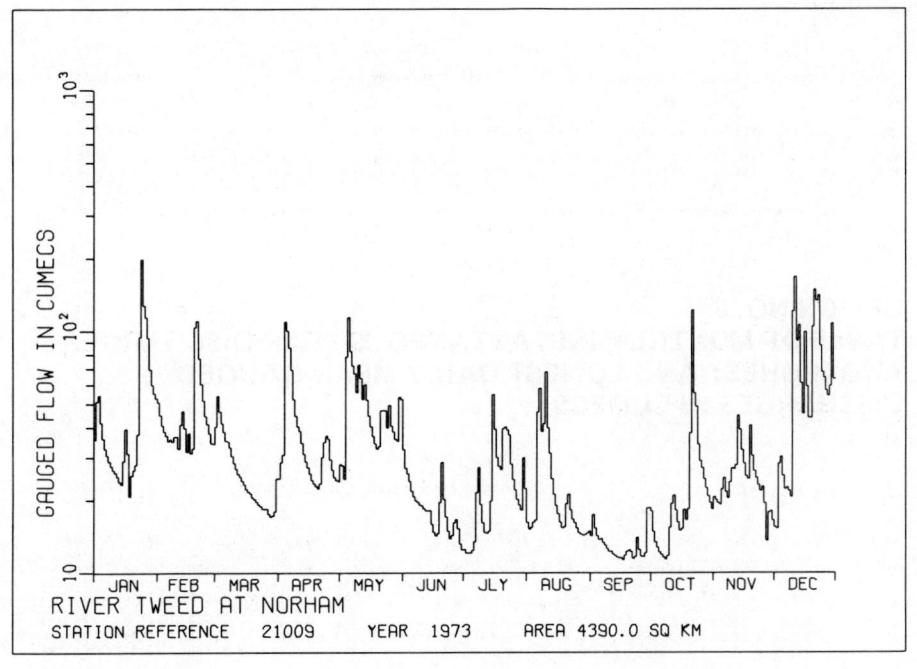

RIVER TWEED AT NORHAM

STATION REFERENCE 21009   YEAR 1973   AREA 4390.0 SQ KM

OPTION NO. 3
TABLE OF DAILY MEAN NATURALIZED DISCHARGES IN CUMECS

```
                    WATER   DATA   UNIT   RETRIEVAL   LISTING

        39001    RIVER  THAMES              AT  TEDDINGTON                 NATURAL   FLOWS
  YEAR   1973
```

DAY	JAN	FEB	MAR	APR	MAY	JUN	JUL	AUG	SEP	OCT	NOV	DEC
1	66.239	68.128	45.872	35.815	47.834	34.705	41.559	30.434	23.591	27.394	26.400	29.514
2	65.355	66.150	48.213	56.682	43.753	34.742	40.534	30.366	22.991	25.211	26.142	29.630
3	64.303	56.477	48.992	60.280	50.128	32.070	31.076	28.041	23.596	27.831	25.958	28.288
4	64.077	52.063	49.491	50.491	81.335	30.008	31.797	27.126	22.844	25.290	27.589	26.531
5	60.779	56.903	50.328	48.287	85.712	28.509	34.542	30.234	23.944	26.242	31.081	27.378
6	61.184	56.077	52.279	40.370	87.779	25.706	39.103	44.047	22.944	31.076	30.571	26.689
7	61.842	55.519	52.716	39.403	100.534	26.926	43.926	55.761	20.556	40.844	27.789	29.982
8	61.410	57.923	51.232	34.374	95.721	26.042	41.854	49.476	20.582	33.206	29.219	39.229
9	60.080	59.864	55.788	38.003	69.537	25.984	41.075	41.328	20.556	30.803	29.009	38.645
10	59.422	57.444	41.002	35.442	66.050	25.921	33.901	31.171	21.198	29.798	29.188	34.064
11	56.487	54.404	44.147	36.662	41.806	26.300	28.236	29.256	20.125	27.026	29.698	32.917
12	42.806	69.379	43.800	37.104	44.252	26.589	28.199	29.630	19.157	28.046	29.761	32.065
13	47.561	81.172	44.074	34.732	45.215	26.300	27.410	31.029	19.962	26.321	26.747	32.312
14	50.822	100.424	44.237	36.241	45.178	25.390	25.869	24.343	21.939	24.317	27.063	33.417
15	85.338	76.317	43.716	34.406	45.657	23.749	62.962	27.594	19.567	26.831	26.526	32.028
16	104.842	71.936	38.566	34.479	42.932	21.193	74.429	26.053	21.755	31.560	27.715	31.171
17	83.550	63.399	39.655	31.455	39.771	22.287	63.415	25.716	22.492	31.260	26.700	31.265
18	75.118	55.724	38.377	33.159	37.693	23.375	40.023	26.605	23.165	28.662	25.690	28.004
19	66.045	54.725	42.022	31.376	38.272	40.513	65.703	26.374	25.963	27.857	25.527	29.751
20	66.013	55.619	41.086	28.104	40.213	109.240	49.449	26.416	45.062	26.852	25.385	35.284
21	90.304	56.045	40.560	28.388	40.470	71.820	42.301	25.500	84.313	26.742	26.395	67.554
22	116.767	54.893	39.392	48.408	37.583	45.473	73.808	24.980	46.551	28.499	24.017	59.470
23	70.142	55.514	38.919	65.555	43.737	39.823	56.766	24.522	30.082	28.772	25.059	90.451
24	72.414	52.384	39.329	82.277	51.459	29.761	42.127	22.087	25.195	27.589	24.417	88.926
25	80.899	50.154	41.354	46.230	37.425	26.274	35.358	23.133	25.085	27.299	24.748	65.918
26	74.908	52.132	41.691	51.942	36.962	29.819	32.954	22.418	27.925	26.421	27.036	54.935
27	73.214	50.848	43.705	44.689	36.678	35.984	29.887	25.695	30.739	27.536	24.953	48.539
28	71.057	47.903	38.929	36.583	30.876	112.154	30.355	29.403	32.307	25.516	26.053	47.235
29	71.194		39.592	40.297	35.363	114.400	28.236	31.344	32.612	26.342	30.613	41.885
30	67.996		34.558	42.953	36.420	72.083	31.413	25.863	29.635	26.389	32.286	43.574
31	62.247		34.548		36.536		30.797	22.486		26.458		48.224

```
  TOTAL  MONTHLY  FLOW:   CUMEC.DAYS

        2154.81  1689.52  1348.17  1264.18  1572.88  1213.14  1279.06   918.43   826.43   873.99   819.33  1284.87

  * AN ASTERISK AT THE HEAD OF A COLUMN DENOTES GAUGED FLOWS SUBSTITUTED FOR NATURAL FLOWS IN THAT MONTH
```

OPTION NO. 4
TABLE OF MONTHLY MEAN GAUGED DISCHARGES IN CUMECS

```
                    WATER   DATA   UNIT   RETRIEVAL   LISTING

        39001    RIVER  THAMES              AT  TEDDINGTON               GAUGED   MEAN   FLOWS
```

YEAR	JAN	FEB	MAR	APR	MAY	JUN	JUL	AUG	SEP	OCT	NOV	DEC
1970	118.665	138.320	98.609	86.783	52.413	17.977	11.463	12.805	13.829	9.523	91.962	93.078
1971	158.144	136.065	106.868	81.938	53.982	124.077	37.339	36.199	16.213	34.253	54.456	52.776
1972	108.203	151.160	131.971	71.924	54.459	30.985	14.387	11.971	9.807	10.570	19.972	113.501
1973	50.139	42.865	25.429	22.012	33.732	21.650	22.616	12.661	11.563	9.800	9.986	20.300

OPTION NO. 5
TABLE OF MONTHLY MEAN NATURALIZED DISCHARGES IN CUMECS

```
                    WATER   DATA   UNIT   RETRIEVAL   LISTING

        39001    RIVER  THAMES              AT  TEDDINGTON               NATURAL   MEAN   FLOWS
```

YEAR	JAN	FEB	MAR	APR	MAY	JUN	JUL	AUG	SEP	OCT	NOV	DEC
1970	134.465	153.504	113.036	101.315	67.854	36.140	32.034	31.701	32.101	26.361	112.333	109.812
1971	174.729	151.785	124.920	98.164	71.206	142.049	56.386	52.593	34.043	51.820	70.421	68.895
1972	124.329	165.341	148.499	89.226	69.992	47.058	32.873	28.006	25.788	25.970	36.178	132.364
1973	69.510	60.340	43.489	42.140	50.738	40.438	41.260	29.627	27.548	28.193	27.311	41.448

```
  * AN ASTERISK FOLLOWING A NUMBER DENOTES GAUGED FLOWS SUBSTITUTED FOR NATURAL FLOWS IN THAT MONTH
```

OPTION NO. 6
TABLE OF MONTHLY INSTANTANEOUS PEAK DISCHARGES
AND HIGHEST AND LOWEST DAILY MEAN GAUGED
DISCHARGES IN CUMECS

```
                    WATER   DATA   UNIT   RETRIEVAL   LISTING

        25001    RIVER  TEES                AT  BROKEN SCAR                       HIGHEST   GAUGED   FLOW
                                                                      MAX. DAILY  MEAN   GAUGED   FLOW
                                                                      MIN. DAILY  MEAN   GAUGED   FLOW
```

YEAR	JAN	FEB	MAR	APR	MAY	JUN	JUL	AUG	SEP	OCT	NOV	DEC
1972	223.004	130.180	163.008	110.087	106.974	105.276	54.619	66.222	5.688	7.471	216.495	283.000
	85.830	68.620	71.400	73.010	58.250	44.900	26.250	26.540	4.595	5.821	138.200	96.620
	5.614	8.815	3.995	2.456	2.759	6.061	1.881	2.116	3.008	2.162	2.116	2.493
1973	111.785	76.976	65.939	164.423	60.562	12.593	170.366	275.925	32.828	149.591	59.519	130.732
	75.500	60.910	35.630	75.250	44.210	8.456	60.800	78.090	18.840	69.290	30.530	55.270
	2.099	3.715	2.215	2.283	1.777	1.372	1.669	2.142	1.788	2.377	1.394	3.030

OPTION NO. 7
TABLE OF CATCHMENT MONTHLY AREAL RAINFALL IN MILLIMETRES

```
                              WATER    DATA    UNIT   RETRIEVAL   LISTING
          39001    RIVER   THAMES                AT  TEDDINGTON                        CATCHMENT  RAINFALL
   YEAR    JAN     FEB      MAR     APR    MAY    JUN     JUL    AUG     SEP    OCT      NOV      DEC
   1970     86      53       46      61     25     38      61     69      53     15      168       38

   1971    104      20       61      56     51    137      23     86      13     69       66       28
   1972     71      69       69      56     56     41      33     25      30     27       67      100
   1973     27      18       14      54     64     74      64     40      57     29       32       48
```

OPTION NO. 8
TABLE OF CATCHMENT MONTHLY AREAL RAINFALL AND NATURALIZED RUNOFF IN MILLIMETRES

```
                              WATER    DATA    UNIT   RETRIEVAL   LISTING
          39001    RIVER   THAMES                AT  TEDDINGTON                     RUNOFF  AND  RAINFALL
   YEAR                        JAN    FEB    MAR    APR    MAY    JUN    JUL    AUG    SEP   OCT   NOV   DEC
   1970    RUNOFF               36     38     31     27     18      9      9      9      8     7    30    30
           RAINFALL             86     53     46     61     25     38     61     69     53    15   168    38

   1971    RUNOFF               47     37     34     26     19     37     15     14      9    14    18    19
           RAINFALL            104     20     61     56     51    137     23     86     13    69    66    28

   1972    RUNOFF               34     42     40     23     19     12      9      8      7     7    10    36
           RAINFALL             71     69     69     56     56     41     33     25     30    27    67   100

   1973    RUNOFF               19     15     12     11     14     11     11      8      7     8     7    11
           RAINFALL             27     18     14     54     64     74     64     40     57    29    32    48
```

OPTION NO. 9
HYDROGRAPHS OF DAILY AND MONTHLY MEAN GAUGED OR NATURALIZED DISCHARGES WITH CORRESPONDING EXTREMES FROM THE PERIOD OF RECORD

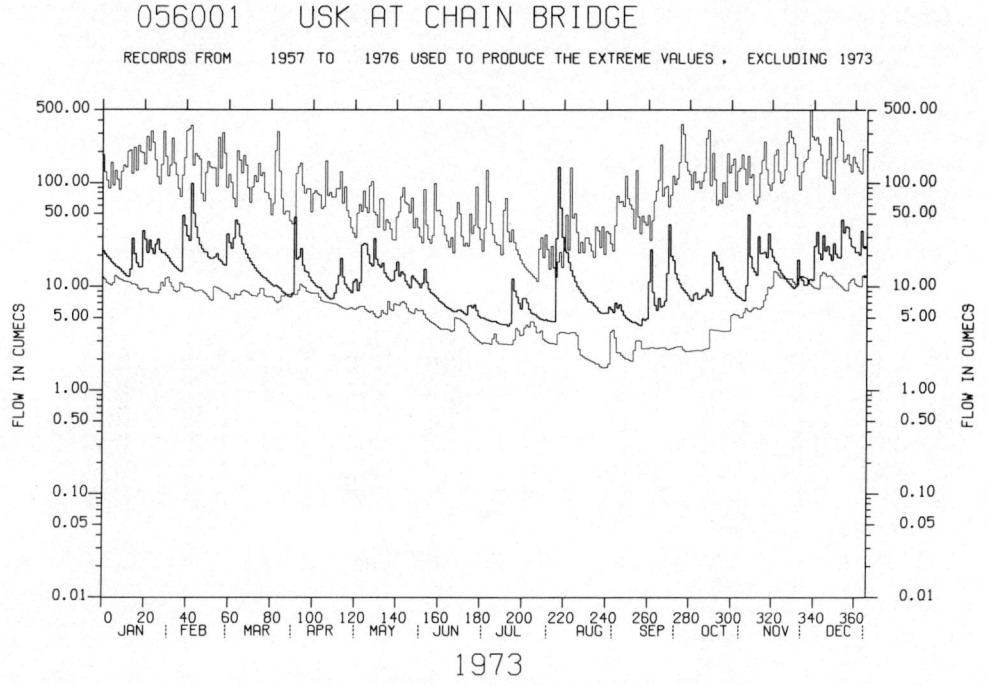

056001   USK AT CHAIN BRIDGE

RECORDS FROM   1957 TO   1976 USED TO PRODUCE THE EXTREME VALUES .   EXCLUDING 1973

1973

OPTION NO. 9—(continued)

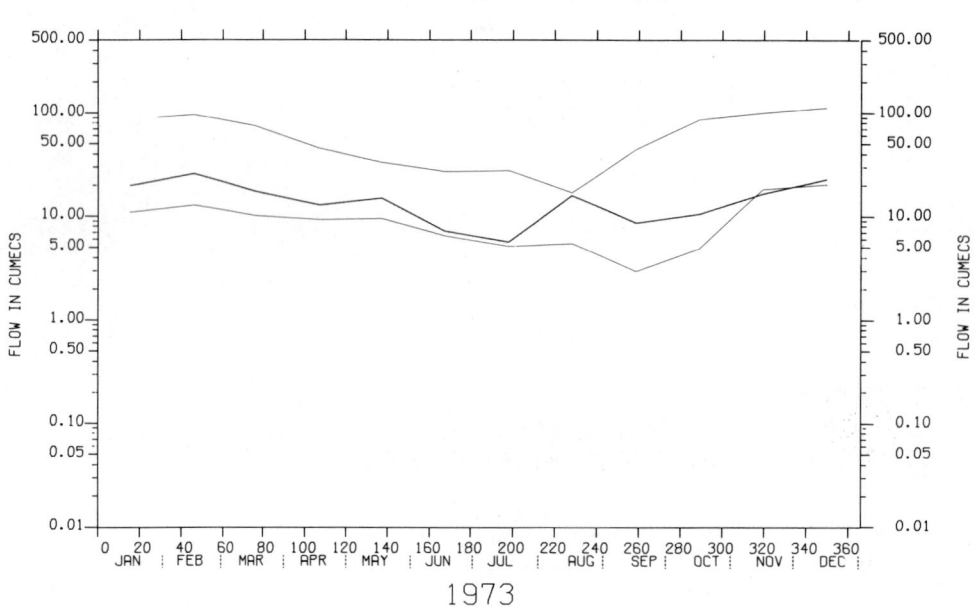

```
           056001    USK AT CHAIN BRIDGE
      RECORDS FROM    1957 TO    1976 USED TO PRODUCE THE EXTREME VALUES .  EXCLUDING 1973
```

1973

OPTION NO. 10
MONTHLY TABLE OF 15 MINUTE AND HOURLY MEAN GAUGED DISCHARGES

```
----------------------------------------------------------------------------------------------------

  STATION NUMBER  54001    SEVERN AT BEWDLEY

   7/OCT/74

           00       15       30       45      MEAN         00       15       30       45       MEAN
  0900   40.386   40.454   40.454   40.386  * 40.420  *  40.319   40.386   40.319   40.454  * 40.370  *
  1100   40.251   40.184   40.184   40.319  * 40.234  *  40.049   40.049   40.116   40.184  * 40.100  *
  1300   40.069   39.982   40.319   40.116  * 40.116  *  39.914   40.049   40.116   39.982  * 40.015  *
  1500   39.982   40.049   40.251   40.184  * 40.116  *  40.251   40.386   40.251   40.319  * 40.302  *
  1700   40.386   40.386   40.522   40.589  * 40.471  *  40.725   40.725   40.929   40.997  * 40.844  *
  1900   41.133   41.337   41.611   41.747  * 41.457  *  42.152   42.417   42.750   43.084  * 42.601  *
  2100   43.485   43.887   44.290   44.762  * 44.106  *  45.304   45.711   46.323   46.870  * 46.052  *
  2300   47.418   47.969   48.590   49.144  * 48.280  *  49.700   50.188   50.818   51.379  * 50.521  *
  0100   51.872   52.366   52.861   53.429  * 52.632  *  53.999   54.427   54.928   55.359  * 54.678  *
  0300   55.646   56.151   56.439   56.801  * 56.259  *  57.163   57.308   57.671   57.962  * 57.526  *
  0500   58.181   58.181   58.473   58.619  * 58.363  *  58.911   58.984   58.984   59.424  * 59.076  *
  0700   59.424   59.424   59.644   59.570  * 59.515  *  59.717   59.717   59.717   59.864  * 59.772  *

  DAILY MEAN FLOW        47.243 CUMECS

  HIGHEST FLOW           59.864 CUMECS

  LOWEST FLOW            39.914 CUMECS

  HIGHEST STAGE           1.034 METRES

  LOWEST STAGE            0.748 METRES

  NUMBER OF READINGS        96

----------------------------------------------------------------------------------------------------

  STATION NUMBER  54001    SEVERN AT BEWDLEY

   8/OCT/74

           00       15       30       45      MEAN         00       15       30       45       MEAN
  0900   59.717   59.864   59.717   59.791  * 59.772  *  59.644   59.644   59.644   59.350  * 59.570  *
  1100   59.350   59.497   59.277   59.131  * 59.314  *  58.911   58.984   58.911   58.692  * 58.874  *
  1300   58.473   58.473   58.327   58.181  * 58.363  *  58.035   57.890   57.890   57.599  * 57.853  *
  1500   57.381   57.308   57.091   56.873  * 57.163  *  56.729   56.729   56.512   56.367  * 56.584  *
  1700   56.295   56.006   55.934   55.790  * 56.007  *  55.718   55.646   55.431   55.287  * 55.521  *
  1900   55.215   55.143   55.000   54.928  * 55.072  *  54.785   54.713   54.642   54.570  * 54.678  *
  2100   54.642   54.713   54.713   54.642  * 54.678  *  54.713   54.785   54.857   55.072  * 54.857  *
  2300   55.215   55.431   55.862   56.151  * 55.665  *  56.512   57.018   57.526   58.181  * 57.309  *
  0100   58.765   59.424   60.232   60.969  * 59.847  *  61.858   62.750   63.721   64.696  * 63.256  *
  0300   65.902   66.735   67.951   68.945  * 67.383  *  70.019   70.944   72.027   73.193  * 71.546  *
  0500   74.208   75.306   76.093   77.040  * 75.662  *  77.991   78.865   79.583   80.303  * 79.185  *
  0700   81.265   81.828   82.392   82.876  * 82.090  *  83.604   83.928   84.415   84.821  * 84.192  *

  DAILY MEAN FLOW        62.268 CUMECS

  HIGHEST FLOW           84.821 CUMECS

  LOWEST FLOW            54.570 CUMECS

  HIGHEST STAGE           1.356 METRES

  LOWEST STAGE            0.961 METRES

  NUMBER OF READINGS        96
```

OPTION NO. 11
FLOW FREQUENCY AND DURATION CURVES WITH TABULATED
DURATION DATA FOR ONE OR MORE YEARS

FLOW DURATION STATISTICS

RIVER SEVERN

    AT BEWDLEY

CATCHMENT AREA 4273.5 SQ KM

    STATION   54001

FLOW EXCEEDED STATED AMOUNT IN CUMECS FOR GIVEN PERCENTAGE OF TIME

	0	1	2	3	4	5	6	7	8	9
0	617.311	311.487	261.083	230.217	211.245	193.688	179.530	170.185	159.708	149.725
10	141.755	135.638	128.276	120.914	115.533	110.436	105.056	101.900	97.900	94.579
20	90.898	87.783	84.385	82.119	79.185	76.456	74.290	72.020	70.280	68.527
30	66.545	64.711	63.147	61.165	59.020	57.740	55.784	54.652	53.470	51.559
40	50.121	48.988	47.600	45.874	44.741	43.891	42.759	41.909	40.776	39.644
50	38.794	37.662	36.959	35.950	35.400	34.547	33.697	33.040	32.560	31.715
60	30.866	30.016	29.450	28.883	28.034	27.160	26.630	26.052	25.202	25.051
70	24.353	24.041	23.503	22.654	22.654	21.804	21.804	20.955	20.655	20.105
80	19.256	19.256	18.406	18.180	17.273	17.183	16.141	16.141	15.291	15.291
90	14.158	13.730	13.026	13.026	12.543	11.893	10.760	10.760	9.911	8.212

AVERAGE DAILY MEAN FLOW   62.053 CUMECS

MAXIMUM DAILY MEAN FLOW   617.311 CUMECS

MINIMUM DAILY MEAN FLOW   7.079 CUMECS

DATA AVAILABLE FOR CALENDAR YEARS 1955-1973

GAUGED FLOWS USED

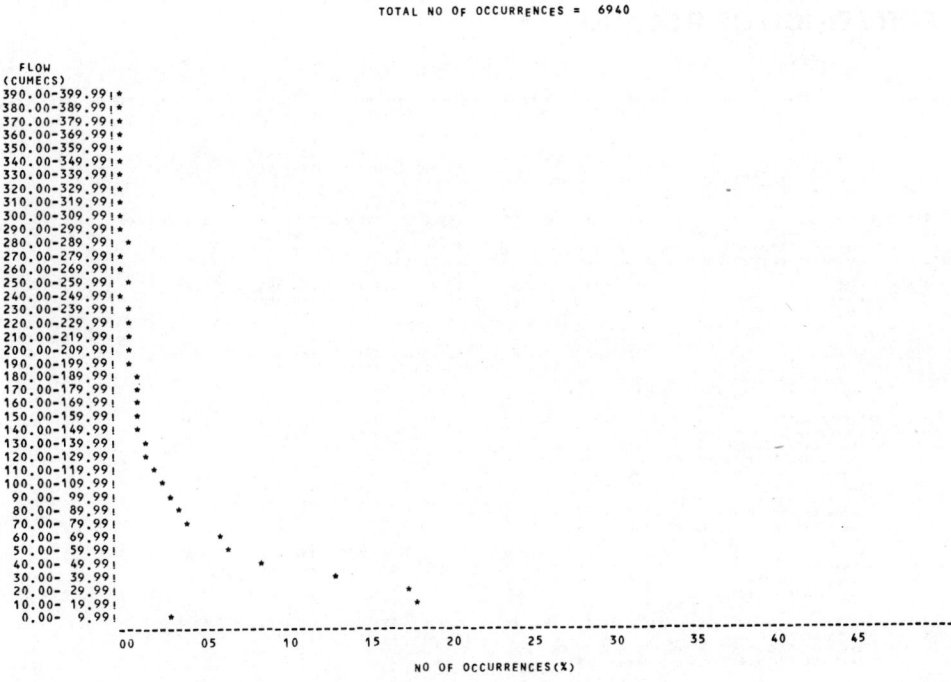

RIVER SEVERN   AT BEWDLEY   FLOW FREQUENCIES   PERIOD 1955-1973

TOTAL NO OF OCCURRENCES =   6940

NO OF VALUES ABOVE RANGE =   21

OPTION NO. 11—(continued)

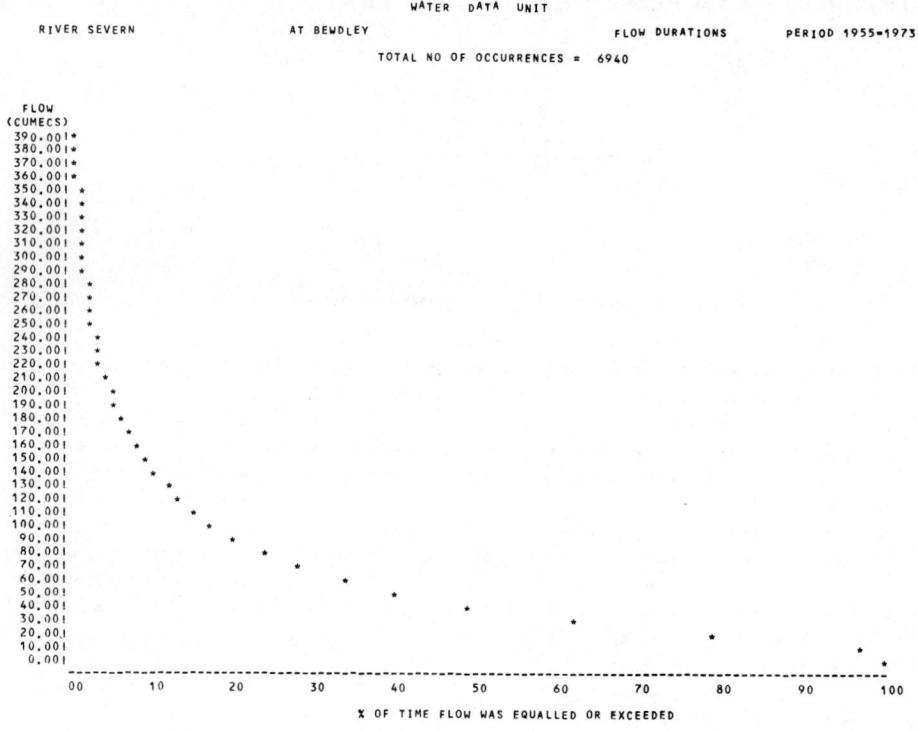

OPTION NO. 12
CONCISE SUMMARY OF STATION GAUGED DISCHARGE DATA
FOR PERIOD OF RECORD

	RIVER/STATION	PERIOD OF RECORD	AVERAGE GAUGED	MINIMUM GAUGED	MAXIMUM GAUGED	HIGHEST INSTANTANEOUS		MISSING OR INCOMPLETE YEARS
21/3	TWEED	1959 1973	14.485	1.928	147.022	481.389	1959	
	AT PEEBLES			7/10/59	10/01/65	15/01/62		
	AREA OF CATCHMENT =	694.0 SQ KM						
	AV RAINFALL (1916-50) =	0 MM						
21/4	WATCH WATER	1965 1968	.102	.025	.736	1.578	1965 1968	
	AT WATCH WATER RESERVOIR			1/10/65	3/11/67	12/05/68		
	AREA OF CATCHMENT =	10.7 SQ KM						
	AV RAINFALL (1916-50) =	C MM						
21/5	TWEED	1961 1973	8.117	1.188	115.817	266.180	1961	
	AT LYNE FORD			7/10/72	15/01/62	15/01/62		
	AREA OF CATCHMENT =	373.0 SQ KM						
	AV RAINFALL (1916-50) =	0 MM						
21/6	TWEED	1961 1973	33.584	3.457	373.784	605.984	1961	
	AT BOLESIDE			7/10/72	24/11/63	16/01/62		
	AREA OF CATCHMENT =	1500.0 SQ KM						
	AV RAINFALL (1916-50) =	1270 MM						
21/7	ETTRICK WATER	1961 1973	14.098	.773	170.752	362.458	1961	
	AT LINDEAN			5/10/72	15/01/62	15/01/62		
	AREA OF CATCHMENT =	499.0 SQ KM						
	AV RAINFALL (1916-50) =	0 MM						
21/8	TEVIOT	1960 1973	18.208	1.784	308.655	475.726	1960	
	AT ORMISTON MILL			25/10/72	6/03/63	6/03/63		
	AREA OF CATCHMENT =	1110.0 SQ KM						
	AV RAINFALL (1916-50) =	1046 MM						
21/9	TWEED	1962 1973	73.849	9.071	1042.066	1186.482	1962	
	AT NORHAM			8/10/72	6/03/63	6/03/63		
	AREA OF CATCHMENT =	4390.0 SQ KM						
	AV RAINFALL (1916-50) =	0 MM						
21/10	TWEED	1963 1973	41.426	4.984	419.092	622.974	1963	
	AT DRYBURGH			5/08/64	24/11/63	11/01/65		
	AREA OF CATCHMENT =	2080.0 SQ KM						
	AV RAINFALL (1916-50) =	1166 MM						
21/11	YARROW	1963 1973	6.224	.407	64.622	102.224	1963	
	AT PHILIPHAUGH			26/10/72	10/01/65	11/01/65		
	AREA OF CATCHMENT =	231.0 SQ KM						
	AV RAINFALL (1916-50) =	0 MM						
21/12	TEVIOT	1963 1973	7.539	.600	115.250	228.600	1963	
	AT HAWICK			6/10/72	23/11/63	27/02/67		
	AREA OF CATCHMENT =	323.0 SQ KM						
	AV RAINFALL (1916-50) =	0 MM						
21/13	GALA WATER	1964 1973	3.375	.374	48.561	62.297	1964	
	AT GALASHIELS			12/09/73	27/03/65	27/03/65		
	AREA OF CATCHMENT =	207.0 SQ KM						
	AV RAINFALL (1916-50) =	0 MM						

6 Directory of Contributors

PRINCIPAL ORGANISATIONS

England and Wales:

Anglian Water Authority (AWA)
Diploma House, Grammar School Walk, Huntingdon, PE18 6NZ

Northumbrian Water Authority (NWA)
Northumbria House, Regent Centre, Gosforth, Newcastle upon Tyne, NE3 3PX

North West Water Authority (NWWA)
Dawson House, Great Sankey, Warrington, WA5 3LW

Severn Trent Water Authority (STWA)
Abelson House, 2297 Coventry Road, Sheldon, Birmingham, B26 3PR

South West Water Authority (SWWA)
P.O. Box 22, 3–5 Barnfield Road, Exeter, EX1 1RE

Southern Water Authority (SWA)
Guildborn House, Worthing, Sussex, BN11 1LD

Thames Water Authority (TWA)
New River Head, Rosebery Avenue, London, EC1R 4TP

Welsh National Water Development Authority (WNWDA)
Cambrian Way, Brecon, Powys, LD3 7HP

Wessex Water Authority (WWA)
Techno House, Redcliffe Way, Bristol, BS1 6NY

Yorkshire Water Authority (YWA)
West Riding House, 67 Albion Street, Leeds, LS1 5AA

Scotland:

Scottish Development Department: Engineering Division (SDD)
Pentland House, 47 Robb's Loan, Edinburgh, EH14 1TY

Clyde River Purification Board (CRPB)
Rivers House, Murray Road, East Kilbride, Glasgow

Forth River Purification Board (FRPB)
Colinton Dell House, West Mill Road, Colinton, Edinburgh, EH13 0NX

 Highland River Purification Board (HRPB)
c/o Town House, Dingwall, IV15 9SD

North East River Purification Board (NERPB)
Woodside House, Mugiemoss Road, Persley, Aberdeen, AB2 2UQ

Solway River Purification Board (SRPB)
39 Castle Street, Dumfries, DG1 1DL

Tay River Purification Board (TRPB)
3 South Street, Perth

Tweed River Purification Board (TWRPB)
Burnbrae, Mossilee Road, Galashiels, TD1 1NF

Department of the Environment for Northern Ireland (DOE(NI))
Stormont, Belfast, BT4 3SS

MEASURING AUTHORITIES

AD	Avon Division, STWA Waveley Road, Coventry, CU1 3AJ
ADD	Avon and Dorset Division, WWA 2 Nuffield Road, Poole, Dorset, BH17 7RL
BAC	British Aluminium Company Lochaber Works, Fort William, PH33 6TH
BAD	Bristol Avon Division, WWA Westmoreland House, Bath, BA2 3HD
BWW	Bristol Waterworks Company GPO Box No 218, Bridgwater Road, Bristol, BS99 7AU
CDC	Cumbernauld Development Corporation, Cumbernauld, Glasgow
CDWC	Corby and District Water Company Geddington Road, Corby, NN18 8ES
CEGB	Central Electricity Generating Board N.W. Region, Llandudno Junction
CRWD	Central Region: Water Department Viewforth, Stirling, FK8 2ET
DCRD	Dee and Clwyd River Division, WNWDA 2 Vicar's Lane, Chester, CH1 1QT
DD	Derwent Division, STWA Raynesway, Derby, DE2 7JA
DGRWD	Dumfries and Galloway Region: Water Division 70 Terregles Street, Dumfries, DG2 9BB
ERD	Essex River Division, AWA Rivers House, 129 Springfield Road, Chelmsford, CM2 6JN
ESWDD	East Sussex Water and Drainage Division, SWA Construction House, Menzies Road, St Leonards-on-Sea, TN38 9BD
EWC	Essex Water Company 342 South Street, Romford, RM1 2AL
FWBA	Freshwater Biological Association Windermere Laboratory, The Ferry House, Far Sawrey, Ambleside, LA22 0LP
GKL	Crane Ltd., Glenfield and Kennedy Works, Kilmarnock, KA1 4DF
GLC	Greater London Council: Rivers Branch (NT) 10 Great George Street, London, SW1P 3AB
GORD	Great Ouse River Division, AWA Great Ouse House, Clarendon Road, Cambridge, CB22 BL
GRD	Glamorgan River Division, WNWDA Tremains House, Coychurch Road, Bridgend, CF31 2AR
GRWD	Grampian Region: Water Division Nicholas House, Broad Street, Aberdeen
GWRD	Gwynedd River Division, WNWDA Highfield, Caernarvon, LL55 1HR

HRWD	Hampshire River and Water Division, SWA Marland House, Civic Centre Road, Southampton, SO9 4XT
HRCWD	Highland Regional Council: Water Division Regional Buildings, Glenurquhart Road, Inverness, IV3 5NX
IH	Institute of Hydrology, NERC Maclean Building, Crowmarsh Gifford, Wallingford, OX10 8BB
IoMWG	Isle of Man Water and Gas Authority 16 Circular Road, Douglas, IoM
IoWRWD	Isle of Wight River and Water Division, SWA St Nicholas, 58 St John's Road, Newport, IoW
ITE	Institute of Terrestrial Ecology, NERC 12 Hope Terrace, Edinburgh, EH9 2AS
IWD	Ipswich Water Division, AWA Cobham Road, Ipswich, IP3 9JE
KRWD	Kent River and Water Division, SWA 54 College Road, Maidstone, ME15 6SN
LD	Lea Division, TWA The Grange, Crossbrook Street, Waltham Cross, Cheshunt, EN8 8LX
LRD	Lincolnshire River Division, AWA 50 Wide Bargate, Boston, PE21 6SA
LRWD	Lothian Region: Water Department Comiston Springs, 55 Buckstone Terrace, Edinburgh, EH10 6QS
LU	Leeds University Department of Geography, Leeds
NGWC	Newcastle and Gateshead Water Company P.O. Box 10, Allendale Road, Newcastle-upon-Tyne, NE6 2SW
NSHEB	North of Scotland Hydro Electric Board 16 Rothesay Terrace, Edinburgh, EH3 7SE
NSRD	Norfolk and Suffolk River Division, AWA Yare House, Thorpe Road, Norwich, NR1 1SA
NWD	Northampton Water Division, AWA Cliftonville, Northampton, NN1 5BH
NWSWD	North West Sussex Water Division, SWA Hurst Road, Horsham, RH12 2DP
NWWAED	Eastern Division, NWWA Oakland House, Talbot Road, Old Trafford, Manchester, M16 0QE
NWWAPD	Pennine Division, NWWA London House, Oldham Road, Middleton, M24 1BD
NWWARBD	Ribble Division, NWWA Pennine House, Stanley Street, Preston, PR1 4DR
NWWARD	Rivers Division, NWWA New Town House, Buttermarket Street, Warrington, WA1 2QQ
NWWAWD	Western Division, NWWA Merton House, Stanley Road, Bootle, Merseyside, L20 3NH
RFR	River Flow Records c/o Professor P O Wolf, The City University, London, EC1Y 4PB
SAU	Severn Area Unit, Resource Planning, STWA 64 Albert Road North, Malvern, WR14 2BB

SD	Somerset Division, WWA The Watergate, West Quay, Bridgwater, TA6 3HN
SRCWD	Strathclyde Regional Council: Water Department 419 Balmore Road, Glasgow, G22 6NU
SRWD	Sussex River and Water Division, SWA Falmer, Brighton, BN1 9PY
SSEB	South of Scotland Electricity Board Cathcart House, Glasgow, G44
SSS	Sunderland and South Shields Water Company 29 John Street, Sunderland, SR1 1JU
STWATD	Tame Division, STWA Tame House, 156 Newhall Street, Birmingham, B3 1SE
SWWA	Directorate of Resource Planning, SWWA Matford Lane, Exeter, EX2 4QX
SWWRD	South West Wales River Division, WNWDA Pen-y-fai House, 19 Pen-y-fai Lane, Furnace, Llanelli, SA15 4EL
TAU	Trent Area Unit, Resource Planning, STWA Trentside, West Bridgford, Nottingham, NG2 5FA
TCD	Thames Conservancy Division, TWA Nugent House, Vastern Road, Reading, RG1 8DB
TRRL	Transport and Road Research Laboratory, DOE Crowthorne, Berks, RG11 6AU
TRWSD	Tayside Region: Water Services Department Bullion House, Invergowrie, Dundee, DD2 5BB
TWD	Taff Water Division, WNWDA Pentwyn Road, Nelson, Treharris, CF46 6LY
UE	University of Exeter, Dept. of Geography, Amory Building, Rennes Drive, EX4 4BJ
URD	Usk River Division, WNWDA The Croft, Goldcroft Common, Caerleon, Newport, NP6 1XF
WNRD	Welland and Nene River Division, AWA North Street, Oundle, Peterborough, PE8 4AS
WRD	Wye River Division, WNWDA 4 St John Street, Hereford, HR1 2NE
YWA	Directorate of Resource Planning, Hydrometry Section, YWA 21 Park Square South, Leeds, LS1 2QG
YWAE	Eastern Division, YWA Alfred Gelder Street, Kingston upon Hull, HU1 2AE
YWANC	North Central Division, YWA 'Spenfield', 182 Otley Road, West Park, Leeds, LS16 5PR
YWAS	Southern Division, YWA Castle Market Building, Exchange Street, Sheffield, S1 1GB
YWASW	South Western Division, YWA Thrum Hall Lane, Halifax, HX1 4QX
YWAW	Western Division, YWA P.O. Box 201, George Street, Bradford, BD1 5PZ

7 Hydrographs of Daily Mean Gauged Discharges at Forty-six Selected Stations for 1971, 1972 and 1973

Station Number	River	Station	Water Authority or River Purification Board Area	Page
054001	Severn	Bewdley	Severn Trent WA	141
055003	Lugg	Lugwardine	WNWDA	142
055006	Elan	Caban Coch Reservoir	WNWDA	143
055007	Wye	Erwood	WNWDA	144
056001	Usk	Chain Bridge	WNWDA	145
060001	Tywi	Ty-Castell Farm	WNWDA	146
067015	Dee	Manley Hall	WNWDA	147
071001	Ribble	Samlesbury	North West WA	148
071003	Croasdale Beck	Croasdale Flume	North West WA	149
072001	Lune	Halton	North West WA	150
075002	Derwent	Camerton	North West WA	151
079002	Nith	Friar's Carse	Solway RPB	152
082001	Girvan	Robstone	Clyde RPB	153
084005	Clyde	Blairston	Clyde RPB	154
203014	Upper Bann	Dynes Bridge	DoE, NI	155
205001	Lagan	Dunmurry Lane	DoE, NI	156

008006 RIVER SPEY AT BOAT O'BRIG   DAILY MEAN FLOWS

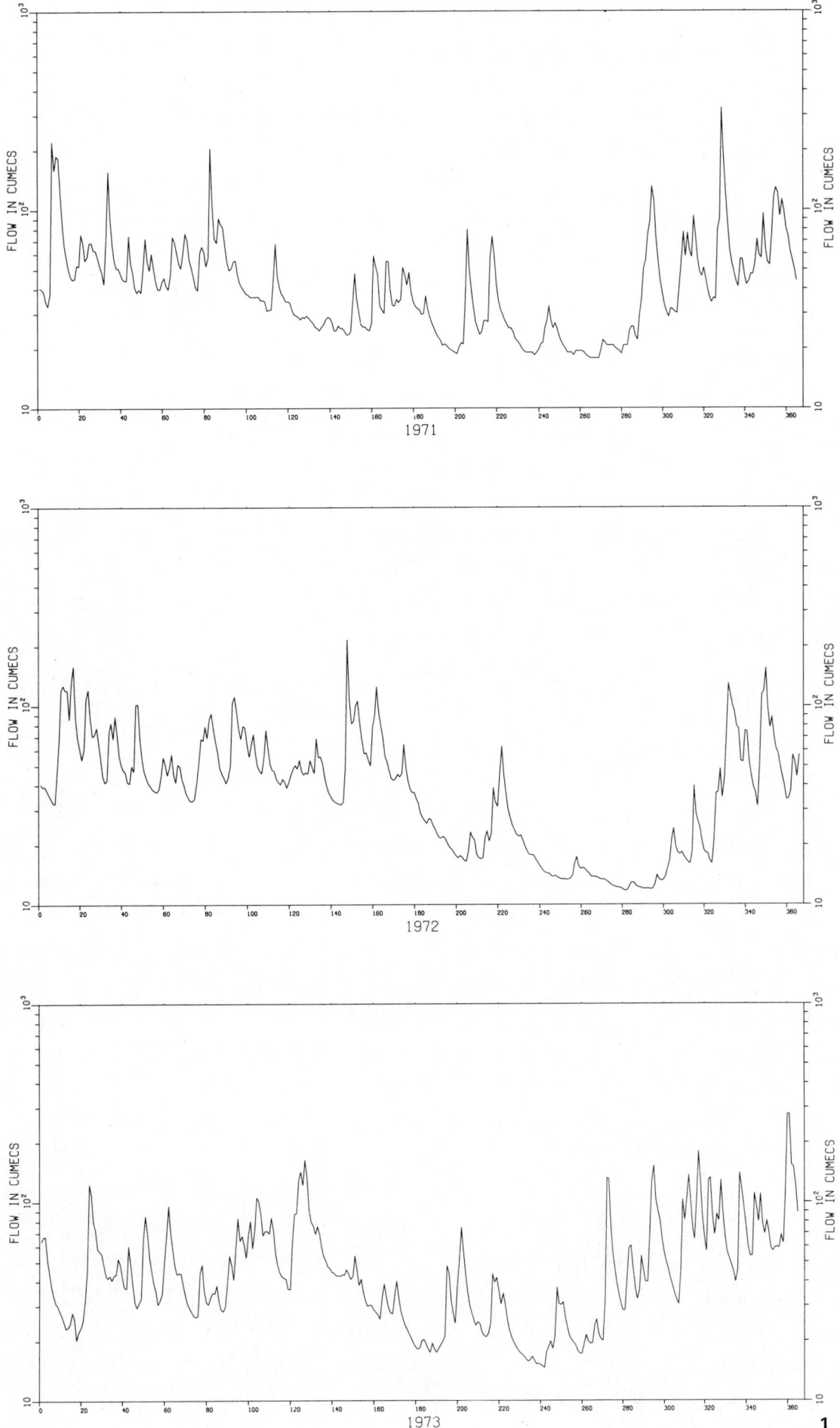

1971

1972

1973

1

111

008009 RIVER DULNAIN AT BALNAAN DAILY MEAN FLOWS

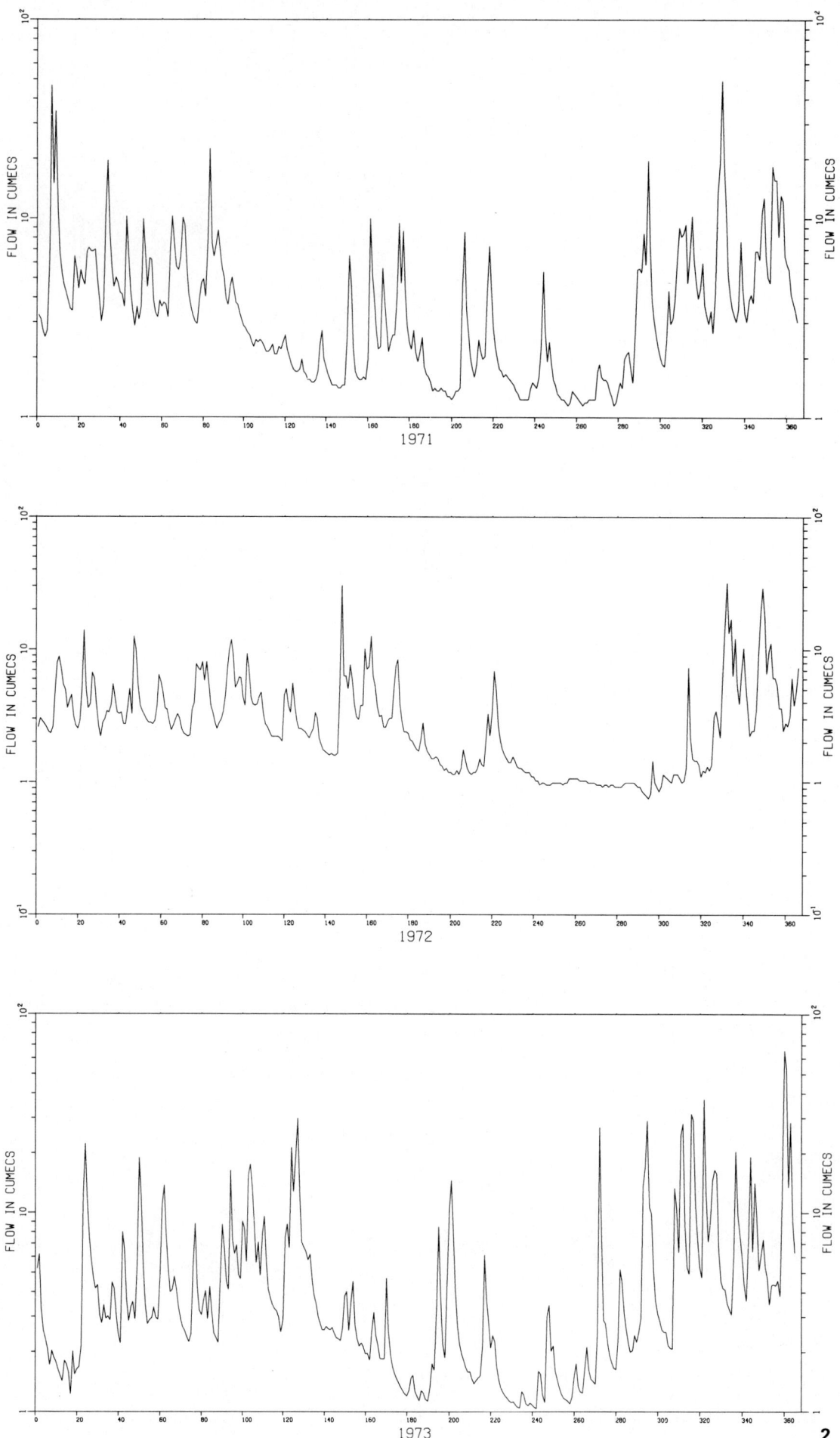

1971

1972

1973

2

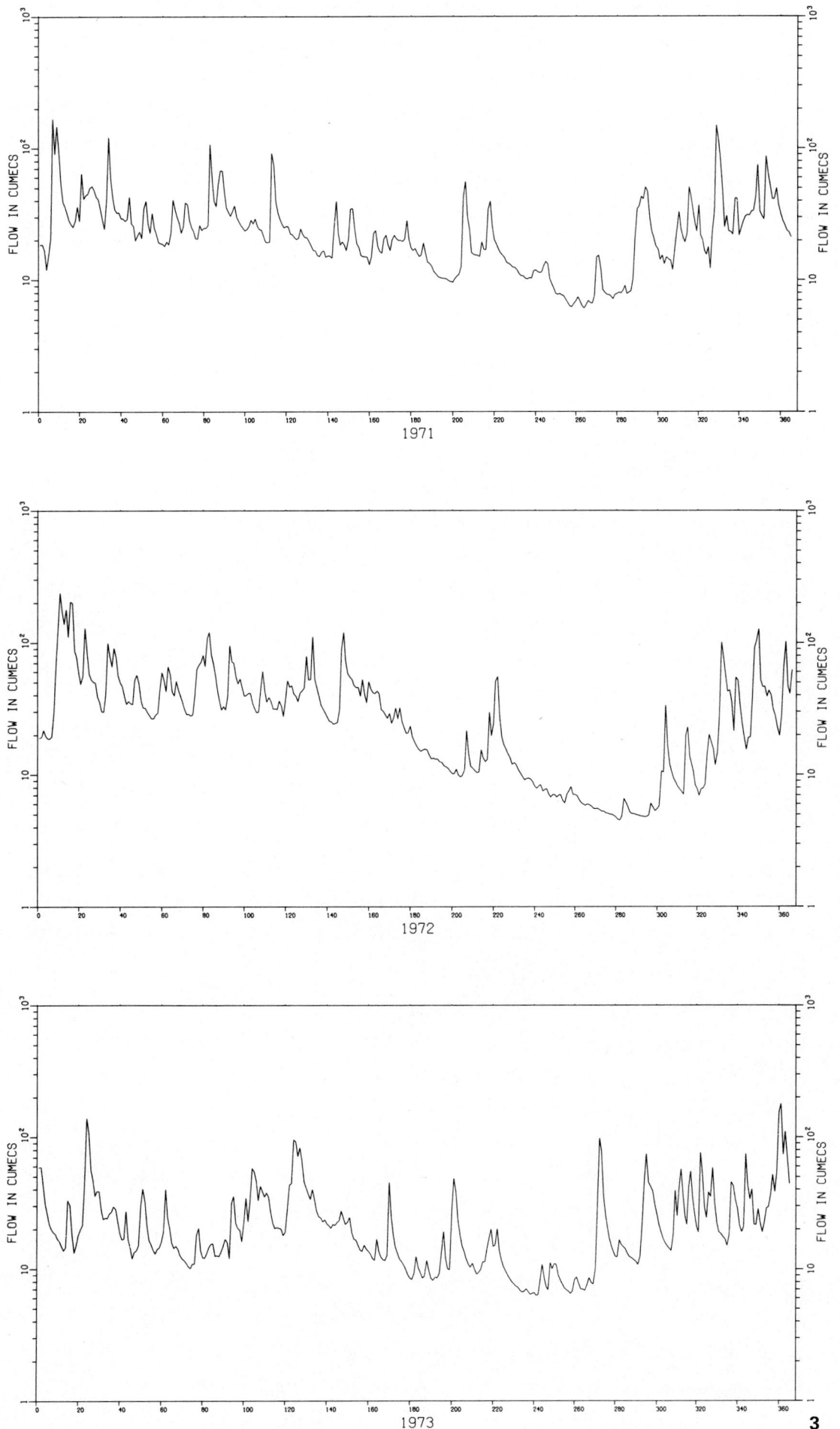

012001 RIVER DEE AT WOODEND   DAILY MEAN FLOWS

FLOW IN CUMECS

1971

1972

1973

3

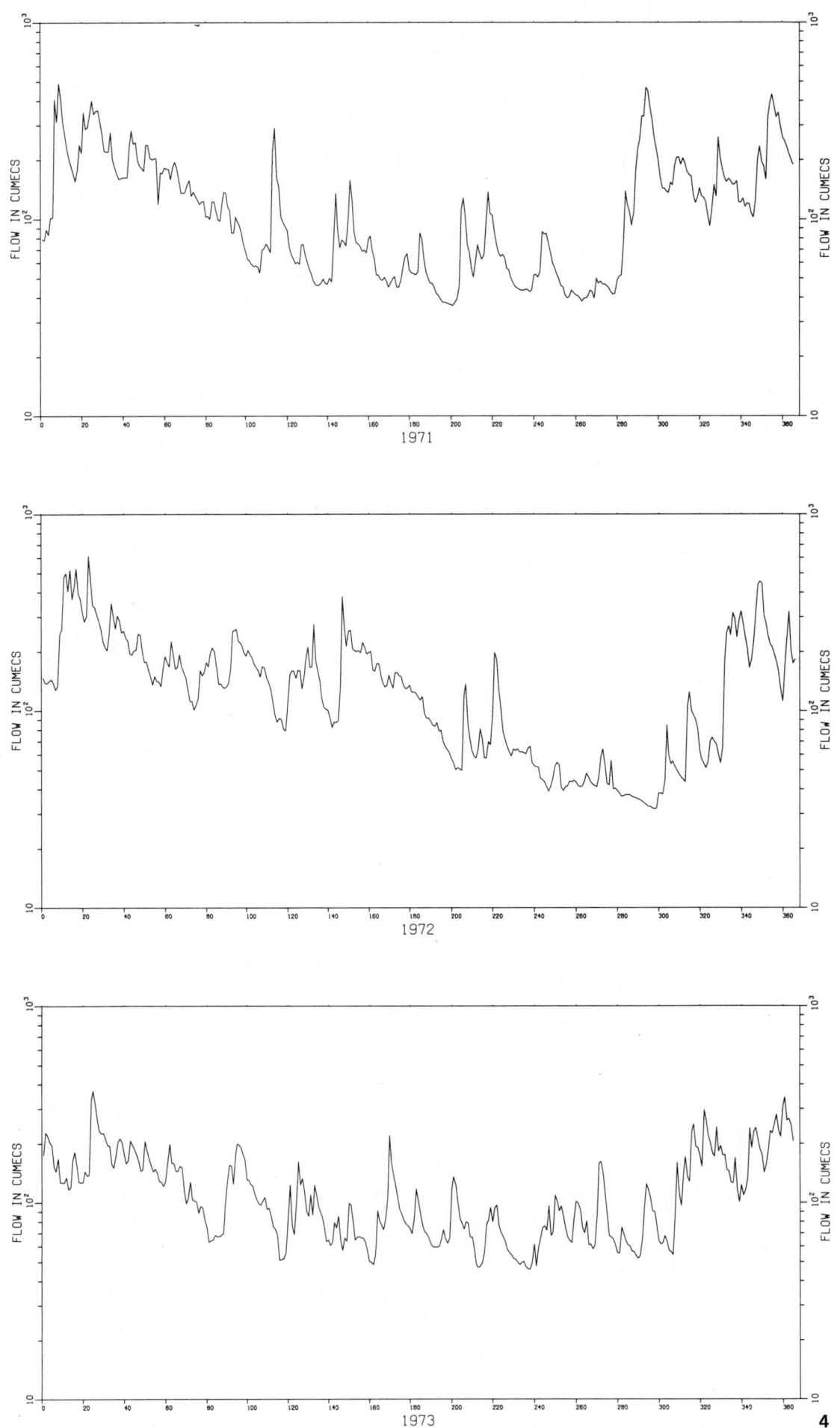

1971

1972

1973

4

019001 RIVER ALMOND AT CRAIGIEHALL   DAILY MEAN FLOWS

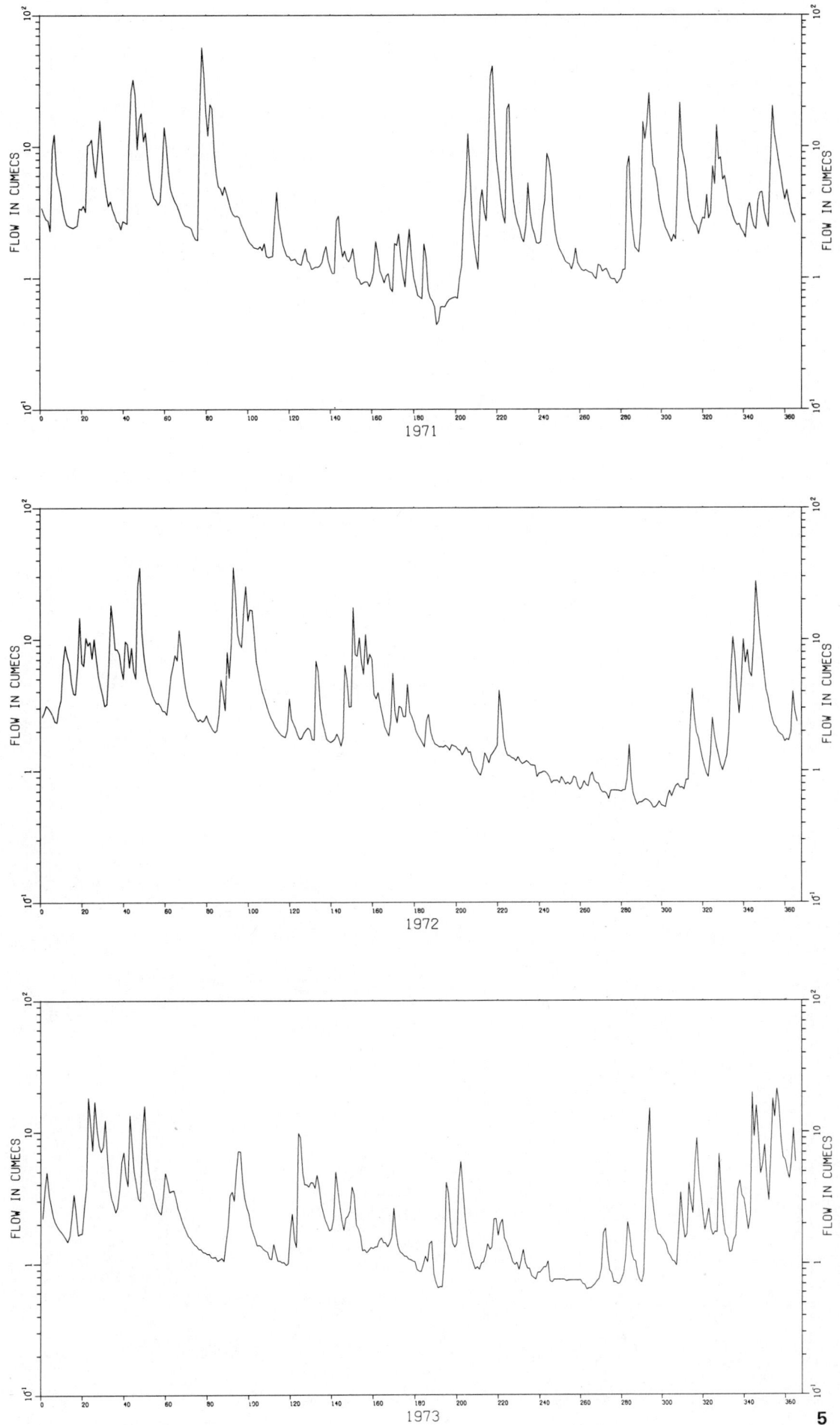

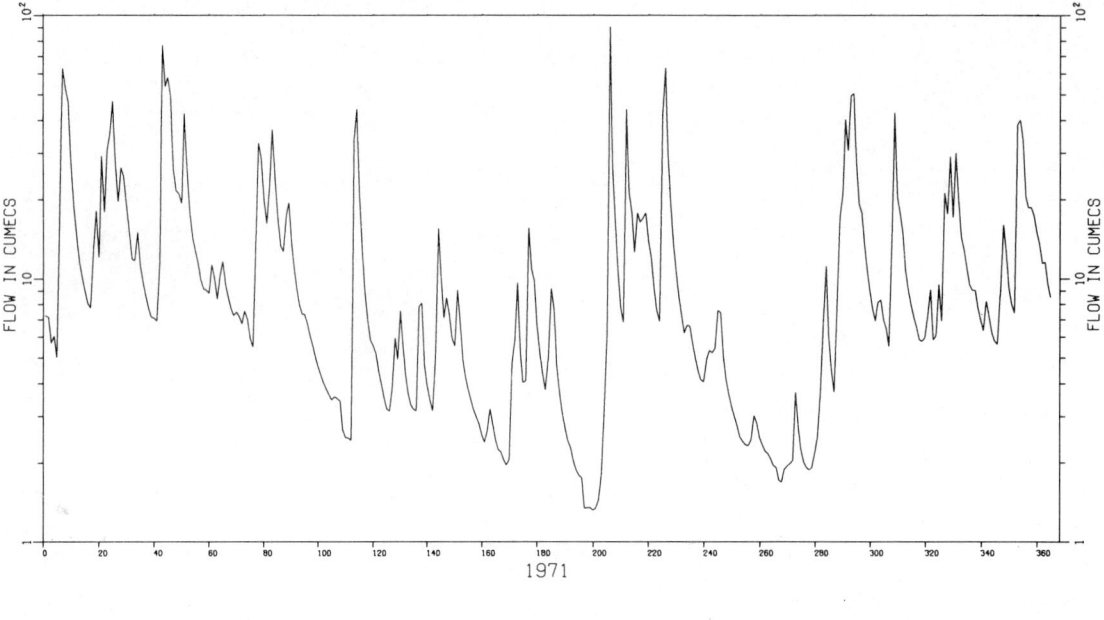

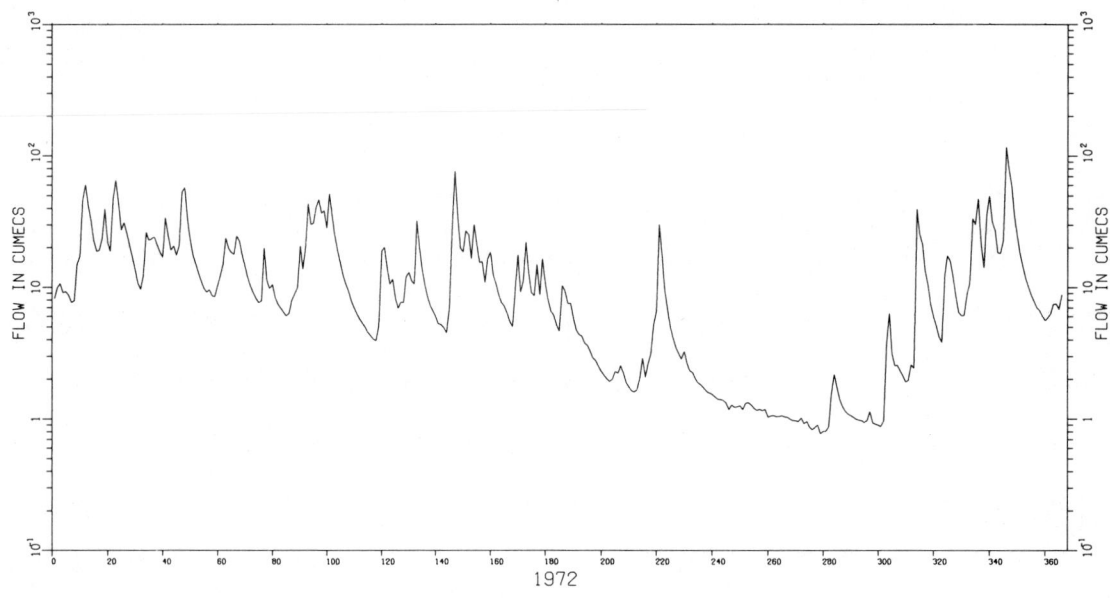

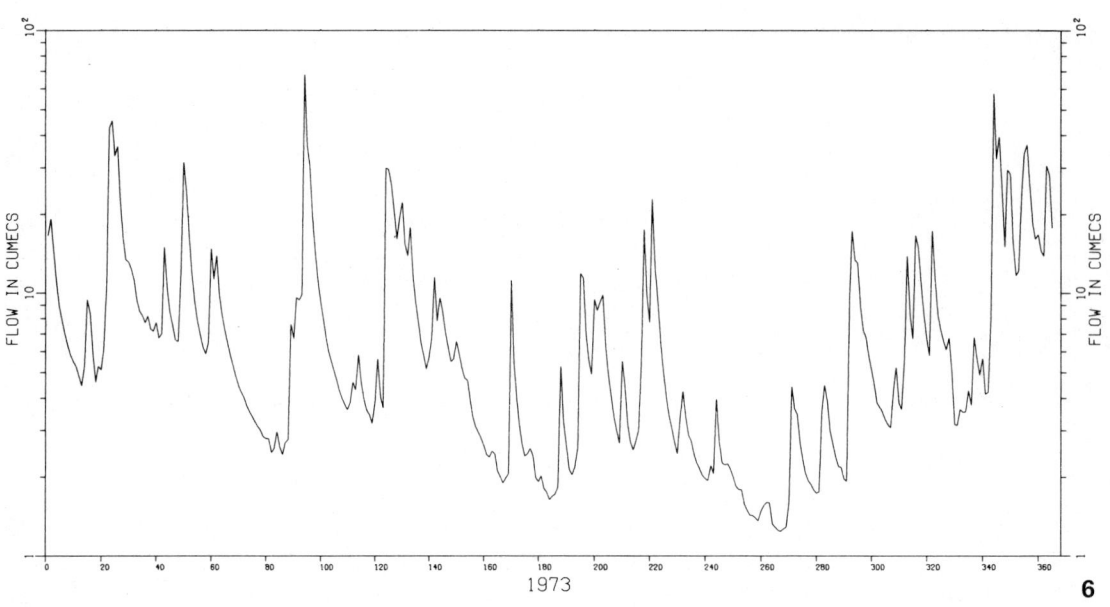

6

021009 RIVER TWEED AT NORHAM DAILY MEAN FLOWS

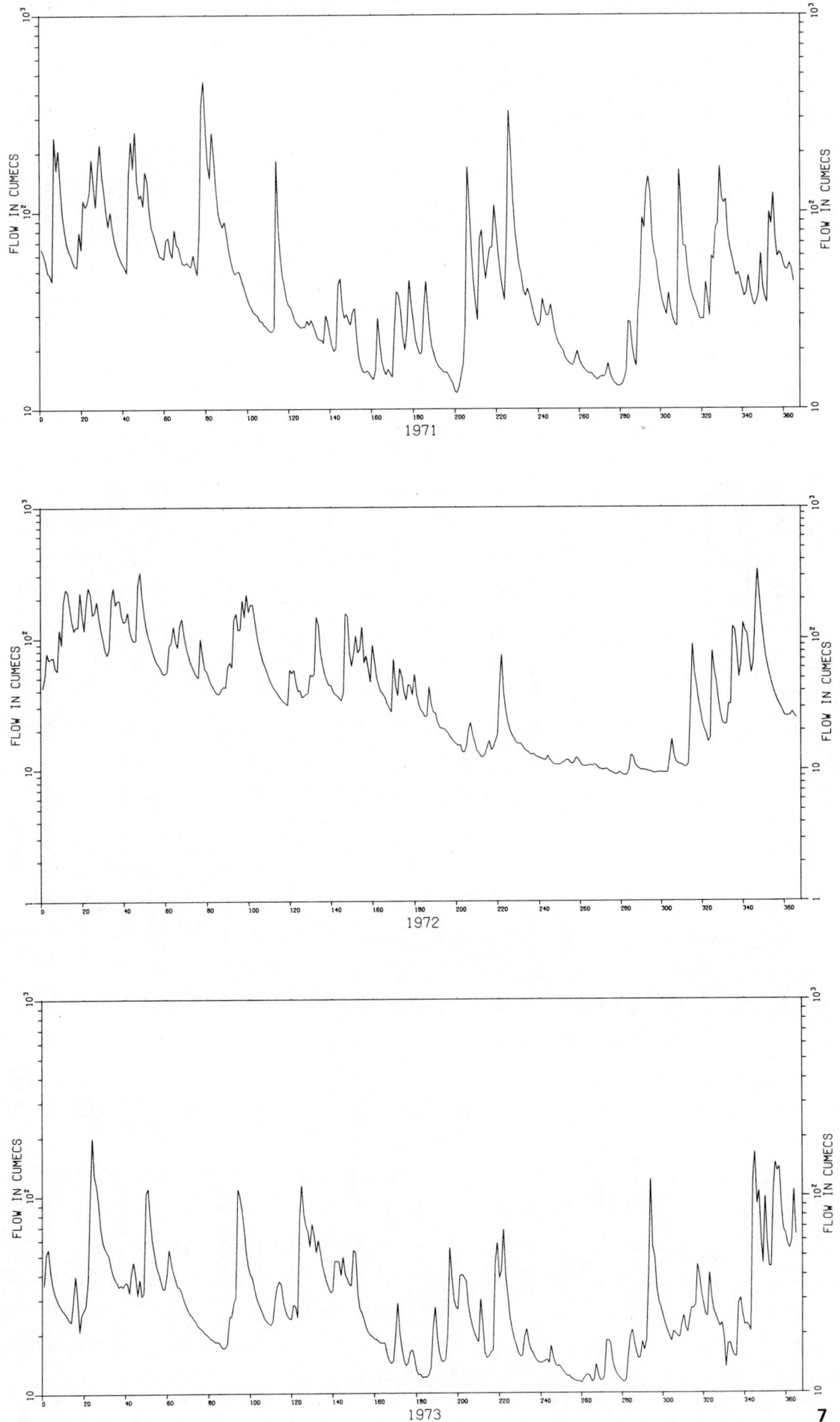

1971

1972

1973

7

022002 RIVER COQUET AT BYGATE   DAILY MEAN FLOWS

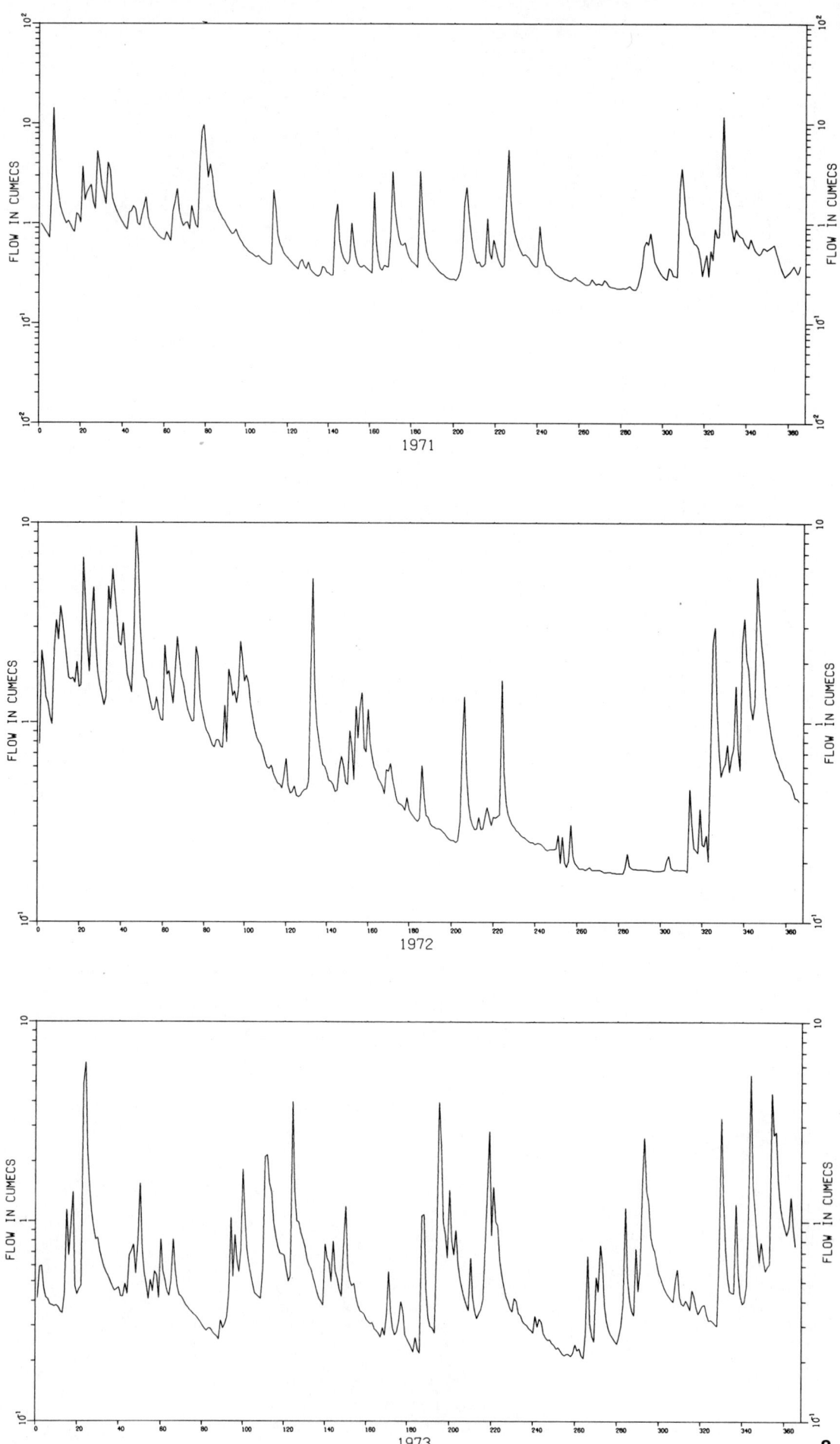

1971

1972

1973

8

023001 RIVER TYNE AT BYWELL DAILY MEAN FLOWS

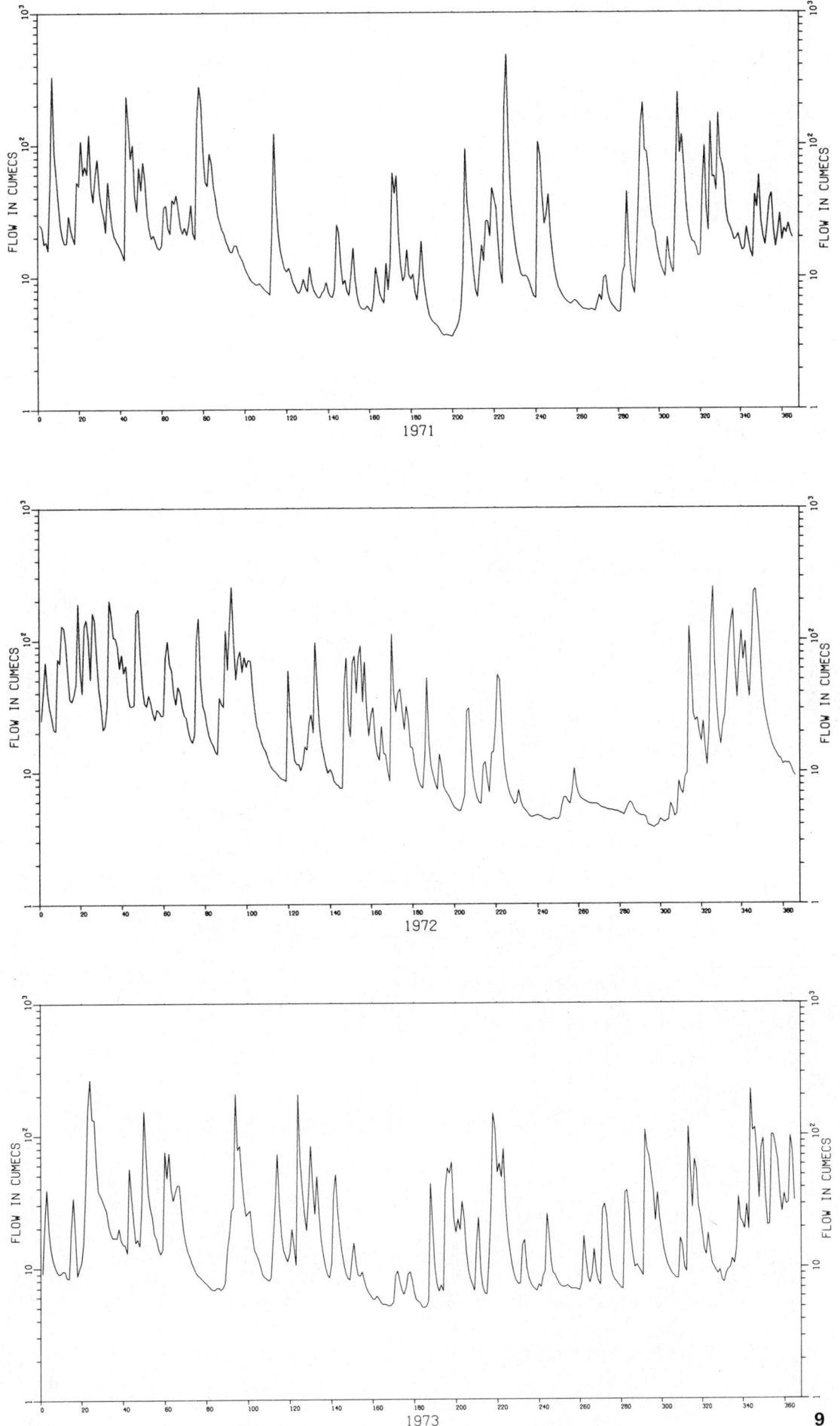

1971

1972

1973

9

025001 RIVER TEES AT BROKEN SCAR DAILY MEAN FLOWS

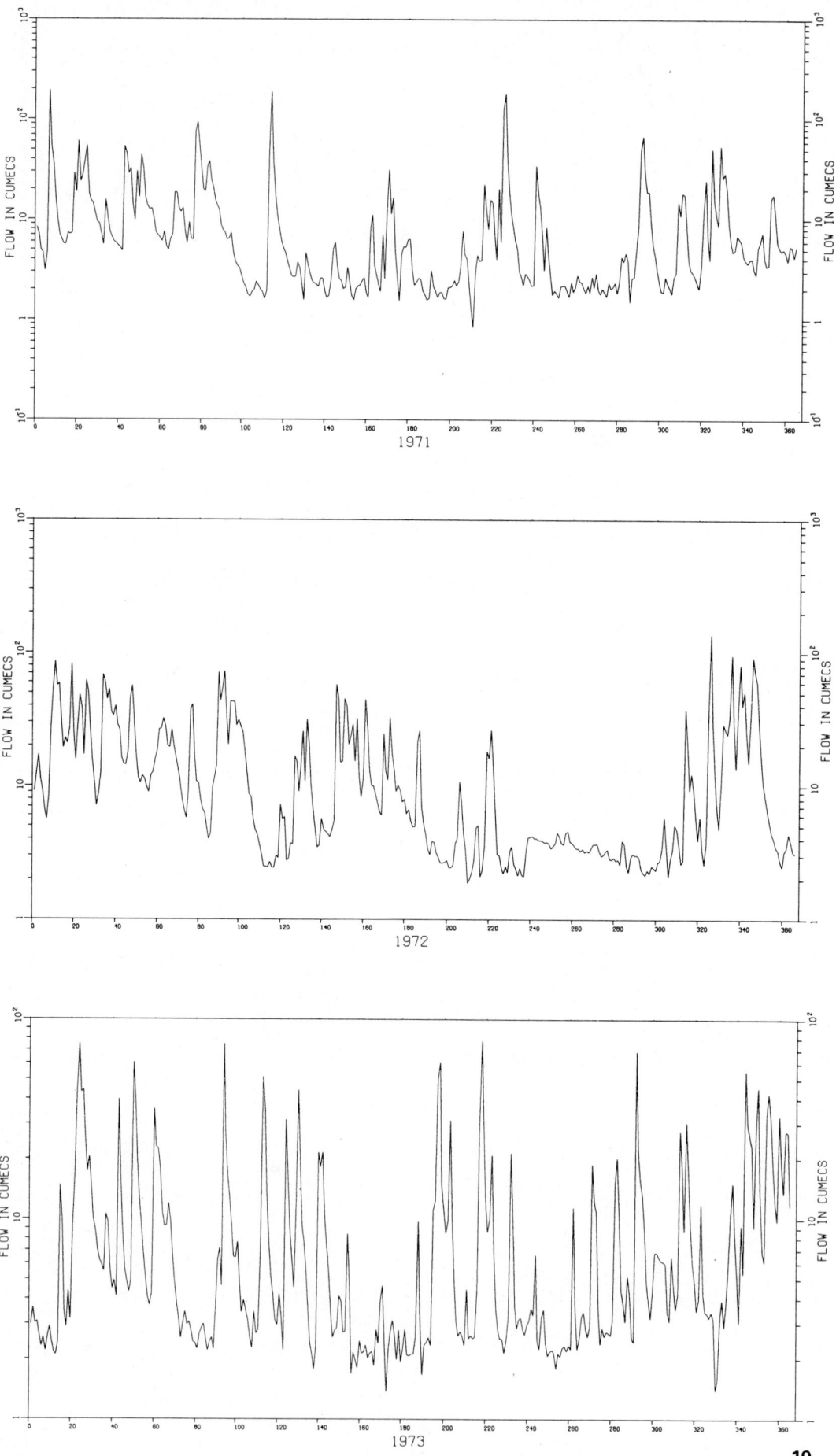

10

027001 RIVER NIDD AT HUNSINGORE WEIR DAILY MEAN FLOWS

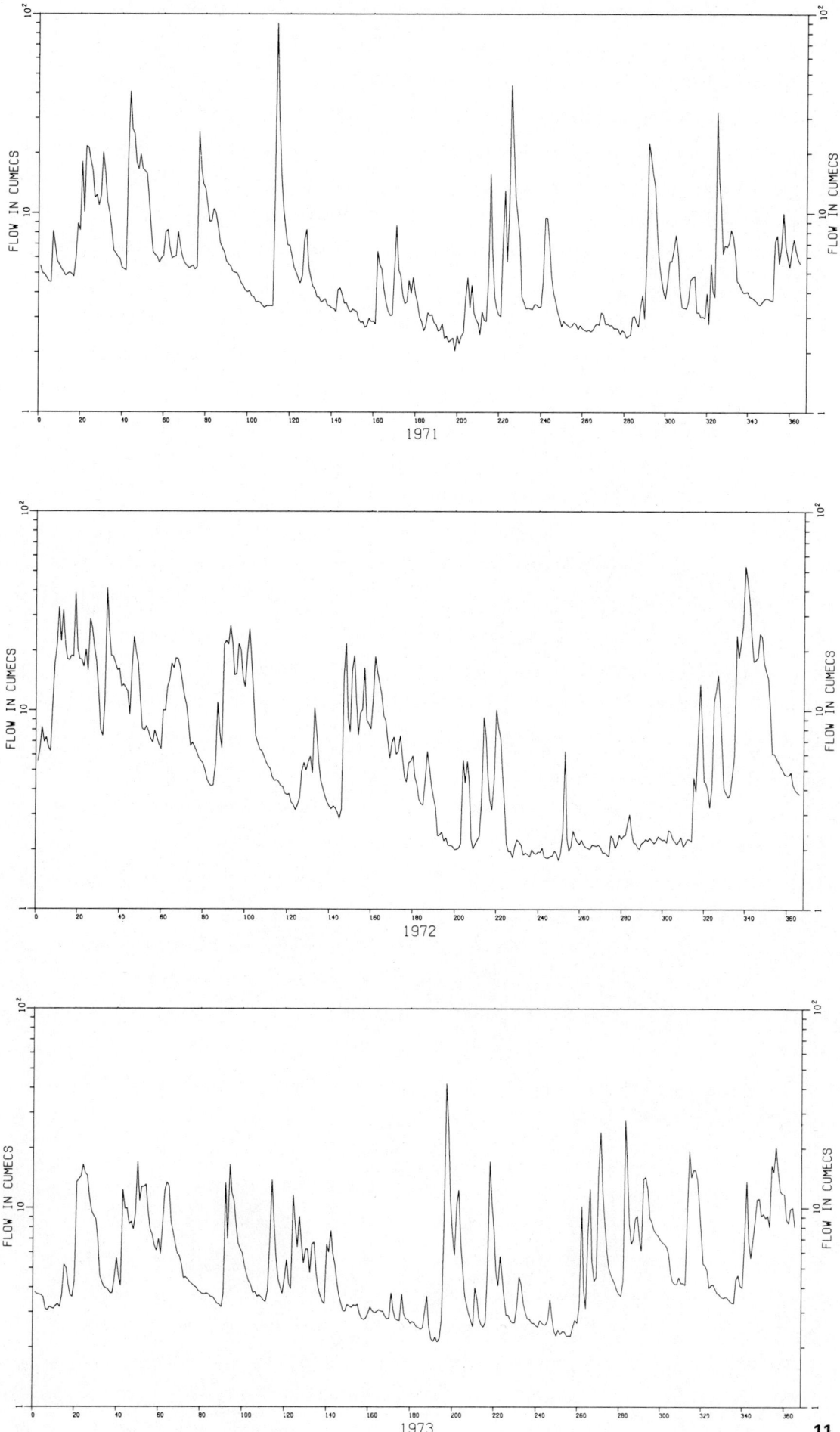

1971

1972

1973

11

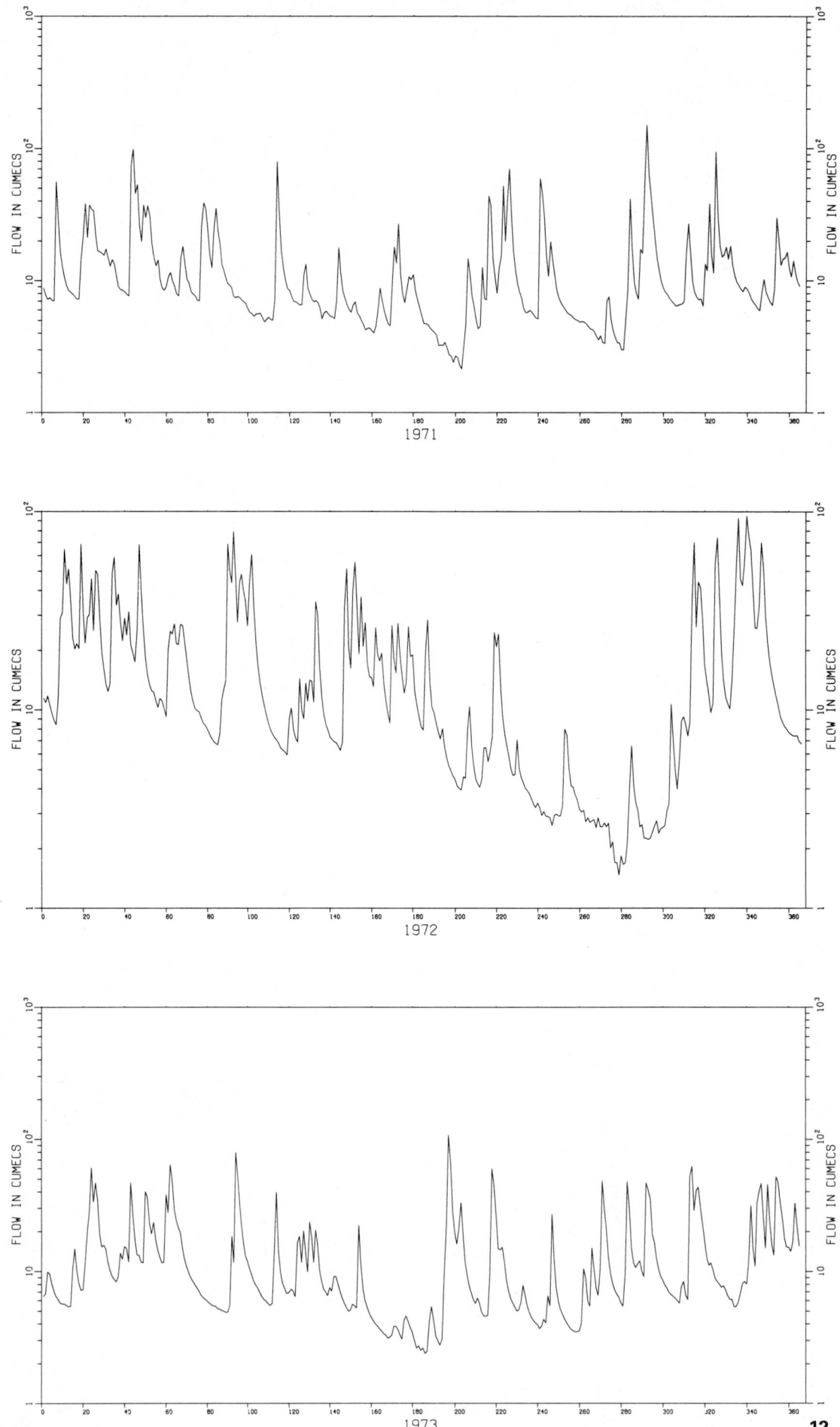

12

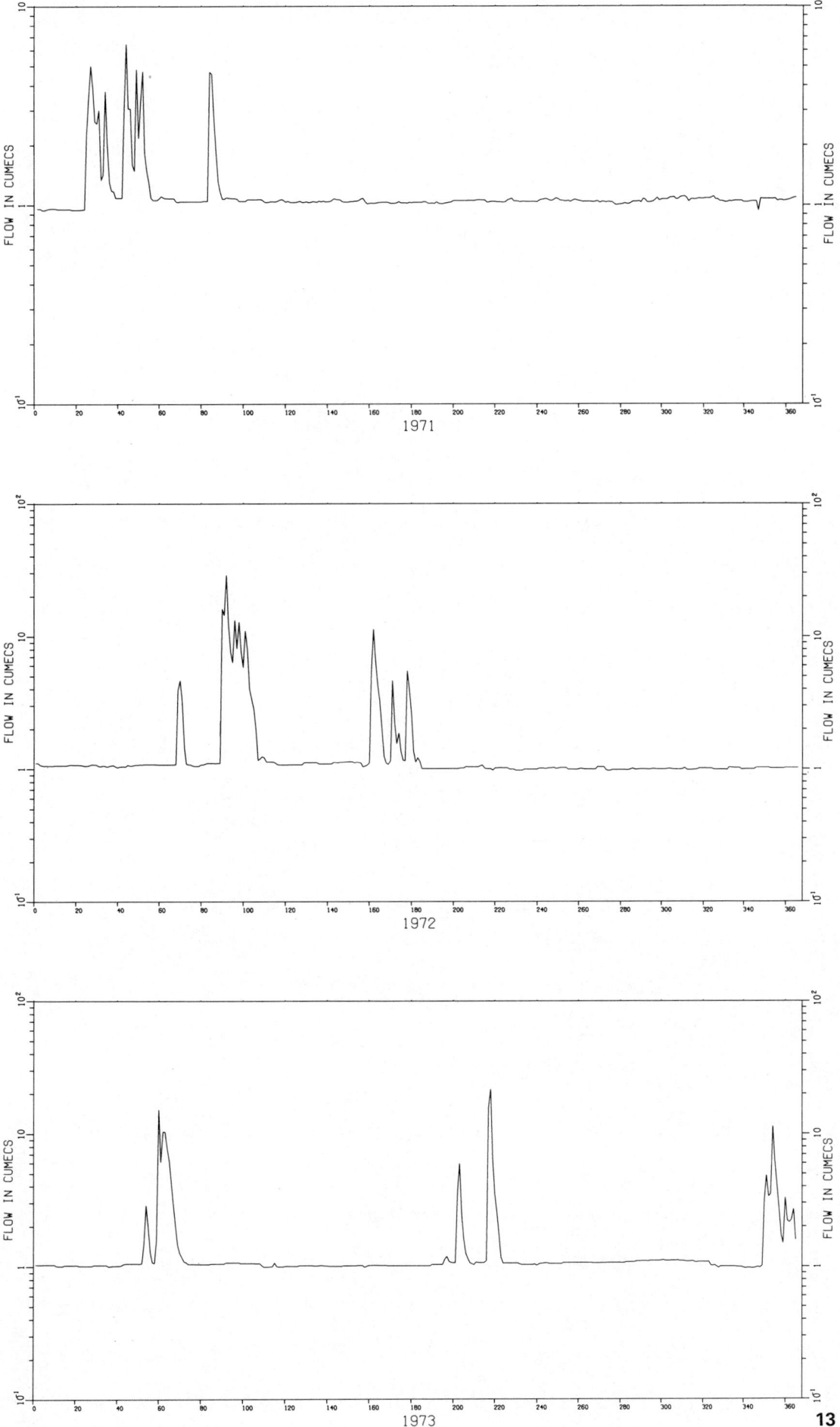

028008 RIVER DOVE AT ROCESTER DAILY MEAN FLOWS

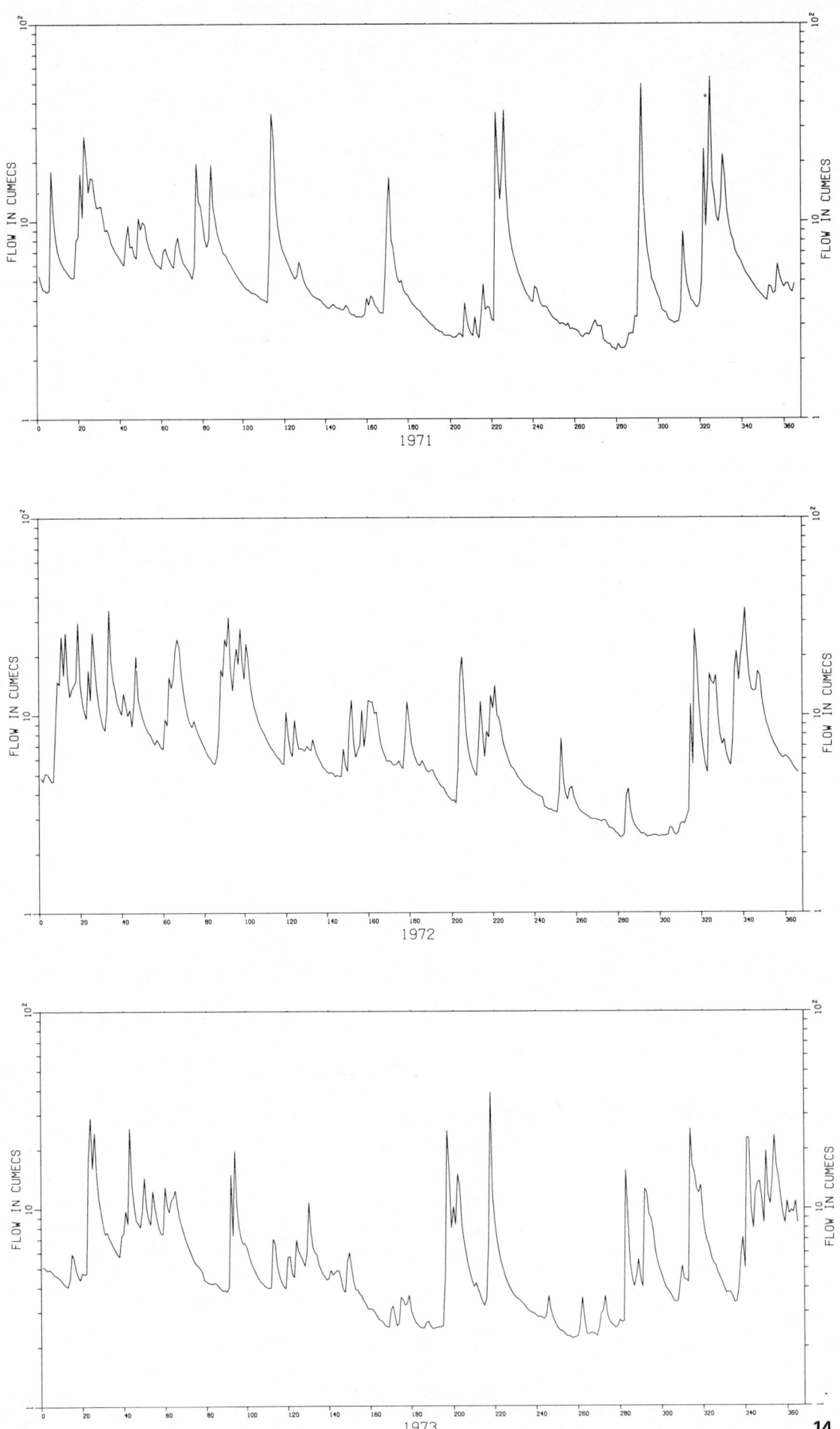

124

14

030001 RIVER WITHAM AT CLAYPOLE MILL   DAILY MEAN FLOWS

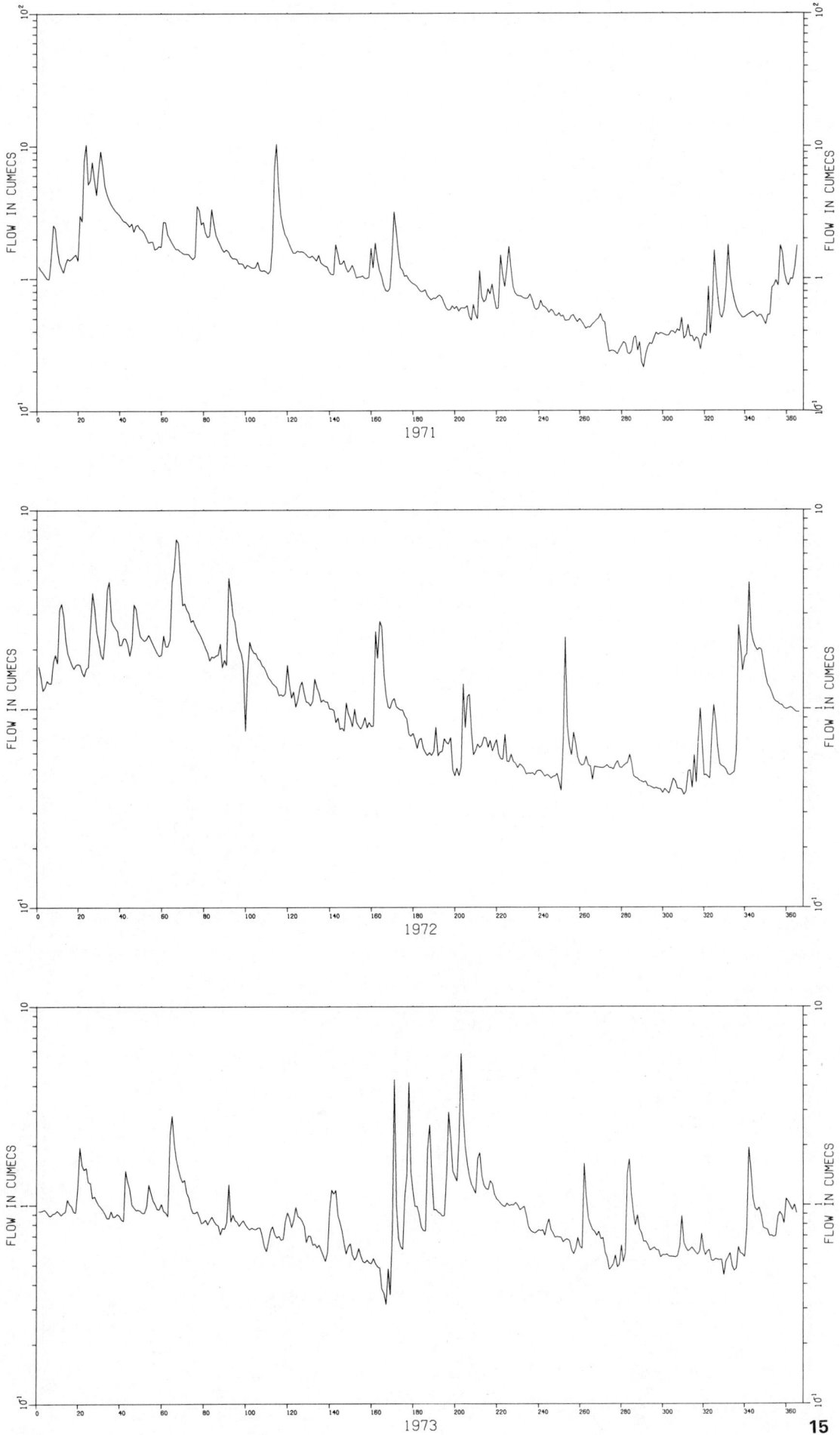

FLOW IN CUMECS

1971

FLOW IN CUMECS

1972

FLOW IN CUMECS

1973

15

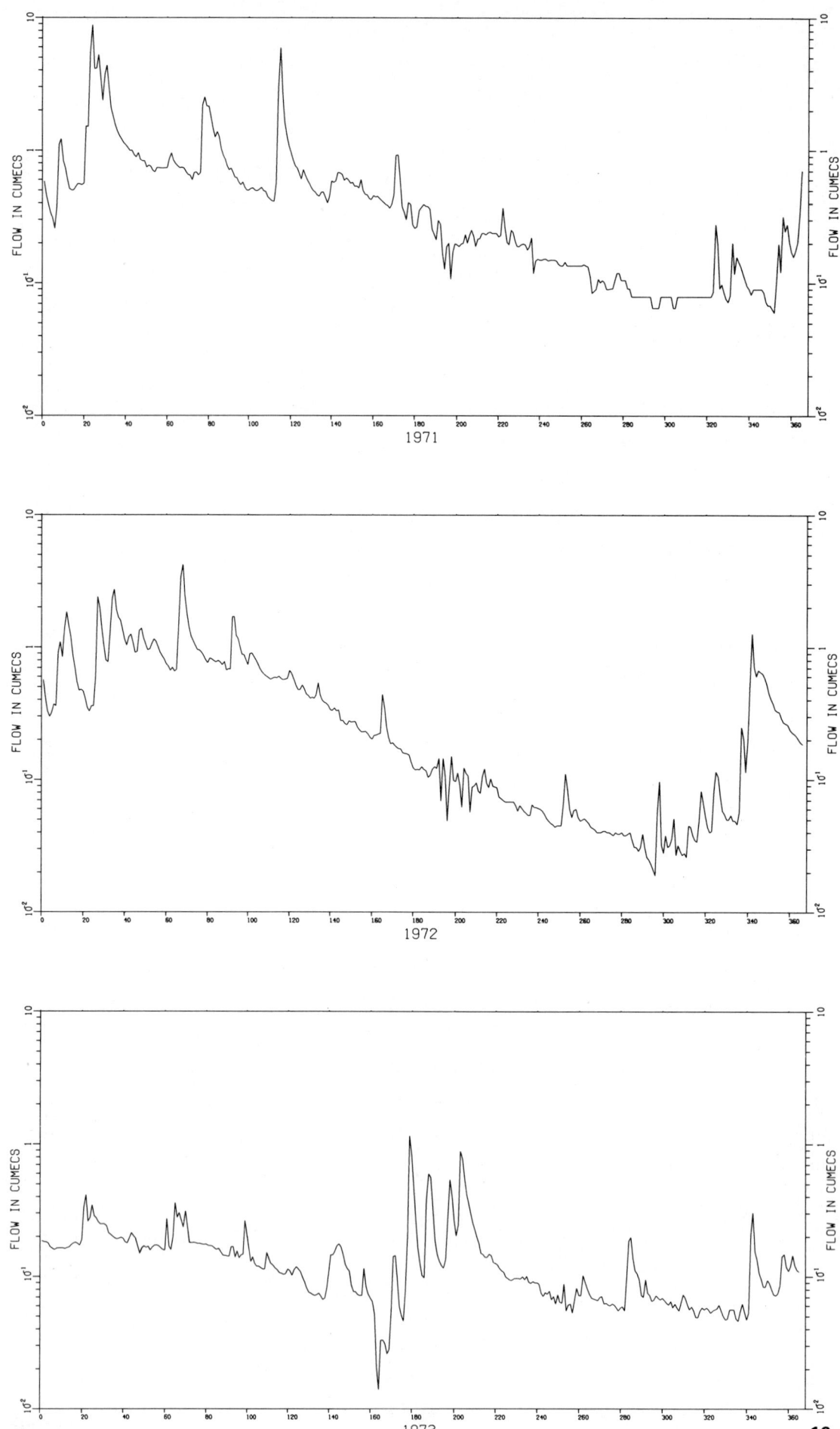

1971

1972

1973

032001 RIVER NENE AT ORTON   DAILY MEAN FLOWS

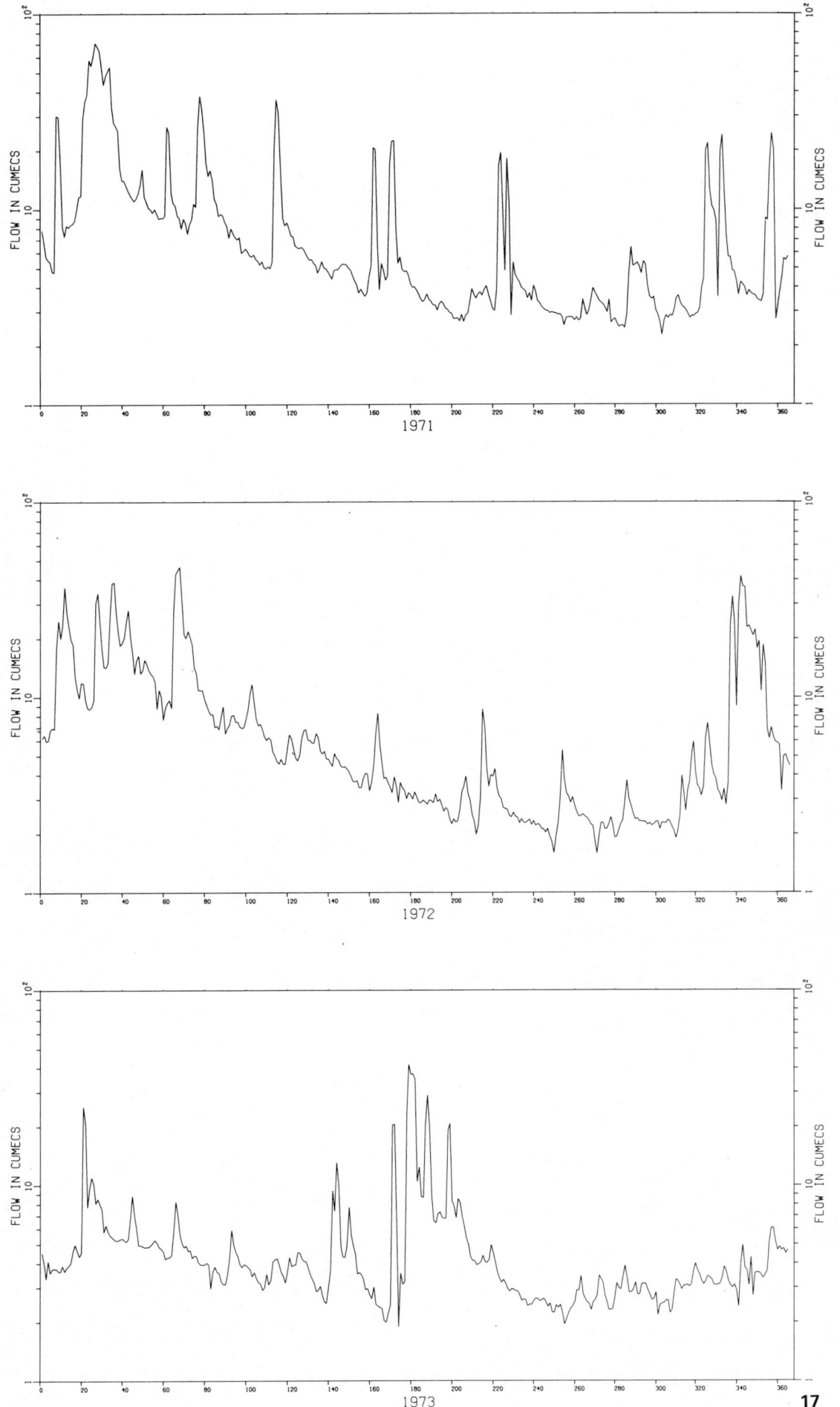

1971

1972

1973

17

033006 RIVER WISSEY AT NORTHWOLD DAILY MEAN FLOWS

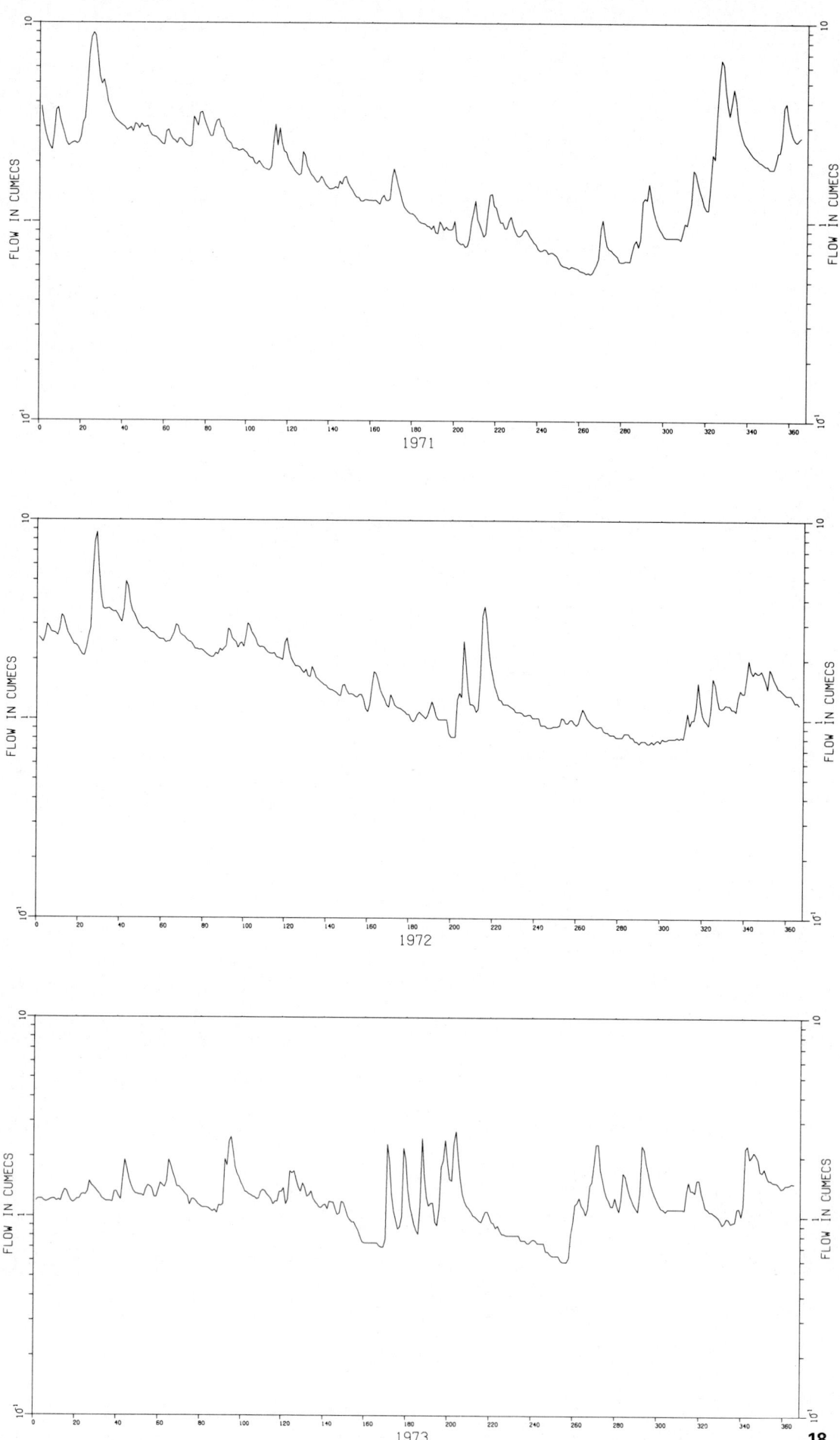

1971

1972

1973

18

033022 RIVER IVEL AT BLUNHAM   DAILY MEAN FLOWS

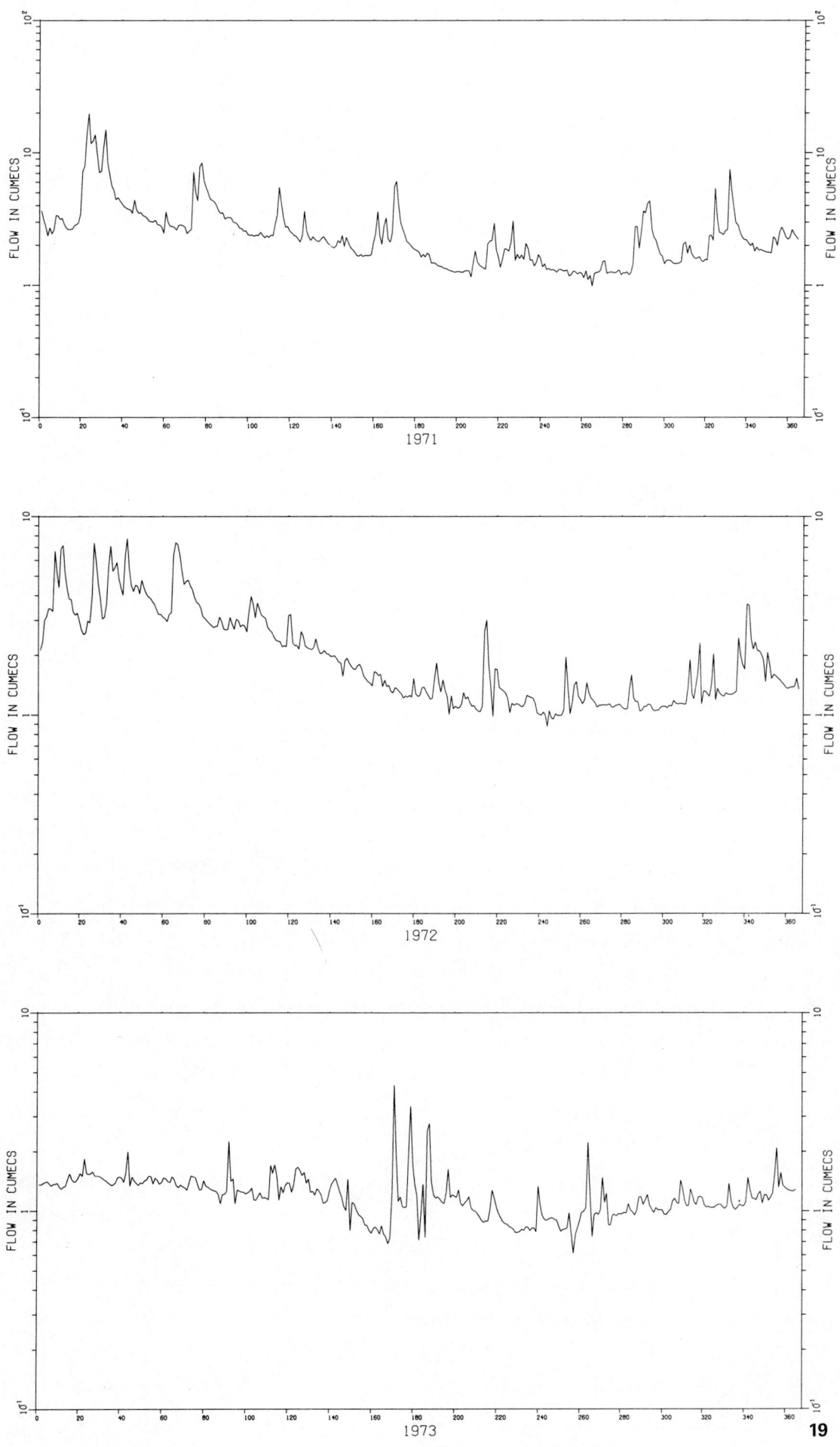

1971

1972

1973

19

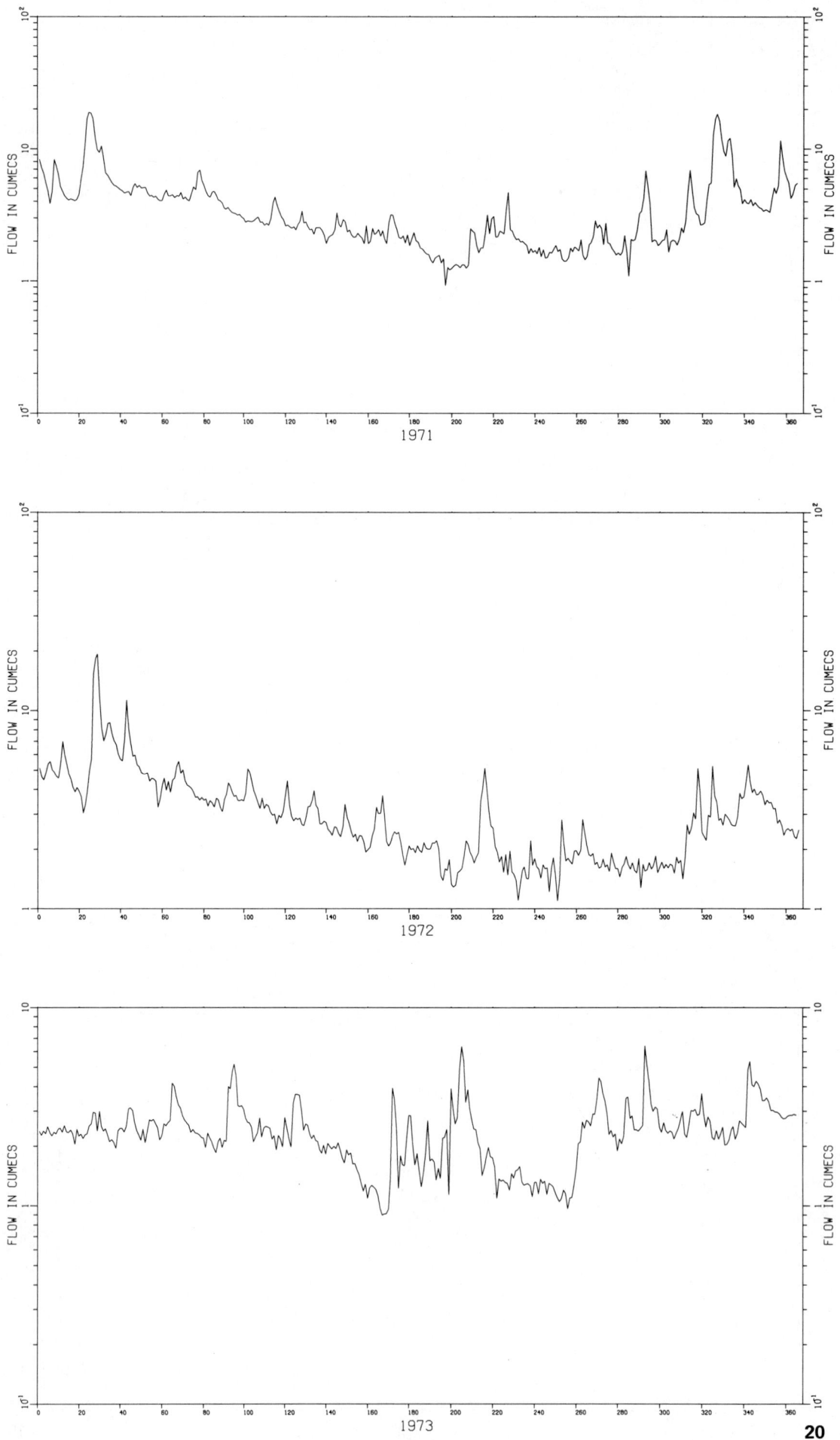

20

036001 RIVER STOUR AT STRATFORD ST MARY   DAILY MEAN FLOWS

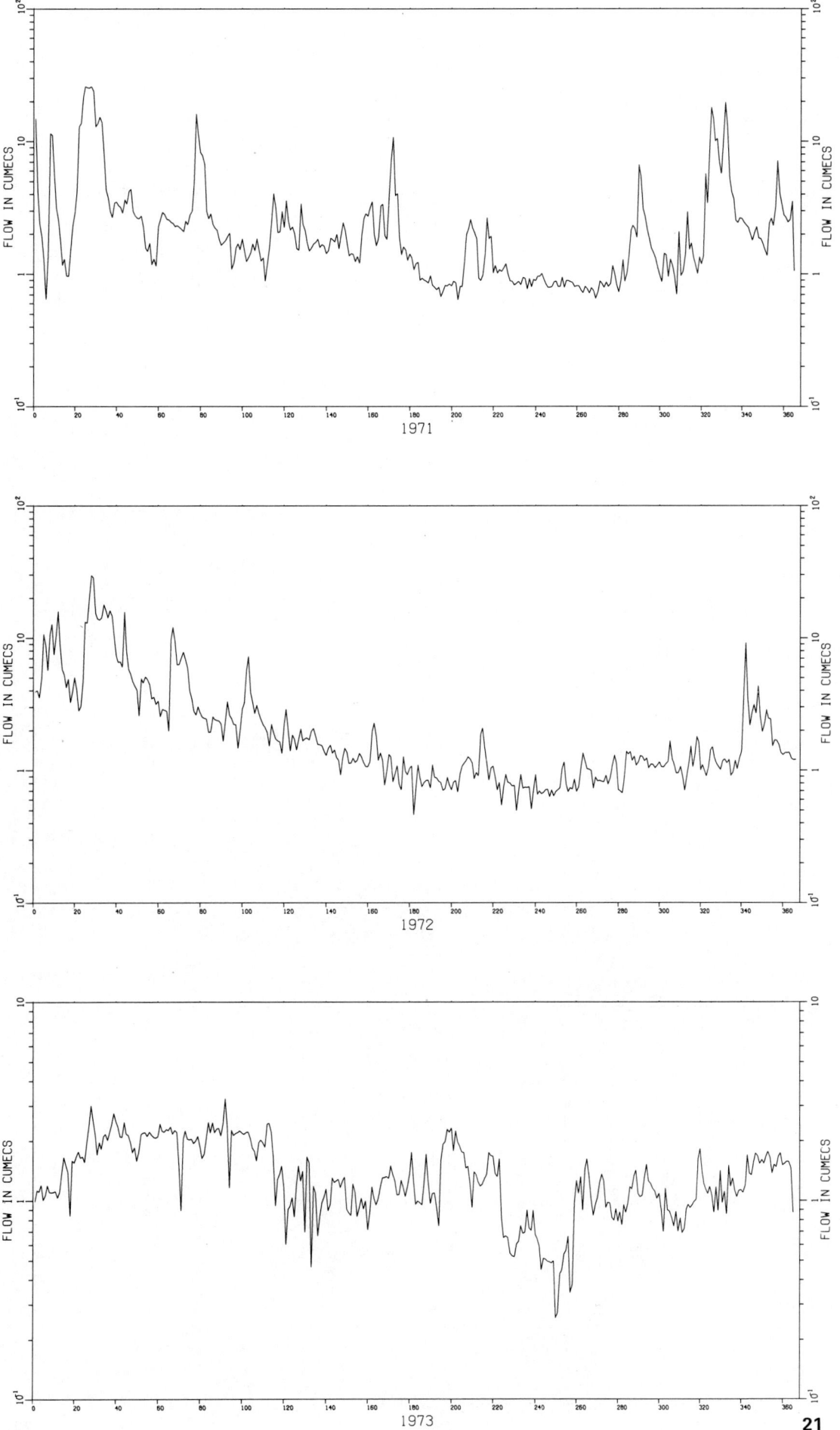

21

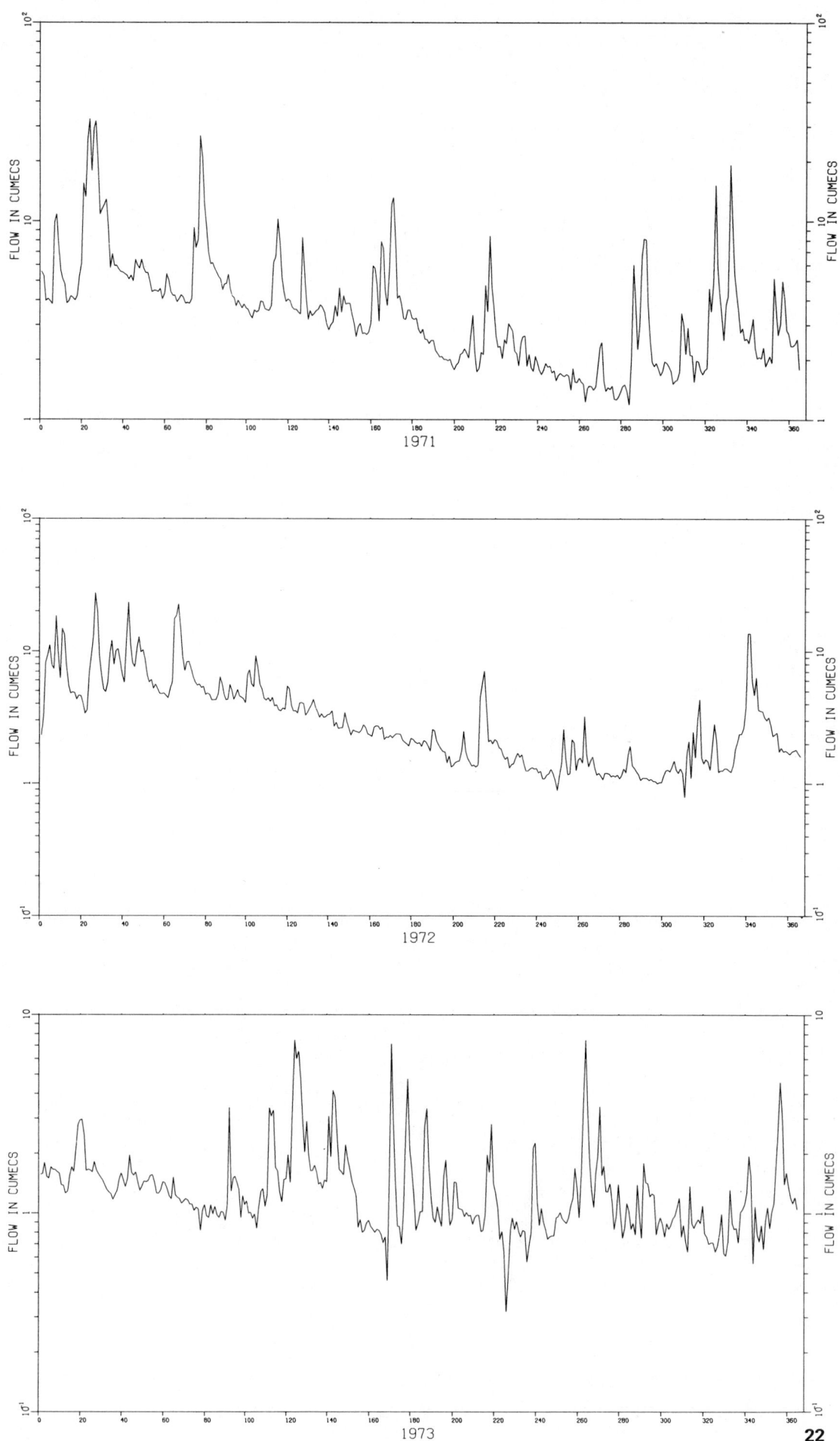

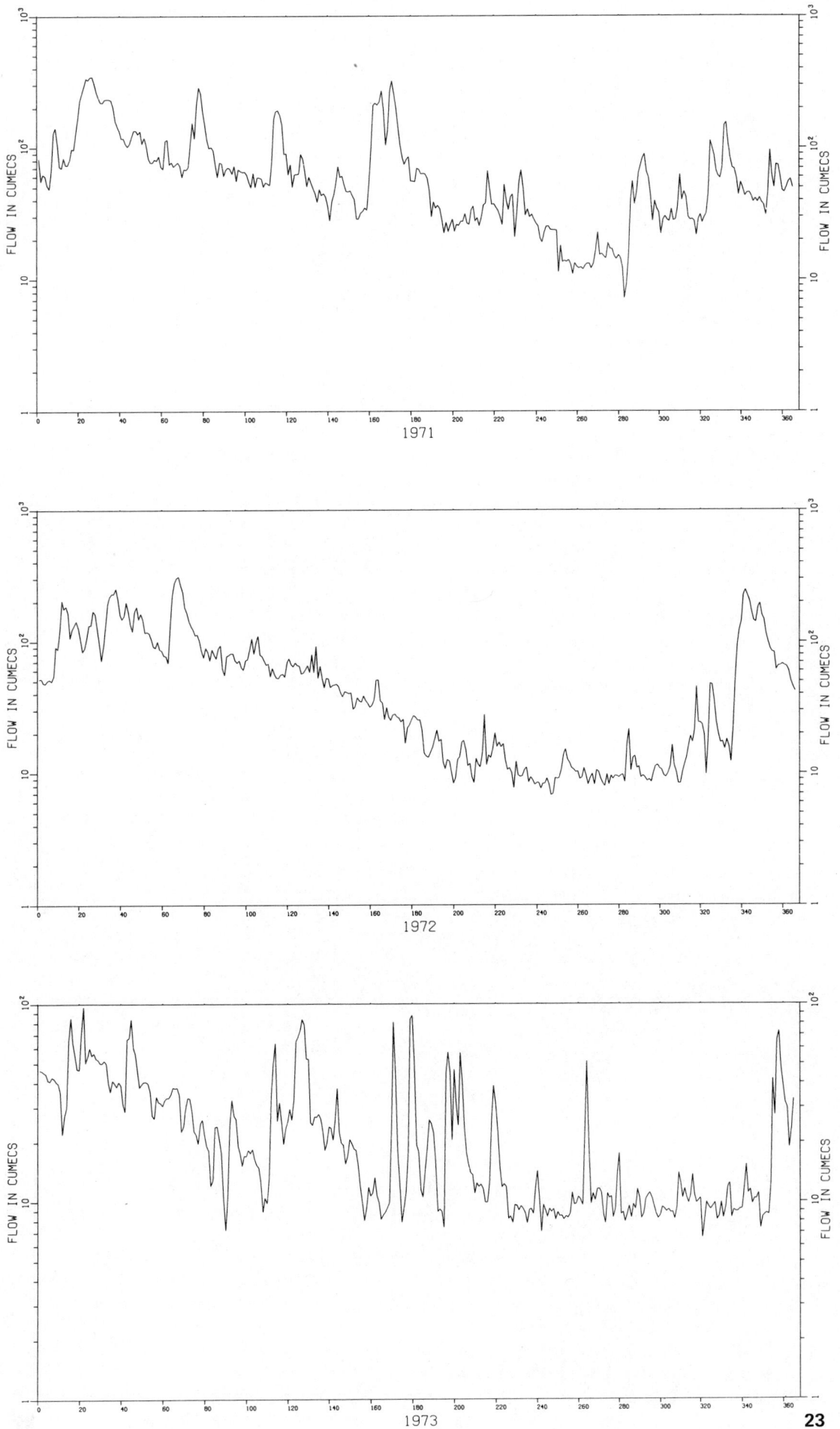

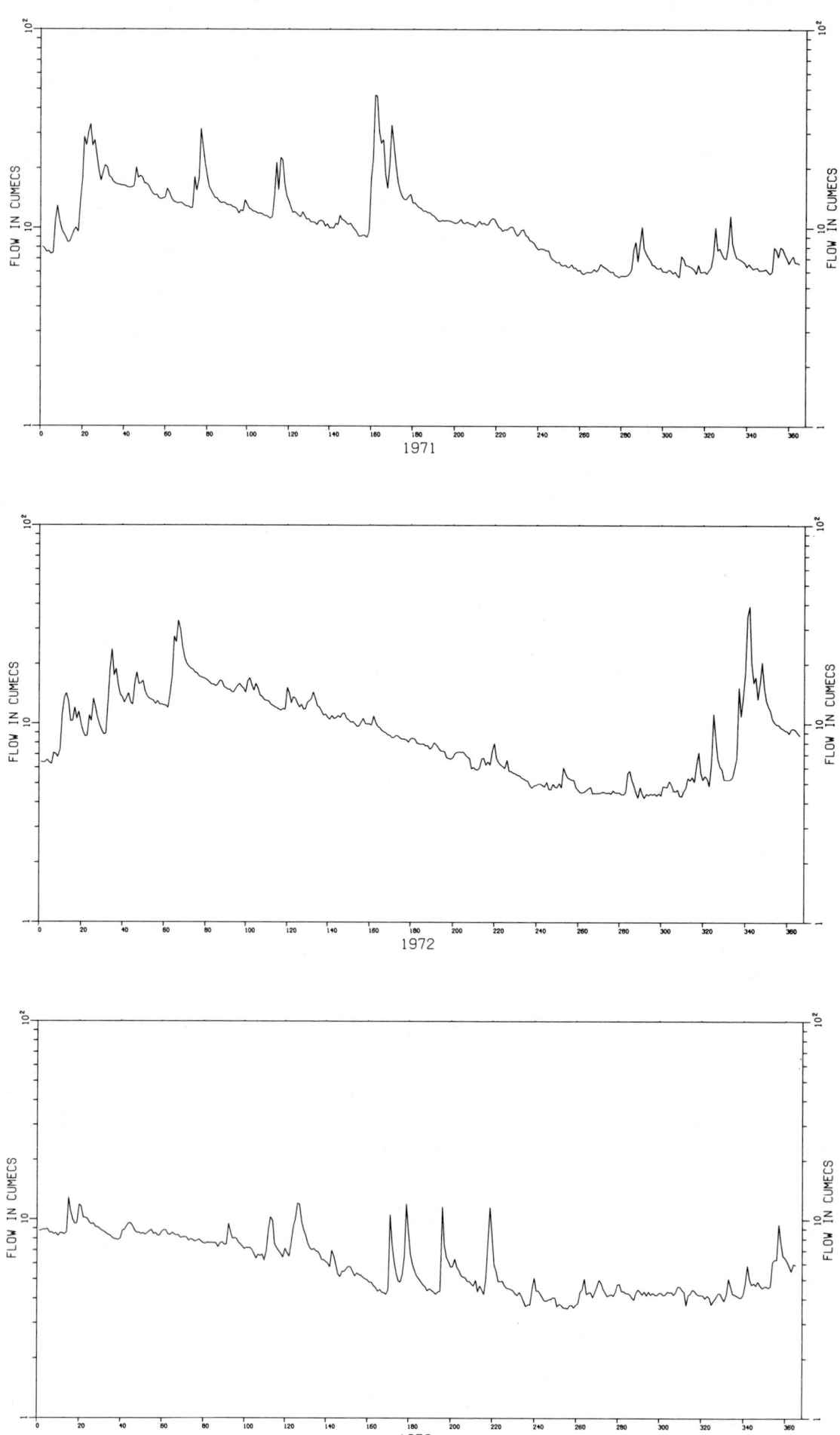

1971

1972

1973

24

040011 RIVER GREAT STOUR AT HORTON   DAILY MEAN FLOWS

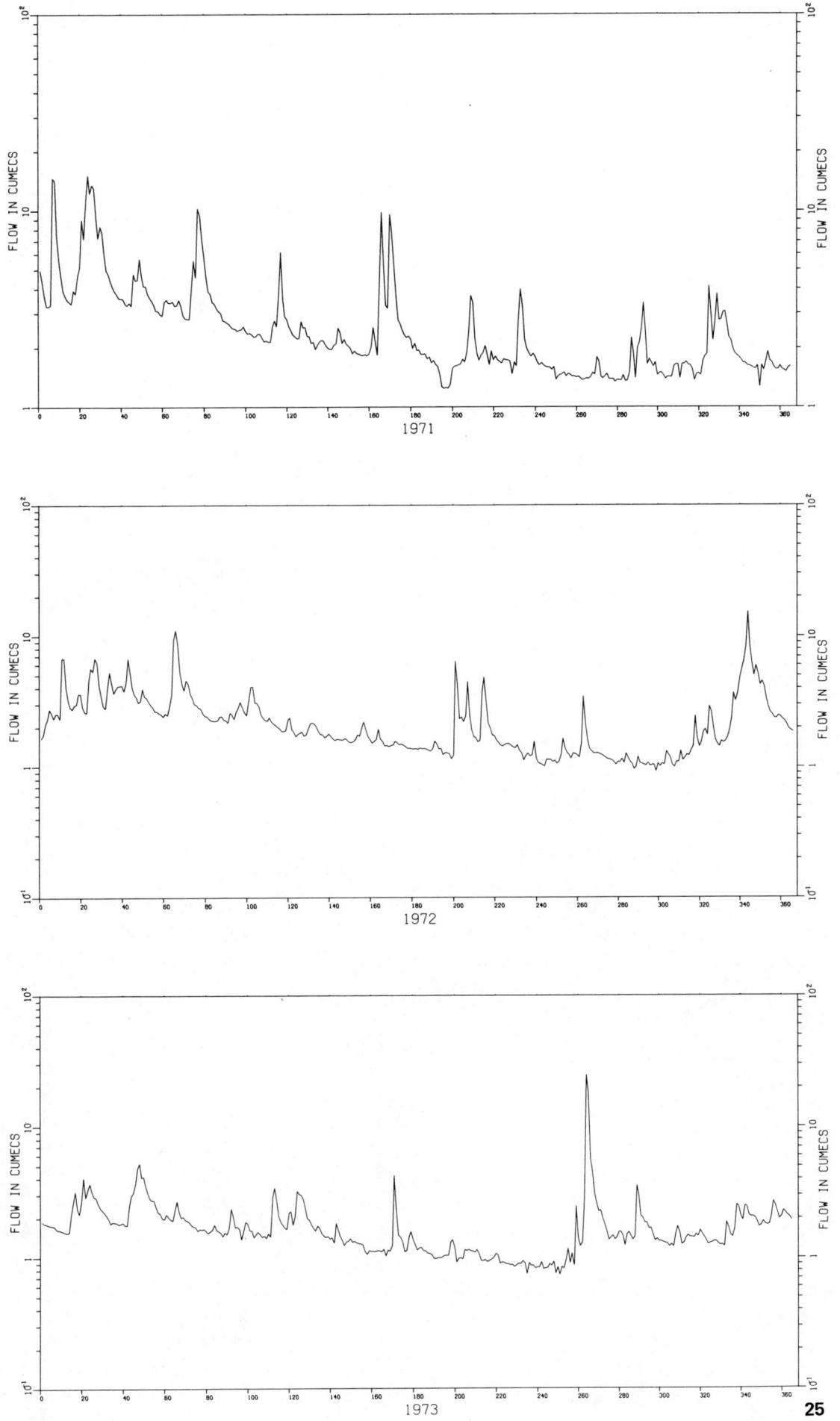

1971

1972

1973

25

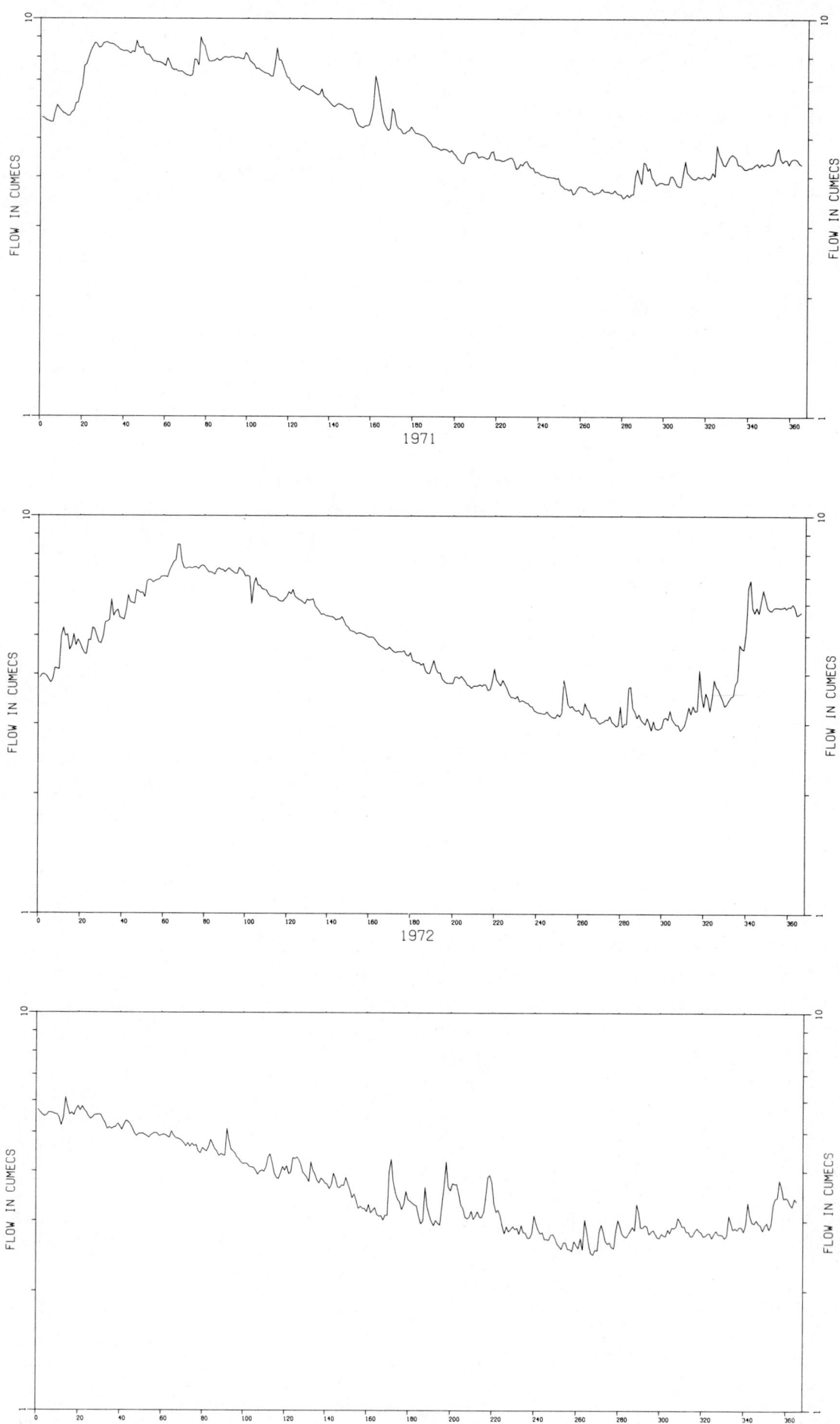

26

043005 RIVER AVON AT AMESBURY DAILY MEAN FLOW

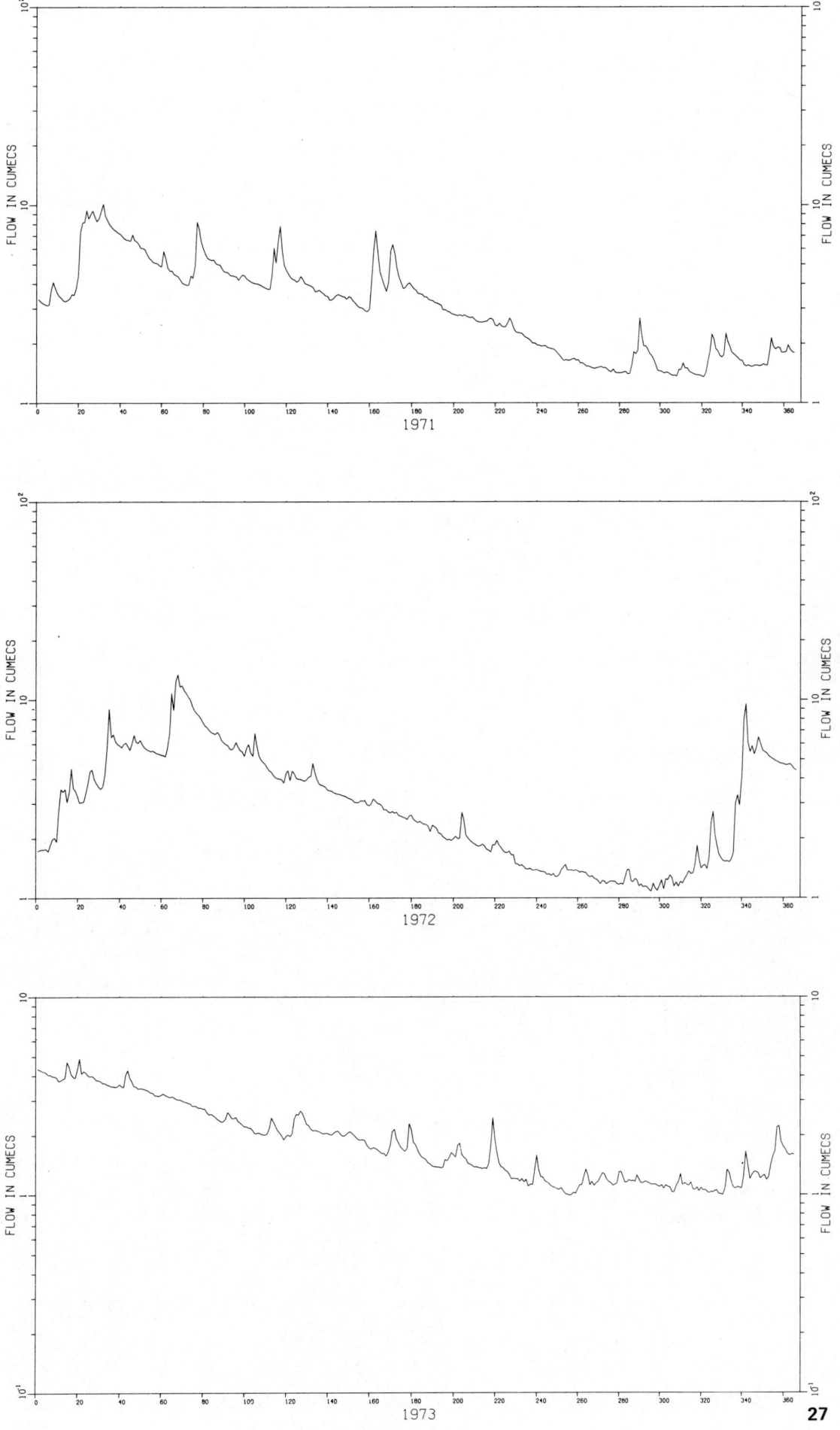

1971

1972

1973

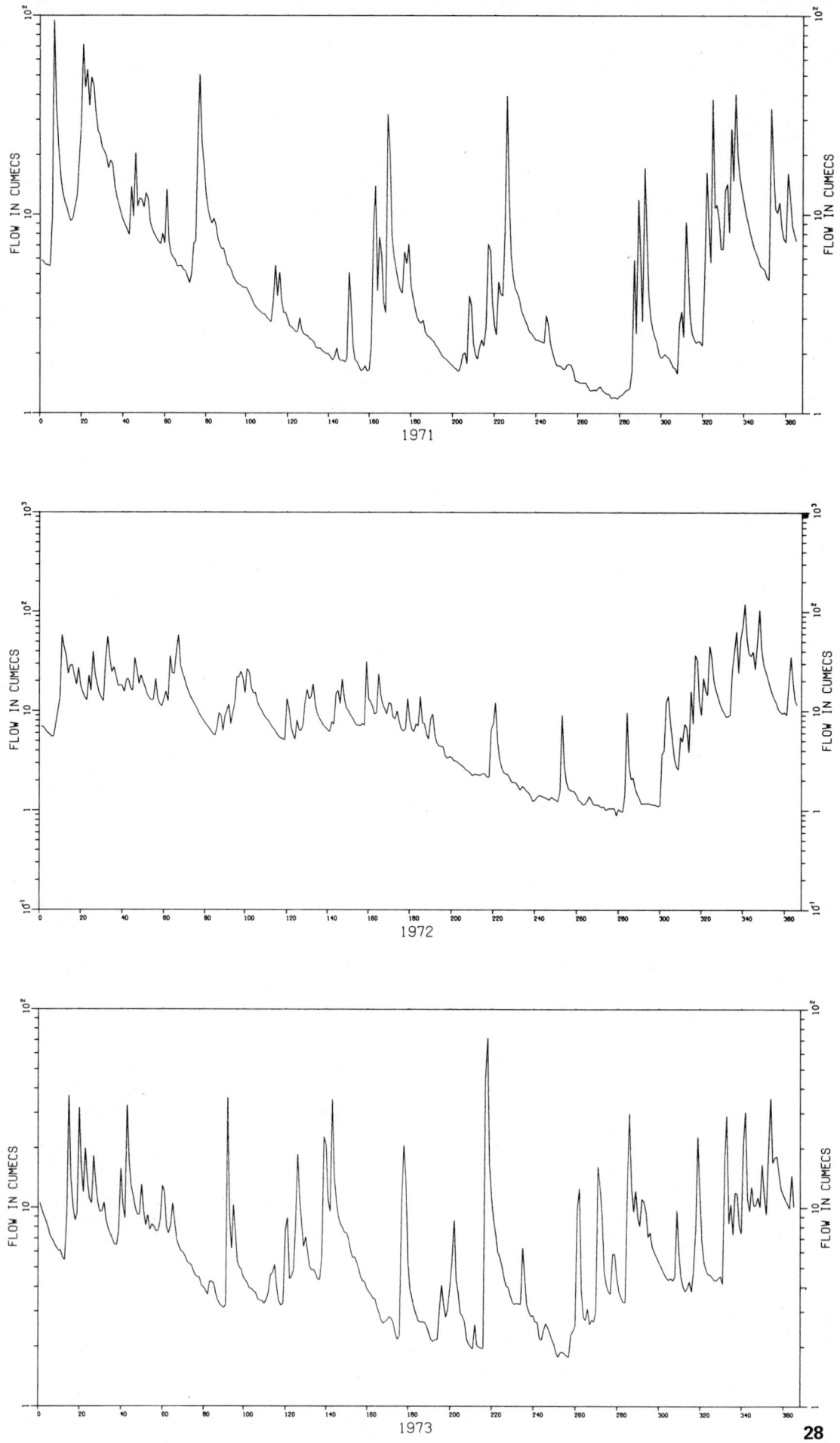

1971

1972

1973

28

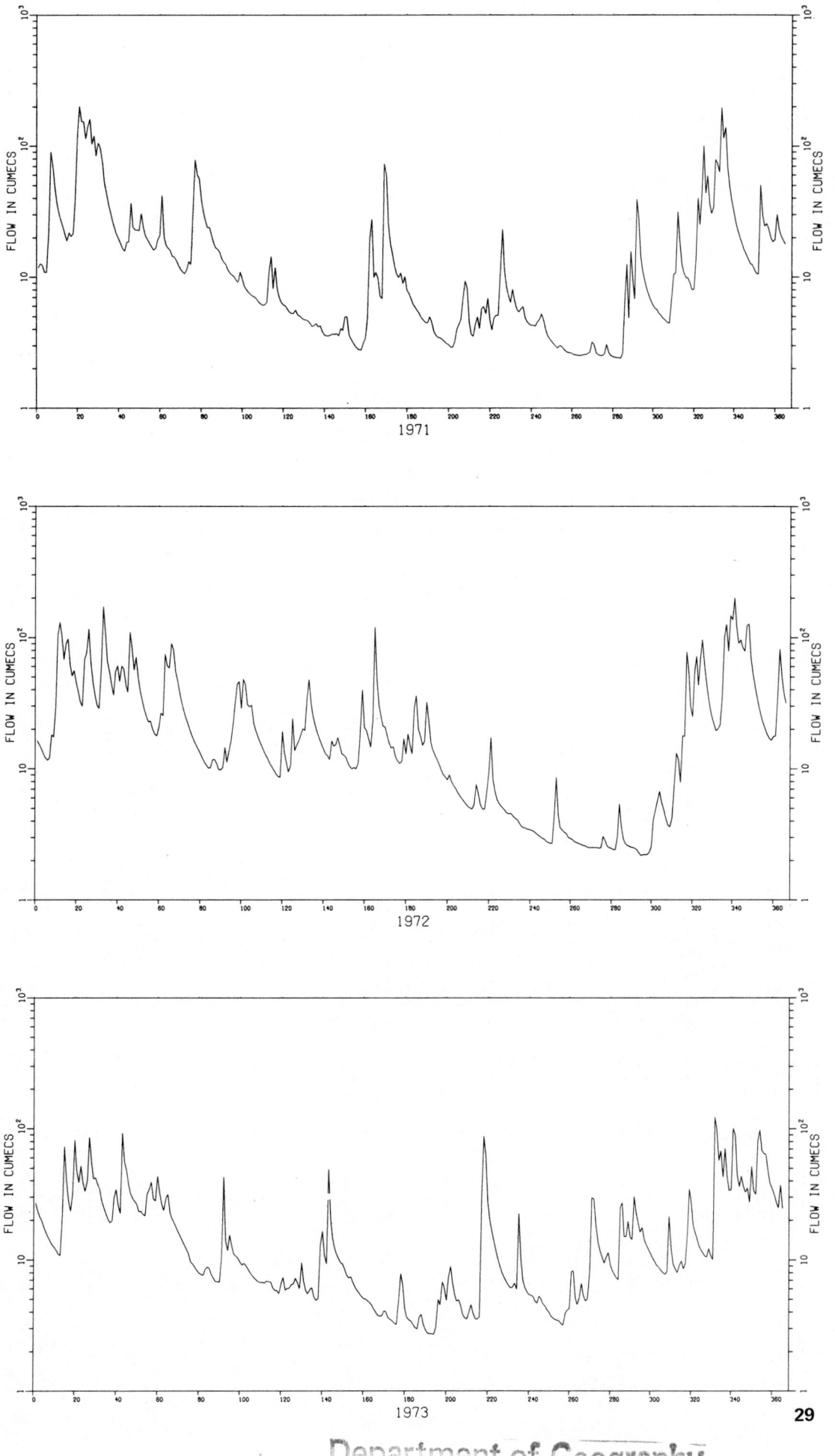

1971

1972

1973

29

139

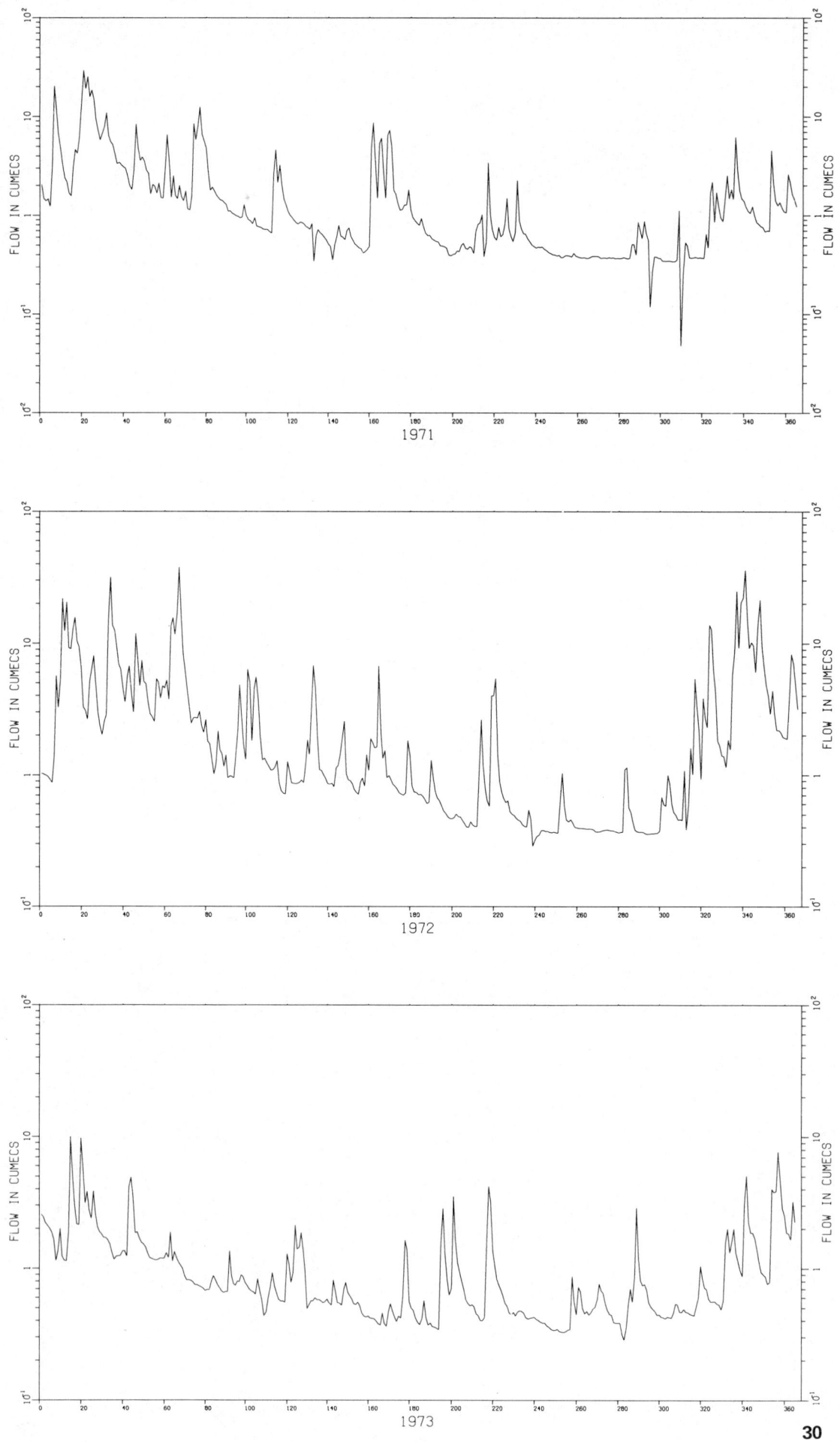

30

054001 RIVER SEVERN AT BEWDLEY DAILY MEAN FLOWS

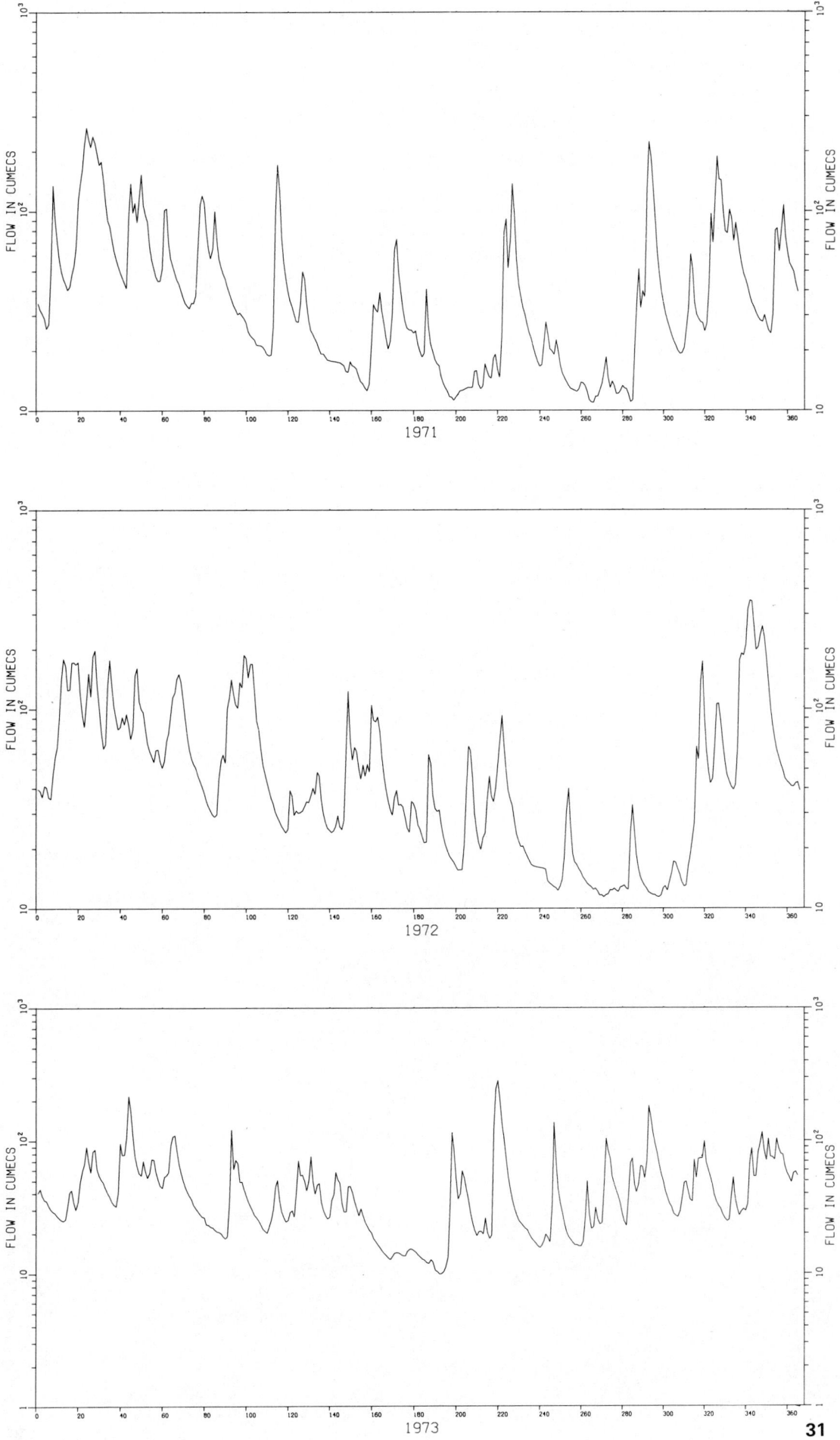

055003 RIVER LUGG AT LUGWARDINE   DAILY MEAN FLOWS

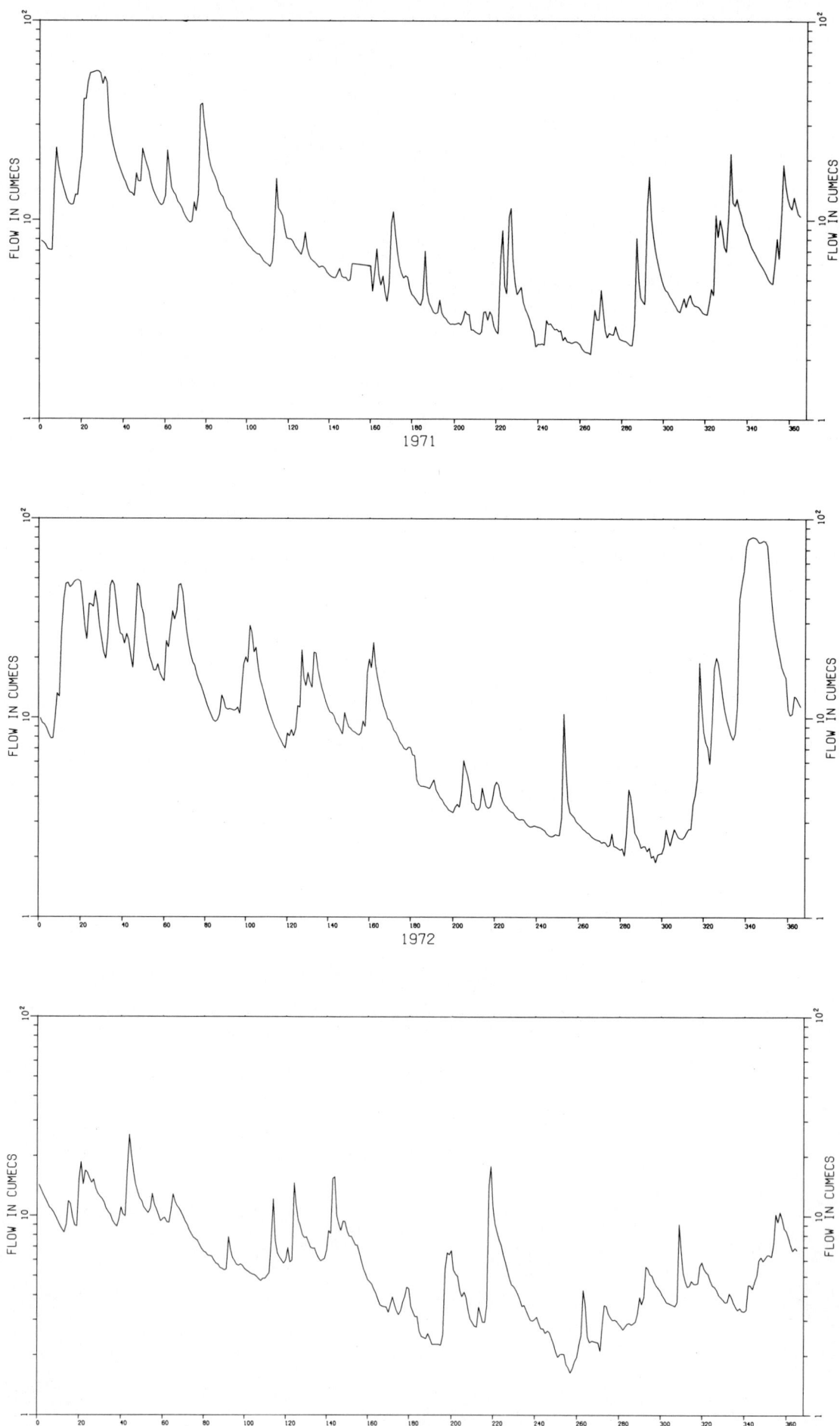

1971

1972

1973

32

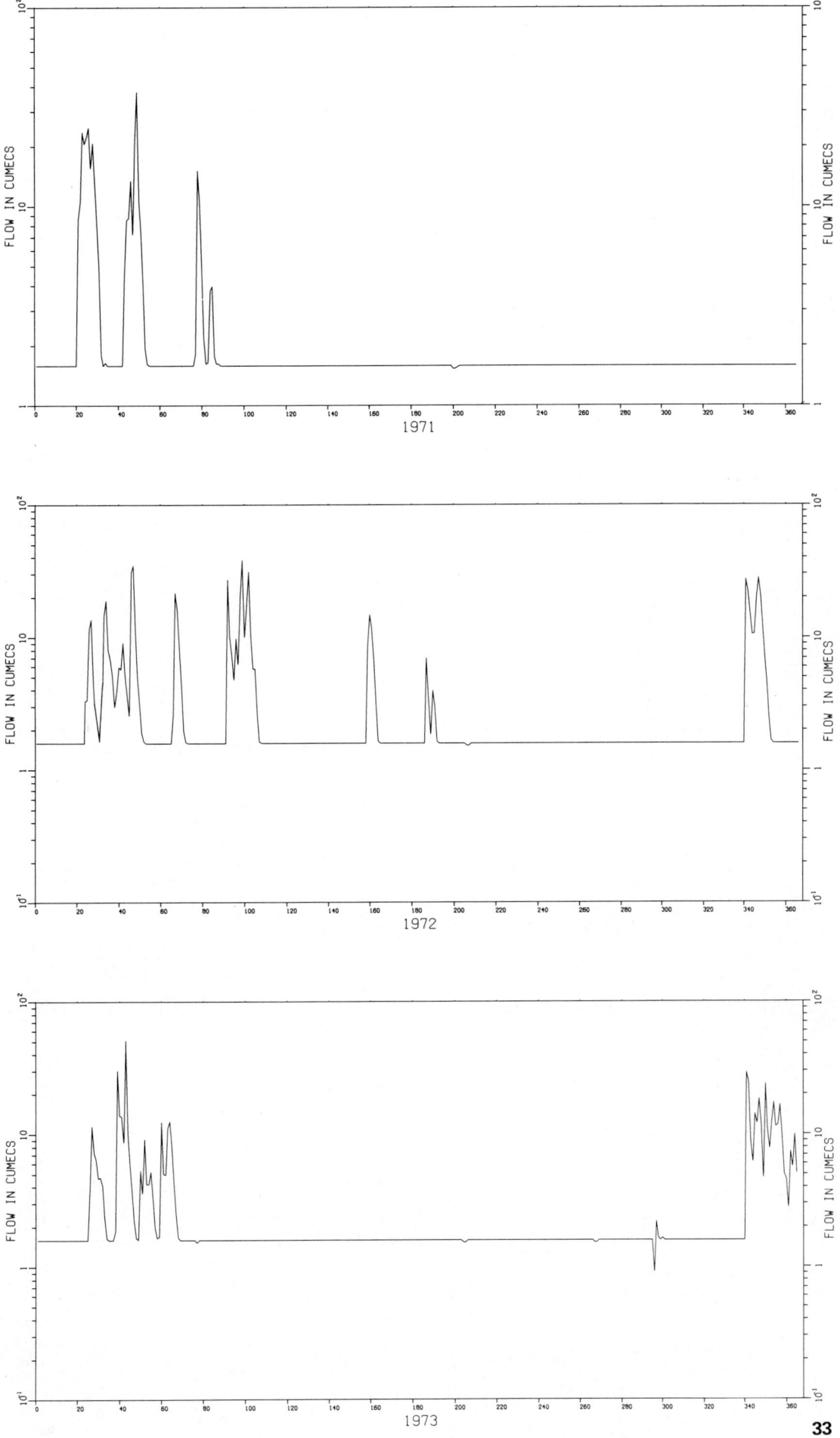

1971

1972

1973

33

055007 RIVER WYE AT ERWOOD DAILY MEAN FLOWS

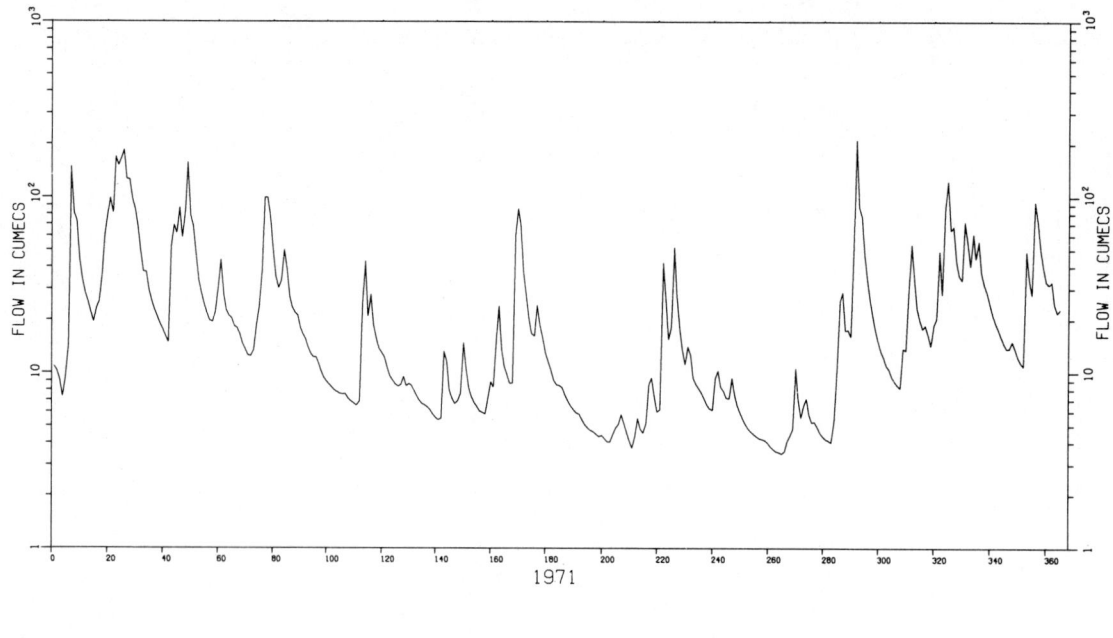

1971

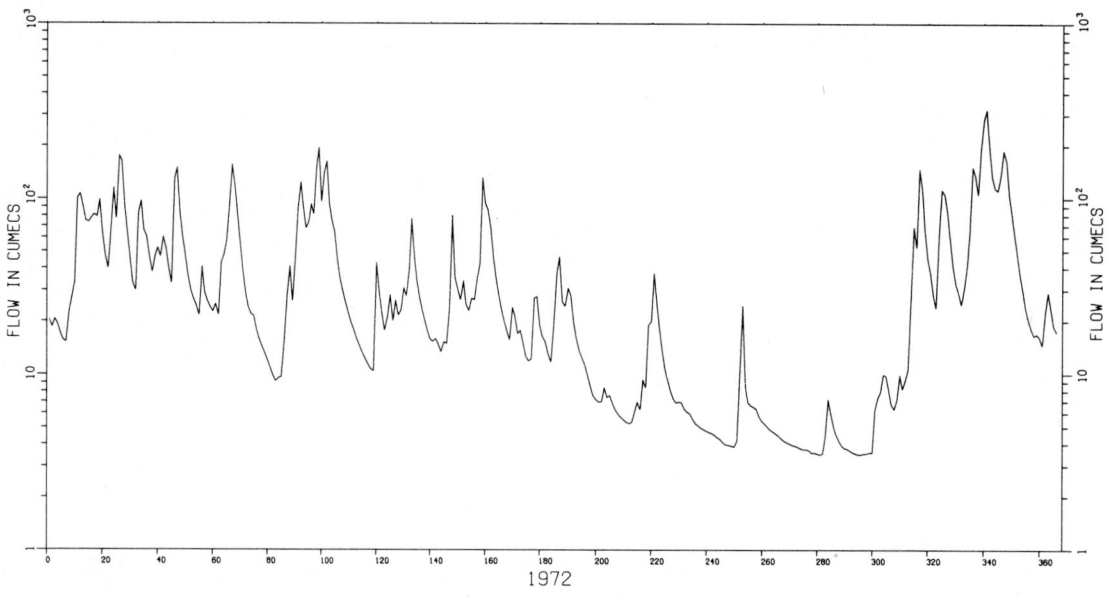

1972

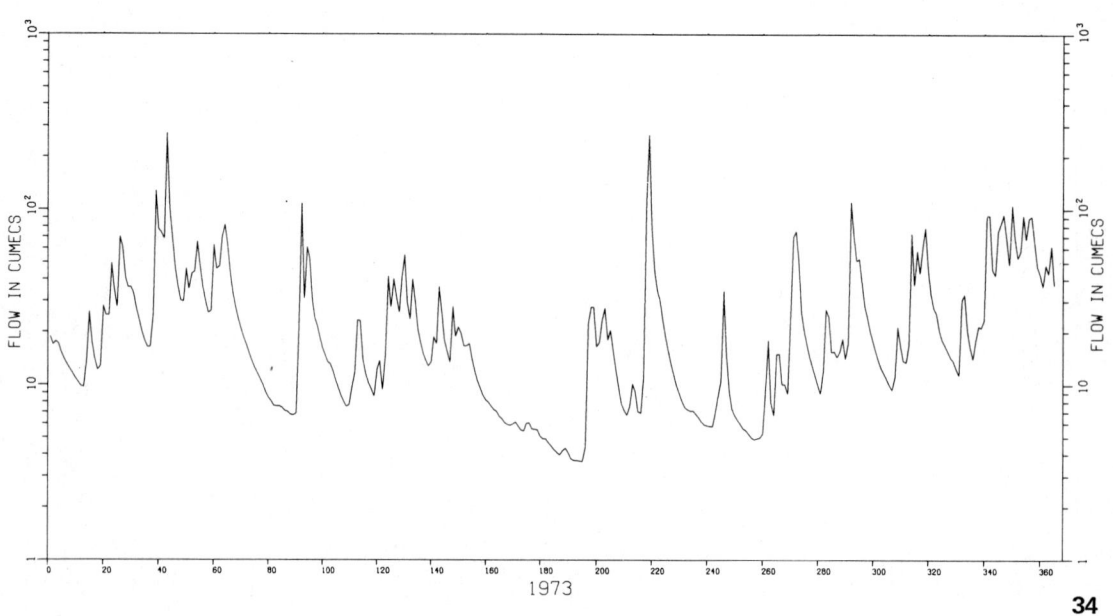

1973

34

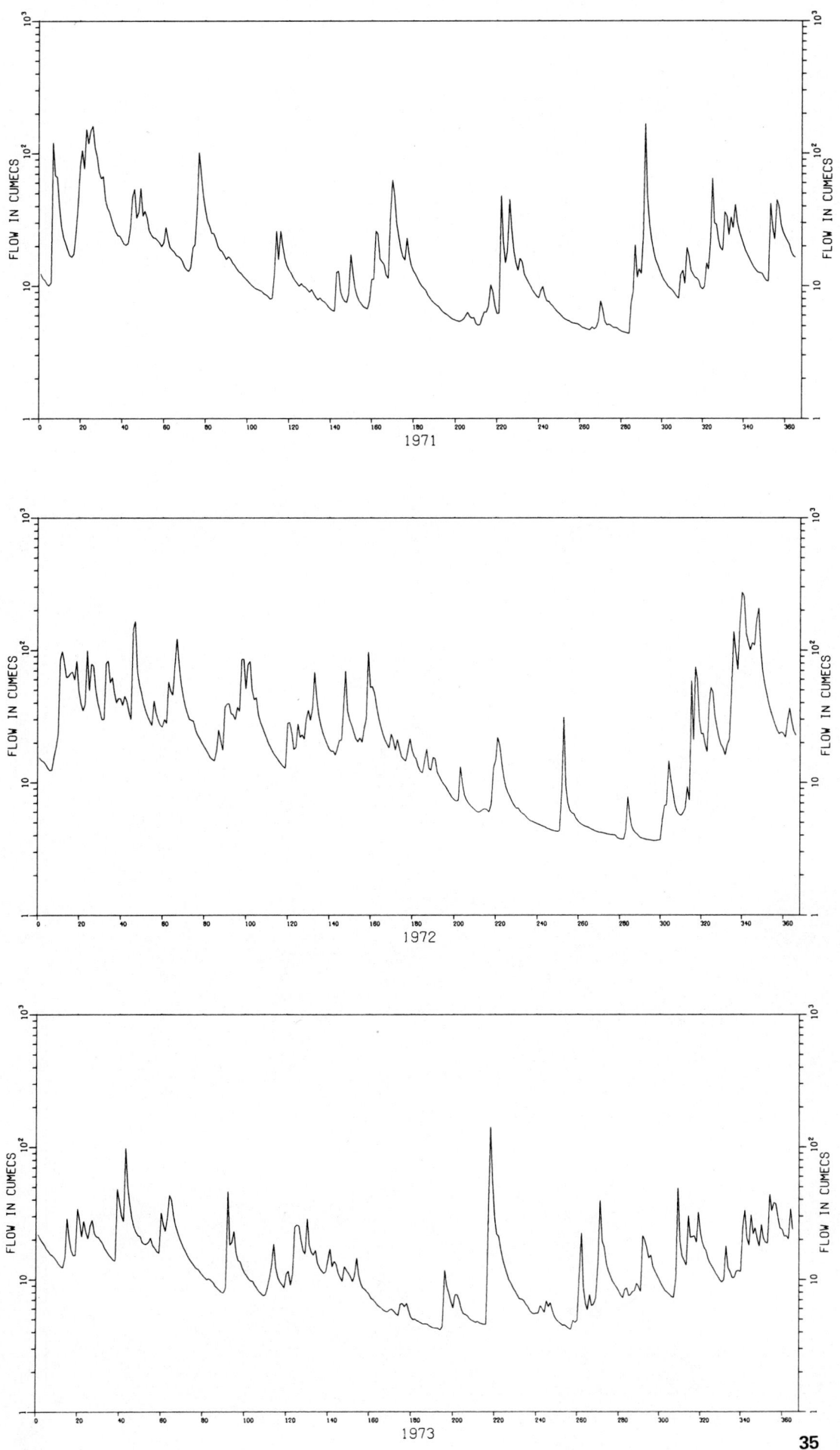

056001 RIVER USK AT CHAIN BRIDGE   DAILY MEAN FLOWS

1971

1972

1973

35

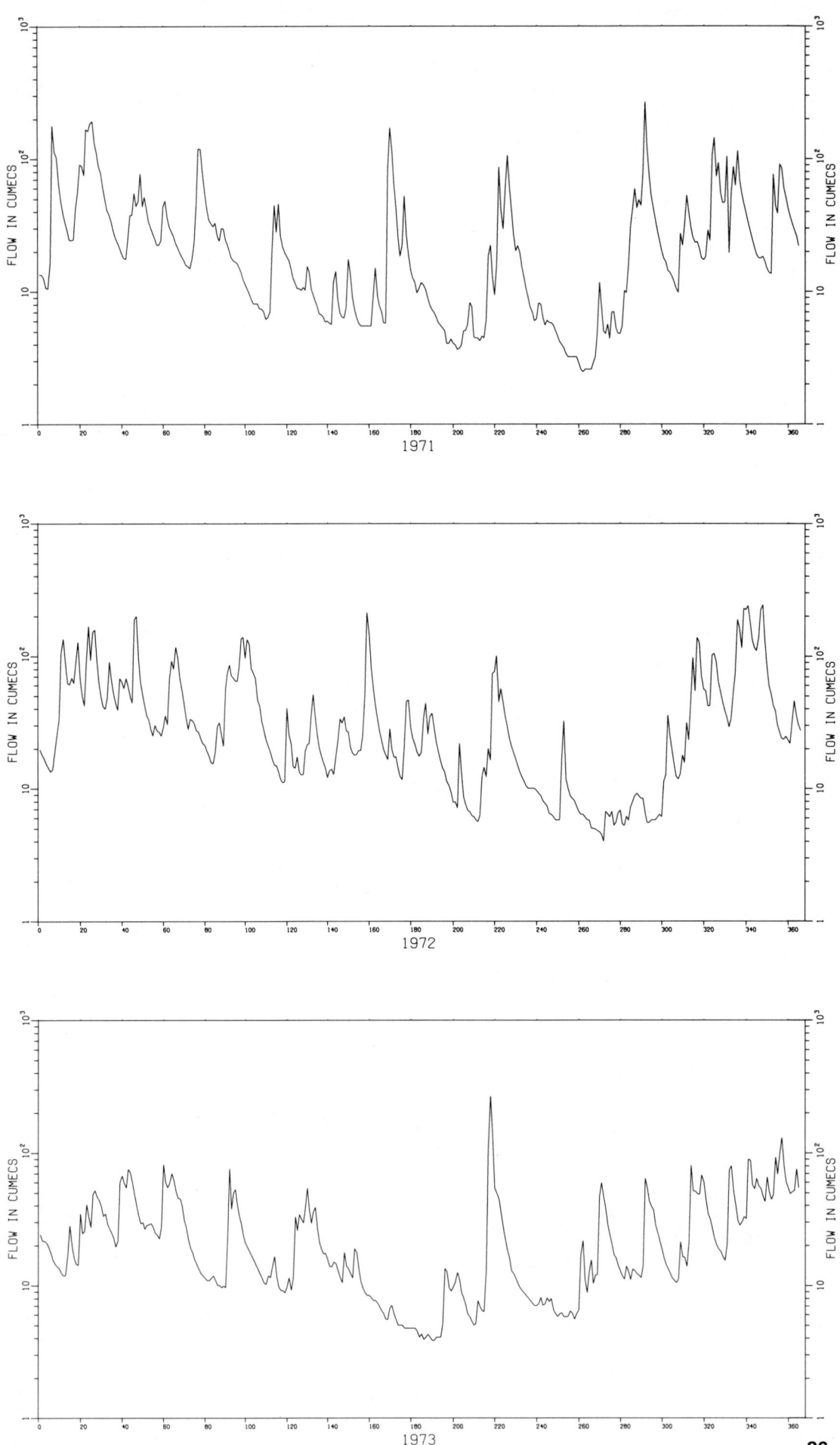

36

067015 RIVER DEE AT MANLEY HALL DAILY MEAN FLOWS

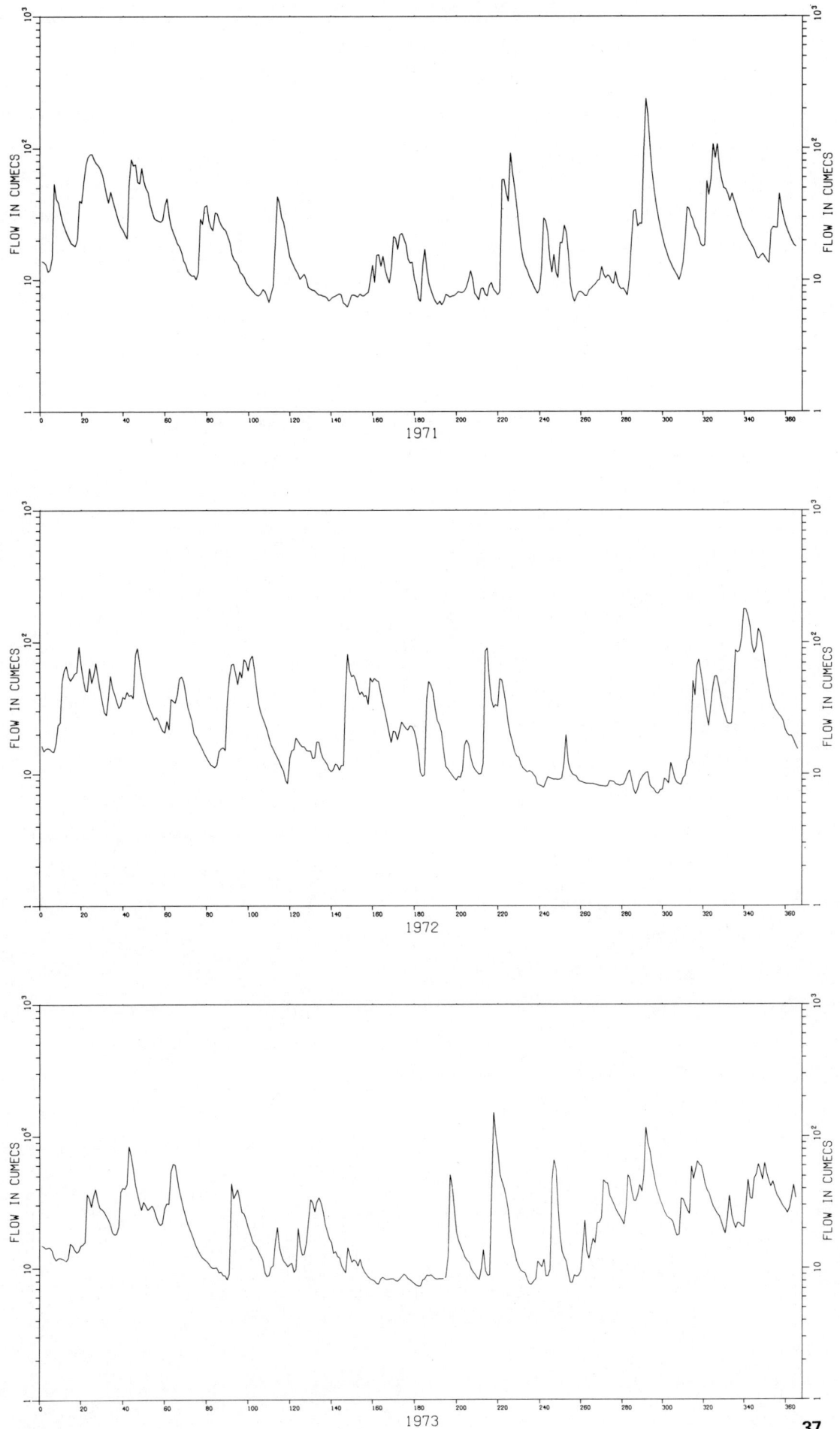

1971

1972

1973

37

071001 RIVER RIBBLE AT SAMLESBURY   DAILY MEAN FLOWS

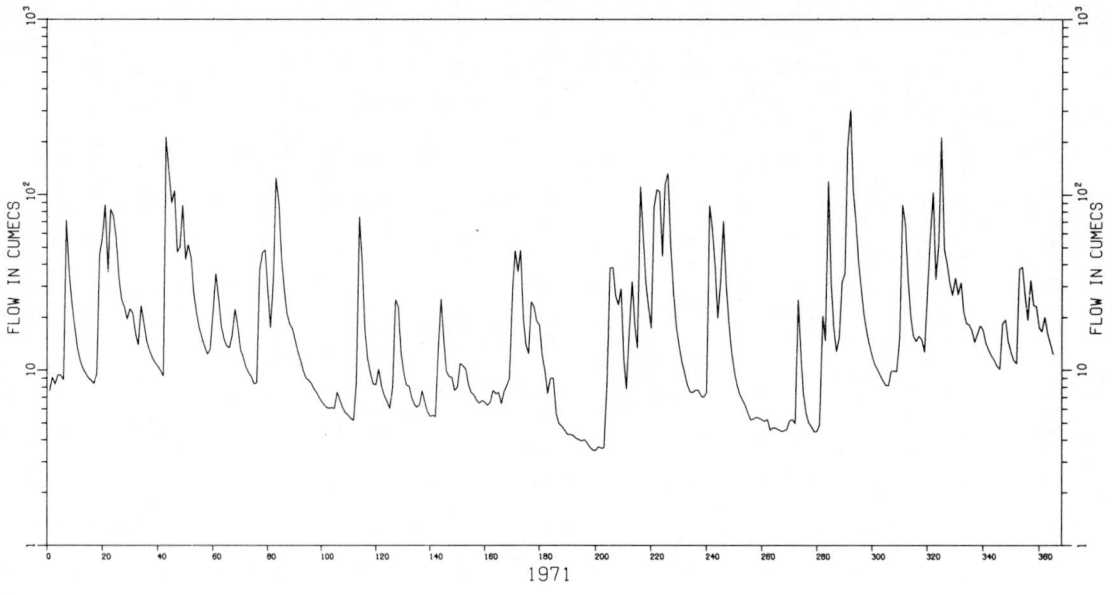

1971

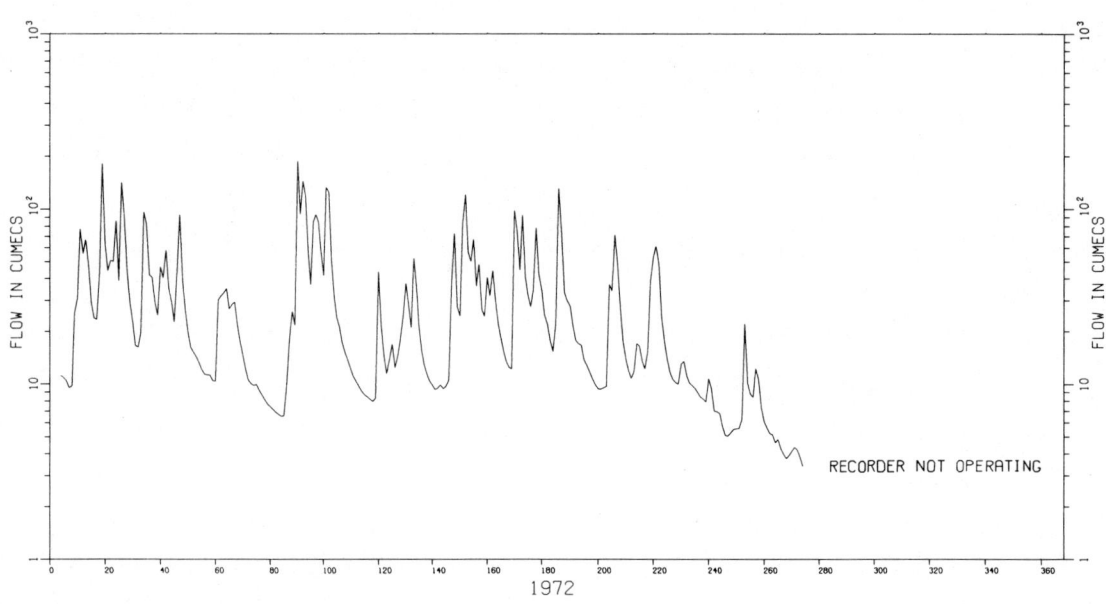

RECORDER NOT OPERATING

1972

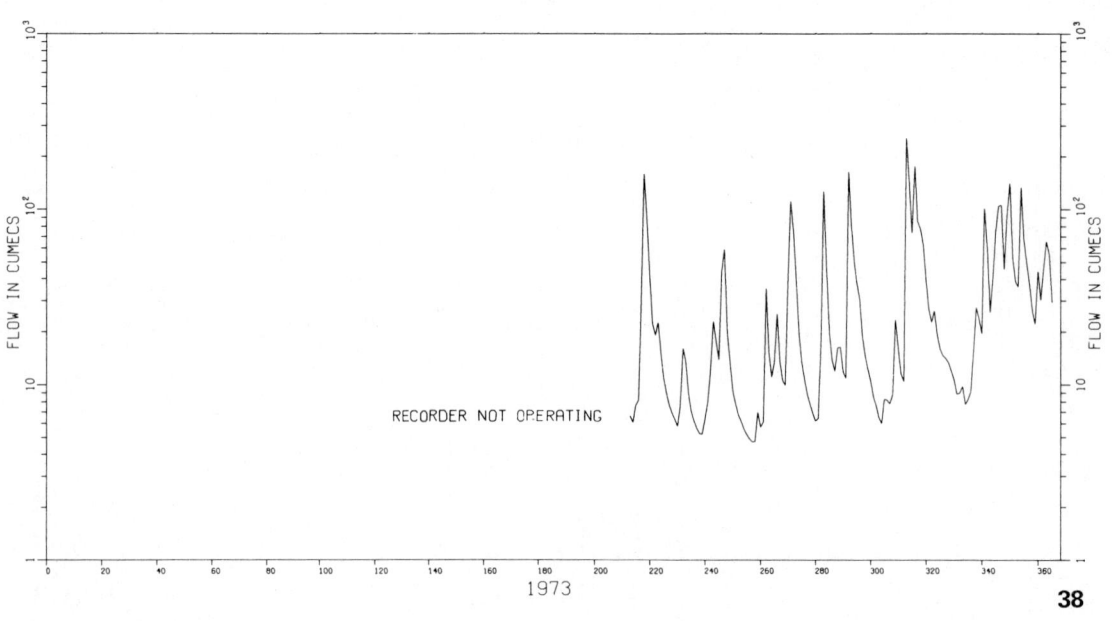

RECORDER NOT OPERATING

1973

38

071003   CROASDALE BECK AT CROASDALE FLUME   DAILY MEAN FLOWS

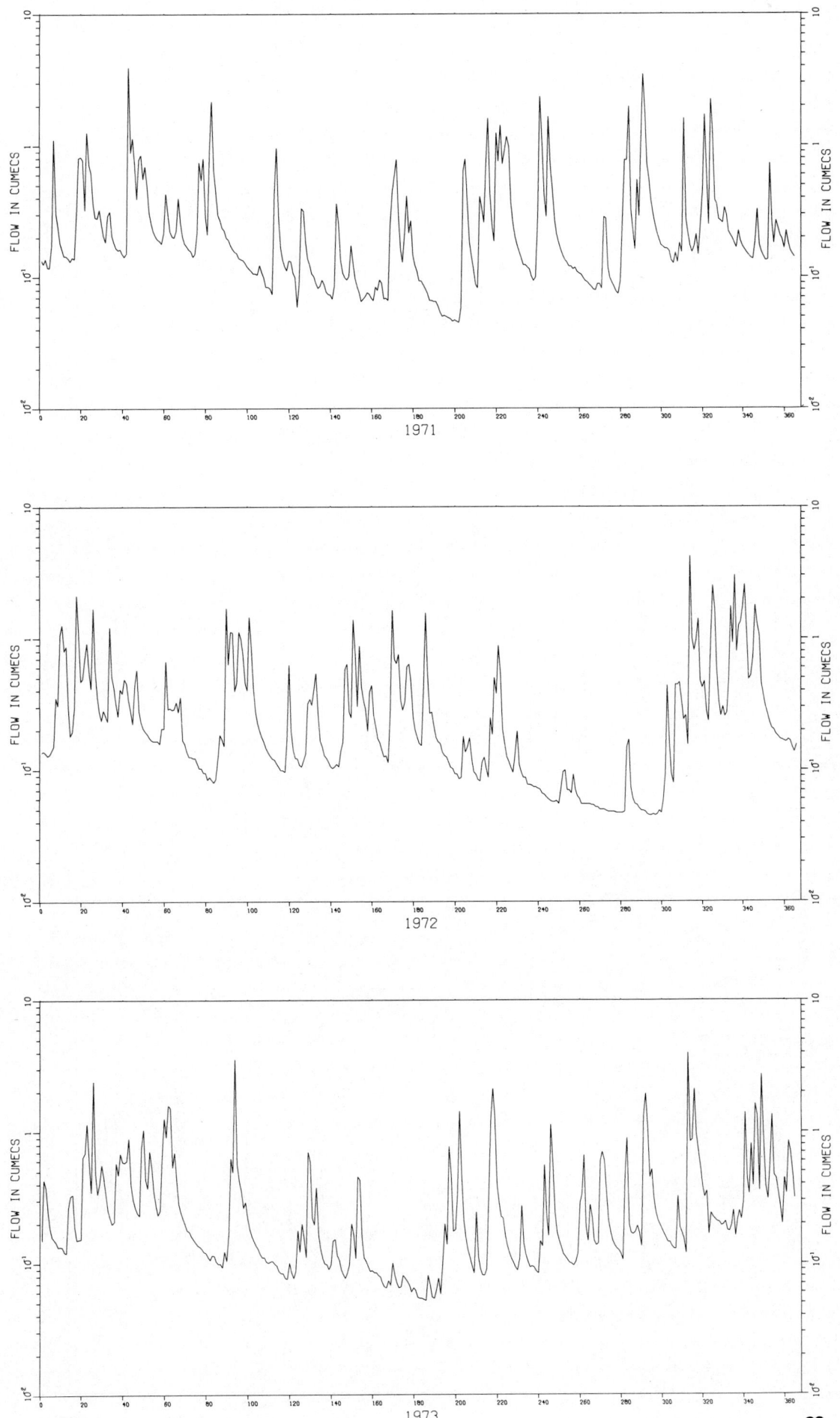

1971

1972

1973

39

072001 RIVER LUNE AT HALTON   DAILY MEAN FLOWS

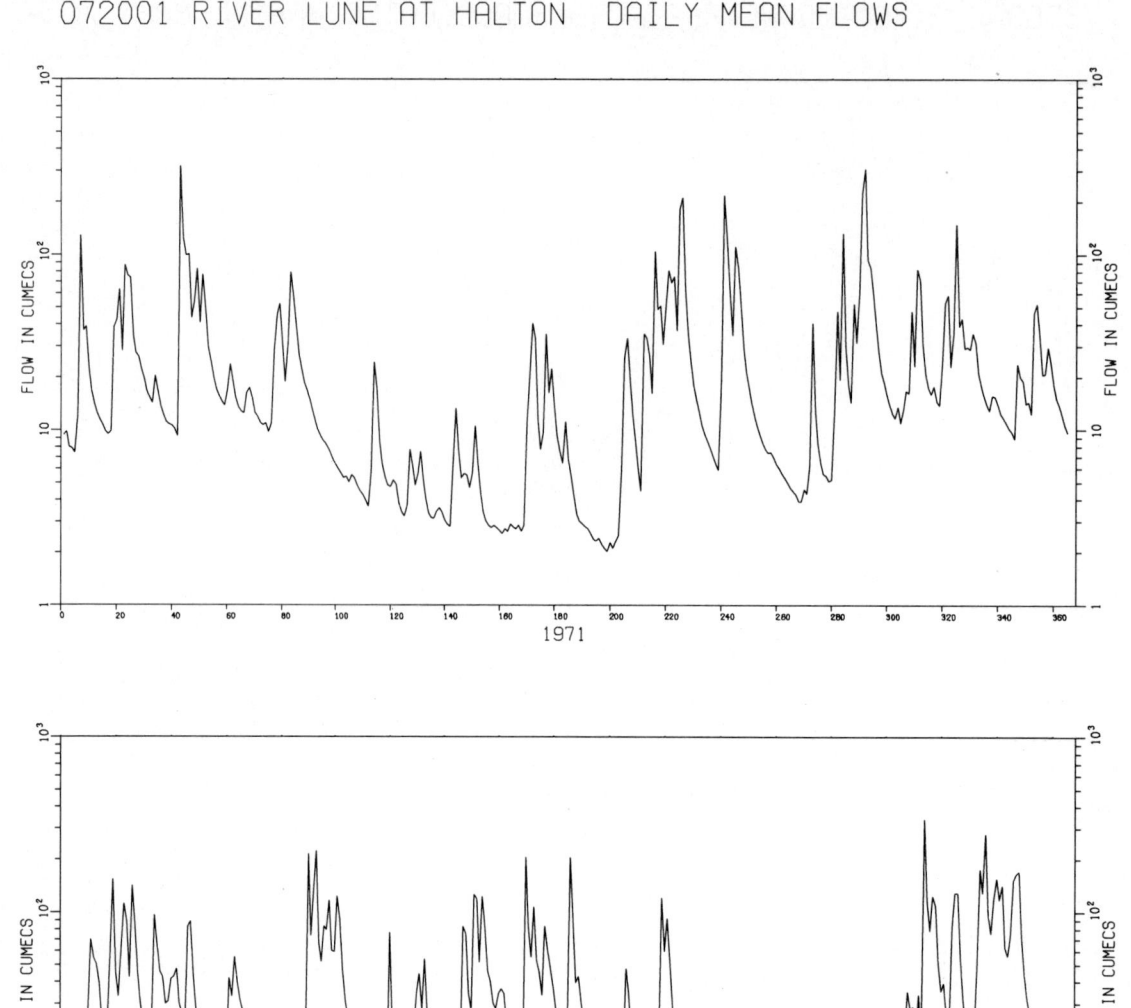

1971

1972

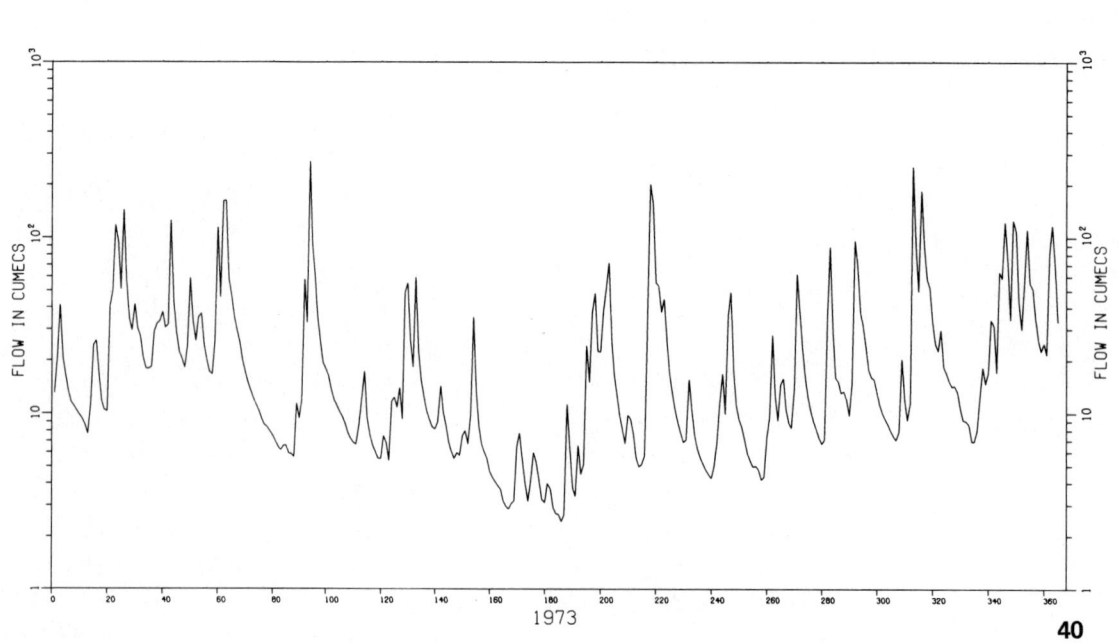

1973

40

075002 RIVER DERWENT AT CAMERTON   DAILY MEAN FLOWS

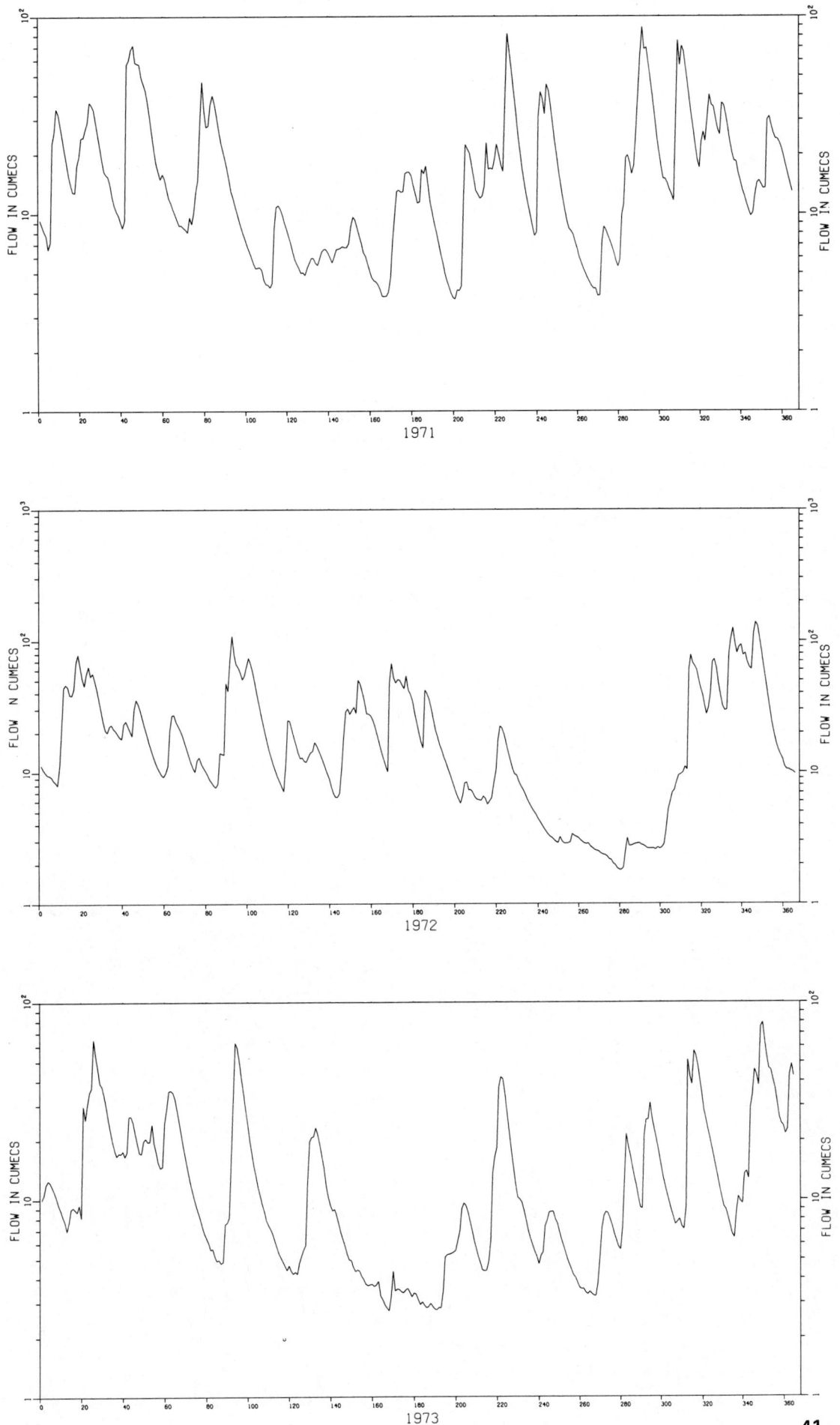

1971

1972

1973

41

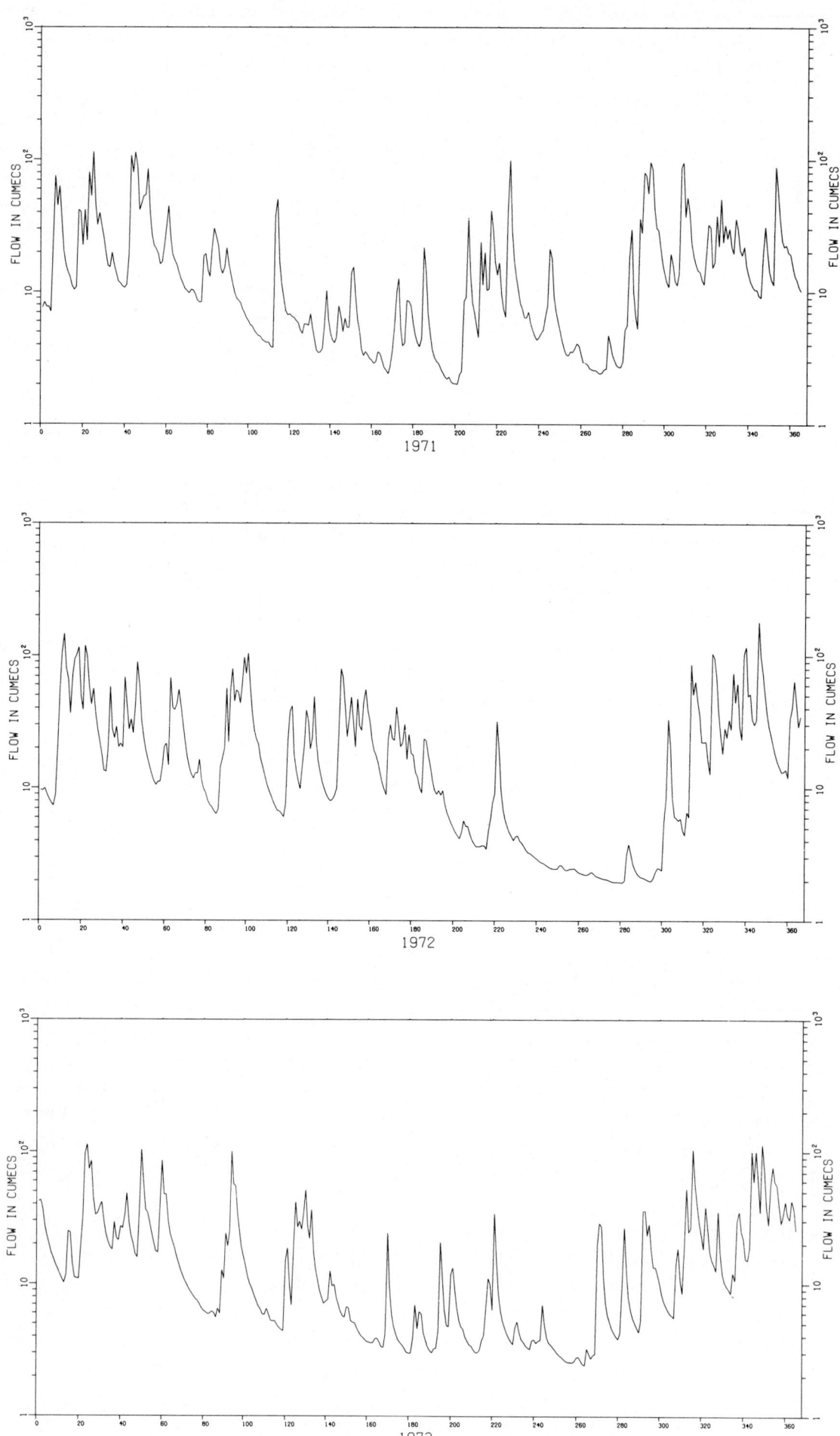

42

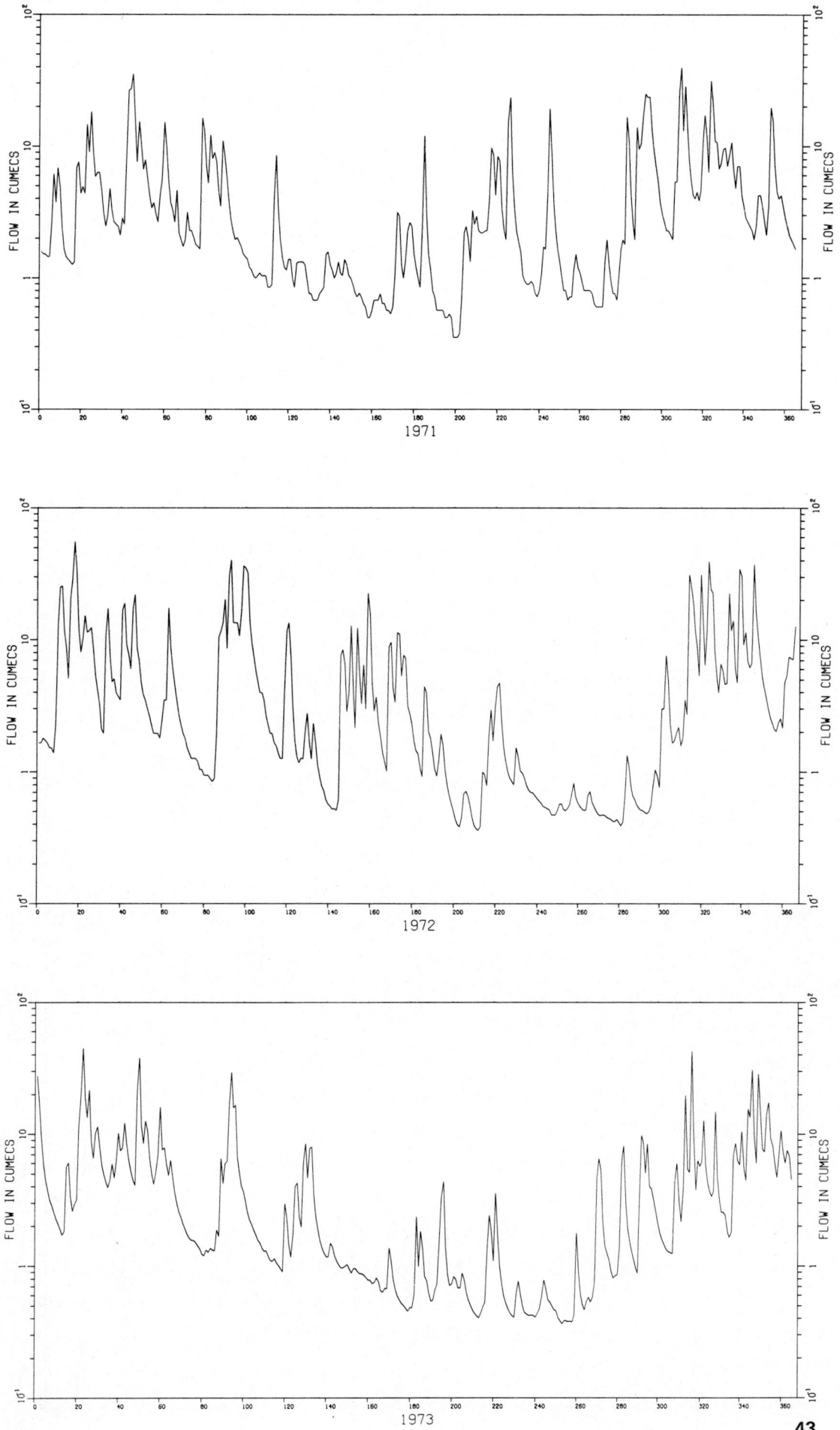

1971

1972

1973

43

084005 RIVER CLYDE AT BLAIRSTON   DAILY MEAN FLOWS

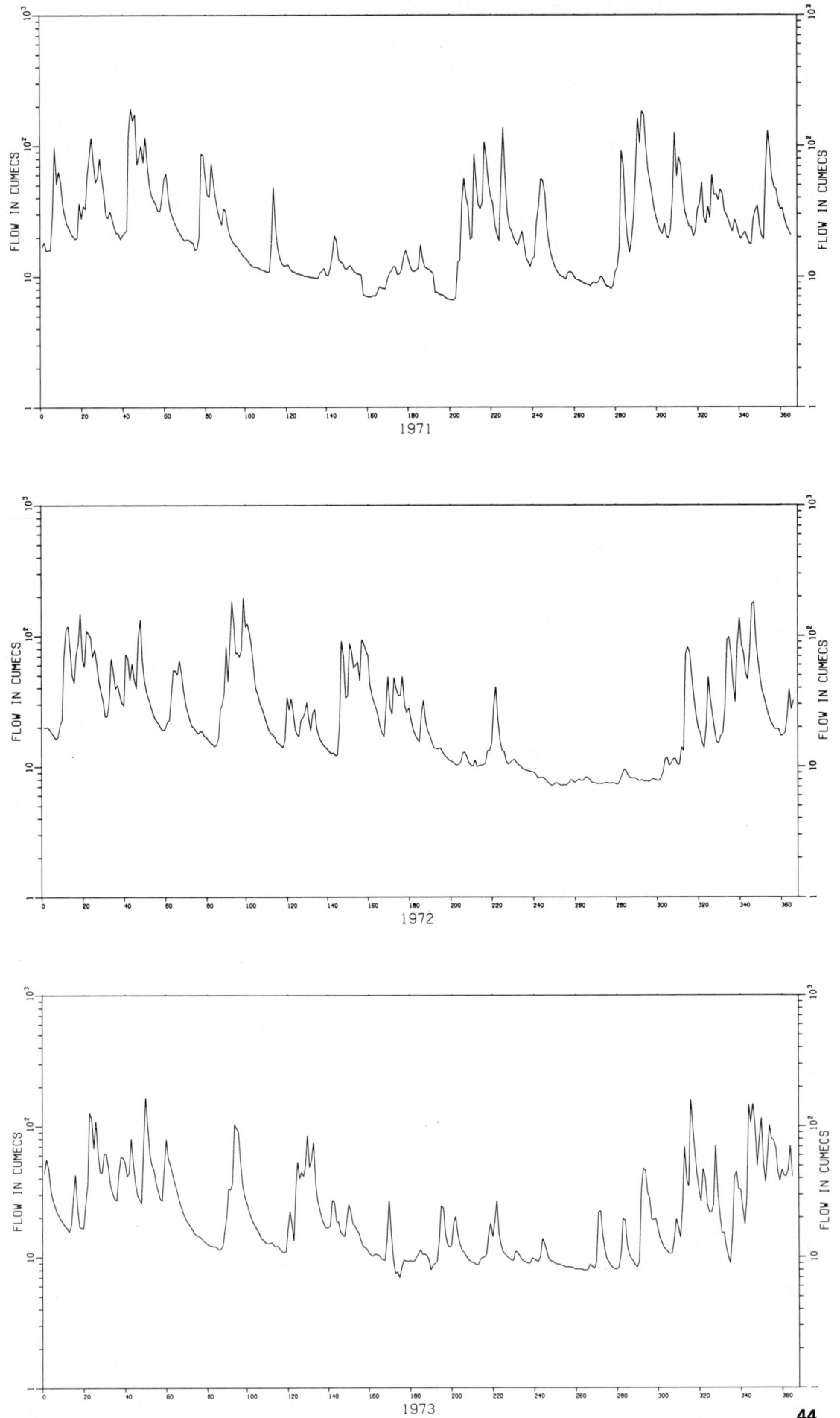

44

203014 RIVER UPPER BANN AT DYNES BRIDGE   DAILY MEAN FLOWS

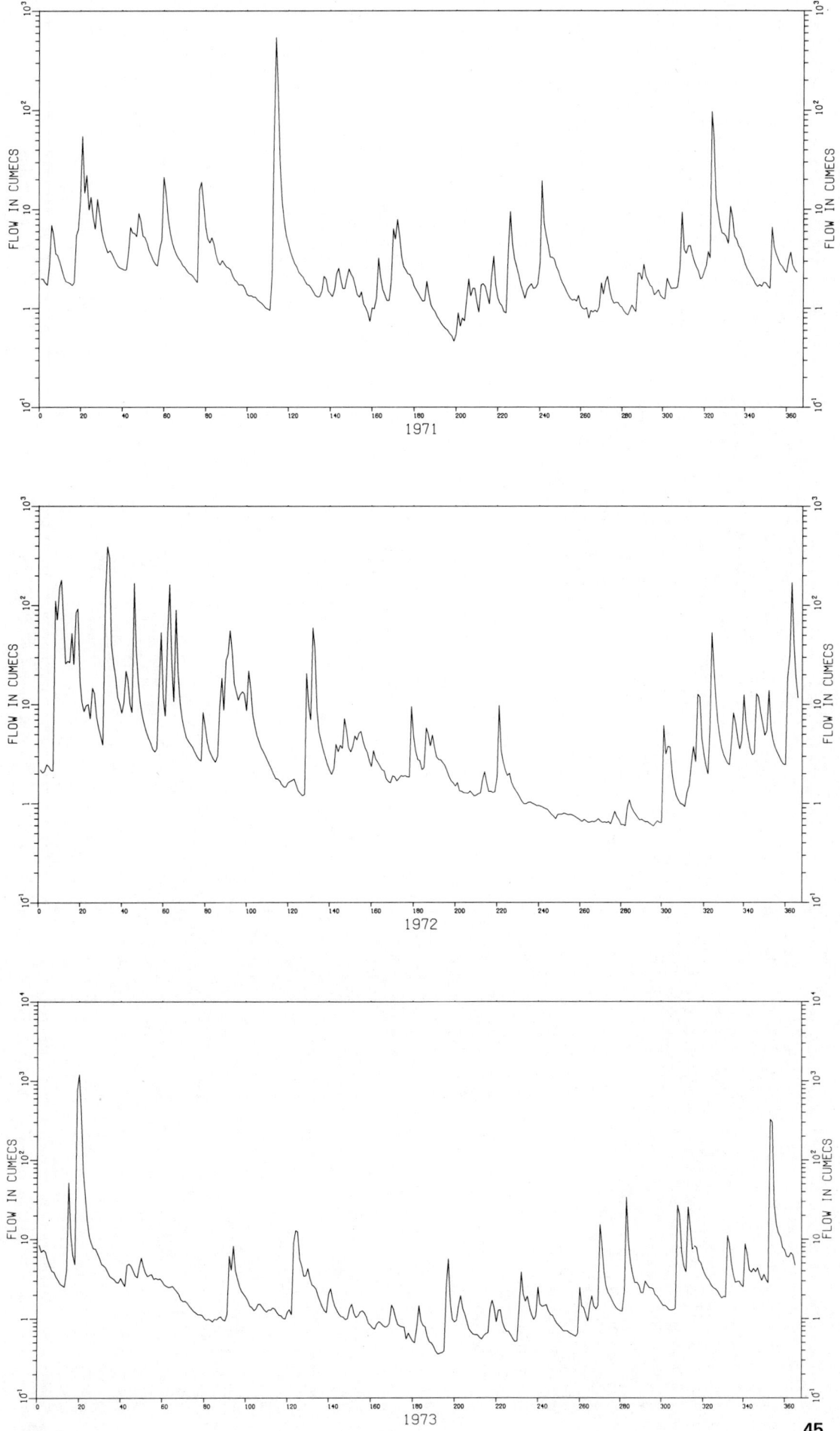

45

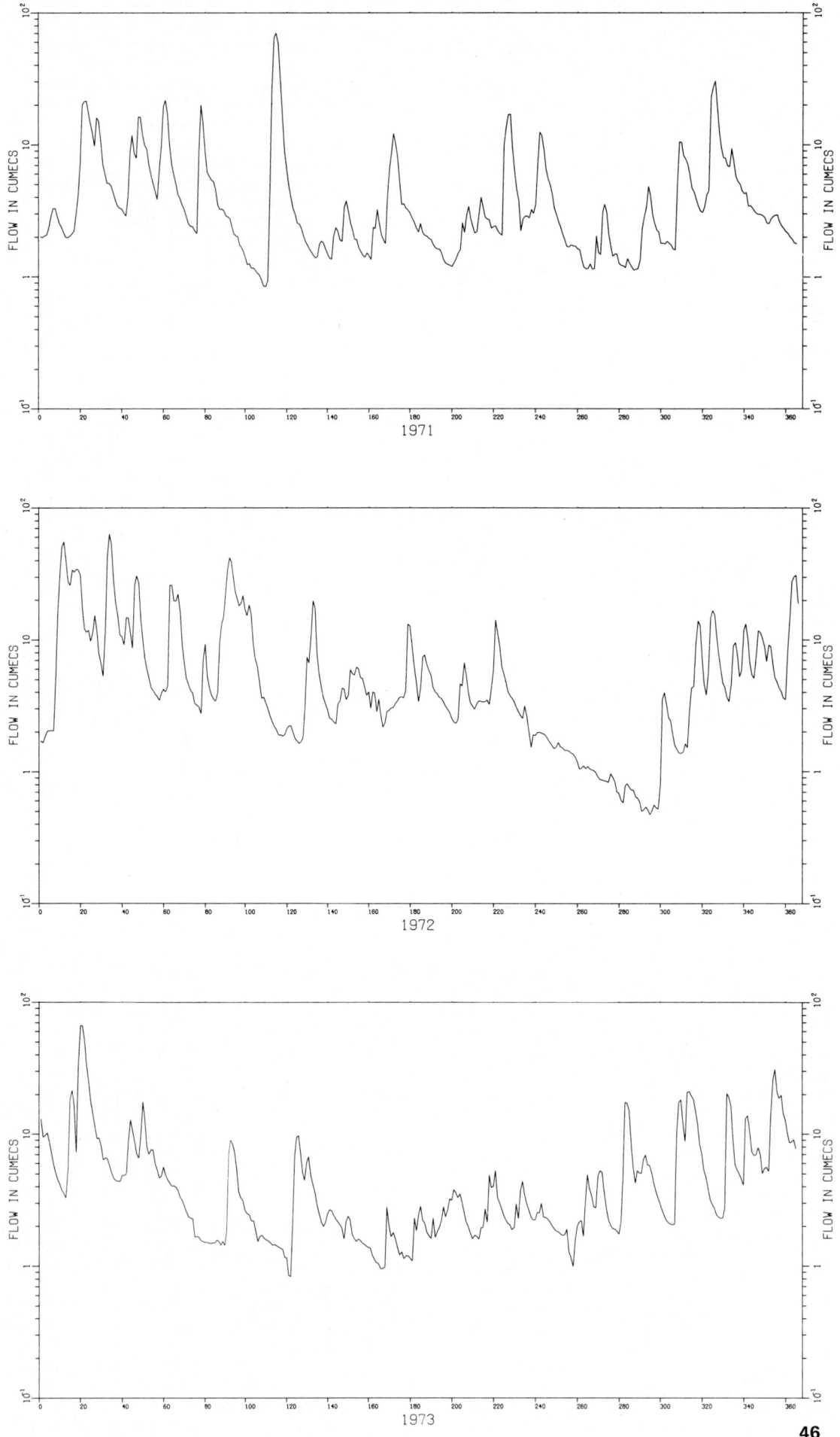

156

8 Graphs for Ten Selected Stations for 1973 Showing

a. weekly areal rainfall with actual and potential evaporation,

b. daily mean gauged discharges with extremes for the period of record,

and

c. monthly mean gauged and natural discharges with extremes for the period of record.

PERIOD OF RECORD   1952 TO 1972

DRAINAGE AREA   2860 km²

GAUGED FLOWS	m³/s	
	PERIOD DISCHARGES	1973
MEAN	63·19	50·87
HIGHEST	1675·00	336·90
LOWEST	9·31	14·62

WEEKLY AREAL RAINFALL/EVAPORATION

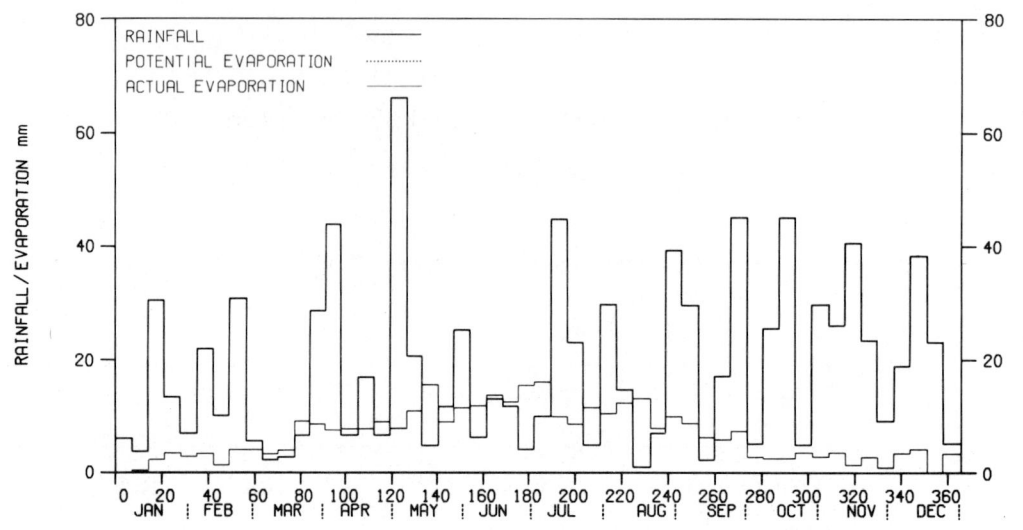

DAILY MEAN FLOW

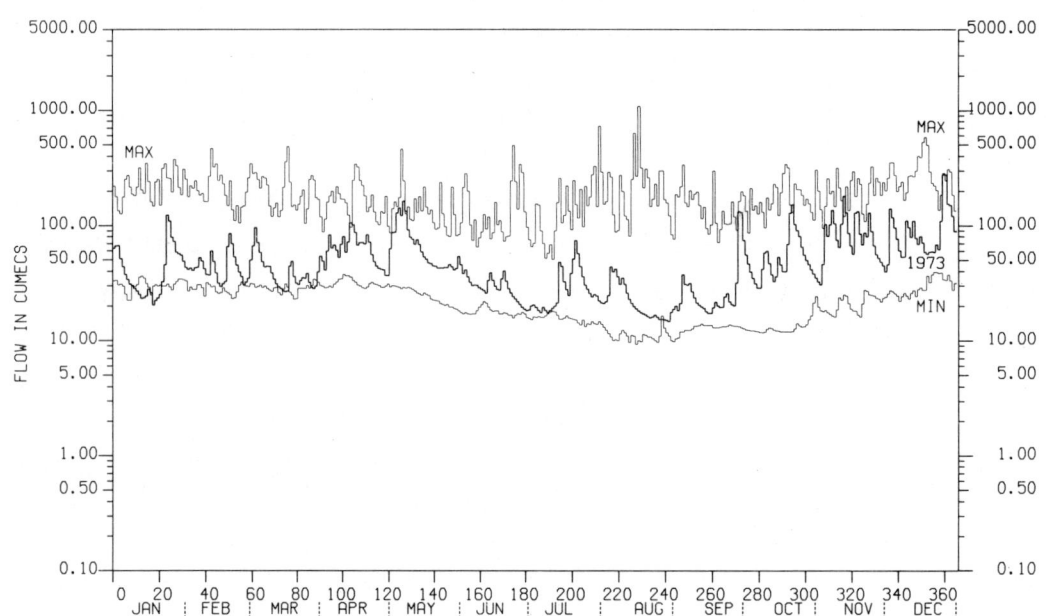

MONTHLY MEAN FLOW

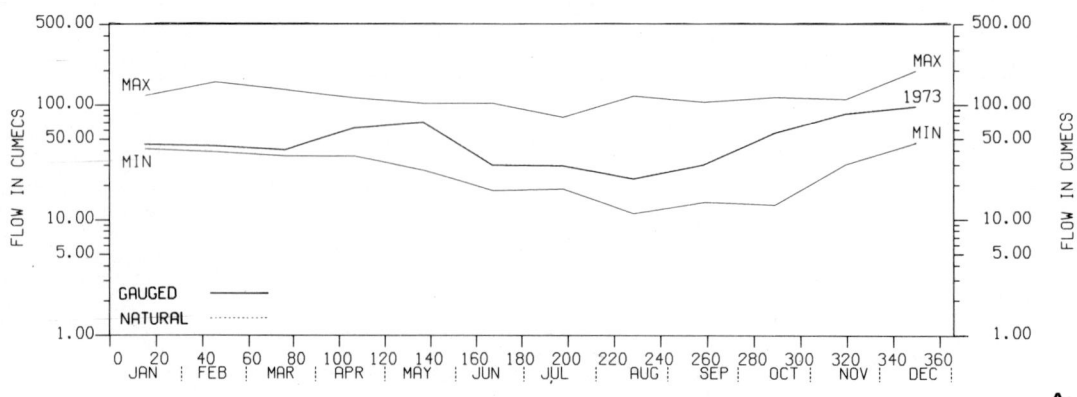

A

PERIOD OF RECORD   1957 TO 1972

DRAINAGE AREA   369 km²

	GAUGED FLOWS	m³/s
	PERIOD DISCHARGES	1973
MEAN	5·04	5·78
HIGHEST	174·80	34·78
LOWEST	0·24	0·64

WEEKLY AREAL RAINFALL/EVAPORATION

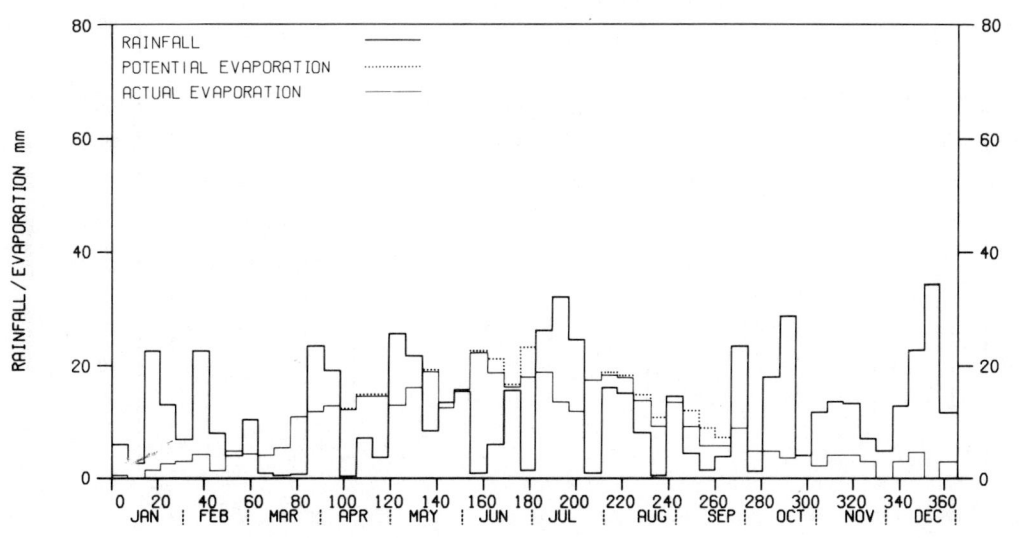

DAILY MEAN FLOW

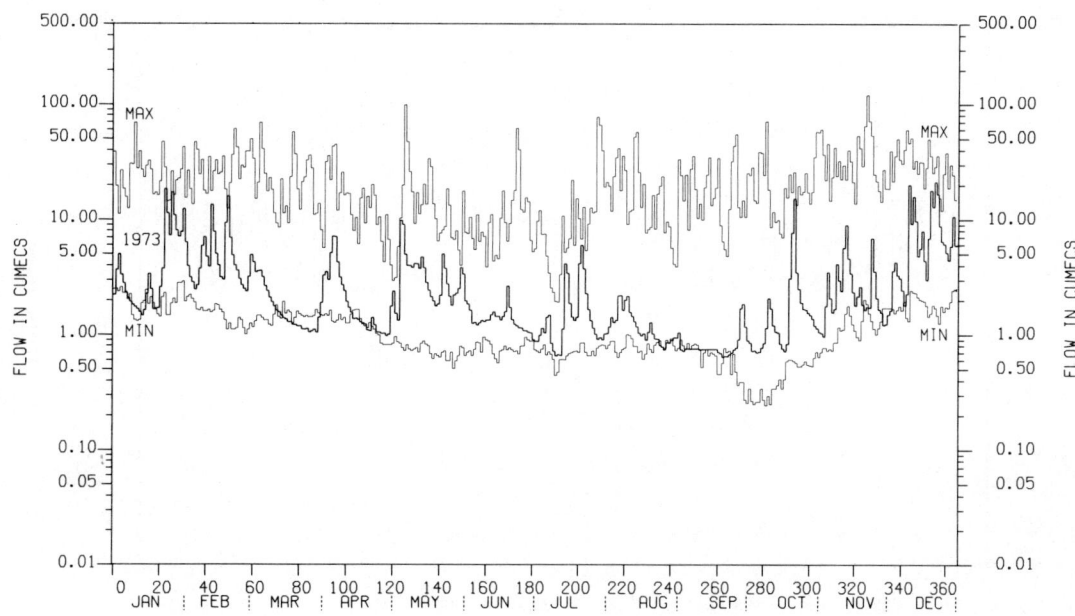

MONTHLY MEAN FLOW

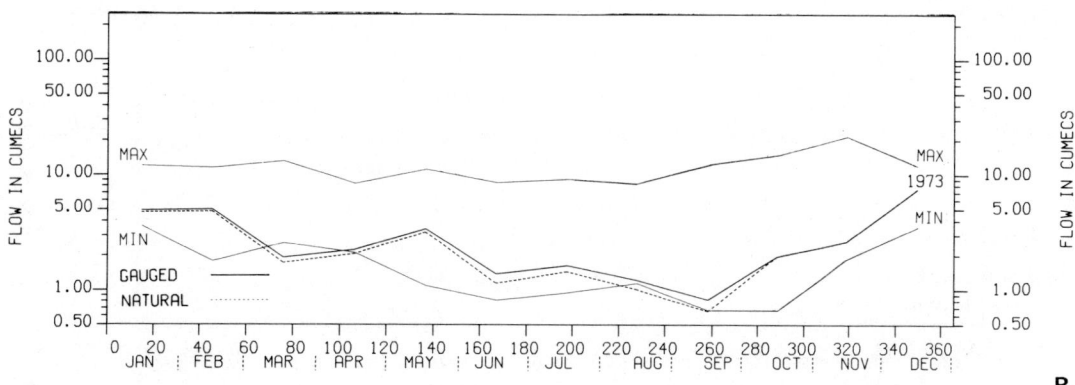

B

159

PERIOD OF RECORD   1956   TO 1972

DRAINAGE AREA   818 km²

GAUGED FLOWS	m³/s	
	PERIOD DISCHARGES	1973
MEAN	16·41	18·76
HIGHEST	679·40	275·90
LOWEST	0·02	1·37

WEEKLY AREAL RAINFALL / EVAPORATION

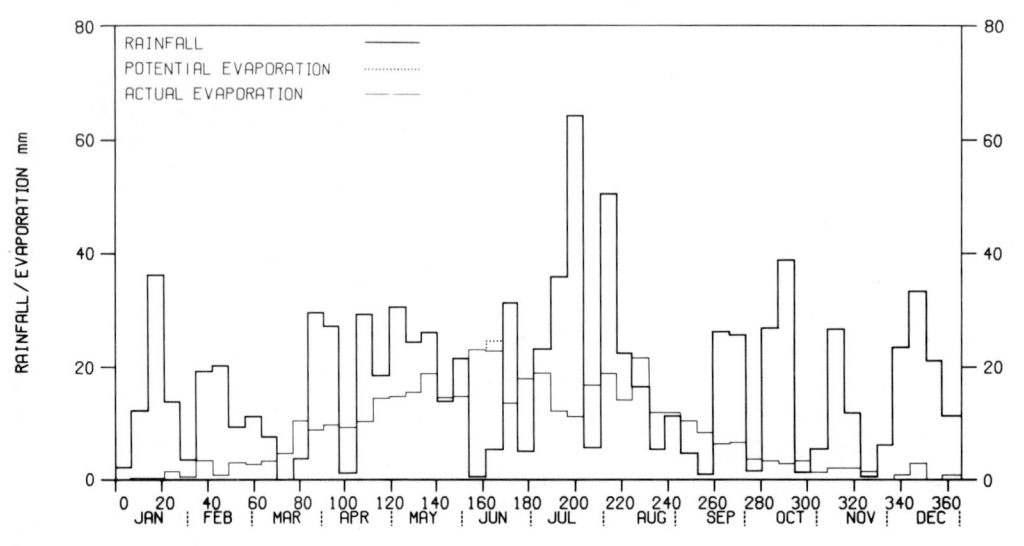

DAILY MEAN FLOW

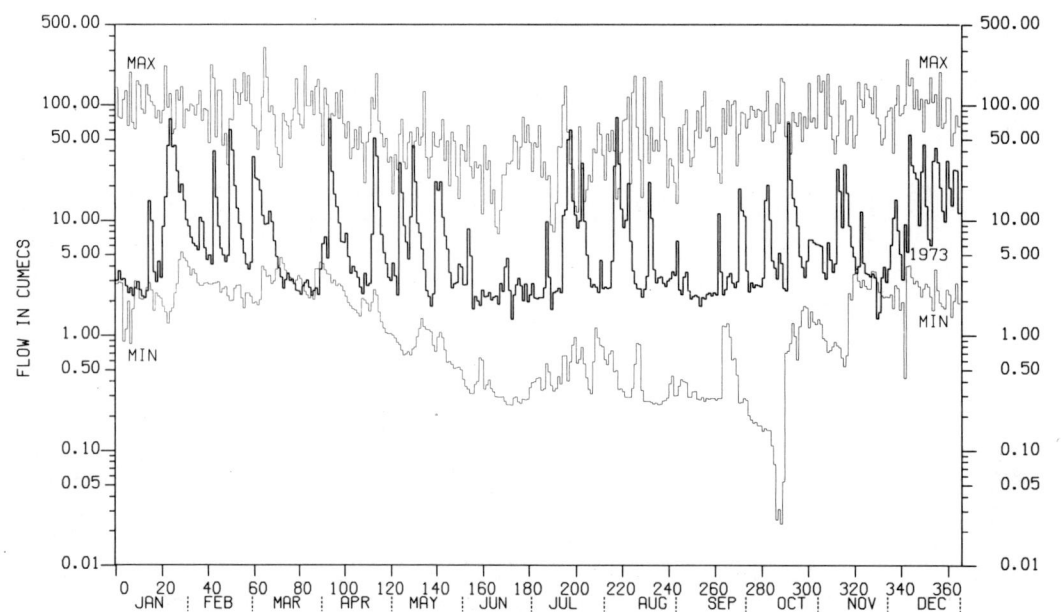

MONTHLY MEAN FLOW

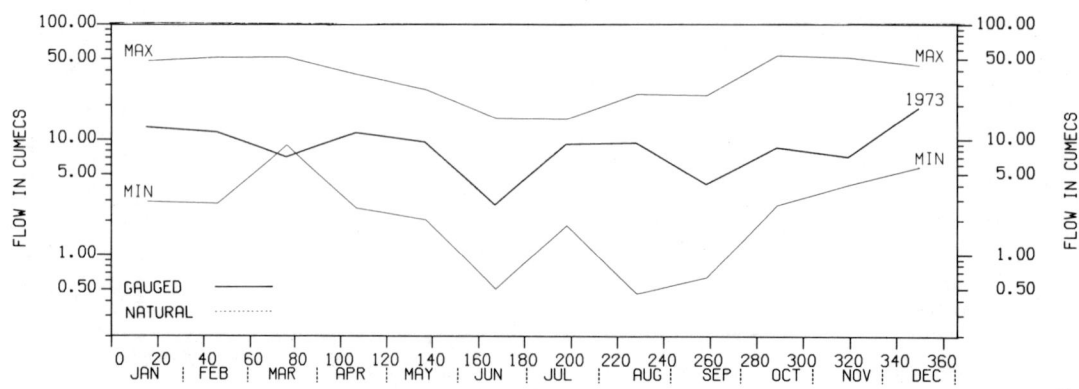

C

160

PERIOD OF RECORD　1956 TO 1972

DRAINAGE AREA　275 km²

	GAUGED FLOWS	m³/s
	PERIOD DISCHARGES	1973
MEAN	1·90	1·24
HIGHEST	9·85	3·50
LOWEST	0·31	0·59

WEEKLY AREAL RAINFALL / EVAPORATION

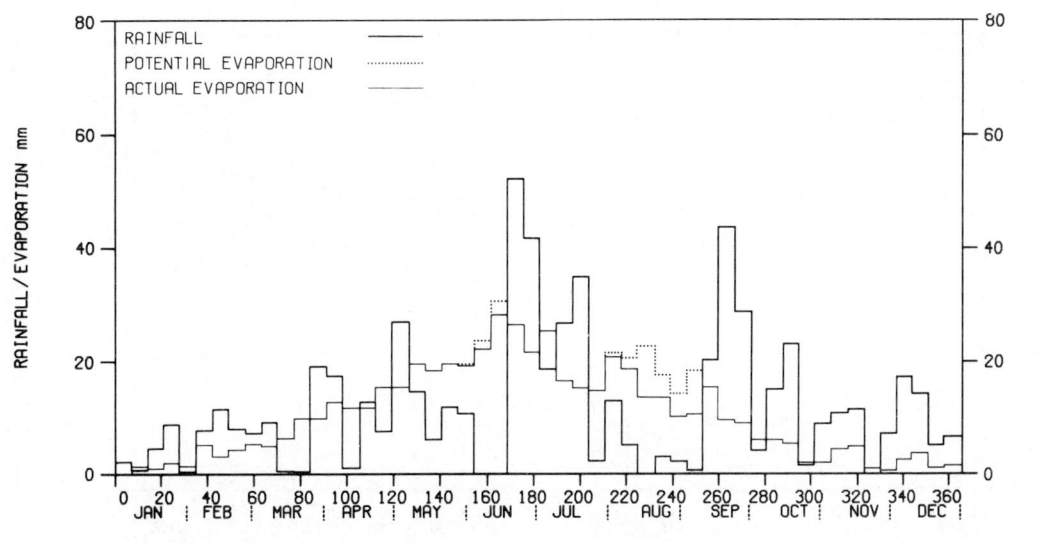

DAILY MEAN FLOW

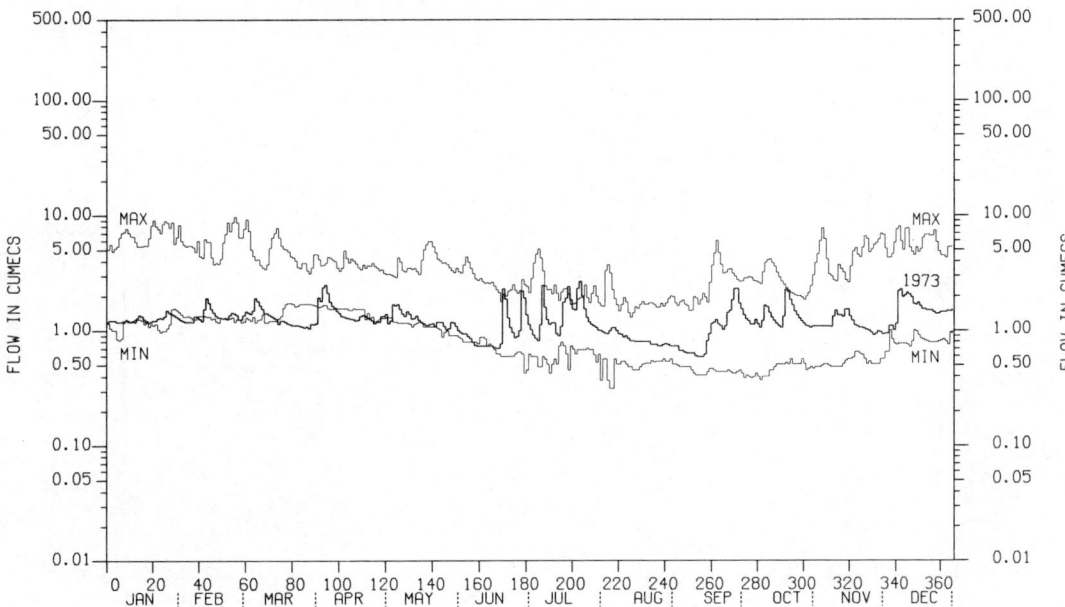

MONTHLY MEAN FLOW

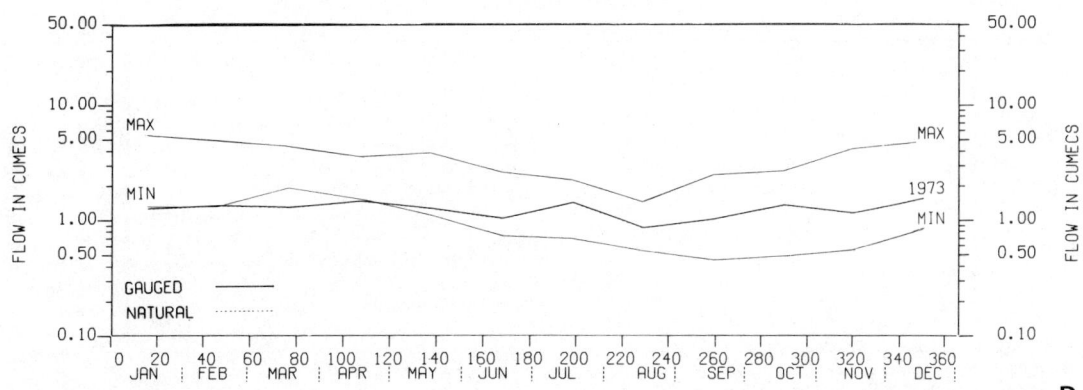

D

PERIOD OF RECORD   1883   TO   1972

DRAINAGE AREA   9950 km²

GAUGED FLOWS		m³/s
	PERIOD DISCHARGES	1973
MEAN	68·09	23·48
HIGHEST		
LOWEST	0·89	6·59

WEEKLY AREAL RAINFALL / EVAPORATION

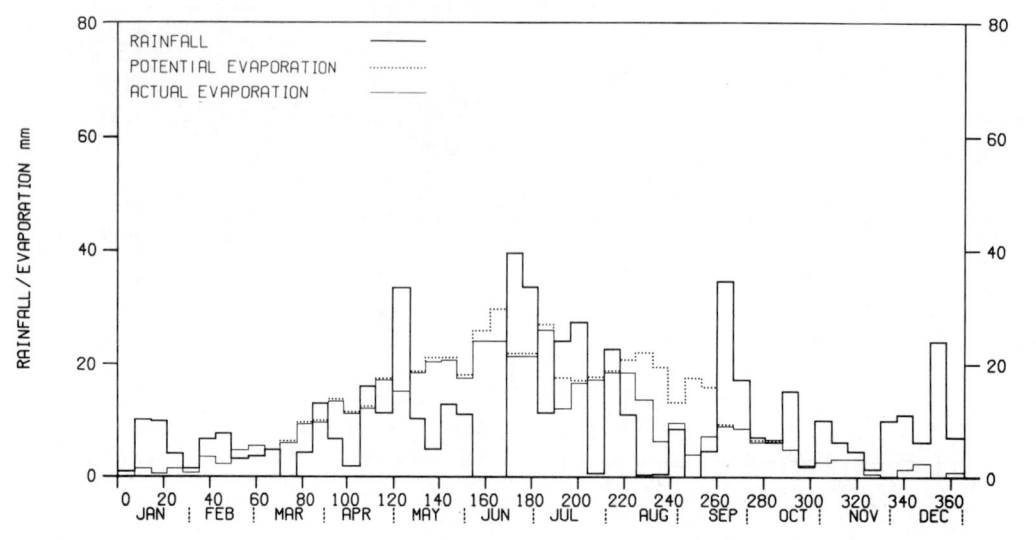

DAILY MEAN FLOW

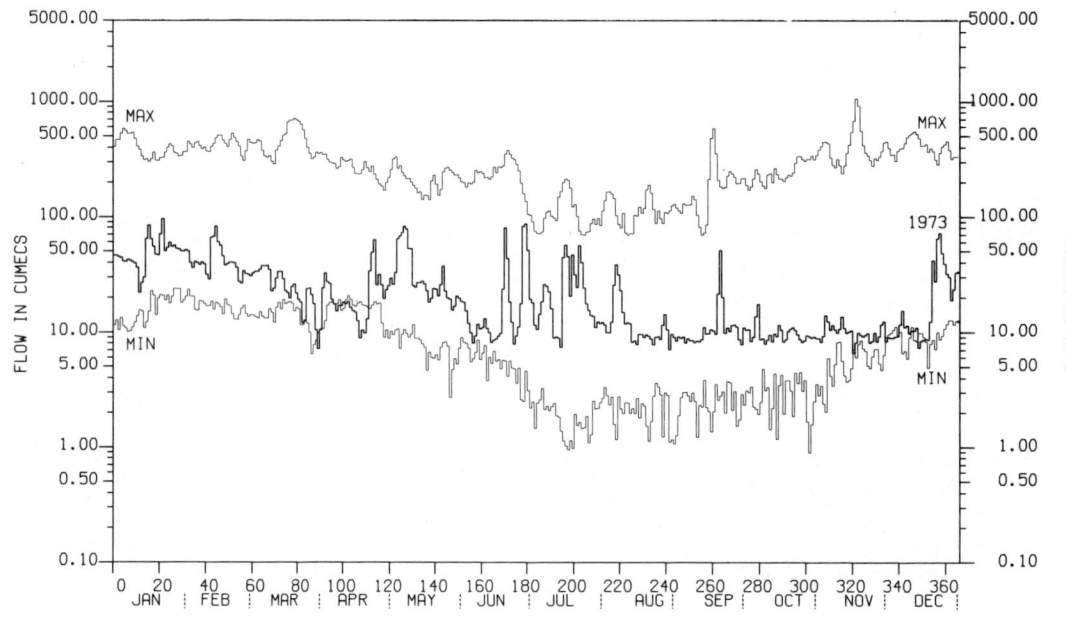

MONTHLY MEAN FLOW

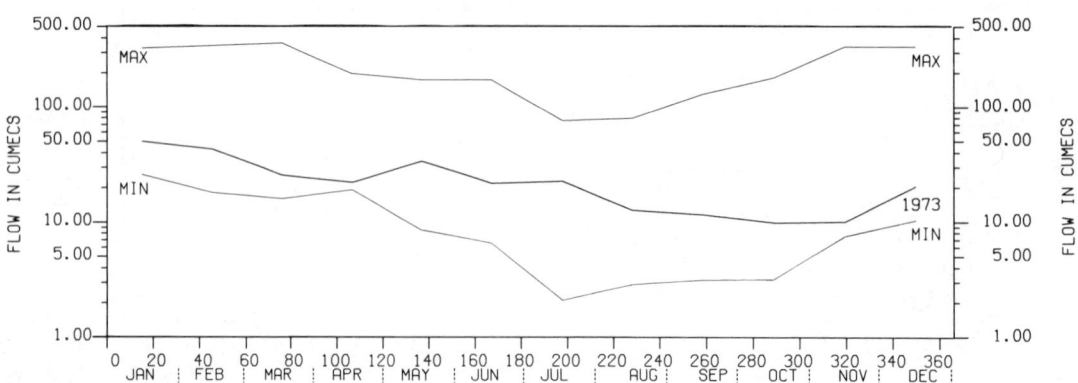

E

PERIOD OF RECORD   1883 TO 1972

DRAINAGE AREA   9950 km²

NATURAL FLOWS	m³/s	
	PERIOD DISCHARGES	1973
MEAN	77·61	41·76
HIGHEST		
LOWEST	7·39	19·16

WEEKLY AREAL RAINFALL/EVAPORATION

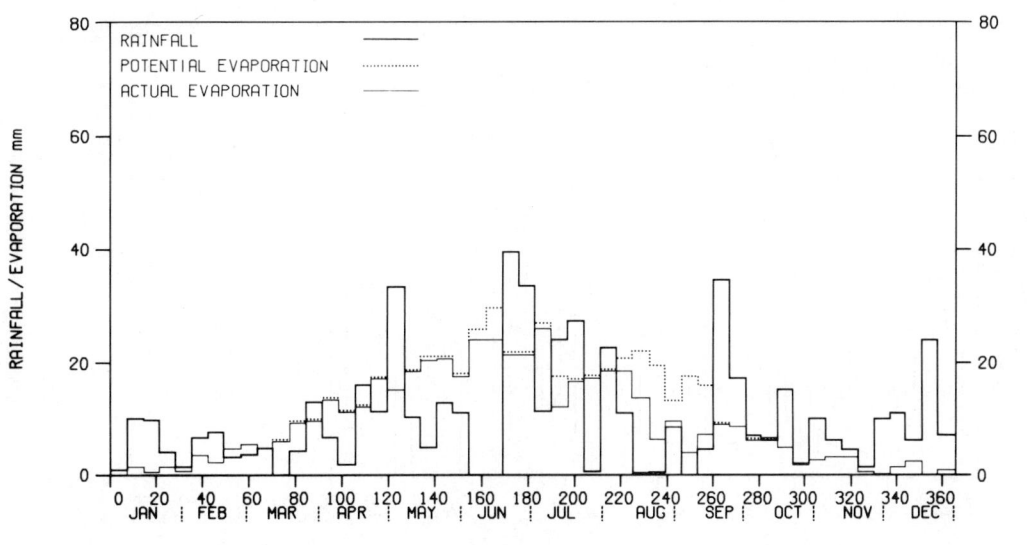

DAILY MEAN FLOW

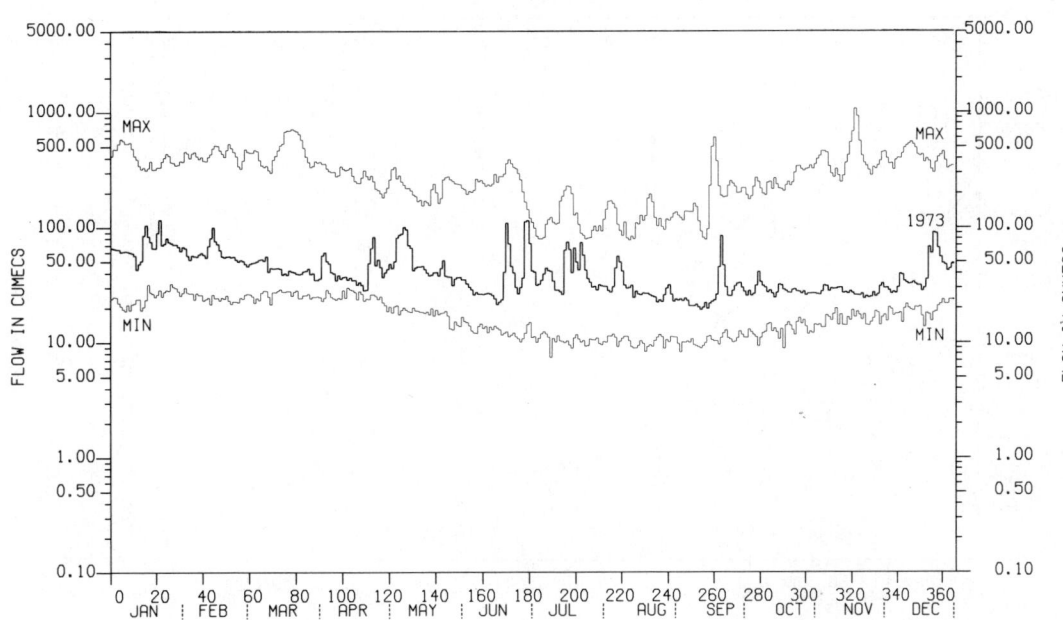

MONTHLY MEAN FLOW

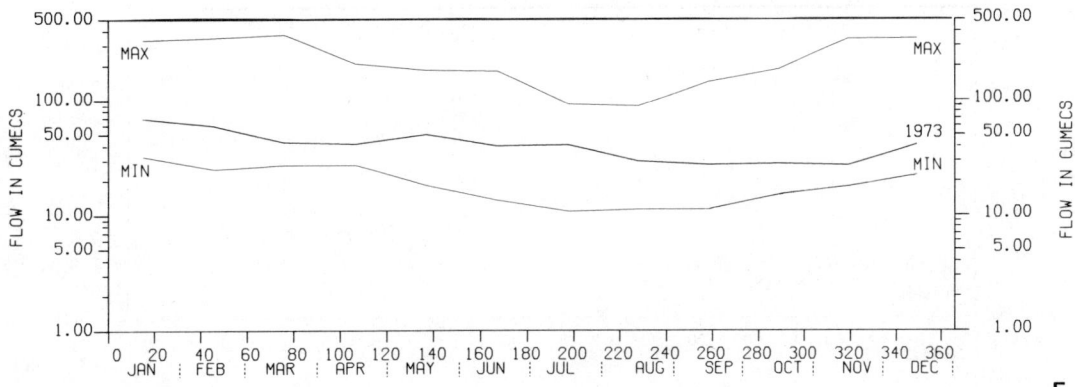

F

PERIOD OF RECORD   1956 TO 1972

DRAINAGE AREA   917 km²

GAUGED FLOWS	m³/s	
	PERIOD DISCHARGES	1973
MEAN	23·62	17·69
HIGHEST	410·60	240·30
LOWEST	0·69	3·18

WEEKLY AREAL RAINFALL/EVAPORATION

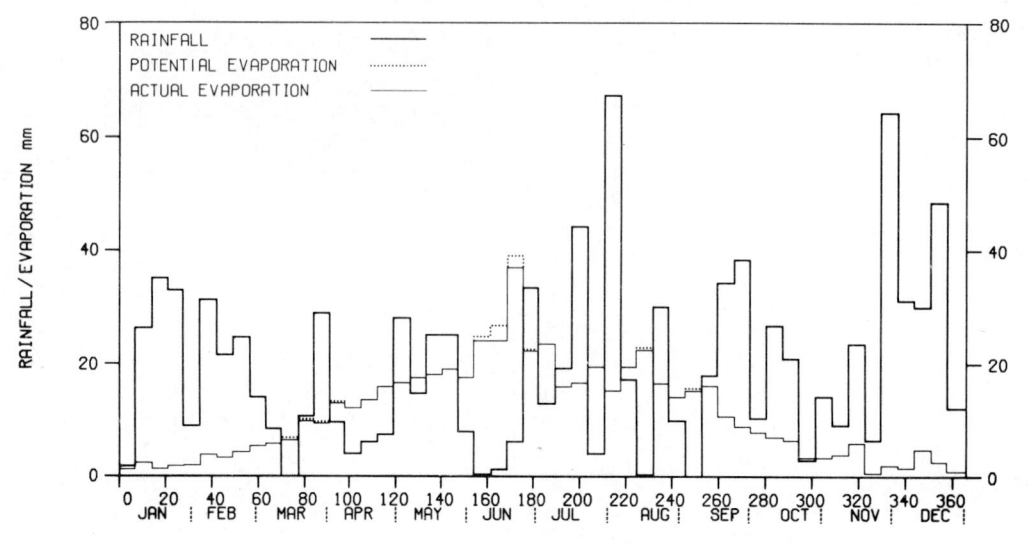

DAILY MEAN FLOW

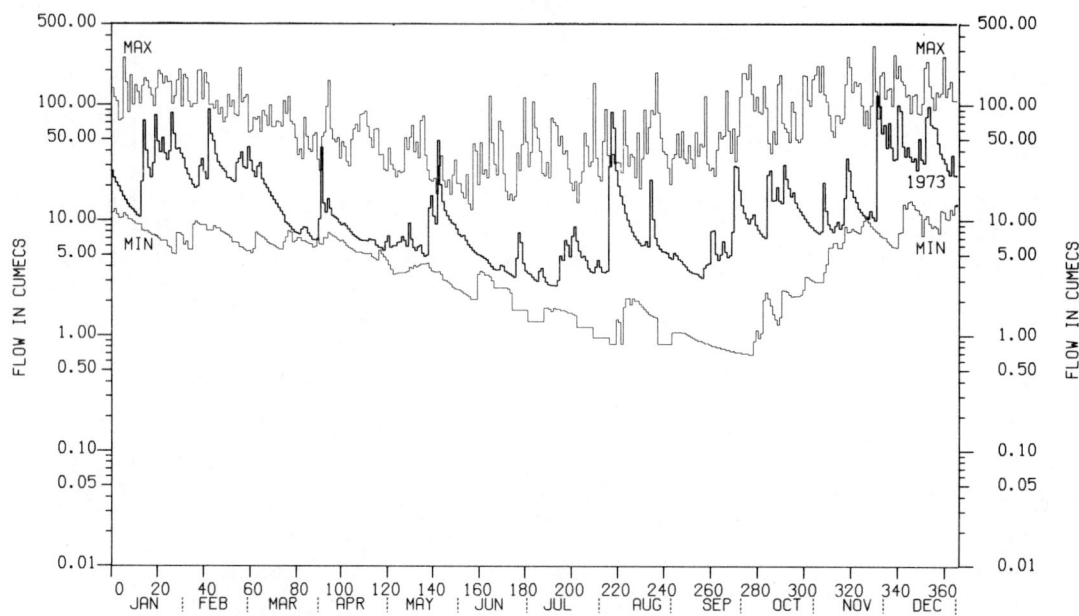

MONTHLY MEAN FLOW

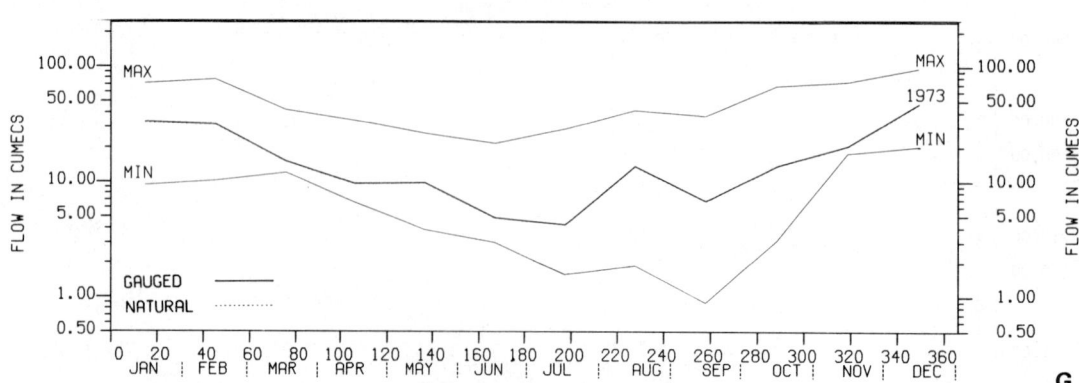

G

PERIOD OF RECORD   1921 TO 1972

DRAINAGE AREA   4330 km²

GAUGED FLOWS	m³/s	
	PERIOD DISCHARGES	1973
MEAN	63·12	45·20
HIGHEST	671·10	289·90
LOWEST	5·38	9·89

WEEKLY AREAL RAINFALL/EVAPORATION

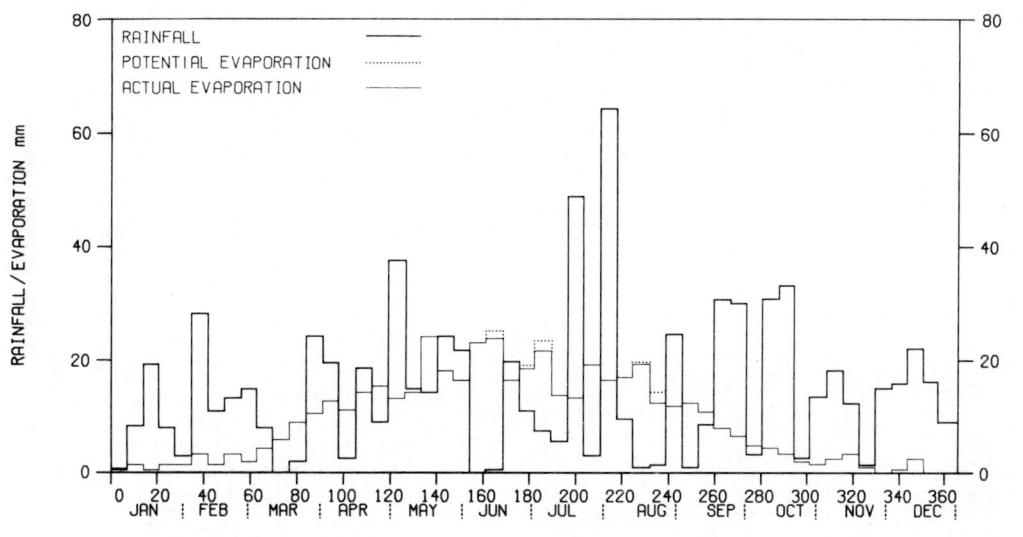

DAILY MEAN FLOW

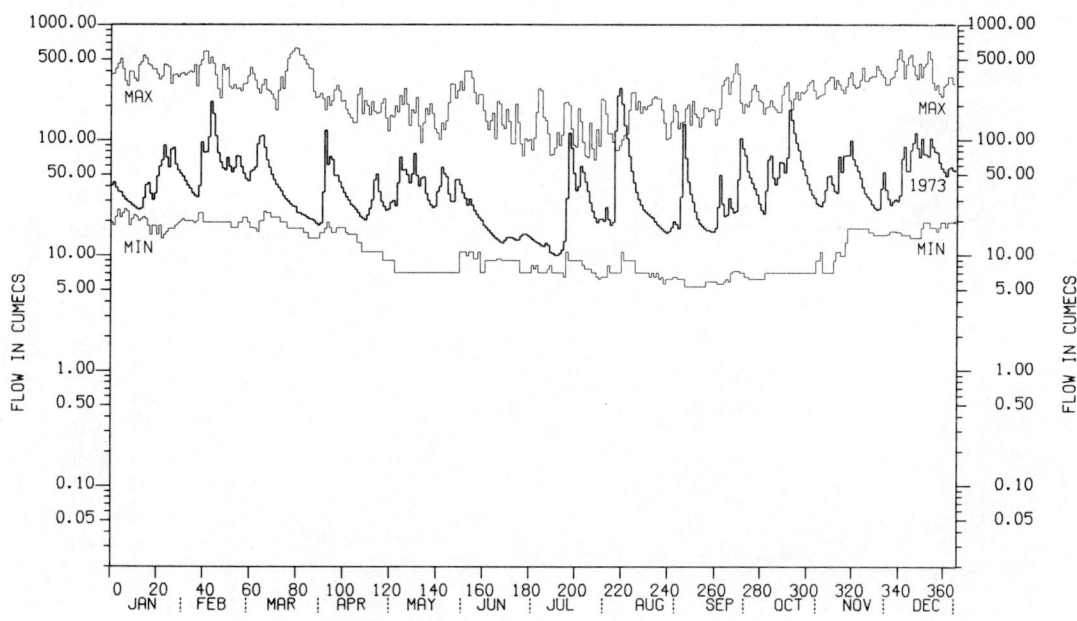

MONTHLY MEAN FLOW

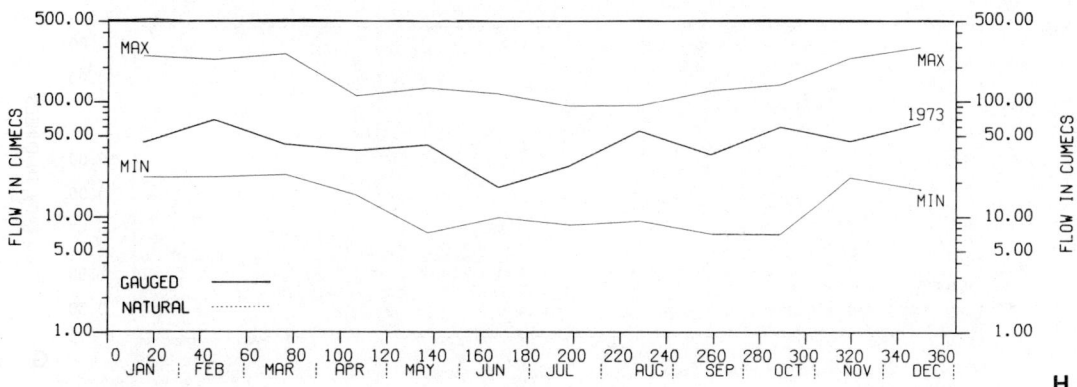

H

PERIOD OF RECORD   1939 TO 1972

DRAINAGE AREA   886 km²

GAUGED FLOWS	m³/s	
	PERIOD DISCHARGES	1973
MEAN	10·63	6·41
HIGHEST	81·22	31·43
LOWEST	0·72	1·63

WEEKLY AREAL RAINFALL/EVAPORATION

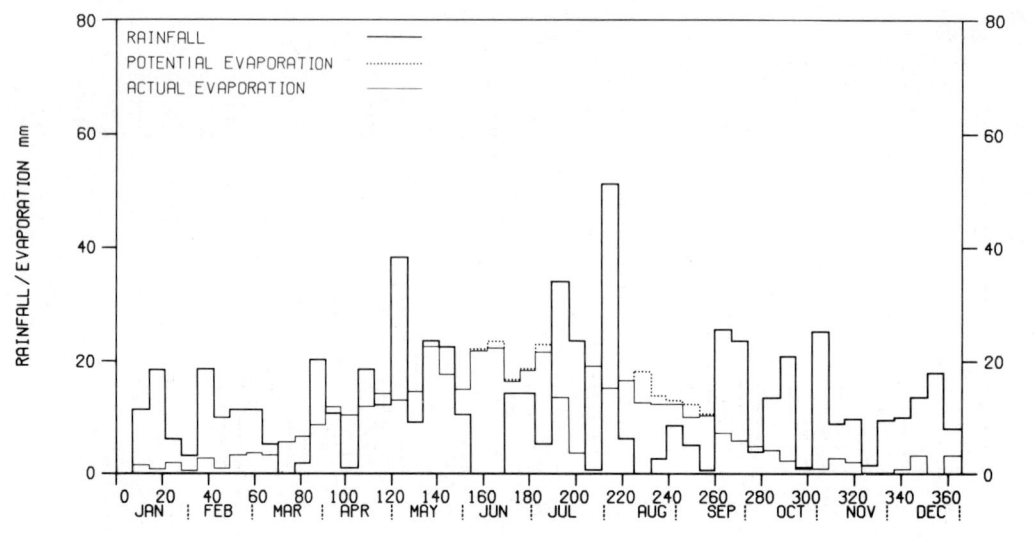

RAINFALL
POTENTIAL EVAPORATION
ACTUAL EVAPORATION

DAILY MEAN FLOW

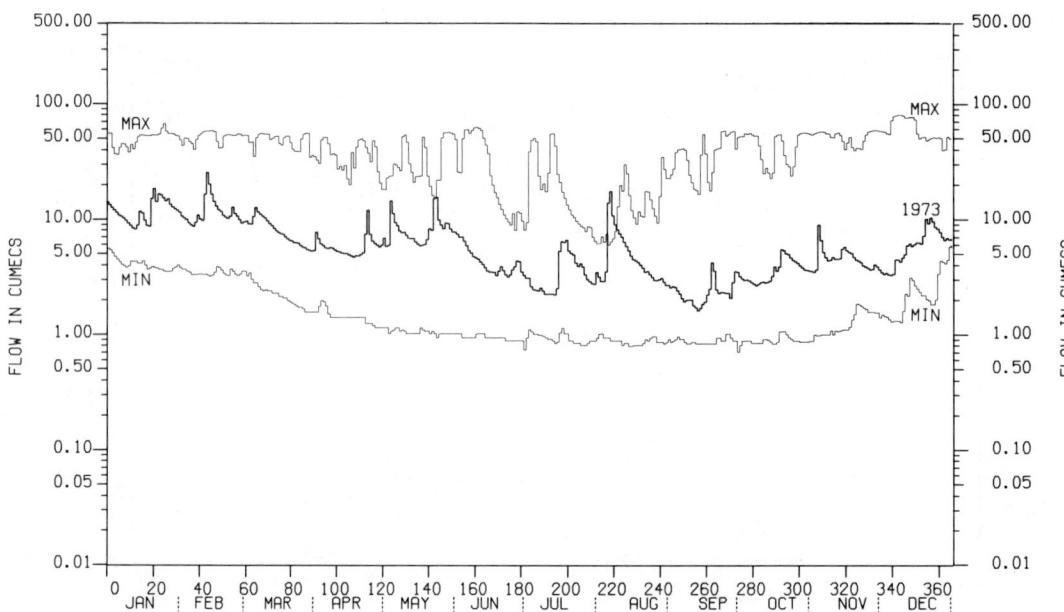

MONTHLY MEAN FLOW

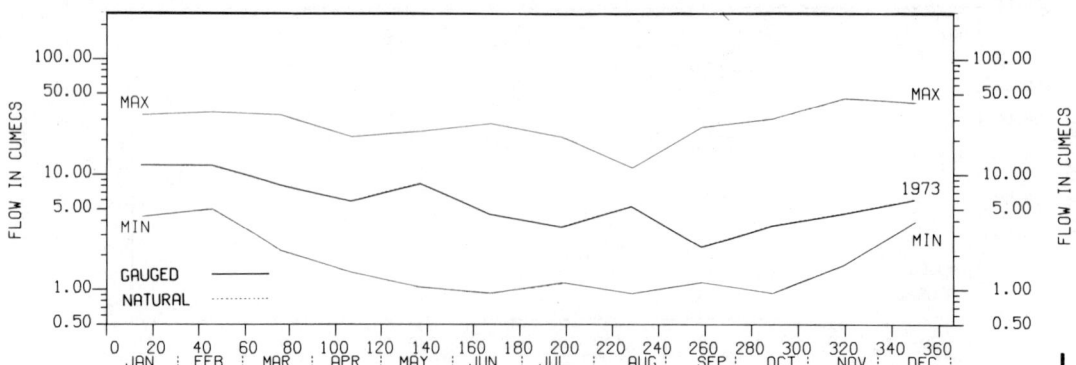

GAUGED
NATURAL

PERIOD OF RECORD　1964　TO　1972

DRAINAGE AREA　1140 km²

GAUGED FLOWS	m³/s	
	PERIOD DISCHARGES	1973
MEAN	31·72	
HIGHEST	891·30	
LOWEST	2·00	

WEEKLY AREAL RAINFALL / EVAPORATION

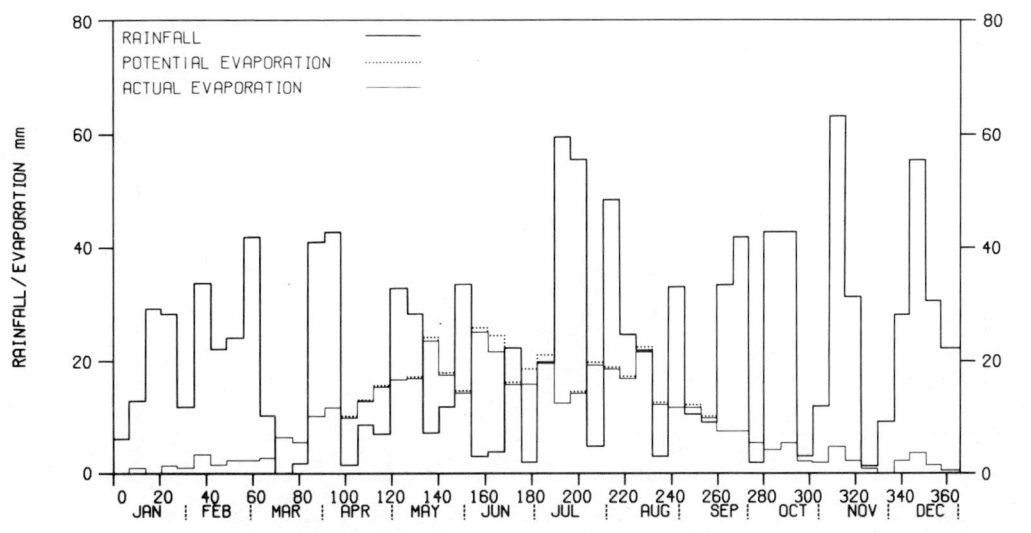

DAILY MEAN FLOW

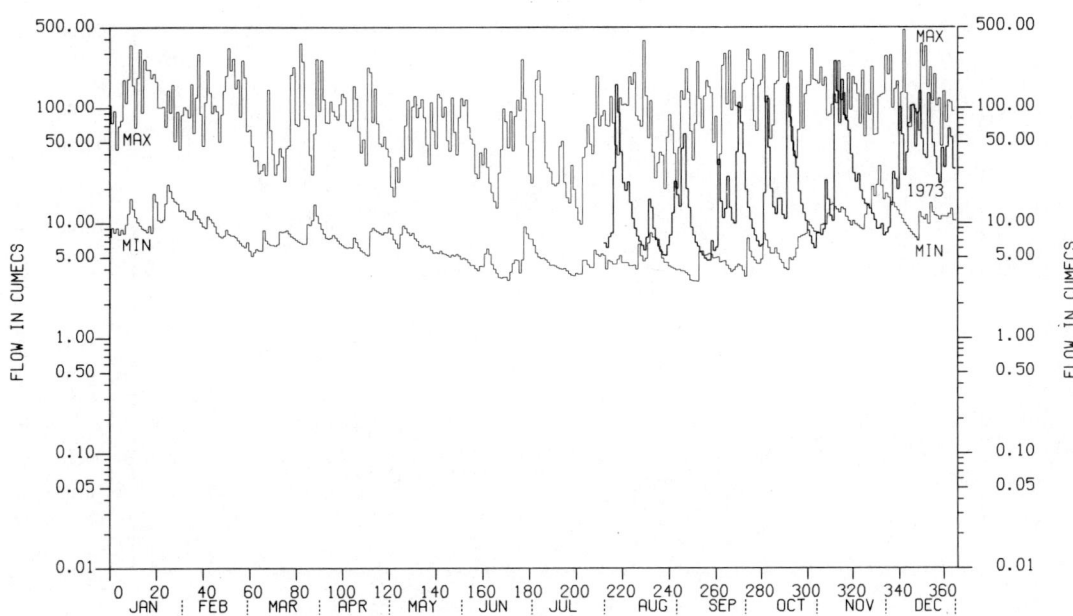

MONTHLY MEAN FLOW

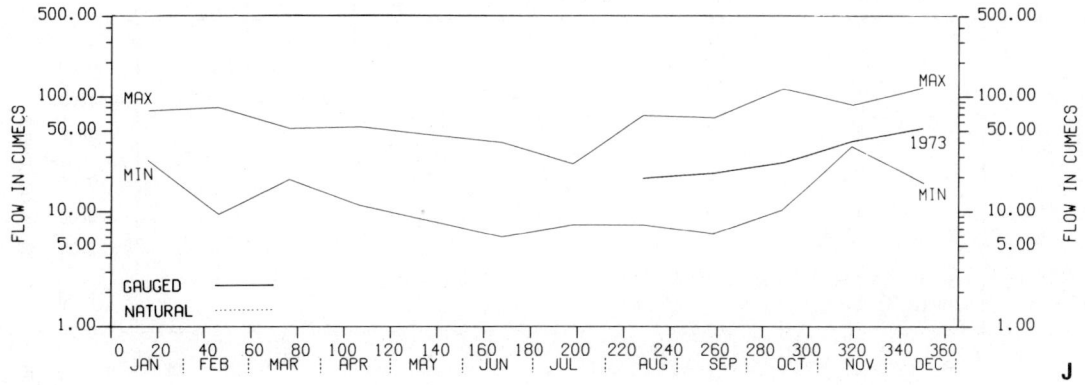

J

167

PERIOD OF RECORD 1957 TO 1972

DRAINAGE AREA 799 km²

GAUGED FLOWS	m³/s	
	PERIOD DISCHARGES	1973
MEAN	24·90	17·60
HIGHEST	1274·00	280·20
LOWEST	1·46	2·43

WEEKLY AREAL RAINFALL / EVAPORATION

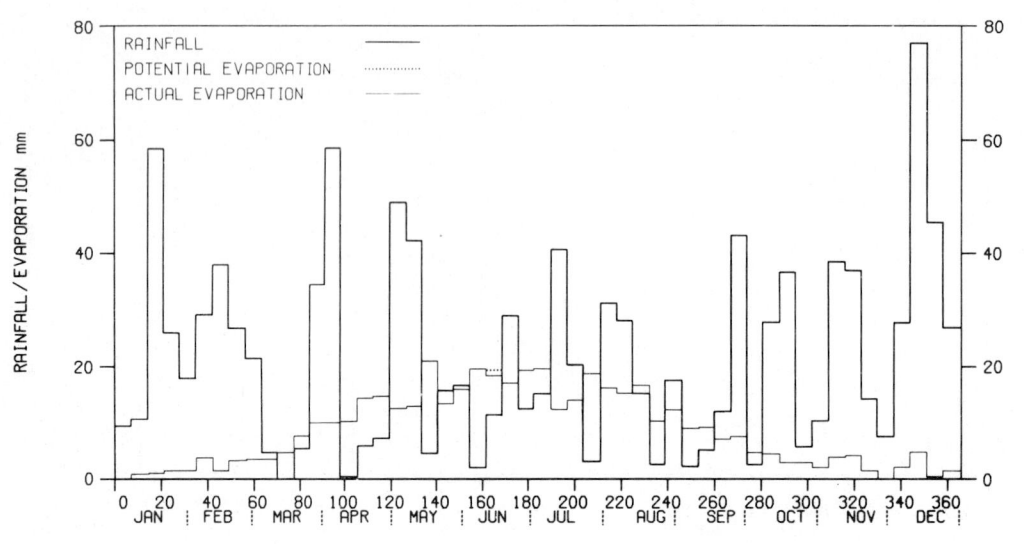

DAILY MEAN FLOW

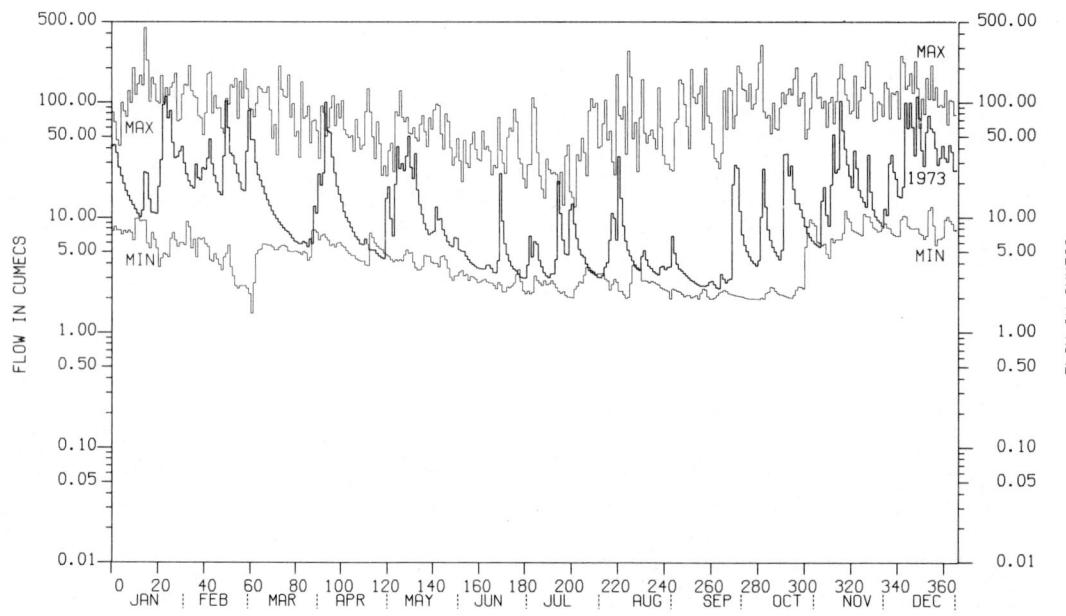

MONTHLY MEAN FLOW

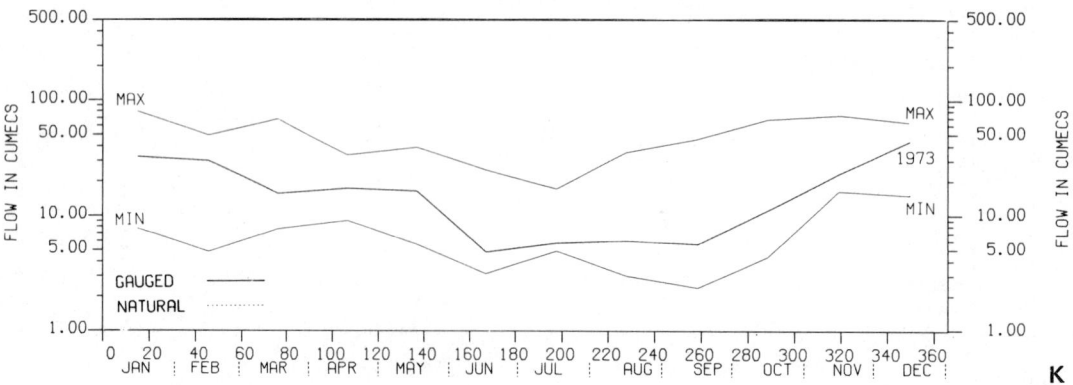

K

9 Register of River Water Temperature Stations

Hydrometric Area (Gauging station number where relevant)	River	Station	National Grid Reference	Records Commence	Method of Measurement	Records at WDU
15	Tummel	Pitlochry Dam	NN 936577	1956	D	1964–1973
19/5	Almond	Almondell	NN 086696	1963	C	1965–1972
19/6	Water of Leith	Murrayfield	NT 228732	1968	C	1968–1973
19/7	Esk	Musselburgh	NT 339723	1968	C	1969–1973
20/3	Tyne	Spilmersford	NT 456689	1963	C	1964–1973
24/1	Wear	Sunderland Bridge	NZ 264376	1958	C	1964–1973
24/3	Wear	Stanhope	NY 984391	1960	C	1964–1973*
25/1	Tees	Broken Scar	NZ 259137	1961	C	1964–1973
25/2	Tees	Dent Bank	NY 932260	1961	C	1964–1973
27/3	Aire	Beal Weir	SE 534255	1972		
27/4	Calder	Kirkthorpe (Newlands)	SE 358212	1972		
27/29	Calder	Elland	SE 124219	1972		
27/31	Colne	Colne Bridge	SE 174199	1972		
27	Calder	Thornhill	SE 233205	1972		
28/4	Trent	Yoxhall	SK 132177	1965	C	
28/5	Tame	Elford	SK 173106	1967	C	
28/7	Trent	Shardlow	SK 446298	1965	C	
28/13	Soar	Zouch	SK 500235	1965	C	
28/18	Dove	Marston-on-Dove	SK 235288	1967	C	
28/804	Trent	Nottingham	SK 582384	1965	C	
31	Welland	Fosdyke Bridge	TF 318323	1960		
32	Nene	Oundle	TL 043888	1937		
32	Nene	Peterborough	TL 193982	1936		
32	Nene	Northampton South Bridge	SP 755597	1938	D	1958–1973*

C = continuous recording thermometer
D = daily read thermometer
* Graphs of long term and 1973 data for these stations are presented on the following pages

Hydrometric Area (Gauging station number where relevant)	River	Station	National Grid Reference	Records Commence	Method of Measurement	Records at WDU
34/4	Wensum	Costessey Mill	TG 177128	1969		1969–1973
34/6	Waveney	Needham	TM 229811	1969		1969–1970 and 1972–1973
35/10	Gipping	Bramford	TM 127465	1970		1970–1973
39/19	Lambourn	Shaw	SU 470682	1972		
39/32	Lambourn	Shefford	SU 390745	1972		
40	Stour	Chartham Mill	TR 097554	1958	D	1964–1969
40/7	Medway	Chafford	TQ 517405	1964	D	1964–1972
42	Test	Burnt Mill (Romsey)	SU 348214	1952	D	1964–1972
42/2	Itchen	Otterbourne (Allbrook)	SU 470233	1964	D	1959–1964 and 1966–1973*
42/3	Lymington	Brockenhurst	SU 318019	1966	D	1966–1972
42/6	Meon	Mislingford	SU 589141	1966		1967–1972
47/1	Tamar	Gunnislake	SX 426725	1968	C	1968–1973
47/2	Plym	Carnwood	SX 521611	1972		1973
48/2	Fowey	Restormel	SX 108613	1968	C	1968–1973
49/1	Camel	Denby	SX 017682	1968	C	1968–1973
52	Tone	Knapp Bridge	ST 302261	1970		
52	Glastonbury Mill Stream	Glastonbury	ST 493396	1968		
52	Parrett	Westover	ST 416265	1971		
52	Parrett (Tidal)	West Quay	ST 300372	1972		
52	Yeo	Yeovilton	ST 545227	1969		
53	Avon (Bristol)	Holt	ST 871615	1953		1953–1955
53/3	Avon (Bristol)	Bath (Bathwick)	ST 757658	1952	D	1952–1968
54/802	Severn	Shrewsbury	SJ 495127	1959	C	1960–1973
54/2	Avon	Evesham	SP 034431	1963	C	1962–1973*
54/903	Teme	Bransford Bridge	SO 804532	1961	C	1961–1973
59/1	Tawe	Ynys Tanglws	SS 685998			
60/3	Taf	Clog y Fran	SN 238160			
60/4	Dewi Fawr	Glasfryn Ford	SN 290175			

C = continuous recording thermometer
D = daily read thermometer
* Graphs of long term and 1973 data for these stations are presented on the following pages

Hydrometric Area (Gauging station number where relevant)	River	Station	National Grid Reference	Records Commence	Method of Measurement	Records at WDU
60/6	Gwili	Glangwili	SN 431220	1974		
60/12	Twrch	Ddol Las	SN 650440			
60/13	Cothi	Pont Ynys Brechfa	SN 537301			
60	Towy	Manoravon	SN 657240			
61/4	Western Cleddau	Redhill	SM 942184	1971		
62/2	Teifi	Llanfair	SN 433406			
66/1	Clwyd	Pont y Cambwll	SJ 069709	1968		
67/1	Dee	Bala (Flume)	SH 942357	1971		
67	Dee	Summers Jetty	SH 292705	1972		
67/2	Dee	Erbistock	SJ 357413	1959	C	1964–1970† ⎫
67/15	Dee	Manley Hall	SJ 348415	1967	C	1970–1973* ⎭
75	Eden	Willow-Holme	NY 385566	1969		
84/11	Gryfe	Craigend	NS 414664	1966		1966–1973
84/12	White Cart	Hawkhead	NS 499629	1966	C	1966–1973
84/14	Avon Water	Fairholm	NS 755518	1964		1964–1973
85/1	Leven	Linnbrane	NS 394803	1963	C	1964–1973*

† = Manley Hall replaced Erbistock 1970

10 Six Graphs of Monthly Data for selected River Water Temperature Stations

(All temperatures are in degrees Celsius)

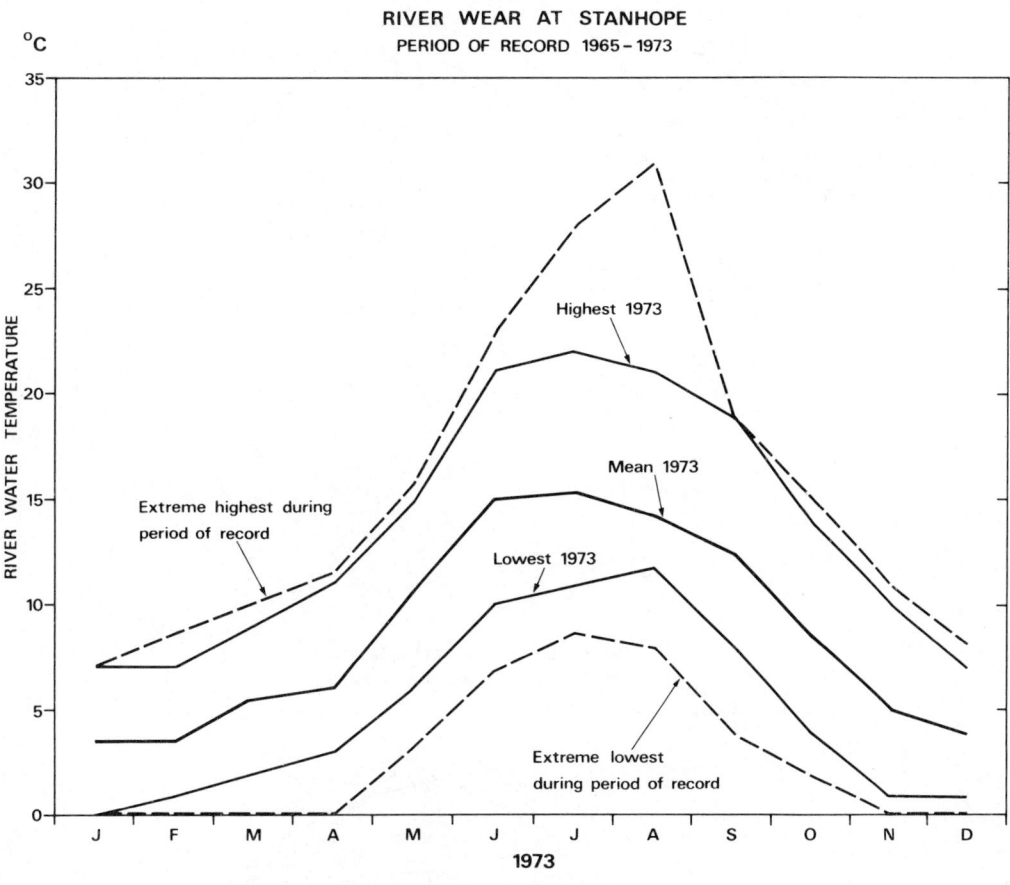

RIVER WEAR AT STANHOPE
PERIOD OF RECORD 1965 – 1973

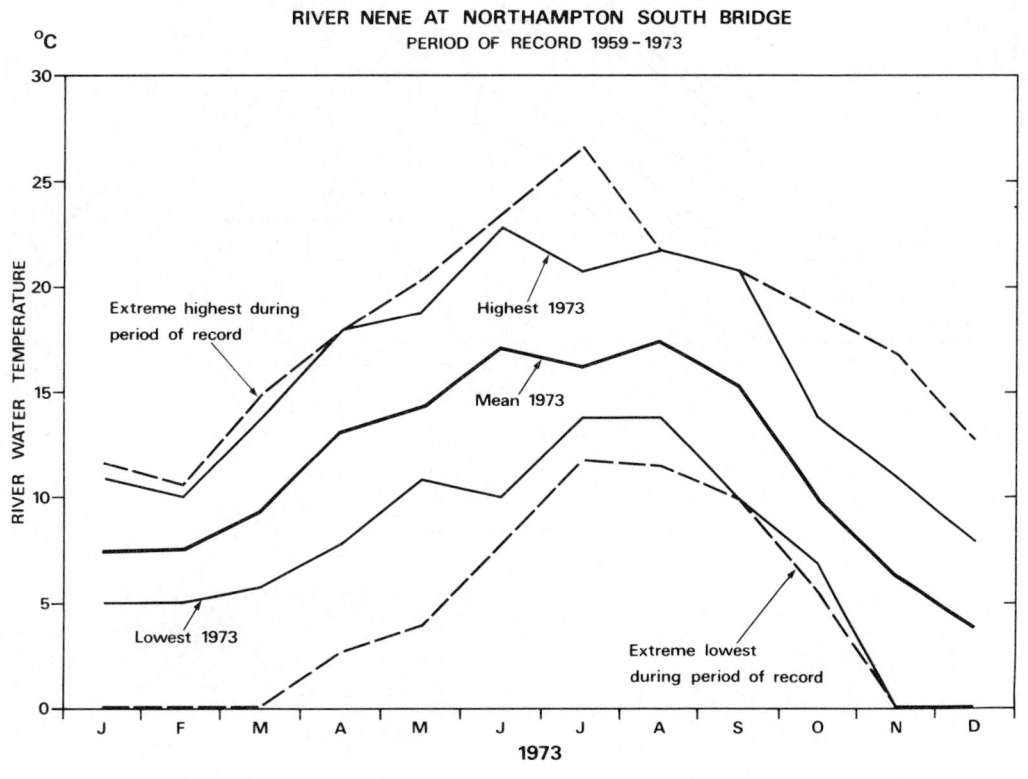

RIVER NENE AT NORTHAMPTON SOUTH BRIDGE
PERIOD OF RECORD 1959 – 1973

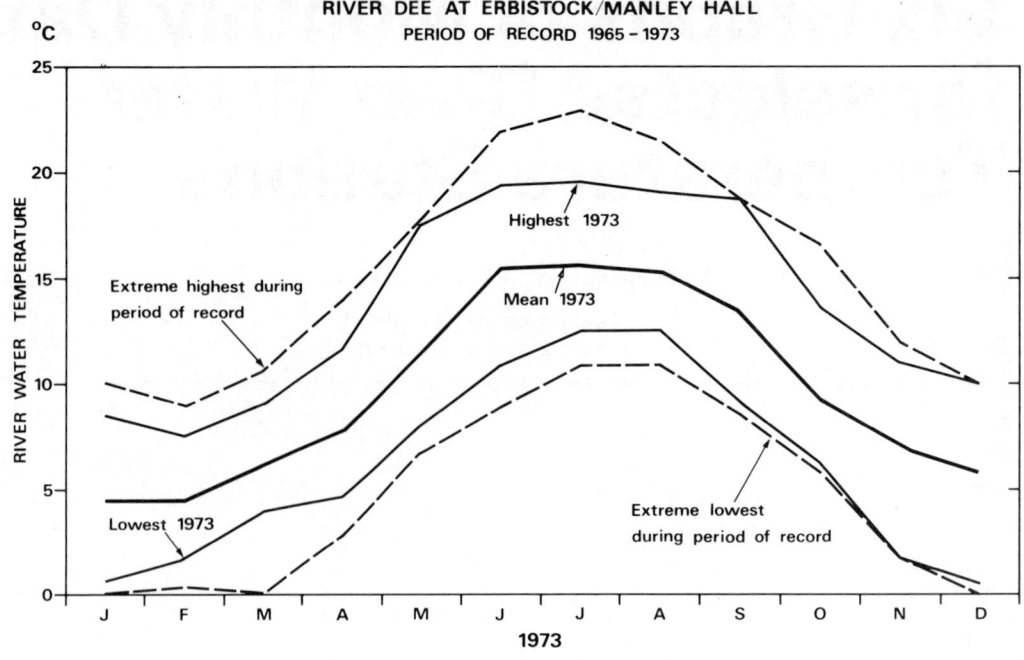

RIVER DEE AT ERBISTOCK/MANLEY HALL
PERIOD OF RECORD 1965 – 1973

°C

RIVER WATER TEMPERATURE

Extreme highest during period of record

Highest 1973

Mean 1973

Lowest 1973

Extreme lowest during period of record

J F M A M J J A S O N D

1973

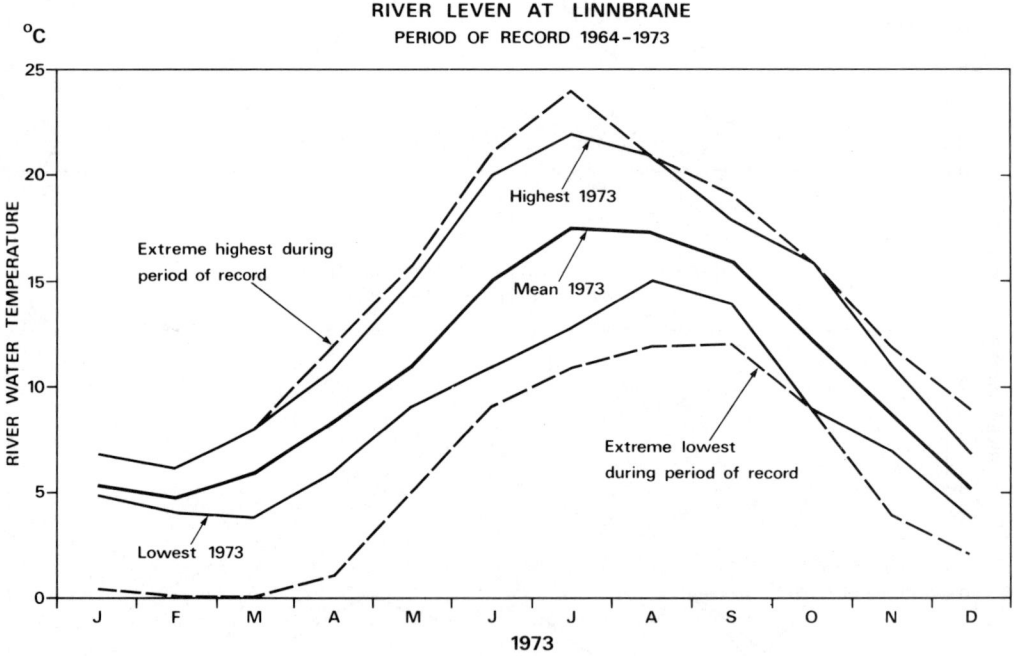

RIVER LEVEN AT LINNBRANE
PERIOD OF RECORD 1964 – 1973

°C

RIVER WATER TEMPERATURE

Extreme highest during period of record

Highest 1973

Mean 1973

Lowest 1973

Extreme lowest during period of record

J F M A M J J A S O N D

1973

174

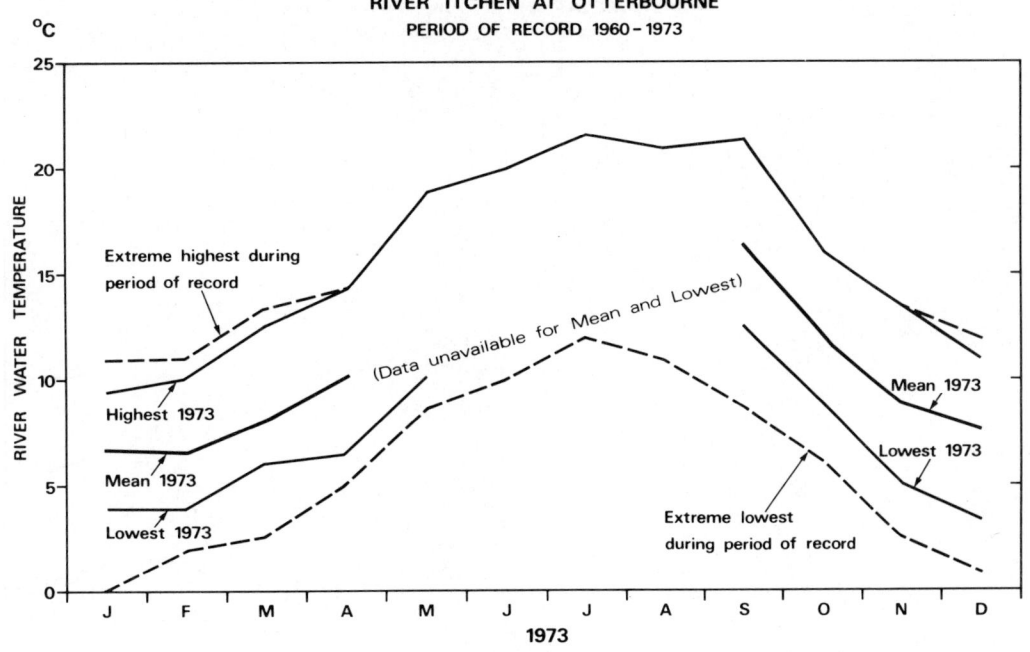

RIVER ITCHEN AT OTTERBOURNE
PERIOD OF RECORD 1960 – 1973

°C

RIVER WATER TEMPERATURE

25

20

15

Extreme highest during
period of record

(Data unavailable for Mean and Lowest)

10

Highest 1973

Mean 1973

5

Lowest 1973

Extreme lowest
during period of record

Mean 1973

Lowest 1973

0

J   F   M   A   M   J   J   A   S   O   N   D

1973

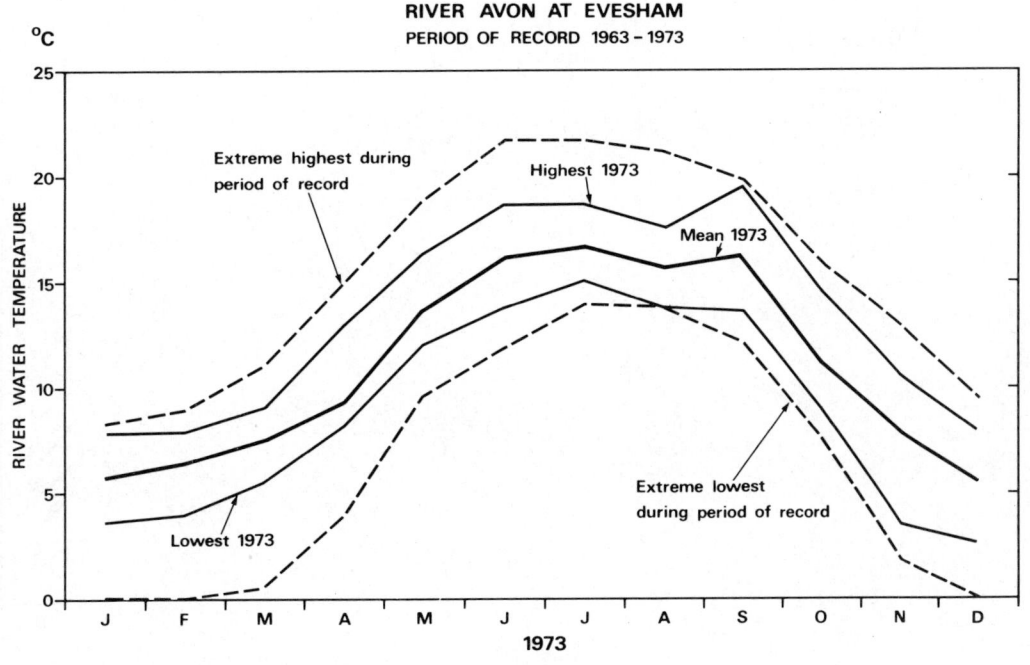

RIVER AVON AT EVESHAM
PERIOD OF RECORD 1963 – 1973

°C

RIVER WATER TEMPERATURE

25

20

Extreme highest during
period of record

Highest 1973

Mean 1973

15

10

Lowest 1973

Extreme lowest
during period of record

5

0

J   F   M   A   M   J   J   A   S   O   N   D

1973

11 Alphabetical Index of Gauging Station Names

Station name	Station number	River
Abbey Bridge	034322	Dove
Abbey Heath	033034	Little Ouse
Abercynon	057004	Cynon
Aberlour	008001	Spey
Abermule	054014	Severn
Abernant	055004	Irfon
Aberuchill	016002	Earn
Abingdon	039018	Ock
Adderbury	039051	Sor Brook
Adelphi Weir	069002	Irwell
Adwick	027030	Dearne
Afton Reservoir	079001	Afton Water
Agivey Bann Bridge	203302	Lower Bann
Airyhemming	081003	Water of Luce
Albany Park	038021	Turkey Brook
Albury	039036	Law Brook
Alfodean	041019	Arun
Allbrook	042002	Itchen
Allford	054359	Allford Brook
Almondbank	015013	Almond
Almondell	019005	Almond
Almond Weir	019002	Almond
Alness	004003	Alness
Alscot Park	054010	Stour (Warwicks)
Alston	023009	South Tyne
Alverstone Mill	101001	Yar (Eastern)
Alwen Reservoir	067004	Alwen
Ancrum	021025	Ale Water
Andraid	203013	Main
Anie	018008	Leny
Antrim	203018	Six Mile Water
Appleford Bridge	037010	Blackwater
Ardingly	041024	Shell Brook
Ardlethen	010001	Ythan
Ardwick	069020	Medlock
Arlesey	033033	Hiz
Armley	027028	Aire
Arnford	071011	Ribble
Ascott-under-Wychwood	039356	Evenlode
Ashbrook	068001	Weaver
Ashford	028023	Wye
Ashford Hill	052004	Isle
Ashley	031021	Welland
Ashton Weir	069007	Mersey
Ashwell	033040	Rhee
Auchendrane	082002	Doon
Auckley	028050	Torne
Audlem	068005	Weaver
Austin's Bridge	046003	Dart
Avochie	009001	Deveron
Avon Intake	046806	Avon
Avon Reservoir	046004	Avon
Bacup	069021	Stake Brook
Baggs Mill	044002	Piddle
Bagnor	039033	Winterbourne
Bala Flume	067001	Dee
Bala Intake	046805	Bala Brook
Bala Lake	067901	Dee
Bala Weir X	067019	Afon Tryweryn
Balderhead Reservoir	025022	Balder
Balfour Bridge	017004	Ore
Ballathie	015006	Tay
Ballee	203027	Braid
Ballinderry Bridge	203012	Ballinderry
Ballinluig	015012	Tummel
Ballyclare	203329	Six Mile Water
Ballymena	203306	Braid
Balmossie Mill	014002	Dighty
Balnaan Bridge	008009	Dulnain
Balnowlart	082003	Doon
Banbury	039026	Cherwell
Barcombe	041004	Ouse
Barden Bridge	071010	Pendle Water
Bardfield Bridge	036007	Belchamp Brook
Barford Bridge	032018	Ise
Barnard Castle	025008	Tees
Barnsley Weir	027023	Dearne
Barrasford	023902	North Tyne
Barrowden	031007	Welland
Bartley Mill	040024	Bartley Mill Stream
Bastreet	047013	Withey Brook
Bath	053903	Avon
Battleford Bridge	203303	Blackwater
Bayfield	034016	Glaven
Beach's Mill	037006	Can
Beal Weir	027003	Aire
Beam Bridge	068008	Weaver
Beck Bridge	033023	Lea Brook
Bedburn	024004	Bedburn Beck
Beddgelert	065001	Glaslyn
Beddington	039004	Wandle

Station name	Station number	River	Station name	Station number	River
Bedford	033002	Great Ouse	Bridgend (High Farm)	075012	St. John's Beck
Beechamwell	033805	Beechamwell Brook	Bridgend	058001	Ogmore
Beetham	073008	Bela	Bridge of Alford	011003	Don
Beggearn Huish	051801	Washford	Bridge of Allan	018005	Allan Water
Belle Isle	236303	Upper Erne	Bridge of Teith	018003	Teith
Bellever Bridge	046005	East Dart	Bridgham	033044	Thet
Belmesthorpe	031006	Gwash	Bridlington	026004	Gypsey Race
Belmont	055002	Wye	Bridport	044003	Asker
Belsteam	035011	Belstead Brook	Brigg Flatts (Sedburgh)	072011	Rawthey
Belton House	020006	Biel Water			
Benhall Bridge	035316	Fromus	Brigsley	029001	Waithe Beck
Berrygrove	039013	Colne	Brimpton	039025	Enborne
Besford Bridge	054015	Bow Bridge	Brinksway	069028	Mersey
Beversham Bridge	035004	Ore	Bristol	053021	The Malago
Bewdley	054001	Severn	Brixworth	032026	Nene, Brampton Branch
Bibury	039020	Coln			
Billingford Bridge	034010	Waveney	Broad Green	036010	Stour
Binfield	039052	The Cut	Broadlands	042004	Test
Bishop Auckland	024002	Gaunless	Broadraine	072804	Lune
Bishopbridge	029004	Ancholme	Brockenhurst Park	042003	Lymington
Bishopbridge	029005	Rase	Brockhoperig	021017	Ettrick Water
Bishop's Frome	055028	Frome	Bodfari	066004	Wheeler
Bishop's Hull	052003	Halse Water	Broken Scar	025001	Tees
Bishop's Hull	052005	Tone	Bromham Mill	033010	Great Ouse
Bitton	053017	Boyd	Bromley South	039824	Ravensbourne East
Blaby	028054	Sence	Broom	054007	Arrow
Blackford Bridge	069023	Roch	Broughton	042005	Wallop Brook
Blackwater Reservoir	090001	Leven	Brown How	073004	Coniston Water
Blairston	084005	Clyde	Brownshill Staunch	033001	Great Ouse
Blaris	205306	Lagan	Brydekirk	078003	Annan
Blatherwyke	032009	Will Brook	Bryn Aled	066003	Aled
Blunham	033022	Ivel	Brynkinalt Weir	067005	Ceiriog
Blyford Bridge	035009	Blyth	Brynmenyn	058005	Ogmore
Blyth	028047	Oldcoates Dyke	Buckenham Tofts	033349	Stanford Water
Boat o'Brig	008006	Spey	Burbage	028070	Burbage Brook
Boat of Garten	008005	Spey	Burcote	054024	Worfe
Bodenham	043011	Ebble	Burn Bridge, Harrogate	027051	Crimple
Bodfari	066004	Wheeler			
Boleside	021006	Tweed	Burn Hall	024005	Browney
Bonnybridge	017003	Bonny Water	Burnham Overy	034012	Burn
Bontnewydd	065004	Gwyrfai	Burnhope Reservoir	024801	Burnhope Burn
Booth Wood Mill Reservoir	027019	Booth Dean Clough			
			Burnt Mill	033021	Rhee
Borough Bridge	042009	Andover Brook	Burton Coggles	031011	West Glen
Bothamsall	028045	Meden	Burton-in-Lonsdale	072012	Greta
Bottisham	033003	Cam	Burwash	040017	Dudwell
Bottoms Beck	071005	Bottoms Beck	Bury Bridge	069035	Irwell
Bottoms Reservoir	069004	Etherow	Bury Weir	033809	Bury Brook
Bounstead Bridge	037021	Roman	Buttercrambe	027041	Derwent
Bradbury	025021	Skerne	Butts Bridge	055021	Lugg
Braithwaite	075006	Newlands Beck	Bygate	022002	Coquet
Bramford	035010	Gipping	Byton	055014	Lugg
Brampton	033020	Alconbury Brook	Bywell	023001	Tyne
Bramshill	039044	Hart	Caban Coch Reservoir	055006	Elan
Bransdale Weir	027010	Hodge Beck			
Bray	039009	Thames	Cademuir	021019	Manor Water
Breich Weir	019003	Breich Water	Cadora	055001	Wye
Bretons Farm	037019	Beam	Calder Hall	074006	Calder
Bridgend	084006	Kelvin	Calderpark	084019	North Calder Water

Station name	Station number	River	Station name	Station number	River
Caledon Bridge	203307	Blackwater	Clywedog Dam	054042	Clywedog
Callan New Bridge	203025	Callan	Coalburn	076011	Coal Burn
Calthorpe Park	028039	Rea	Cobbinshaw	019009	Bog Burn
Cambusnethan	084806	Clyde	Cockfield	036009	Brett
Camerton	075002	Derwent	Coldstream	021023	Leet Water
Camowen Terrace	201005	Camowen	Coleshill	028066	Cole
Campsie Bridge	201006	Drumragh	Coleshill	039355	Cole
Canaston Bridge	061002	Eastern Cleddau	Colindeep Lane	039049	Silkstream
Canonbie	077001	Esk	Colne Bridge	027031	Colne
Capel Dewi	060010	Tywi	Colney	034001	Yare
Capenoch	079004	Scar	Colwick	028009	Trent
Cappenham Bridge	033018	Tove	Compstall	069015	Etherow
Caputh	015003	Tay	Compton Dando	053004	Chew
Carn Wood	047011	Plym	Comrie Bridge	015011	Lyon
Carreg-y-Wen	055017	Chwefru	Condorrat	084016	Luggie Water
Carshalton	039832	Wandle	Congleton Park	068018	Dane
Cassington Mill	039034	Evenlode	Connolly's Mill	039003	Wandle
Castle Mill	039364	Mill	Constantine Weir	035001	Gipping
Catbridge	034326	Thorndon Watercourse	Cookston	015008	Dean
Catcleugh Reservoir	023903	Rede	Copford Hall	037016	Pant (Upper Blackwater)
Caton	072004	Lune	Corwen	067014	Dee
Catrine	083003	Ayr	Costessey Mill	034004	Wensum
Causey Bridges	069030	Sankey Brook	Costessey Park	034005	Tud
Cefn Brwyn	055008	Wye	Cotham	028017	Devon
Cemaes Road	064004	Twymyn	Cottesmore Farm	039360	Ewelme Brook
Central Park	070003	Douglas	Cowbeech	041016	Cuckmere
Cerney Wick	039035	Churn	Cow Green Reservoir	025023	Tees
Chadkirk	069009	Goyt	Cowley	045806	Creedy
Chafford	040007	Medway	Coytrahen	058007	Llynfi
Chain Bridge	056001	Usk	Crabb's Bridge	037003	Ter
Chalk Bridge	038008	Lee	Crabb Mill	053019	Woodbridge Brook
Charr	012801	Glen Dye	Cradle Bridge	037330	Holland Brook
Chart Leacon	040022	Great Stour	Craig Douglas	021034	Yarrow Water
Chatsworth	028043	Derwent	Craigend	084011	Gryfe
Cheadle	069011	Micker Brook	Craigiehall	019001	Almond
Cheddleton	028042	Churnet	Craigshill Wood	048009	St. Neot
Chess Bridge	041028	Chess Stream	Crayford	040016	Cray
Chesterford	033051	Cam	Cream Poke Farm, Stainfield	030012	Stainfield Beck
Chesterton	032027	Billing Brook			
Chester Weir	067020	Dee	Cribynau	054013	Severn
Chinbrook Meadows	039829	Quaggy	Cricklade	039040	Thames
Chipping Ongar	037015	Cripsey Brook	Croasdale Flume	071003	Croasdale Beck
Chiselborough	052007	Parratt	Croft	025007	Clow Beck
Cholstrey Mill	055020	Pinsley Brook	Cromwell Lock	028057	Trent
Churchend	037011	Chelmer	Cross Inn	057803	Clun
Church Warsop	028032	Meden	Croston Mill	070004	Yarrow
Church Wilne	028067	Derwent	Crowford Bridge	047010	Tamar
Cilfrew	058008	Dulais	Crowhurst	041017	Combe Haven
Cilmery	055012	Irfon	Croxley Green	039030	Gade
Cilrhedyn Bridge	061003	Gwaun	Crummock Water	075015	Crummock Water
Clappers Bridge	041020	Bevern Stream	Cuckney	028044	Poulter
Clatworthy Reservoir	052008	Tone	Cultybraggan	016003	Ruchill
Claughton	072812	Stubbins Brook	Currys Bridge	203021	Kells Water
Claypole Mill	030001	Witham	Currypool	052016	Currypool Stream
Claythorpe Mill	029002	Great Eau	Cwm Llanerch	066011	Conwy
Clennell	022008	Alwin	Cwmavon	058004	Afan
Clipstone	033030	Clipstone Brook	Cynefail	067010	Afon Celyn
Clog y Fran	060003	Taf	Dalbeattie	080001	Urr
Clungunford	054356	Clun	Daldowie	084013	Clyde

Station name	Station number	River	Station name	Station number	River
Dalinlongart	086001	Little Eachaig	East Mill	015809	Muckle Burn
Dalkeith Palace	019011	North Esk	East Mills	043003	Avon
Dalmore Weir	019004	North Esk	East Shefford	039032	Lambourn
Dalnas Hugh	008004	Avon	East Stoke Mill	044001	Frome
Dalry	083002	Garnock	Easton Wood	031023	West Glen
Damflask Reservoir	027017	Loxley	Eaton Mill	054041	Tern
Darwell Reservoir	040002	Darwell	Earlston	021015	Leader Water
Day's Weir	039002	Thames	Ebley Mill	054027	Frome
Ddol Farm	055026	Wye	Eccles	069019	Worsley Brook
Ddol Las	060012	Twrch	Eckford	086002	Eachaig
Deephope	021026	Tima Water	Eddy's Bridge	023002	Derwent
Denby	049001	Camel	Edmonton (Silver Street)	038022	Pymmes Brook
Denham	039010	Colne	Edmonton	038014	Salmon Brook
De Lank	049003	De Lank	Eel House Bridge	073006	Cunsey Bridge
Dent Bank	025902	Tees	Elford	028005	Tame
Denver	033035	Great Ouse	Elizabeth Way	038007	Canons Brook
Dernford	033024	Cam	Elland	027029	Calder
Derryadd Bay	203614	Lough Neagh	Ellingham Mill	034013	Waveny
Derrymeen Bridge	203922	Blackwater	Elshieshields	078302	Water of Ae
Devonvale	018904	Devon	Empingham	031016	North Brook
Disserth	055016	Ithon	Enfield	038015	Intercepting Drain
Diversion Works	080801	Pullaugh Burn	Enfield Lock	038024	Small River Lee
Dodford	032008	Nene, Kislingbury Branch	Ennerdale	074003	Ehen
Dolau Hirion	060007	Tywi	Ensbury	043002	Stour
Dolgellau	064005	Wnion	Enslow Mill	039021	Cherwell
Dolybont	064006	Leri	Enterwell	045006	Quarme
Dol y Mynach	055030	Claerwen	Erbistock Rectory	067902	Dee
Doncaster	027021	Don	Erchless	005901	Beauly
Dorchester	044004	Frome	Erme Intake	046801	Erme
Dotton	045005	Otter	Ermington	046006	Erme
Dovey Bridge	064001	Dovey	Erwood	055007	Wye
Dowles	054034	Dowles Brook	Euston County Bridge	033011	Little Ouse
Drakelow Park	028019	Trent	Etal	021031	Till
Draycott	028021	Derwent	Evesham	054002	Avon
Dromona	203011	Main	Ewelme	039361	Ewelme Brook
Drove Lane	042007	Alre	Ewenny Priory	058003	Ewenny
Druid	067006	Alwen	Ewood Bridge	071013	Darwen
Drumlanrig	079006	Nith	Eye	034325	Yaxley Watercourse
Drungewick	041025	Loxwood Stream	Eye Brook Reservoir	031001	Eye Brook
Dryburgh	021010	Tweed	Eyemouth Mill	021016	Eye Water
Dryfield	084015	Kelvin	Eynsham	039008	Thames
Duddon Hall	074001	Duddon	Fairbrook Farm	040015	White Drain
Dudgeon Bridge	201002	Fairy Water	Fairholm	084014	Avon Water
Duffield	028055	Ecclesbourne	Fakenham Mill	034011	Wensum
Dunadry	203330	Six Mile Water	Farndon	067024	Dee
Dunham Massey	069006	Bollin	Farnham	035003	Alde
Dunkerton	053016	Spring Flow	Farnworth Weir	069024	Croal
Dunmurry Lane	205003	Lagan	Far Sawrey	073012	Windermere
Dunnabridge	046007	West Dart	Fawe Park	075011	Derwent Water
Durley Mill	042011	Hamble	Featherstone	023006	South Tyne
Durlock	040014	Wingham	Feildes Weir	038001	Lee
Dynes Bridge	203017	Upper Bann	Felin-Mynachdy	060002	Cothi
Eamon Bridge	076004	Lowther	Felin y Cwm	060009	Sawdde
Earls Colne	037024	Colne	Felsted	037020	Chelmer
Easby	025019	Leven	Feltham	039837	Duke of Northumberland Stream
Easneye	038005	Ash			
East Gate	024006	Rook Hope Farm			
East Linton	020001	Tyne	Feltham	039838	Longford

Station name	Station number	River	Station name	Station number	River
Fenny Castle	052009	Sheppey	Gorhuish	050804	Hookmoor Brook
Fernworthy Reservoir	046001	South Teign	Goulceby Bridge	030011	Bain
			Gouthwaite Reservoir	027005	Nidd
Feshie Bridge	008902	Spey	Grange	009003	Isla
Fiddlers Elbow	057007	Taff	Grantown	008010	Spey
Fiddlers Ford	079005	Cluden Water	Graylingwell	041023	Lavant
Fledborough	028062	Trent	Great Bridgford	028052	Sow
Flint Mill Weir	027002	Wharfe	Great Haywood	028006	Trent
Flixton Bridge	069029	Mersey	Great Oakley	036016	Ramsey
Flore Experimental Catchment	032029	Unnamed tributary	Great Sampford	037036	Ely-Ouse Outfall
Florida Bridge	205907	Blackwater (Ards)	Great Somerford	053008	Avon
Footholme	071804	Dunsop	Greenham	052014	Tone
Ford	068010	Fender	Greenhaugh	023010	Tarset Burn
Forge, Brecon	056003	Hondda	Greenholme	076008	Irthing
Forgewood	084007	South Calder Water	Greens Bridge	069031	Netherley Brook
Fornalls Green	068016	Birket	Grendon Underwood	039017	Ray
Forres	007002	Findhorn	Grimsthorpe Park	031014	Grimsthorpe Brook
Forter	015001	Isla	Grosmont	055029	Monnow
Forteviot Bridge	016004	Earn	Guithavon Valley	037009	Brain
Fosters Bridge	031010	Chater	Gunnislake	047001	Tamar
Foston Mill	026003	Foston Beck	Gwills	049004	Gannel
Fotheringay	032002	Willow Brook	Hadfields Weir	027006	Don
Frenchay	053006	Frome (Bristol)	Hadleigh	036005	Brett
Friar's Carse	079002	Nith	Hadlow	040006	Bourne
Fruid	021901	Fruid Water	Halfway Bridge	041022	Lod
Fullerton	042012	Anton	Halkirk	097002	Thurso
Fulling Mill	038011	Mimram	Hall Bridge	079003	Nith
Fulsby Lock	030003	Bain	Halton	072001	Lune
Gaidrew	085002	Endrick Water	Halton upon Weir	073803	Lune
Gairlochy	091901	Mucomir Cut	Halton West	071802	Ribble
Galashiels	021013	Gala Water	Hammer Wood Bridge	041002	Ash Bourne
Galesyke	074002	Irt	Hammoon	043009	Stour
Galgate	073017	Conder	Hamstall Ridware	028002	Blithe
Gallica Bridge	052020	Gallica Stream	Hansteads	039014	Ver
Gambles Bridge	203024	Cusher	Hanwell	039834	Brent
Ganllwyd	064003	Mawddach	Harford Hill	054011	Salwarpe
Garstang	072008	Wyre	Harraby Green	076010	Petteril
Gatehouses	027038	Costa	Harrold Mill	033009	Great Ouse
Gatwick	039024	Gatwick Stream	Harrowden Old Mill	032004	Ise Brook
Gatwick Airport	039054	Mole	Hartford Bridge	022006	Blyth
Gaynes Park	037018	Ingrebourne	Harwood Beck	025012	Harwood Beck
Gethin's Bridge	066012	Lledr	Hatfield Peverel	037901	Ter
Gilsburn	076912	Irthing	Hatterell Bridge	041010	Adur
Glangwili	060006	Gwili	Haughton	011002	Don
Glan Teifi	062001	Teifi	Haughton	028034	Maun
Glasfryn Ford	060004	Dewi Fawr	Haw Bridge	054357	Severn
Glashagh Bridge	201303	Derg	Hawick	021012	Teviot
Glemsford	036002	Glem	Hawkerland	045801	Back Brook
Glenavy	203026	Glenavy	Hawkhead	084012	White Cart Water
Glenbreck	021029	Tweed	Hawk Hill	022004	Aln
Glen Cottage	017007	Red Burn	Hawkridge	052803	Aisholt Brook
Glen Falloch	085003	Falloch	Hawkridge	052804	Merridge Brook
Glenochil	018002	Devon	Hawley	040012	Darent
Glenone Bridge	203019	Claudy	Hawley Road Bridge	039363	Cove Brook
Glyndyfrdwy	067907	Dee	Haydon Bridge	023004	South Tyne
Gold Bridge	041005	Ouse	Hayes Lane	039825	Ravensbourne West
Gordon Bridge	021020	Yarrow Water	Hazelbank	084003	Clyde
Gore Farm	068011	Arley Brook	Heacham Mill	033032	Heacham

Station name	Station number	River	Station name	Station number	River
Headsor Mill	039023	Wye	Inverugie	010002	Ugie
Headswood	017001	Carron	Iping Mill	041011	Rother
Hebden	027032	Hebden Park	Irlam Weir	069001	Mersey
Helmshire	069034	Musbury Brook	Irnham	031013	East Glen
Helston	048006	Cober	Irwell Vale	069022	Irwell
Hempholme	026002	Hull	Isfield	041006	Uck
Hendal Bridge	040020	Medway	Isleham	033004	Lark
Henderland	021030	Megget Water	Iwood	052017	Congresbury Yeo
Hendon Lane Bridge	039820	Dollis Brook	Izaak Walton	028046	Dove
Henley Bridge	041013	Huggletts Stream	Jedburgh	021024	Jed Water
Henthorn	041006	Ribble	Jeffy Knots	073014	Brathay
Herts, Training School	038006	Rib	Jerretspass (River)	206002	Jerretspass
			Jerretspass (Canal)	206003	Newry Canal
Higham	036013	Brett	Jesus Lock	033016	Cam
Highbridge	042002	Itchen	Jumbles Rock	071009	Ribble
High Hodder Bridge	071803	Hodder	Kate's Bridge	031002	Glen
Highford Dam	022005	Wansbeck	Kearsley	069026	Irwell
High Greenwood	027012	Hebden Water	Kedington	036012	Stour
High Keer Bridge	073015	Keer	Keepers Lodge	058009	Ewenny
High Ongar	037014	Roding	Kemback	014001	Eden
High Wycombe	039039	Wye	Kendal	073805	Kent
Hindley Wrae	023013	West Allen	Kenmore	015016	Tay
Hinton-on-the-Green	054036	Isbourne	Kentchurch	055009	Monnow
Hockcliffe Weir	033030	Clipstone Brook	Kettering	032019	Slade Brook
Hodder Foot	071007	Ribble	Kidderminster	054006	Stour
Hodder Place	071008	Hodder	Kielder	023011	Kielder Burn
Hodnet	054361	Hodnet Brook	Kielder	023314	North Tyne
Hollingsclough	028033	Dove	Kilbreece	055019	Gamber Brook
Holm Hill	076009	Caldew	Kildwick Bridge	027035	Aire
Holton	035013	Blyth	Kilgram Bridge	027034	Ure
Holywell	031024	Holywell Brook	Killermont	084001	Kelvin
Holywell	041026	Cockhaise Brook	Killington New Bridge	072005	Lune
Hookagate	054018	Rea Brook			
Hopemill Bridge Sandhurst	040021	Hexden Channel	Killymore Bridge	201001	Owenkillew
			Kilmarnock	083082	Irvine
Horley	039053	Mole	Kilphedir	002001	Helmsdale
Hornby	072807	Wenning	Kinbuck	018001	Allan Water
Horning Lock	034008	Ant	King Street Bridge	031003	Glen
Horton	040011	Great Stour	Kingledores	021014	Tweed
Hulme End	028038	Manifold	Kingsford Bridge	009801	Allt Deveron
Hulme Walfield	068006	Dane	Kingston Hall	028029	Kingston Brook
Hungerford	039028	Dun	Kingston-on-Thames	039012	Hogshill
Hungry Snout	021902	Whiteadder Water	Kinkell Bridge	016001	Earn
Hunsingore Weir	027001	Nidd	Kinnersley Manor	039365	Mole
Hutton Castle	021022	Whiteadder Water	Kinrara	008002	Spey
Huxley	068015	Gowy	Kinross	017308	South Queich
Hydro-Electric Scheme	065901	Dwyryd	Kirkby	069032	Alt
			Kirkby Lonsdale	072006	Lune
Ilam	028031	Manifold	Kirkby Mills	027042	Dove
Ilkley	027027	Wharfe	Kirkby Stephen	076014	Eden
Ingworth	034003	Bure	Kirkmuirhill	084009	Nethan
Intake	003804	Cassley	Kirknewton	021032	Glen
Intake	091802	Alt Leachdach	Kirk Smeaton	027037	Went
Intake	087801	Alt Uaine	Knighton	039043	Kennet
Intake	021033	Baddingsgill Burn	Knightsford Bridge	054029	Teme
Invergarry	006904	Garry	Knockenden Reservoir	083001	Caaf Water
Invermoriston	006906	Allt Bhlaraidh	Lady Bridge	032012	Wootton Brook
Invermoriston	006903	Moriston	Laggan Bridge	008901	Spey
Invertruim	008007	Spey	Lairg	003901	Shin

Station name	Station number	River	Station name	Station number	River
Lamarsh	036015	Stour	Lough MacNean Lower	236604	Arney
Lambeth Road	037332	Eastwood Brook	Loughton	037023	Roding
Lanchester	024007	Browney	Loverley Mill	043010	Allen
Langdon Beck	025011	Langdon Beck	Lovington	052010	Brue
Langford	037904	Blackwater	Low Briery	075009	Greta
Langham	036006	Stour	Low Houses	027047	Snaizeholme Beck
Langholm	083004	Lugar	Lowdham	028060	Dover Beck
Langsett Reservoir	027852	Little Don	Low Nibthwaite	073002	Crake
Langworth Bridge	030002	Barling's Eau	Low Worsall	025009	Tees
Laverstock Mill	043004	Bourne	Ludlow	054353	Corve
Lea Marston	028004	Tame	Luffness	020002	Peffer West
Lechlade	039042	Leach	Lugwardine	055003	Lugg
Leckby Grange	027008	Swale	Luton Hoo	038013	Upper Lee
Lednoch Intake	015808	Almond	Lullingstone	040018	Darent
Lennoxlove	020007	Gifford Water	Lyne Ford	021005	Tweed
Letcombe Basset	039357	Letcombe Brook	Lyne Station	021018	Lyne Water
Leven	017002	Leven	Maentwrog	065002	Dryryd
Leven Bridge	025005	Leven	Main Road Bridge	037329	St. Osyth Brook
Lexden	037005	Colne	Manchester Racecourse	069025	Irwell
Liberton	019010	Braid Burn	Manley Hall	067015	Dee
Lifton Park	047006	Lyd	Manor Farm, Wantage	039358	Tributary of Letcombe Brook
Lilford	032014	Nene			
Lindean	021007	Ettrick Water	Manor House Gardens	039828	Quaggy
Lindley Wood Reservoir	027011	Washburn			
			Mansfield	028059	Maun
Linnbrane	085001	Leven	Manthorpe Bridge	031008	East Glen
Little Bytham	031012	Tham	Mardock	038002	Ash
Little Habton	027014	Rye	Margaretting	037902	Wid
Little Walsingham	034320	Stiffkey	Marham	033007	Nar
Little Woolden Hall	069005	Glaze Brook	Market Harborough	031022	Jordan
Llanbadarn Fawr	063002	Rheidol	Marlborough	039037	Kennet
Llandetty	056004	Usk	Marple Bridge	069017	Goyt
Llandewi	055011	Ithon	Marsh Farm	039822	Crane
Llandovery	060005	Bran	Marshfield Bridge	068004	Wistaston Brook
Llanederyn	057008	Rhymney	Marton on Dove	028018	Dove
Llanfair	062002	Teifi	Matlock Bath	028011	Derwent
Llanrhystyd	063003	Wyre	Mattersey	028015	Idle
Llanwern	056008	Monks Ditch	Maydown Bridge	203010	Blackwater
Llanyblodwel	054038	Tanat	Meagre Farm	033012	Kym
Llwynon Reservoir	057002	Taf Fawr	Medbourne	031019	Medbourne Brook
Llyn Celwyn Outflow	067017	Afon Tryweryn	Melandra	069016	Etherow
			Meldreth	033813	Mel
Llyn Gwellyn	065903	Gwyrfai	Melford Bridge	033019	Thet
Lobby Bridge	073803	Winster	Melksham	053001	Avon
Lochaber W.P.A.	091001	Lochy	Menzion Farm	021028	Menzion Burn
Loch Calder	097001	Calder Burn	Middleton-in-Teesdale	025018	Tees
Loch of Lintrathen	015004	Inzion			
Loch of Lintrathen	015005	Melgam	Midford	053005	Midford Brook
Lochhouses	020004	Peffer East	Milford	028014	Sow
Lodge Farm	039015	White Water	Millbrook	056012	Grwyne
Longbridge Deverill	043015	Wylwye	Miller Bridge House	073013	Rothay
Longbridge Weir	028010	Derwent			
Longhill Weir	017006	Carron	Millikin Park	084017	Black Cart Water
Long Melford	036004	Chad Brook	Mint Bridge	073011	Mint
Longworth Clough	069036	Eagley Brook	Mislingford	042006	Meon
Lopwell	047003	Tavy	Mitchel Troy	055022	Trothy
Lostock Gralam	068007	Wincham Brook	Mitford	022007	Wansbeck
Louth	029003	Lud	Moar	015902	Lyon
Loughan Island	203301	Lower Bann			

Station name	Station number	River	Station name	Station number	River
Mogden (Lower Dukes)	039836	Duke of Northumberland Stream	Old Mill Bridge	032003	Harper's Brook
			Old Ship	041021	Clayhill Stream
Molingey	048008	White	One Barrow	028030	Blackbrook
Monks Park	039821	Brent	Onibury	054354	Onny
Montford	054005	Severn	Orchard Mill	033902	Ouzel
Moor Bridge	203021	Torrent	Ormiston Mill	021008	Teviot
Moor House	025003	Trout Beck	Orton	032001	Nene
More Hall Reservoir	027013	Ewden Beck	Otford	040013	Darent
			Ouse Bridge	075003	Derwent
Moreton	068017	Arrowe Brook	Pallingham Quay	041014	Arun
Morwick	022001	Coquet	Pangbourne	039027	Pang
Mount Mill Bridge	206001	Clanrye	Panshanger Park	038003	Mimram
Mouth Bridge	021027	Blackadder Water	Pant Mawr	055010	Wye
Movanagher Weir	203004	Lower Bann	Pant-yr-Onen	066002	Elwy
Mowden Bridge	025010	Baydale Beck	Park	012002	Dee
Moy Bridge	004001	Conon	Parkham	050801	Yeo
Moyola New Bridge	203020	Moyola	Parkhill	011001	Don
Muiresk	009002	Deveron	Partington	069013	Sinderland Brook
Muirshiel	084002	Calder	Partney Mill	030004	Partney Lymm
Mundesley Hospital	034321	Mundesley Beck	Peebles	021003	Tweed
Murrayfield	019006	Water of Leith	Peil Wyke	075008	Bassenthwaite
Musselburgh	019007	Esk	Pencaenewydd	065005	Erch
Muxworthy	050904	Hole Water	Penkridge	028053	Penk
Mytham Bridge	028037	Derwent	Pen Mill	052006	Yeo
Nant Aberderfel	067011	Nant Aberderfel	Penshurst	040010	Eden
Narborough	028051	Soar	Penwhirn Reservoir	081001	Penwhirn
Naunton Hall	035002	Deben	Perces Bridge	037325	Bourne Brook
Needham Mill	034006	Waveney	Perry Farm	054045	Perry
Neen Sollars	054355	Rea	Philiphaugh	021011	Yarrow Water
Ness Castle Farm	006901	Ness	Pickering Wood	028068	Lathkill
Ness Side	006007	Ness	Picton	068002	Gowy
Netherby	077001	Esk	Pillaton Mill	047004	Lynher
Netherton	018306	Goodie Water	Pitnacree	015007	Tay
Newbourn	035314	Mill River	Plas Rhiwaedog	067013	Afon Hirnant
Newbourn	035315	Newbourn Stream	Platt	054366	Platt Brook
Newbridge	054028	Vyrnwy	Plynlimon	054022	Severn
Newbridge	039006	Windrush	Pointon	030014	Pointon Lode
Newby Bridge	073001	Leven	Polesworth	028026	Anker
Newferry	203305	Lower Bann	Polmonthill	017005	Avon
Newforge	205004	Lagan	Polstead	036003	Box
New Inn	067018	Afon Dyfrdwy	Ponsanooth	048007	Kennall
Newlands	027004	Calder	Pontaryscir	056013	Yscir
Newport Pagnell	033037	Great Ouse	Pont-hen-hafod	056007	Afon Senni
Newton	015002	Newton	Ponthir	056005	Afon Lwyd
Newton-le-Willows	069018	Newton Brook	Pont Llolwyn	063001	Ystwyth
Newton Stewart	081002	Cree	Pontneath-vaughan	058006	Mellte
New Viaduct	069901	Medlock	Pontypridd	057005	Taff
Norham	021009	Tweed	Pont-y-Cambwll	066001	Clwyd
Northampton	032005	Nene	Pont-y-Capel	067008	Alyn
North Fareham	042001	Wallington	Pont y Garth	064002	Dysynni
North Muskham	028022	Trent	Pont-y-Gwyddel	066006	Elwy
Northampton	032005	Nene	Pont Ynys Brechfa	060013	Cothi
Northwich	068804	Dane	Pont y Rhuddfa	067003	Brenig
Northwold	033006	Wissey	Poolewe	094001	Ewe
Norton Bavant	043012	Wylye	Pooley Bridge	076015	Eamont
Oakley Park	034007	Dove	Pool Street	037012	Colne
Offenham	054023	Badsey Brook	Portinscale	075005	Derwent
Offord	033026	Great Ouse	Portna	203308	Lower Bann
Ogston Reservoir	028071	Amber	Portora	236302	Lower Erne

Station name	Station number	River	Station name	Station number	River
Portwood	069027	Tame	Saltersford	030005	Witham
Potford Bridge	054360	Potford Brook	Saltoun Hall	020005	Birns Water
Prendergast Mill	061001	Western Cleddau	Saltwater Bridge	037328	Bentley Brook
Preston	046002	Teign	Samlesbury	071001	Ribble
Prestonholm	019008	South Esk	Sandbach	068014	Sandersons Brook
Preston-le-Skerne	025020	Skerne	Sandford Bridge	055027	Rudhall Bridge
Prestwood Hospital	054363	Stour	Saxon's Lode	054032	Severn
Princes Marsh	041027	Rother	Scarborough	027033	Sea Cut
Puslinch	047007	Yealm	Scorton Weir	072809	Wyre
Queen's Falls	043005	Avon	Scotland Weir	069003	Irk
Quidenham	033045	Whittle	Scout Dike Reservoir	027020	Scout Dike
Quoile Barrier, Lr	205301	Quoile	Sedgwick	073005	Kent
Quoile Barrier, Up	205302	Quoile	Sefton	069033	Alt
Ratcliffe Culey	028025	Sence	Semington	053002	Semington Brook
Ravenscroft	068012	Dane	Seneirl	204001	Bush
Ravernet	205005	Ravernet	Serlby Park	028016	Ryton
Reaverhill	023003	North Tyne	Sewards Bridge	042008	Cheriton Stream
Euston Rectory Bridge	033013	Sapiston	Sewardstone Road	038020	Cobbins Brook
			Sgodachail	003002	Carron
Red Bridge	033046	Thet	Shabbinton	039038	Thame
Redbridge	037001	Roding	Shalford	039029	Tillingbourne
Rede Bridge	023008	Rede	Shardlow	028007	Trent
Redbrook	055023	Wye	Shaw	039019	Lambourn
Redburn	004302	Glass	Sheaveshill Road	039833	Silk Stream
Redhall	078004	Kinnel Water	Sheepbridge Hill	039022	Loddon
Redhill	061004	Western Cleddau	Sheepmount	076007	Eden
Red Lees	084008	Rotten Calder Water	Shefford	033028	Flit
Resolven	058002	Neath	Shenachie	007001	Findhorn
Restormel 1	048002	Fowey	Sherman Bridge	041003	Cuckmere
Restormel 2	048011	Fowey	Sherriffmills	007003	Lossie
Revesby Reservoir	030803	Miningsby Beck	Shewalton	083005	Irvine
Rhayader	055005	Wye	Shillingthorpe	031009	West Glen
Rhiwderyn	056002	Ebbw	Shillmoor	022003	Usway Burn
Rhos y Pentref	054025	Dulas	Ship House Bridge	037327	Sixpenny Brook
Rhuddlan Bridge	066707	Clwyd	Shottesham	034002	Tas
Rhydymwyn	067009	Alyn	Shottisham	035317	Shottisham
Richmond	027024	Swale	Sills	084004	Clyde
Ridlington	031015	Chater	Skelton Railway Bridge	027009	Ouse
Ringwood	043901	Avon			
Rivington Reservoir	070001	Douglas	Slate Mill	054026	Chelt
Robstone	082001	Girvan	Sleights Weir	027050	Esk
Rocester	028020	Churnet	Somerford	043013	Mude
Rocester Weir	028008	Dove	Somerton	052011	Cary
Rodbourne	053020	Gauze Brook	South Luffenham	031020	Morcott Brook
Rodington	054016	Roden	South Newton	043008	Wylye
Rosscor	236301	Lower Erne	South Park	025004	Skerne
Rothbury	022009	Coquet	South Willesborough	040023	East Stour
Rotherham	027022	Don	Southwaite Bridge	075004	Cocker
Rothley	028056	Rothley Brook	Southwick Brook	032024	Southwick Brook
Rowanburnfoot	077003	Liddell	Spilmersford Bridge	020003	Tyne
Rowland's Gill	023007	Derwent	Springs	038016	Stansted Mountfitchet
Roxton	033039	Great Ouse	Springfield	037008	Chelmer
Rudheath	068003	Dane	Spring Mill	073009	Sprint
Rushes Lock	037002	Chelmer	Spring Valley	037035	Salary Brook
Rutherford Bridge	025006	Greta	Sprouston	021021	Tweed
Ruthven Bridge	008003	Spey	St. Andrew's Mill	032007	Nene, Brampton Branch
Ryburn Reservoir	027018	Ryburn			
Ryholmes Bridge	032023	Grendon Brook	St. Erth	049002	Hayle
Sakenham	041012	Adur (East Branch)	St. Ivel Staunch	033017	Great Ouse

Station name	Station number	River	Station name	Station number	River
St. Michael's	072002	Wyre	Theale	039016	Kennet
St. Mungo's Manse	078301	Annan	The Moor Bridge	203023	Torrent
Stamford Bridge	027015	Derwent	Thetford No. 1 Staunch	033008	Little Ouse
Standwell Green	034323	Dove			
Stanhope	024003	Wear	Thetford Bridge	033901	Little Ouse
Stanion Lane	032016	Willow Brook	Thirlmere Reservoir	075001	Greta (St. Johns Beck)
Stanley	053013	Marden			
Stanneylands	069008	Dean	Thornborough Mill	033005	Great Ouse
Stanton	054365	Roden	Thornthwaite	076001	Haweswater Beck
Stapleford	028027	Erewash	Thorpe Langton	031018	Langton Brook
Stapleford	033353	Granta	Thorpe-le-Soken	037022	Holland Brook
Stareton	054019	Avon	Thorpe Thewles	025313	Billingham Beck
Staveley	027040	Doe Lea	Thorverton	045001	Exe
Sticklepath	050003	Taw	Three Ashes	053014	Spring Flow
Stile Bridge	040005	Beult	Three Cocks	055025	Llynfi
Stisted	037017	Blackwater	Three Elms	055031	Yazor Brook
Stocks Reservoir	071002	Hodder	Threlkeld	075007	Glenderamackin
Stoke	054362	Stoke Brook	Throop Mill	043007	Stour
Stoke Ash	034324	Finningham Watercourse	Tibberton	054040	Meese
			Tideford	047009	Tiddy
Stoke on Trent	028040	Trent	Tilford	039011	Wey
Stoke Park	054358	Stoke Park Brook	Tilley Bridge	041001	Nunningham Stream
Stone Bridge	033348	Larling Brook	Tinhay	047008	Thrushel
Stone Bridge	040009	Teise	Tirydail	059002	Loughor
Stone Bridge	201304	Strule	Tiswell	053015	Spring Flow
Stoneleigh	054004	Sowe	Titley Mill	055013	Arrow
Stoodleigh	045002	Exe	Tixover	031005	Welland
Stowmarket (I.C.I.)	035008	Gipping	Tongwynlais	057003	Taff
Stratford St. Mary	036001	Stour	Toome (Lower Bann)	203315	Lower Bann
Sturmer	036011	Stour Brook	Toome (Lough Neagh)	203616	Lough Neagh
Sunderland Bridge	024001	Wear			
Surney Bridges	032025	Nen, Whilton Branch	Torksey	028065	Trent
Sutton Bingham Reservoir	052002	Yeo	Torrington	050002	Torridge
			Trallong	056006	Usk
Swaffham Bulbeck	033052	Swaffham Lode	Trebrownbridge	048010	Seaton
Swallowfield	039007	Blackwater	Tregony	048003	Fal
Swanton Morley	034014	Wensum	Trehafod	057006	Rhondda
Swill Bridge	051001	Doniford Stream	Trekeivesteps	048001	Fowey
Swincombe Intake	046802	Swincombe	Trengoffe	048004	Warleggan
Swindon	054367	Smestow Brook	Trent Bridge	028804	Trent
Sydling St. Nicholas	044006	Sydling Water	Triumph Road, Nottingham	028035	Leen
Syston Mill	028024	Wreake			
Sywell Reservoir	032902	Sywell Brook, Sywell	Tromie Bridge	008008	Tromie
Taf Fechan Reservoir	057001	Taf Fechan	Trostrey	056010	Usk
Tafolog	055015	Honddu	Troutbeck Bridge	073007	Troutbeck
Tallington Weir	031004	Welland	Truro	048005	Kenwyn
Tamworth	028069	Tame	Tulliford Mill	084018	Clyde
Tanyards	041018	Kird	Tunwell Loop	032015	Willow Brook
Tarset	023005	North Tyne	Twyford Bridge	028036	Poulter
Tebay	072010	Lune	Ty-Castell Farm	060001	Tywi
Teddington	039001	Thames	Udford	076003	Eamont
Tellisford	053007	Frome (Somerset)	Udiam	040004	Rother
Temple Mills	038010	Dagenham Brook	Ullock	075010	Marron
Temple Sowerby	076005	Eden	Umberleigh	050001	Taw
Temple Weir	033014	Lark	Underbank Reservoir	027016	Little Don
Tenbury Wells	054008	Teme	Upavon	043014	East Avon
Tenpenny Bridge	037326	Tenpenny Brook	Upavon	043017	West Avon
Ternhill	054352	Bailey Brook	Upper Shide	101001	Medina
Teston	040003	Medway	Upper Tryweryn	067112	Afon Tryweryn

Station name	Station number	River	Station name	Station number	River
Upton Mill	032006	Nen, Kislingbury Branch	West Luccombe	051002	Hornet Water
			West Mill	036008	Stour
Upton-on-Severn	054043	Severn	West Newton Mill	033025	Babingley
Urieside	011304	Urie	Westwick Lock	027007	Ure
Usk Reservoir	056014	Usk	West Wycombe	039039	Wye
Vellake	050802	West Okement	Whalley	071004	Calder
Verners Bridge	203309	Blackwater	White Bridge	033029	Stringside
Vyrnwy Reservoir	054003	Vyrnwy	White Hill	203028	Agivey
Wades Mill	038004	Rib	Whitford	045004	Axe
Wadhams Farm	052801	Tone	Whittington	027026	Rother
Walcot	054012	Tern	Whitwell	038017	Mimram
Wandle Park (Wimbledon)	039901	Wandle	Wickford	037331	Crouch
			Wide Eals	023012	East Allen
Wanes Blades Bridge	070002	Douglas	Willen Weir	033015	Ouzel
Wanlip	028028	Soar	Wilmslow	069012	Bollin
Wansford	032020	Wittering Brook	Wilton Park	043006	Nadder
Wansford Bridge	026001	West Beck	Wimbledon Common	039005	Beverley Park
Warham	034018	Stiffkey	Wimpole	033027	Rhee
Warwick Bridge	076002	Eden	Wingfield Park	028048	Amber
Watch Water Reservoir	021004	Watch Water	Winterbourne	039362	Winterbourne Stream
			Witton Park	024008	Wear
Water Hall	038018	Lee	Wollaston	032013	Nene
Waterhouses	028041	Hamps	Woodend	012001	Dee
Water Orton	028003	Tame	Woodhead	069802	Etherow
Wattsville	056011	Sirhowy	Woodhouse Mill	027025	Rother
Wedderburn Bridge	054017	Leadon	Woodleigh	050803	Mole
Weir Wood Reservoir	040001	Medway	Woodmill	045003	Culm
Welford	039031	Lambourn	Wookey	052001	Axe
Welham Road Bridge	031017	Stanton Brook	Worksop	028049	Ryton
Welham Road Bridge	031018	Langton Brook	Worthenbury	067016	Worthenbury Brook
Wellow	053009	Wellow Brook	Wraxall	052015	Land Yeo
Wennington Road Bridge	072009	Wenning	Wray	072003	Hindburn
			Writtle	037007	Wid
Werrington	047902	Tamar	Wye	040008	Great Stour
Werrington Park	047005	Ottery	Yarkhill	055018	Frome
West Ayton	027048	Derwent	Yeaton	054020	Perry
West Baldwin Reservoir	103801	Glass	Ynys Tanglws	059001	Tawe
			Ystrad Ffin	060008	Tywi
Westbourne	041015	Ems	Yorkshire Bridge	028001	Derwent
West Challom	039359	Childrey Brook	Yoxall	028012	Trent
West Cardean	015010	Isla	Zouch	028013	Soar

12 Publications of the Water Data Unit

'Groundwater Year Book 1968–70', 1975. Her Majesty's Stationery Office, £12.50

'Groundwater: United Kingdom 1971–73' Her Majesty's Stationery Office. 1977. £21.00.

'The Surface Water Year Book of Great Britain 1966–70', 1974, with the Scottish Development Department. Her Majesty's Stationery Office, £6.50.

'Water Data 1974', 1975. £1.05.

'Water Data 1975', 1977. Her Majesty's Stationery Office, £4.75.

'Water Data 1976'. 1978. £2.00.

Map of Gauging Stations in the United Kingdom, 1973. Scale 1:1250000

TECHNICAL MEMORANDA

No. 1 Data Processing and Computing Capabilities. April 1975.

No. 2 Water Demand in England and Wales 1973. August 1975.

No. 3 A Review of Fish Counter Development. September 1975.

No. 4 A Guide to Metric Units in the Water Industry. December 1976.

No. 5 Surface Water Data Processing – A Guide to Practice. April 1976.

No. 6 Punched Tape River Level Recorders: Report of the Instrument Sub-Group of the Water Archive Development Working Group. May 1976.

No. 7 An Evaluation of the Braystoke Current Meter. May 1976.

No. 8 The Design of Crump Weirs. (Revision of WRB TN8). February 1977.

No. 9 Water Demand in England and Wales 1974. December 1976.

No. 10 The Effect of Pulsations on the Accuracy of River Flow Measurement. In press.

No. 11 An Outline of the Water Archive. In preparation.

No. 12 Method of Flow Computation in the River Pollution Survey. In preparation.

No. 13 Autographic Water Level Recorders. December 1976.

No. 14 A Bibliography of Biological Surveillance Methodology for Macro-Invertebrates in Running Waters. July 1977.

No. 15 Weed Growth on River Flow Measurement Structures. August 1977.

No. 16 Interrogable Devices for the Transmission of River Level and Rainfall Data. August 1977.

No. 17 Portable Current Meter Cableways and Winches. August 1977.

WATER ARCHIVE MANUALS

No. 1 Chemical Determinand Dictionary for use with Water Quality Archive System. June 1976.

The following Technical Notes issued by the Water Resources Board are also available on request to the Water Data Unit.

TN1   Rating of Current Meters 1970

TN2   Morphometric Analysis of River Basin Characteristics 1971

TN3   Logarithmic Plotting of Stage-Discharge Observations 1970

TN4   Estimating Frequencies using Probability Paper 1972

TN5   The Measurement of River Water Temperature 1972

TN6   Wind Set-up in Relation to River Gauging 1970

TN7   The Magnitude of Probable Errors in Water Level Determination at a Gauging Station 1970

TN9   Metrication 1969

TN10   River Water Quality 1971

TN11   The Magnitude of Errors at Flow Measurement Stations 1971

TN12   Dry Weather Flows 1970

Appendix

Publications of the International Standards Organization and of the British Standards Institution relating to methods of measurement of Liquid Flow in Open Channels

The various standards are available on payment with order from:

British Standards Institution
Sales Department
101 Pentonville Road
London N1 9ND (Tel: 01–837 8801)

The prices are subject to Currency Exchange fluctuations based on the Swiss Franc and should be checked with BSI Sales prior to ordering. (See also the Note at the end of Appendix). Subscribing members receive a discount of 30% on these prices.

INTERNATIONAL STANDARDS

ISO	555/I	1973	Liquid flow measurement in open channels – Dilution methods for measurement of steady flow – Part I: Constant rate injection method	£15
ISO	555/II	1974	Liquid flow measurement in open channels – Dilution methods for measurement of steady flow – Part II: Integration (Sudden injection) method	£15
ISO	748	1973	Liquid flow measurement in open channels by velocity area methods	£19.50
ISO	748(R)	1977*	Ditto	
ISO	772	1973	Liquid flow measurement in open channels – Vocabulary and symbols	£21
ISO	772(R)	1977*	Ditto	
ISO	1070	1973	Liquid flow measurement in open channels – Slope area method	£7.50
ISO	1088	1973	Collection of data for determination of errors in measurement of liquid flow by velocity area methods	£12.75
ISO	1100	1973	Liquid flow measurement in open channels – Establishment and operation of a gauging station and determination of the stage-discharge relation	£22.50
ISO	1438	1975	Liquid flow measurement in open channels using thin-plate weirs and venturi flumes	£26.00
ISO	1438(R)	1977*	Thin-plate weirs	
ISO	2425	1974	Measurement of flow in tidal channels	£14.25
ISO	2537	1974	Liquid flow measurement in open channels – Cup-type and propeller-type current meters	£6.00
ISO	3454	1976	Liquid flow measurement in open channels – Sounding and suspension equipment	£6.00
ISO	3455	1976	Liquid flow measurement in open channels – Calibration of rotating element current meters in straight open tanks	£9.00
ISO	3716	1977*	Liquid flow measurement in open channels – Functional requirements and characteristics of suspended sediment load samplers	
ISO	3846	1977*	Liquid flow measurement in open channels by weirs and flumes – Free overfall weirs of finite crest width (rectangular broad-crested weirs)	

ISO	3847	1977*	Liquid flow measurement in open channels by weirs and flumes — End depth method for estimation of flow in rectangular channels with a free overfall	
ISO	4359	1977*	Liquid flow measurement in open channels using flumes	
ISO	4360	1977*	Liquid flow measurement in open channels by weirs and flumes — Triangular profile weirs	
ISO	4361	1977*	Liquid flow measurement in open channels by weirs and flumes — Round nosed broad-crested weirs	
ISO	4363	1977*	Liquid flow in open channels — Methods of measurement of suspended sediment	
ISO	4364	1977*	Liquid flow in open channels — Bed material sampling	
ISO	4369	1977*	Liquid flow measurement in open channels by the moving boat method	
ISO	4373	1977*	Liquid flow measurement in open channels — Water level measuring equipment	
ISO	4375	1977*	Liquid flow measurement in open channels — Cableway system	
ISO	4377	1977*	Liquid flow measurement in open channels — Flat-V weirs	
ISO	5168	1977*	Calculation of the uncertainty of a measurement of flowrate	

REPORTS

ISO	Data 2	1977*	Investigation on the total error in measurement of flow by velocity area methods

BRITISH STANDARDS

BS 3680   **Methods of Measurement of Liquid Flow in Open Channels**

Part 1	1964	Glossary of terms	£2.20
Part 1	1977*(1)	Vocabulary and Symbols	
Part 2		Dilution methods	
2A	1964 (2)	Constant rate injection	£4.70
2C	1967	Radioisotope techniques	£4.70
Part 3	1964†	Velocity area methods	£4.70
Part 4		Weirs and flumes	
4A	1965†	Thin plate weirs and venturi flumes	£6.60
4B	1969†	Long-base weirs	£4.70
4C	1974†	Flumes	£6.60
Part 5	1973 (3)	Slope area method of estimation	£2.20
Part 6	1973 (4)	Measurement of flow in tidal channels	£4.70
Part 7	1971†	Measurement of liquid level (stage)	£2.20
Part 8		Current meters	
8A	1973†	Current meters incorporating a rotating element	£2.70
8B	1973†	Current meters: suspension equipment	£2.70
8C	1977*	Calibration of current meters	

Part 9   Water level instruments

    9A   1971   Specification for the installation and performance of pressure actuated
                              liquid level measuring equipment   £2.20

    9B   1977*   Float operated water level recorders

(1) Identical to ISO 772 – 1977*
(2) Corresponds to ISO 4555/I – 1973
(3) Corresponds to ISO 1070 – 1973
(4) Corresponds to ISO 2425 – 1974

†   See also similar ISO Standards
R   Currently under review
*   Expected publication date

NOTE:
BSI is pursuing a policy of publishing corresponding identical ISO Standards as British Standards with a joint ISO/BS number. For example, the revised Vocabulary and Symbols will be published by BSI as 'BS 3680 : Part 1 : 1977/ISO 772 – 1977 Vocabulary and Symbols'. The BSI price normally will be cheaper than the ISO one and intending purchasers should consult BSI Sales before ordering.

Printed in England for Her Majesty's Stationery Office
by Hobbs the Printers of Southampton
(310) Dd496286 K7 5/78 G3313